CHANEL AND THE TWEEDMAKER

Weavers of Dreams

Patricia M. Hitchon

With best wishes
Patricia M. Hitchon

**For
Gil and Liz**

CHANEL AND THE TWEEDMAKER

Weavers of Dreams

Patricia M. Hitchon

P3 Publications

First Published in Great Britain
in September 2012 by:

P3 Publications
13 Beaver Road
Carlisle
Cumbria,
CA2 7PS

Typeset in Verdana

Printed and bound in China by
Hong Kong Graphics and Printing Ltd.

www.p3publications.com

Contents

Foreword

This book tells much more than the story of the enduring relationship between the House of Chanel and Linton Tweeds: it gives the historical context - regionally, nationally and internationally - interweaving it with the glamorous world of the Paris fashion houses.

It offers a rare description of the growth, decline and (more recent) transformation of the tweed industry, inextricably linked with the fortunes of haute couture and prêt-à-porter, as well as tracing the lives and fortunes of the founding figures: William Linton and Coco Chanel.

Tweed production on both sides of the Border has always relied on three elements coming together effectively: wool, free-running rivers and people with the energy and vision to change the mundane into the magical. The story of Linton Tweeds epitomises this: for a century its fortunes have been guided by just two families - the Lintons and the Walkers, both steeped in the traditions of the region's textile industry. But, as this book makes clear, there have been many other contributors to its success, at home and abroad.

The Border textile industry was made up of many families financing and running mills. For example, my grandfather, David Walker, started Heather Mills in Selkirk during the 1880s. It wove its own designs to keep in stock and took swatches to tailors throughout the UK, for their clients to make their choice. The mill would then cut and send the fabric on to them.

William Linton, however did not have his own woollen spinning mill: hence the lengthy relationship with Robert Todd & Sons, who spun his yarn in Shaddon Mills - yarn that was then transformed into the tweed Linton used to chase business in Paris, America and Canada.

Latterly, under my son's leadership, we have extended into other markets in the Far East, making use of the latest internet technology to access tailors on a global scale never envisaged by my grandfather.

We are very proud of our association with Chanel - keeping them happy formed a large part of my working life, as it does for my son and – hopefully – for the generation beyond.
Pat has written a fascinating and thoroughly researched book. I am happy to recommend it.

Leslie H. Walker
Chairman, Linton Tweeds

Introduction

I have long been a believer in the American notion of 'happenstance', and this belief was confirmed, when on a soft autumn day in 1995, I had to go to the Royal Mail depot in Junction Street, Carlisle, to pick up a package. It turned out to be from Phillips Auctioneers about Sam Bough paintings - the book I was researching, and my brother, Gil, was writing at the time. On the way back, I decided to call in at the Bobbin Coffee Shop at Linton Tweeds.

As I was having my coffee, a party of Asian ladies was being given a tour of the adjoining showroom, and listening to a talk on the use of the different fabrics, such as silk tweed. Samples were being passed around to look at - and unable to restrain my curiosity and my interest, I joined on the back of the party, to listen to the talk - the next words burned into my mind:

'What Chanel does, even today - the world wants.'

And from those words of Carole Walker came the inspiration for this book.

My interest in fashion, and particularly French fashion, goes back to my earliest years. At the tender age of three or four my favourite occupation was to look through my mother's wardrobe and finger the fabrics of her clothes - the soft silks

The author with her mother, Teresa M. Hitchon

and crêpe-de-chines, and the nubbly tweeds and wools. I also loved to watch my grandfather, Gig Hitchon, who had been a master shoemaker, as he sat at his last, working with soft leather.

My mother's aunt, Margaret Shane, had been a tailoress, and my grandmother Polly O'Neill, although a teacher by profession was also a gifted amateur milliner who transformed the hats of her friends.

The French connection held up when the Hitchon aunts, who lived in Paris and were smart and formidable Parisian ladies, visited us with their son, Pierre, who looked like the young Yves Saint Laurent. There was much kissing and bowing, and overwhelmed at four years old by all this French *politesse*, I hid behind my mother's skirts.

My father, as a young man in the 1930s, had worked at Morton Sundour Fabrics in Carlisle. Morton Sundour supplied many of the top London fashion houses, such as Matita, with luxury fabrics. He was often allowed to buy 'end-of -line' fabric, which my mother had made up into fashion dresses and coats, in the years before her marriage in 1940.

The first French couturier I ever heard of was Christian Dior. In February 1947, after the austerity of the war years, he launched 'The New Look'. Later that year, my mother bought a fine grey herringbone tweed coat in this style. I can still see her twirling round to let my father see the flowing, feminine lines, and the laughter and delight in her eyes. There was something to celebrate and fashion had returned.

This book is the product of all those early influences and subsequent interests: the true but amazing story of how a small firm in Carlisle, in the North of England, would have an impact on one of the greatest couture houses of the 20th century and on the most famous fashion 'look' in the world.

When William Linton's tweeds met with Coco Chanel's vision - the rest, as they say, was history.

The story that follows traces the fortunes of this company, Linton Tweeds, founded in 1912, in a city that emerged from being a Roman town, to a Border fortress, through the industrial revolution in the 19th century, to the growth of its boundaries, and the prosperity of its citizens in the 20th century, and which looks forward to a bright future with its further development into a University city in the 21st century.

The House of Chanel came into being through the gifted designer, Gabrielle Chanel, who revolutionised the style of women's clothes in 1920s Paris, and developed this into a worldwide fashion experience.

She was responsible for many of the fashion ideas that we take for granted today. These include, quilted leather bags, glittering costume jewellery, sling-back shoes, long strings of pearls, the little black dress, the world's best loved perfume and, of course, brilliantly coloured braided tweed jackets.

Now, in the 21st century, this happy marriage of brilliant design and fabulous fabric is still a potent force in the world of fashion.

Patricia M. Hitchon

***

If there's one thing no one cares about it's someone's life. If I wrote a book about my life, I would begin with tomorrow'
Coco Chanel

Rob Irvine, the Head Designer at Linton Tweeds, glances out of his office window. Across the yard he can see the old mill and Dixon's Chimney. On his desk, strands of coloured yarn lie among photographs, slight sketches, all the makings of a new design. A new tweed.

Tomorrow the design must be in Paris.

Karl Lagerfeld has sent through his latest requirements. A thought, a hint, a small sketch of the brilliant tweed he wants for his latest creation. Rob and the weavers are hard at work, creating the cobweb weave designs; the yarn colours are chosen; the machines set up - ready to roll.

Tomorrow, this must be in Paris.

The House of Chanel and Linton Tweeds. It's a relationship that goes back over 80 years. A story with a fascinating past, present and future. But mostly about the future. Mostly to-morrow.

This is that story.

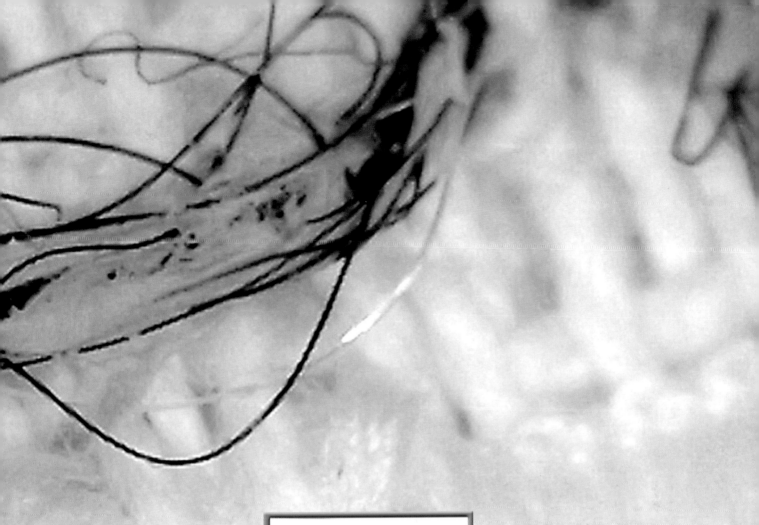

Part One

The tweedmaker and ...

William Linton and Gabrielle 'Coco' Chanel

1

The time when it all began

Today, looking at beautiful, leggy models sashaying down the catwalks in Paris, New York, Milan or at London's Fashion Week, wearing the latest creations of talented designers, in a myriad of zinging, luscious fabrics, it is hard to imagine the time when it all began – back in the 1750s.

When the Industrial Revolution started, Britain was at its spearhead. Improved transport systems coupled with new farming methods and the development of steam-powered machinery, created the revolution. After centuries of exporting wool and trading cloth all over the world (and becoming rich in the process), the cotton manufacturers kick-started mechanised large-scale production and stepped firmly into the future.

By the beginning of the nineteenth century that revolution had spread throughout Europe and the New World. In the years that followed, the textile industry went from strength to strength and, in the middle of this maelstrom of change, the world of fashion was born.

The developments that changed the lives of millions of workers also gave rise to a multi-billion-dollar, global industry. Not only did it provide work and economic growth for nations, wealth for manufacturers, and developments for technology, but it also gave the women of the world access to those most desired commodities, glamour and style.

As with most things in the world of haute couture, the beginnings of this story were much less spectacular than the outcome.

Linton's beginnings

Edinburgh was bathed in bright sunlight on that fine June morning in 1865 when Marion Pringle wed William Linton. It was a day of celebration as both families crowded into Drum Gardens, Liberton, for the wedding ceremony. The old words of the Church of Scotland rites resonated in the hearts of William and Marion, as the minister pronounced them husband and wife: they were married and the future was theirs to shape.

The old town, with its narrow passageways, alleys, and steep, crowded streets, was a

...the couturière

hive of activity. Across the bridges, the Georgian New Town, not long built, with its wide streets, spacious squares and charming crescents, had brought new homes and development. Even the railway had come in 1836. And the Industrial Revolution had introduced its own measure of elegance, prompting Robert Louis Stevenson to describe it as 'this profusion of eccentricities, this dream of masonry and living rock, not a drop scene in a theatre, but a city in the world of everyday reality.' [1]

The everyday reality for Marion was working long hours as a domestic servant, and she looked forward to moving to William's hometown of Selkirk, where he worked as a gardener. They were both twenty-four and fortunate to have all their parents with them on that happy day, John and Margaret Linton having travelled from Selkirk for the event. Marion's father, Alexander Pringle, had something in common with his new son-in-law: he too was a gardener, in Liberton.

Selkirk was a Scottish border town famous for its tweed industry. It was very different from 'Auld Reekie'. Yet Marion liked the place, the expanse of green hills and the way the grey stone streets stretched down to the valley of the Ettrick and Yarrow Waters. Gardening and the outdoor life were William's passions, and his job at Ettrick Lodge, a large mansion owned by the Brown family, was one he loved. But he harboured ambitions to set up his own market garden and now, with a wife and perhaps a family in the future, he hoped to fulfil his ambitions.

Before long they started a family. By 25 May 1872 when William Linton, junior, was born at Bridge Road Cottage, they already had a daughter, Katherine, and two sons, John and Alexander Pringle. After William's birth, Marion was to have four more children, Lillie, Robert, Margaret and the youngest girl, born in 1881, Mary H. Linton.

The Linton family was now complete and living comfortably in Ettrick Lodge Garden House, located on Ettrick Terrace, next to the County Buildings and just north of the busy Market Square. William had achieved his ambition: he was a self-employed market gardener and, by 1888, he was listed in the town's Almanac as Vice-President of the Selkirk Horticultural Association.

By 1901, the family had moved to Linton Court, Old Bridge Road and only Alexander,

Selkirk, birthplace of William Linton

Lillie, Robert, Maggie and Mary still lived at home, the others having grown up and fled the nest. In this, they were no different from many other families in the town, where the main employment was in the spinning and weaving mills, in woollen manufacture.[2] Some of William and Marion's eight children became apprenticed as designers, weavers and spinners in the local tweed mills, while others trained in the professions: Maggie as a milliner, Robert becoming a solicitor in Edinburgh and Mary, the youngest, a teacher at Hawick High School.

But it was William junior who was to make his mark in the world of textiles and fashion, and who would keep the Linton name forever associated with tweed.

Enter the French connection

When William Linton was just eleven years old and running along to school in Selkirk without a care in the world, an event was taking place in France which, in the far off future, would not only change the world of fashion, but enrich his whole life. The strange thread of connections that would bind him and Coco Chanel together in the world of haute couture was about to start.

Gabrielle Chanel was born in 1883 in the garrison town of Saumur in the lush green Loire Valley. She would grow up to be a beautiful girl with dark hair and a fine-featured, somewhat aristocratic face offsetting expressive, watchful eyes. She had verve and energy, but with a down-to-earth outlook on life which would serve her well in the years to come. She was also inclined to secrecy by nature.

The Chanels were country people earning their living in the village of Ponteils, tucked into the Cévennes mountains, north of Nîmes in southern France. A simple life and a hard life with few luxuries.

Ponteils had developed at the centre of a large forest of chestnut trees - their autumn harvest was the lifeblood of the working people of the village. The local tavern keeper was a popular man, often requested to act as witness to the many marriages and baptisms taking place at the church across the square. The Catholic faith was an ever-present part of the villagers' lives, and the local church the hub of the community. It was here, in the church records, that his name would be preserved for posterity. He had not married until he was nearly forty, and with money from his wife's dowry had rented part of the solid, stone house which became the tavern.

His name was Joseph Chanel and he was Gabrielle Chanel's great-grandfather. Joseph was born in Ponteils in 1792, and over the next sixty years many Chanels were born and worked on the land in the surrounding area. By 1854, when Joseph's second son, Henri-Adrien, was twenty two years old the chestnut trees, which had supported the close knit community for so many years began to die out, attacked by chestnut blight and black canker.[3]

It was time to move on, and many of the young men of the village thought so. Henri-Adrien was one of them. But where to go? And what to do? His older brother Joseph had followed his father as tavern keeper, and with no real skills Henri-Adrien felt a confusion about the direction his life was taking. He travelled thirty miles from home, but local jobs were scarce and he did not want to go to the coalmines at Ales.

On his travels he met the Fournier family who had a silkworm factory at Saint-Jean-de-Valériscle , and they offered him a job. The farmer had a pretty sixteen-year-old daughter, Virginie-Angelina, and when Henri-Adrien's flirtatious ways led to seduction, the Fourniers insisted on marriage. His parents were sent for and a hasty marriage took place at Gagnières, after which the young couple moved south to Nîmes in 1854.

Nîmes was an historic town, the centre of a textile industry that gave its name to one of today's best-loved fabrics, 'de Nîmes' or denim. Henri-Adrien and Angelina settled in lodgings at 4 rue du Bat d'Argent and he embarked on a new career as a market trader. Gabrielle's first cousin, Mme Adrienne Valet, would describe his work: 'My grandfather, who was also Coco's, bought fabric rejects from silk manufacturers in Lyon and sold them through itinerant vendors. Then he followed the vendors all over the country in order to recover his money and claim his profits. Finally we settled in Vichy.' [4]

Many of the Chanel's extended family had also settled in Nîmes, as well as other neighbours and friends from Ponteils: together they formed a close-knit community. But on the day her first son, Albert, was born in 1856, Angelina was alone. Henri-Adrien was away selling his wares at a village fair, and the teenage girl was admitted to the Hospice d'Humanité of Nîmes where she gave birth to Gabrielle's father. No other Chanel was present, so the infant's birth was registered by three illiterate hospital staff, who wrongly gave his name as Charnet.

There was to be no settled life in Nîmes for Angelina to bring up her baby. Before long, Henri-Adrien returned and the little family took off, to travel the roads to the local fairs and eke out a living. They had only been in Nîmes for a year, but leaving was no sad occasion, rather the road to adventure and a life spent following carnivals and fêtes in the beautiful villages and towns of the Cévennes and the south of France.

The festivals, often with religious symbolism, were part of life and provided a good living for a trader such as Henri-Adrien. Flowers were strewn on the streets; the statue of the Blessed Virgin, clothed in silk and hung with jewels would be carried with pride to the local church, where it would be set among flickering candles for the service of benediction. The crowds, in holiday mood, would mill around the traders' stalls, looking to buy souvenirs, to sample the local food, drink the wine and laugh with their friends, amid the perfume of buckets of flowers and the pungent aromas of fruit and spices.

Another daughter, Louise, was born in 1863, followed by two more sons, Hippolyte in 1872 and Marius in 1877. Albert and Louise were the closest in age and, as they grew older, they worked together and gave each other moral support. They had to supplement the family income and it was not unusual to find them doing seasonal work, such as helping the farmer in his fields or assisting the farmer's wife in the kitchen.[5]

The close bond between them would last until Louise's wedding, when she married Paul Costier from Ponteils. Paul worked for the railway company at Clermont-Ferrand, a busy commercial centre previously two separate cities, but joined together in 1731. The wedding party was attended by friends and neighbours from Ponteils, as well as most of the extended Chanel family, with the many small children clinging to their mothers. Albert turned up, but was soon on the road again, following the fairs. Inspired by the example of his father, he went in search of the crowds attending all those religious festivals: this was what he knew, this was his life.

When Jeanne met Albert

In November 1881, the last fair of the autumn was at Courpière and, with winter approaching, Albert decided to make this his base for a few months. It was a small town a few miles east of Clermont-Ferrand, and here he got to know twenty-three year old Marin Devolle who had inherited his father's carpentry business at a young age. Left orphans, Marin's young sister, Jeanne, lived with her Uncle Augustin, but each day she went to Marin's to cook and clean for him. Jeanne planned to follow her mother in making her living as a seamstress.

Before long, Albert had swept the young Jeanne off her feet and they were caught up in a passionate love affair. But by January 1882 Albert began to feel the wanderlust again; he wanted to get back to the towns and the religious fairs which were starting up before Lent. With typical Chanel male insouciance, off he went, leaving no address and, although he may not have known it, leaving the pretty nineteen year old Jeanne pregnant.

Once Jeanne's condition became apparent, the Devolle family were up in arms, even enlisting the help of the local Mayor to locate Albert. His parents told the Devolles that he was in Aubenas, a town in the shadow of the Cévennes mountain range in the Ardèche region. Jeanne, eight months pregnant, went looking and found him where he would so often be in the future, conducting his business in the local tavern. To her disappointment, and her parents' anger, he would not agree to marry her, but agreed to accept her as his common-law wife and to recognise Julia, who was born in the tavern on 11 September 1882, as their daughter.

The wrath of his own parents and the Devolle family, as well as the newfound responsibilities of a family, did not sit well with Albert. He decided to make a break with the familiar area of his youth and travel north to Saumur to seek new opportunities. Jeanne had no option but to follow him, or lose him. And, besides, she loved him. By January 1883, they were in Saumur and Jeanne was pregnant again.

Saumur was a beautiful stone city with an impressive château towering above the town and the river. Famed for its troglodyte dwellings, carved out of the soft limestone and providing cheap accommodation for some of the townspeople, it was even more famous for its National Riding School, the École Nationale d'Équitation, where the English

Saumur, birthplace of Gabrielle Chanel

influence on saddle making was beginning, and English horses were being imported. The cavalry garrison gave it the buzz of a military town, and the music halls and café-bars were open late. It was wine-producing country and Albert's greatest wish was to become a wine merchant. They found lodgings at 29 rue St Jean, and Albert started to sell his wares in the nearby market at the Place de la Bilange, using his market trader's charm and patter to entice the ladies to buy. Jeanne, taking the toddler Julia with her, took on whatever work she could find, helping in kitchens, with laundry or sewing.

Gabrielle is born

On 19 August, at the Maison-Dieu Hospice, run by the Sisters of Providence, and without Albert present, Jeanne gave birth to her second daughter, Gabrielle. The next day, Albert had still not arrived when three hospital employees took the baby to the town hall to be registered by the Deputy Mayor. As no one knew the correct spelling of her surname, it was written as Chasnel. The illiterate witnesses signed with an X - and history had repeated itself. On the 21 August, Gabrielle was baptised by the hospital chaplain - and so Gabrielle Chanel came into the world.

For the next year life continued on an even keel. The couple decided to make Saumur their base to bring up the two little girls, Albert went off with his horse and cart to trade at the local fairs and Jeanne kept the home going. By spring, with Gabrielle a little older, Jeanne would join Albert selling in the market place.

The market traders' wives saw nothing unusual in their husbands' constant absences, however. After all, the nature of their work demanded it and, while making a home base for the children, they joined them whenever possible. Life was exciting and happy, and absences were understood. It was a far cry from the solid Scottish roots and settled life that the young William Linton was living in Selkirk.

But a wedding ring was what Jeanne really wanted, and when she found herself pregnant for the third time, Albert agreed. This was a child too far, and surrounded by the Chanel and Devolle families, the couple were married at Courpière on 17 November 1884. Julia and Gabrielle were now legitimate.

The Devolles were not without means, and Jeanne brought a 5,000 franc dowry with her, as well as furniture and personal objects valued at 500 francs. The children were legalised and their names entered in the *livret de famille*, the record book given to every family to record births and deaths.[6] At the marriage, Henri-Adrien and Angelina, Gabrielle's grandparents (by now celebrating their thirtieth wedding anniversary) announced that they too had another daughter, Adrienne, born at Saintes the previous year. Adrienne was not only Gabrielle's aunt, but she would become her best friend.

With Jeanne five-months pregnant and winter approaching, they decided to move some twenty miles south of Clermont-Ferrand to Issoire. It not only had a busy market each day, but the Paris-Lyon-Méditerranée railway line passed through, making it a busy commercial centre. The old town still had its medieval walls and the market place was surrounded with houses with deep, tiled eaves. It was also close to Albert's favourite territories, the country markets and fairs of the Auvergne region, and a good starting point for his journeys.

They set up home in a small house on rue du Perrier and here, on 15 March 1885, their first son, Alphonse, was born. Shortly after, they moved to rue du Moulin Charrier, a narrow damp street near the river with its mills, an area inhabited by craftsmen trying to eke out a living. There were hemp weavers, candle makers, rope makers, potters and hat makers and from them Albert bought stock to sell in the markets.[7]

In 1887, a third daughter, Antoinette was born in Saintes, Adrienne's birthplace. Now, with four children to look after and Albert often away on his trading trips, Jeanne's health began to cause her trouble, as she suffered bouts of breathlessness.[8] As her condition worsened, and with little treatment available, the family decided to move back to the country air of Courpière, and Jeanne's uncle, Augustin Chardon, offered to have them back to live in her old home. Jeanne's health was a source of anxiety for the whole family. She suffered from a form of asthma which her mother, Gilberte, had died of, and her appearance had changed, with her eyes sunken into her thin face. Producing four children in five years and constant moves with her small brood had weakened her. It was hoped that with rest and home comforts her health and strength would be restored.

But Jeanne could not trust Albert. She knew what a magnet his charming, flirtatious ways were to the women he met at the market. She was determined to fight for her marriage, and she missed the charming rogue that he was. Before long she decided to leave the four children in the safe hands of her family and follow him on the road again. By now he was at a fair in Guéret, north east of Limoges, so they took rooms in a country inn, and it was here that she gave birth to their second son Lucien in 1889.

Gabrielle had taken well to living in the country with Uncle Augustin: the older children attended the local school and spent summer days helping their uncle in the garden. This was a new kind of settled happiness for them. Jeanne shuttled back and forth between Albert and the children, but this and her numerous pregnancies had taken a harsh toll on her health. She came back to Courpière in March 1891 and in May another son, Augustin, named for her uncle, was born but died in infancy.

In spite of all her family's exhortations, Jeanne was anxious to get back to Albert once more. She had received a letter from him saying that he had set up business as an innkeeper with his brother, the twenty-one year old Hippolyte, at Brive-la-Gaillarde, a town halfway between Clermont-Ferrand and Bordeaux. He had lodgings, and Jeanne was excited at the thought of a steady living and settled home life. So in 1893 she set out again, taking Julia and Gabrielle with her. It was not to be, of course. Albert was a waiter at the inn and wanted his wife to work there also. It was winter and soon Jeanne was ill again. Albert was away and, feeling faint and short of breath, she took to her bed. Trying to avoid the expense, she would not let anyone call the doctor. For several days she had a high fever and asthma attacks, and on 16 February 1895 she was found dead in her room. It is not known if Julia and Gabrielle saw her die but, in Albert's absence, Hippolyte was left to make arrangements for her funeral. Jeanne was just thirty-two years old and left five young children to their father's care.[9]

**

2
The valley of the mills

The unsettled lives of the Chanel family could not have been in starker contrast to the solid Scottish roots of the Linton family. Young William's birthplace, the Royal Burgh of Selkirk, had long been an important Border town. In ancient times it was surrounded by the magnificent Ettrick Forest; by the 13th century it was where William Wallace was declared 'King of the Scots'; and in 1721 it was the birthplace of the explorer Mungo Park. It also became the place where Sir Walter Scott worked as Sheriff of Selkirkshire until his death in 1832.

A mill town stretching from its hilltop location down to the valley of the Ettrick Water, Selkirk had long been a centre for textile milling. Ettrick Water was a tributary of the Tweed, which wended its way through the town, its banks lined with mill buildings. These were all family businesses, often changing hands as the fortunes of individual families ebbed and flowed. But overall they brought stability to the development of the town.

In 1767 the first woollen mill had been established in the valley and by 1872, when William was born, there were seven mills making the beautiful fine tweeds, and employing over a thousand people. The road to Edinburgh had been in place since the 1830s and the rail network arrived in 1856, enabling the mill owners to reach a wider market for their products, surmounting the formidable distribution problems that had previously existed. With the rapid expansion of new mills in this period, the town's population almost doubled between 1841 and 1851, rising to a total of 3,314.[10] Not surprisingly, the mill owners in the Scottish Border towns at this time were often men

Views of Heather Mills, Selkirk - founded in 1894 by David Walker

of substance and pillars of the local community.

The sights and sounds of Selkirk's textile industry had a great impact on young William Linton in his early years. The mill buildings and their chimneys billowing smoke, the expanse of water alongside, the mill horn blasting, weavers hurrying to work, the pungent smell of oil and wool, bales of tweed being packed up and loaded onto horse-drawn carts, the bustle and noise, the sheer excitement of it all. This would impress the young boy as he made his way to school, and that feeling for textiles would never leave him. He knew that this was where his destiny lay. By the time he was 18, his future was already mapped out: the 1891 Census records him as a 'woollen millworker'.

Selkirk's textile dynasties

Selkirk's woollen mills at this time were in the hands of a number of prominent families who controlled development and production. Many of the town's young people would look for no other career than to be part of this great textile boom.

Ettrick Lodge, where William's father worked, was a large house owned by the Brown family. The brothers James and Henry were woollen manufacturers who had moved from nearby Galashiels and, along with partners, started the company J. & H. Brown & Co. at Ettrick Mill in 1835. The mill was to become known as the largest and finest mill in the Scottish Borders.[11]

The firm became extremely successful, exhibiting and winning a medal for their products at the Great Exhibition held at the Crystal Palace, Hyde Park, London in 1851, which was a showcase for the best of British manufacturing. When it was opened in May by Queen Victoria, the first World's Fair, or 'The Great Exhibition of the Industry of All Nations,' was intended to stimulate trade between nations, and was seen as a vehicle for world peace. The brainchild of Queen Victoria's husband, Prince Albert, it also sought to display and promote all that was best in design in manufactured goods. A specially designed iron and glass modern structure, it was spread over twenty-one acres of Hyde Park, and many of the exhibits later became part of the collection which eventually was housed in the new Victoria and Albert Museum. More than six million people were to visit the exhibition during its six months' run, and it was a huge success.[12]

The interest created by the Great Exhibition increased demand for tartans, tweeds and other Scottish cloths, and many of the manufacturers appointed London agents where customers could consult pattern books and place orders.[13] This was an exciting time of rapid development in industry, technology and the arts, and the effects were felt throughout the United Kingdom.

The Brown family became prominent in local affairs, with William Brown, the owner in 1888, being a Justice of the Peace, a committee member of the Parochial Board, and Chairman of the Selkirkshire Building and Investment Company. Another member of the family, James B. Brown, a talented tweed designer, became renowned as the Selkirk poet, J. B. Selkirk, using the town's name as his nom-de-plume.[14]

After the construction of Ettrick Mill in 1835, Dunsdale Mill was built in 1837 by the Inglis brothers at Dunsdale Haugh, followed by Forest Mill in 1838. Dunsdale Mill was eventually bought by William Waddell and Richard Turnbull in 1865. Cheviot Mill, built in 1864, eventually became known as Heather Mills under the Walker family and the connections with the story of Linton Tweeds were assembling.

The woollen trade was booming and another prominent family, the Roberts, was taking great strides to secure the Selkirk trade. Forest Mill, downstream from the Selkirk Corn Mill, was sold to George Roberts and Andrew Dickson in 1838, and the company George Roberts & Co. was born. George Roberts became Provost of Selkirk and was a leading protagonist in securing the railways for the town. In his efforts to get them extended over the Border to Carlisle, he put forward as evidence that the population of the town in 1858 was 3,800, and that five mills employed 770 workers with an annual wage bill of £22,000.[15] The Lintons knew the Roberts family, as in later years William Linton's brother, John Linton, was employed by George Roberts as Head Designer.

As demand for greater volumes and variety grew, the development of new machinery became crucial to the industry, and the woollen manufacturers and employees were constantly looking for ways of solving technical problems. A particular instance was wool fibre, which was carded or disentangled before being spun into yarn. A persistent problem occurred with the wool slivers which required reducing into a viable thread before being spun. In 1842, two of the towns manufacturers, Henry Brown and Thomas Walker came up with an invention known as the 'Scotch Feed' to obviate this and had it patented in October of that year.[16] By 1853, David Walker had started a spinning mill at Philiphaugh, a few miles outside town, but later went out of business and by 1870 George Roberts and his brother James had bought the mill.[17]

Scottish mill owners had long been men of foresight and innovation, and when the quality of the fleece produced by local farmers did not meet up with their standards, they began to look elsewhere for supplies. The age-old custom of 'tarring' the sheep with a mix of butter and tar, to help them survive the cold Scottish winters, had died out by the early 1800s but, even with the improved quality of Cheviot fleece, the manufacturers still sought new supplies much further afield in Australia and New Zealand, where the Roberts family would become prominent in sheep farming and wool exporting.[18]

Opening up international markets

The Selkirk trade soon established an international reputation for quality, with tweeds popular in Europe and Russia, as well as America. The thirty years from 1864 to 1894 saw eleven new mills open in Selkirk, and by 1885 the trade had reached its pinnacle of prosperity.

Many factors transpired to account for this surge of popularity, including the expansion of the railways, leading to the growth of fashionable resorts and, with it, a demand by the fashion–conscious public for tweed travelling coats and suits, as well as sports clothes made from woollen cloth.[19]

By 1890, however, America's McKinley Act imposed heavy duties on the import of high class woollen goods, a serious setback causing a slump in the industry. These were the years when many of Selkirk's young men emigrated to the Dominions and to America. The glory days of the wool industry seemed over and the decline would last until 1902.[20]

But even in the hardest times, enterprise could still pay off. By 1894 for example, David Walker, another Selkirk man, had set up Heather Mills and started a family tradition for manufacturing beautiful tweed.[21] Born in Edinburgh in 1860, by 1885 he lived in Innerleithen in the Tweed Valley. He was president of the Innerleithen Debating Society at this time, and an interesting surviving document shows his involvement in local affairs. Innerleithen in the 1880s had five mills and a population of over 1,000. However, David was looking to expand and moved to Selkirk, a larger town with greater opportunity. Here he married Helen Hope (known in the family as Nellie). He was to gain a considerable reputation in the textile world, and the family tradition he established was to play a major part in the story of Linton Tweeds generations later.

By 1902 the tide had started to turn, with a growing market for fancy weaves, some with silk decoration pioneered in Selkirk. These expensive cloths were popular with the rich and fashionable in Europe at the luxury end of the market. The Borders woollen industry was in the hands of this group of families, with a variety of partnerships and links. This pioneering spirit, introducing new types of wool, with Merino from Australia, and half-bred wool from New Zealand, to supplement the fine home-grown Cheviot wools, saw it succeed for another hundred years, gaining worldwide renown, before the pressures of commerce in the late twentieth century produced a decline.

***

Dean Mills - formerly Howlands Mill, where William Linton started working when he moved to Hawick

3

At home in Hawick

Young William Linton was one of those who decided to look further afield during the slump years. Instead of heading to America, however, he moved much closer to home: just eleven miles south of Selkirk, to Hawick, home of tweedmaking.

Hawick is the largest town in the Scottish Borders and its position at the meeting of the River Teviot and the Slitrig Water was the key to its development as a town and the hub of the textile industry in Scotland. A grey, stone-built town, nestling in the lush green of the Teviotdale Valley, for hundreds of years its industry had been based on textiles. By 1800 there were three thousand people employed in producing hosiery, carpets, linen and woollen goods in the town's 50 textile mills.[22] The name 'tweed' was born here in 1832.

According to legend, Messrs William Watson & Sons of Dangerfield Mills invoiced the London firm of James Locke, Regent Street, for a consignment of twill cloth, or 'tweel' as it was known. This was misread by Locke's invoice clerk and re-ordered as 'tweed', which the company and the other Hawick manufacturer's then decided to adopt as the new name.[23] Scotch tweed had arrived and the Hawick textile industry boomed.

Steam power replaced water power. The size and number of the mills grew. Now-famous names, such as Pringle, first made their impact on the fashionable public, as wool and tweed became sought-after fabrics. The tweed glistened and glinted with the colour palette of the natural world, reflecting the tones of the earth, shades of leaves, bracken and heather, mountains and mists, streams and stones, clouds and sky – the awesome beauty of nature in a piece of cloth. Together and skilfully blended, these tones gave tweed its initial universal fascination. It was these very qualities, together with the warmth and hard-wearing properties of the wool and inspired design in weaving intriguing textures, which ensured tweed's place in the gallery of the world's classic textiles.

The coming of the railway link between Edinburgh and Hawick in 1849 and its extension to Carlisle in 1862 meant that raw materials and finished products could be easily transported. The expansion of the tweed mills at that time was similar to that in Selkirk. Entrepreneurs flocked to Hawick to be part of the action and created great wealth for the tweed manufacturers who built imposing mansions around the town.[24]

After training as a tweed designer and working in the mills in Selkirk, and being a hardworking, energetic and ambitious young man, William Linton, moved to Hawick to work in this booming industry with Messrs Greenwood, Watt & Co. as a tweed pattern designer. He was no doubt attracted by the new building programme of the firm, widely seen as a forward-thinking company.

The company had built Teviotdale Mills on Commercial Road in 1877 but, as their business grew, they decided to extend and erected an extension on a vacant site on Victoria Road in 1880. A local road surveyor, John Manuel, was engaged to design the new mill and, when Howlands Mill opened in 1880, it was linked to Teviotdale Mills by telephone. It was large and modern, with 78 looms plus the ancillary machinery and the potential for 300 looms in its three large bays. By 1888, Greenwood and Watt removed to Howlands Mill and sold Teviotdale Mills.

Development on this scale shows the confidence that manufacturers felt in the future of the industry. It was in this state-of-the-art mill that William Linton worked, doing the job he loved most, designing tweed.[25]

William weds Helen

On 1 July 1898, the local newspaper, *The Hawick News*, carried a report of a presentation made to William by his fellow workers at Greenwood, Watt & Co. It stated that, on the day before his marriage, Thursday 23 June, the employees met in their dinner hour, and Mr Black, the company cashier presented William with a handsome aneroid barometer. William gave a suitable speech thanking his colleagues for their generous gift.[26]

That night he returned to Selkirk from his home at Howlands, Hawick, for his marriage to Helen Horsburgh of Backrow, Selkirk on 24th June 1898. Helen was a talented dressmaker, twenty-five years old, and William was twenty-six when they wed. Born on 18 September 1872, at 28 High Street, Selkirk, Helen was the daughter of Agnes Stoddart and Hugh Horsburgh. The Horsburghs were both born in 1833, Hugh in Haddington and Agnes in Selkirk. They had married in Edinburgh in November 1854 and had nine children, including twins and Helen, who was the youngest. Hugh had been a groom, but by 1881 was an unemployed woollen mill worker. Later he became a groom and coachman at Kirkbrae. Several of the children made their living in the local mills, one becoming a power-loom tuner, others weavers and dyers.

By the time of Helen's marriage to William, her mother was dead and her father retired. William's parents, William and Marion, were at the wedding and by now William senior had his own market-gardening business. The Marriage Register was signed by the witnesses Robert Linton, William's brother, and Margaret Horsburgh, Helen's sister.

The young couple returned to live in Hawick and, while William worked as a tweed pattern designer, Helen probably continued working as a dressmaker. They set up home at 25 Beaconsfield Terrace, a row of stone-built houses within walking distance of the mill. The property was let out as apartments as, by 1901, three families are shown on the census return as occupants. As well as the Lintons, there was forty-year-old Margaret Horsburgh, Helen's older sister, a housekeeper, as by this time, their father Hugh had died in Selkirk, and she too had moved to Hawick. Walter Atkinson, a teacher of a brass band, his wife Sarah, and their two children were the other occupants of the house.[27]

Joy and tragedy

After four years of marriage, their happiness was complete when, on 10 November 1902, their first child, Agnes Helen Pringle Linton, was born at the family home. William and Helen's joy at the birth of their infant daughter was to be short-lived, as Helen became seriously ill.

25 Beaconsfield Terrace, Hawick - home of William and Helen Linton, where Agnes was born

On the morning of 7 December, tragedy struck the small family when, with William at her bedside and barely four weeks after her daughter's birth, Helen died from puerperal septicaemia at the age of thirty. William was devastated by this tragedy, and had to rely on other members of his family to take care of the infant Agnes, while he earned his living at the mill. Life was not easy, but he was driven by a burning ambition: one day he planned to own his own tweed mill, and Agnes would follow him into the business. Helen's loss had hit William hard and he would never remarry, instead, devoting his life to his work and his daughter.

Nothing is ever stable in the textile industry and the mills in

Hawick were no exception. In 1906, when James Edgar, the founder of the Hawick Callants Club, published his *Hawick Guide and Directory,* he listed eleven manufacturers producing tweed in the town.[28] But by 1910 Hawick's tweed trade was facing a serious decline and there was a scaling down of the industry. Howlands Mill was sold on to another manufacturer, Messrs Sime, Williamson & Co., who had been in business at Weensland Mills since 1889. In a change of name, Greenwood, Watt & Co.'s Howlands Mill became Dean Mills.[29] By 1909, when Mr John Farrar Blenkharn died, Mr Greenwood was head-hunted by one of his former rivals, Messrs Blenkharn, Richardson & Co. of Eastfield Mills, to join their sales staff, and Messrs Greenwood, Watt & Co. closed. Mr Greenwood's hopes for the future had not withstood the economic pressures on the trade. As the mill families grouped and re-grouped in an attempt to create stability, William was out of a job.[30] Undeterred, he decided to look further afield to fulfil his dream and, by 1912, he had moved across to the English side of the border to the city of Carlisle.

***

4
A child of the orphanage

Albert Chanel was a big disappointment: as he had been to his wife, so he was to his children. Overwhelmed by the enormity of his responsibilities, instead of trying to shoulder them, he did what he had always done and took off. In all the accounts of Gabrielle's early life, her father is denigrated as abandoning his children. But would Gabrielle say that was true? She would recall:

> *'Like all children, I listened at closed doors. I learned that my father had ruined my mother – 'poor Jeanne'. All the same she married the man she loved. And having to hear people call me an orphan! They felt sorry for me. I had nothing to be pitied for – I had a father. All this was humiliating. I realized no one loved me and I was being kept out of charity.'* [31]

She would, in fact, make up stories to account for her father's absence, and in these tales he was always something of a knight in shining armour. 'He really loved me. I represented the good days, fun, happiness. When I was born everything was going well.' [32] It would be difficult for any man to care for five children aged between six and twelve, without family support, and also earn a living to keep the family together. It was not in Albert's nature to even try, and he went back to the markets.

In later years, Gabrielle recalled the day when, at eleven years old and with her two sisters riding along, her father drove them in the horse-drawn buggy along the nine miles from Brive to the convent in the mountains.[33] The girls must have found it a forbidding view as they neared the entrance. The high, isolated abbey, sited on a plateau encircled by deeply wooded hills, stood like a vast stone fortress, with its steep-pitched roofs and high walls guarding its own, menacing in the bleak February light.

Aubazine in 1895 was an orphanage run by the sisters of the Congregation of the Religious of the Sacred Heart of Mary. The congregation had been founded in 1849 by Père Pierre Jean Gailhac who was a priest in Béziers, part of the diocese of Montpellier, the capital of Languedoc-Roussillon on the southern coast of France. His co-founder was a young widow, Madame Apollonie Pelissier-Cure: she and her husband had been close friends of Père Gailhac, and after her husband's death she took the religious name of Mother St John. The religious order they founded grew and received final approbation of the Holy See in 1899. Often known as the Béziers Sisters, some came to England in 1872, the year of William Linton's birth, and in time opened a convent school in Carlisle.[34]

Consolation, hope and salvation?

The Congregation's motto was 'Salus Consolatio Spes Nostra' (Our consolation, hope, salvation). A painting of Apollonie shows a pretty and determined woman: Gabrielle may well have been familiar with her portrait in Aubazine Convent. Aubazine had been a monastery built by a twelfth-century Cistercian monk, Étienne d'Aubazine, and his followers. Made of local granite in a landscape of forests, rivers and limestone gorges, amid the early morning mists and winds from the west which surround this lovely region of Corrèze. A canal was built by the monks to supply water to the monastery and, in this peaceful setting, they lived a life of silence and solitude, hermits who gave up everything for the love of God. Étienne's influence was still felt, and the sisters read passages to the girls from the *Life of Étienne d'Aubazine*, published in 1888, every day at mealtimes, during walks and in class. To the nuns the book was like a gospel.[35]

The convent was built against the side of the abbey church, and enclosed a courtyard with a fountain and a fishpond fed by the waters of the Coiroux mountain stream. It had high-ceilinged rooms with white walls and scrubbed floors, long corridors and dormitories with tall black doors, everything black and white and clean. On Sundays, the girls were taken for walks, with views of never ending green forests, canopies of trees as far as the eye could see. To Gabrielle, who was used to the colourful, bustling life of the marketplace, with its pungent aromas of mushrooms and wild brambles, the street cries of traders and hawkers, narrow streets and cramped cosy houses, this must have seemed an alien world. But it could grow on you, all this simplicity and perfection.

Although never in her lifetime would Gabrielle ever utter the words 'Aubazine' or 'orphanage', the influences would remain with her for the rest of her life. She would carry them deep within herself, and years later bring them out and use them, in her trade - fashion.

The nuns may have been taking care of the girls' welfare and material needs, but what they were about was education, to equip the girls to hold their own in life. Everything had to be perfect, done to the highest standard. As well as the usual lessons, the nuns taught the girls hand-sewing to a high degree. Beautiful buttonholes, French seams, hems so neat you could scarcely see them and embroidery where the reverse was as perfect as the front. Personal standards were high, with shiny hair, perfect posture, crisp white shirts, pressed black box-pleated skirts - and manners were all.

In summer, lessons might occasionally be taken in the garden, under the shade of the trees, or the girls would set off in long crocodiles taking their walk. Down the country roads where golden Limousin cattle grazed. At night, in the cool dormitory, they would whisper to each other about popular novels they had managed to read, out of sight of the nuns. Sundays would mean early Mass with the priest saying the prayers in Latin, amid the tinkle of the communion bell, fresh flowers and flickering candles. Christmas had them all practicing carols, with visits to the crib and the nuns high-voiced singing at Midnight Mass - *Il est né, le Divin Enfant.* And all around the clean, clean smell of lye soap and beeswax polish. They had to work hard, and learn well, and the nuns hoped that the end product of this strict, settled, ordered life would be - a refined lady.

A refined lady she may have become, but Gabrielle would never forget the deep wounds of bitterness and resentment that she felt, on what she saw as abandonment by her family at a time when she was traumatised by the loss of her mother. She was prickly, suspicious, held back her trust - she wanted to be loved, but was afraid of being hurt, of being rejected. It gave her that backbone of independence and total self-reliance. Later in life, on becoming the successful Coco, she would tell all sorts of stories about her early life, anything but the truth. She was brought up by two strict aunts, who were good people , but without tenderness, she said, 'I got no affection.' [36]

The 'aunts' that she spoke of were actually the nuns of Aubazine, But she acknowledged some benefits from the time spent with them, in particular a desire for order and

Madame Apollonie Pelissier-Cure, co-founder of the religious order at Aubazine, where Chanel was educated

comfort, clean-smelling linen and gleaming floors. And a sense of solid substance that, for her, was the essence of being French.[37]

She would also credit this period in her life with her understanding of independence and the need to earn her living and for the influences on her personal style of dress.

She claimed that money never interested her but remembered vividly the servants in the orphanage planning their independence when they had saved enough. For Coco, money represented just that: a means to independence.

She also claimed that the little tailored suits all girls had to wear at that time were the basis of her own fashion style. [38]

All her would-be biographers were told fantastic tales, even those who became her friends and supporters. Her father was a wine merchant from Béziers, her mother died when she was six years old, her father went to America and she never saw him again, and so it went on, even the date on her birth certificate had been changed to make her appear ten years younger. She was, in fact, creating her own legend. Why did she do this? Perhaps a natural reaction for children separated from their parents and left in an orphanage?

If Gabrielle and her sisters had suffered a strict life at the convent, the fate of her two young brothers was even harder. They became Hospice children, placed in foster care with farming families, who were paid an allowance to keep them until they reached the age when they could be apprenticed to a trade. They were usually children who were orphans or who had been abandoned at birth. Working hard, they were often harshly treated, receiving little education. Alphonse and Lucien were ten and six years old respectively when Albert left them, and it was not until they were thirteen that their grandparents and Aunt Louise arranged for them to leave the farms and become apprenticed to market traders based in Moulins. They were back to the life they had known with their parents, in the markets. Alphonse was later to tell his children, 'I was put on the road at thirteen... always on the road.' [39]

Why none of the Chanel family could take in any of the children remains a mystery, but it was probably due to the fact that they were continually on the move themselves and could not afford to feed and clothe Albert's five children.

Little is known of the children's mother's family, the Devolles, and they do not seem to have featured very much in the Chanel children's lives after their mother's death. Perhaps they were old or there were few of them, as by now Uncle Augustin would be an old man. Uncle Marin, their mother's brother and Albert's old friend appears to have played no part in their lives.

In 1895, paternal grandfather Henri-Adrien was sixty-three years old and his wife was fifty-seven, with their youngest daughter Adrienne at the Nôtre Dame boarding school, run by the Canonesses of St Augustine in Moulins. By 1900, Gabrielle's grandparents were looking for the more settled life of working in the Halles or covered markets, and the one in Moulins was a favourite. They decided to make their home there, living in an attic apartment on rue des Fausses-Braies, where they were near the market, the fairground and Adrienne.

At Aunt Julia's

Louise and Paul Costier were living at Varennes-sur-Allier, only twelve miles away. They had no children and Paul was making a successful career on the railways. Louise was known in the family as 'Aunt Julia' and her home would become the central family meeting place, with Uncle Paul giving the family free passes on the railway and a warm welcome to his many relatives, including his wife's favourite brother, Albert.[40] At last, it seemed that the family were gathering the children back together in Moulins. The boys were back working on their apprenticeships, and it was decided that Julia, Gabrielle and Antoinette would attend Nôtre-Dame, the same boarding school as Adrienne. (The nuns at Aubazine only kept the girls there until they were eighteen, unless they were entering the convent. They did , however, have a wide range of influence locally and would often arrange apprenticeships, while still providing the girls with room and board. Or they would arrange movements to other convents and find work or benefactresses for them. The nuns were a powerful part of the community and their charges were never abandoned.[41])

Gabrielle was growing up. At seventeen she had striking good looks and an innate elegance and sense of style. Adrienne was her mirror image, and it delighted them when they were mistaken for sisters. It was Adrienne, with her affectionate nature, who would make Gabrielle feel at home in Moulins and help her get used to a new school and a new life. The two girls became inseparable, and shared confidences in the dormitory at Nôtre-Dame and in the attic bedroom that they shared in the holidays at Aunt Julia's. They were not alike in nature. Adrienne had not suffered Gabrielle's hardships, and was used to a secure, serene life, giving her an air of self-possession. Gabrielle was an energetic, imaginative, creative creature and could not wait to start living.

But Nôtre-Dame School gave Gabrielle a further hard lesson in life. It had the social split of fee-paying girls, whose parents were wealthy and privileged, and places for more needy young women. The divisions were obvious to her when, even at Sunday High Mass in the Cathedral, the fee-paying girls sat in the centre aisles, with the free-school in the side aisles. But in Moulins life was colourful too – in June, there were the Corpus Christi processions, when the Blessed Sacrament encased in a golden monstrance was carried by the Bishop, under a swaying white and gold canopy, in procession along the streets. With bands playing, flower girls strewing rose petals and hymn singing in the flower-bedecked streets, Gabrielle walked along with the other girls, heading the procession. She sang the hymns with all her heart: she loved to sing because it made her feel as light as air. All the pavements were crowded and the procession wended its way to the grandest of the wayside altars, erected by the cavalry regiments. The preparations and celebrations went on for days.[42]

Over the next two years, holidays would be her escape. Aunt Julia would arrive at school amid general excitement and pick up her four girls, Adrienne, Julia, Gabrielle and Antoinette. Soon they would be on Uncle Paul's railway, off to Varennes.

Aunt Julia did not work: her life was in making a comfortable home for her husband and in her creative skills. Louise Costier was a gifted amateur dressmaker and milliner. This caught the interest of both Adrienne and Gabrielle. Gabrielle's quick mind soon grasped the creative possibilities: she could sew beautifully, but this was something else – a way to express your ideas, your originality, to create. She learnt easily, and soon she could follow Aunt Julia in

Aubazine convent, in the wooded landscape of Corrèze

making fine pleated collars and cuffs from scraps of white linen, spicing up the sombre convent-girl clothes. Or make a flower brooch from a bright handkerchief and pin it to a crisp shirtwaister. With a little ingenuity the possibilities were endless.

The annual trip to Vichy was made to buy basic hat shapes, and from these Aunt Julia showed her nieces how to snip and embellish, until a simple shape became chic, with braid, ribbons and feathers. It was a revelation to Gabrielle and stored away in her memory.[43] In 1903, Gabrielle turned twenty. The next few years were to see her transform her life. The girls left Nôtre-Dame, but still kept in touch with the nuns. Gabrielle was proud to be asked to keep on singing with the free-school choir - she hoped to become a singer. In Scotland, in Hawick, Agnes Helen Pringle Linton was just a few months old. She too was without a mother, but with an ambitious father whose work would one day link these two girls.

***

5
Stepping out in Moulins and Vichy

By now, Julia was working for her grandparents as a market trader, Antoinette was still at Nôtre-Dame, and Adrienne and Gabrielle found their first jobs. The House of Grampayre, on the rue de l'Horloge, was owned by Henri Desboutin and his wife, a respectable couple well known to the nuns, who placed their most talented needlewomen there. The dress shop was known as 'À Sainte Marie' and, at first, the girls were shop assistants selling wedding trousseaux, christening gowns and lace, and living in the attic bedroom above the shop.

Madame Desboutin soon recognised their talents and they were moved to the sewing room, where clothes for ladies and small girls were made. Here Gabrielle came into her own - and word soon got around. Moulins was no provincial backwater. Her employers made sure that she was aware of the importance of the wealthy customers and landed gentry who patronised the shop. Gabrielle was not impressed, of course, but it was a precursor of things to come.

This was châteaux country and had been the seat of the Bourbon Dukes since the 10th century. They are depicted, alongside the saints, in the 15th and 16th century, beautiful stained-glass windows of the Cathédrale Nôtre-Dame, on rue Louis Mantin where Gabrielle had worshipped. Also in the Treasury here is a luminous triptych of the Virgin and Child painted by the 'Master of Moulins' in 1498. The centre panel depicts Pierre, Duke of Bourbon and his wife wearing sumptuous embroidered and jewelled clothes meeting a simply dressed Madonna.

Men were the association that Gabrielle would always have in her mind when she thought of Moulins, for it was here that her first encounters began. Up to now, her glances at the black-bloused, white-collared boys with floating ties, from the rue du Lycée school, across the road from Nôtre-Dame, had been frowned upon. Now with her new-found independence and at the threshold of her twenties, she felt excitement in the air. She needed freedom and was ready to spread her wings. Without the more conservative Adrienne, she rented a cheap room in the rue du Pont Guinguet with views across to the Allier river. Soon approval was given from Aunt Julia and the nuns, and both girls shared the room. Unknown to the Desboutins, they started using their dressmaking skills by taking private clients, making stylish dresses, fitted skirts and jackets - all of the highest quality. The ladies of the châteaux approved.

Moulins buzzed: it was first and foremost a garrison town. Several regiments were billeted on the edges of town, and the most elite of these was the 10th Light Horse at Quartier Villars across the Allier. The attractions of the town brought the cavalry to its bright lights - to the pastry shops, to the Café Chinois for dancing on Saturday nights, and to The Alcazar to dance quadrilles on Sunday. The town was a rendezvous for the young men and their fiancées and sweethearts, for their sisters and mothers. They cut fine figures these young men, sons of the wealthy and the landed gentry, with their high leather boots, stylish braided and buttoned jackets, and rakish peaked caps. The bright young men were not likely to come into the local tailors: private incomes and wealthy parents meant they patronised the best tailors in Paris for their frogged and gilt-buttoned jackets and their sky-blue overcoats. [44]

The horse-racing season was important in Moulins, given its proximity to some major stables, and race days saw many noble visitors attending. On a busy race day, several of the young men found themselves in need of urgent repairs before taking part in the race. Dashing into the Modern Tailleur, a local tailor's shop, they were surprised to see two beautiful girls sewing in the back room. The girls never raised their eyes. On enquiring, they found out that the girls worked at 'À Sainte Marie', a ladies dress shop, and helped out in the tailor's shop at peak times. In time-old tradition, they hung around waiting for them to finish work. It did not take long to persuade the beautiful, polite young women to accept an invitation to watch the next day's jumping events. Gabrielle was to be remembered by these well-bred young lieutenants for many years after, not only for her exceptional beauty, but for the *cachet* of her original qualities. To them we owe the record of her life in Moulins.[45]

Meetings took place, at the sherbet shop - À la Tentation - or at the Grand Café with its wood panelling and bevelled mirrors. It was pretty, it was luxurious and it delighted Gabrielle. Adrienne was more cautious. However, there was safety in numbers and, as their popularity soared, they became part of a wider group enjoying the nightlife of Moulins.

Coco la chanteuse

Gabrielle still harboured an ambition to be a singer: she saw it as a way of making a name for herself, of succeeding in life. There were some ideas she never gave up on. La Rotonde was to be the starting place for those ambitions.

The first time they went there, Gabrielle was mesmerised by the music, the atmosphere and the crowds. She did what she always did: she observed, missing nothing, drinking it all in. A germ of an idea came to her: could she sing here? La Rotonde was originally built as a café and reading room, but with the spread of café-concerts throughout France, it had become a favourite music hall for the men at the garrison.

An elegant young Coco Chanel

It stood, with its trellised walls and pagoda roof, in a tree-lined square, with benches round the lawn and swans on the pool. She approached La Rotonde's Director - encouraged by her group of supporters – and was given a chance. This was the time when Paris was leading the way and young women were becoming famous as music-hall and nightclub singers. They all aspired to have the success of Yvette Guilbert, a fêted Parisian singer and monologuist featured in some of Henri de Toulouse-Lautrec's brilliant posters.

Another favourite was Pauline Polaire, the stage name of the singer Emilie Marie Bouchard. Born in Algiers, she started her career as a café singer at the age of fifteen.

She was also sketched by Toulouse-Lautrec and made her first major stage appearance in 1902, at the Bouffes-Parisiens playing the title role in Colette's play, *Claudine a Paris.*[46] As she wrote in her memoirs, 'Claudines were all the rage... every nightclub and house of ill repute had its "Claudine".'[47] (Colette was the author of the series of Claudine books, although this was not known at the time they were published in the early 1900s. The fictional Claudine was a precocious sixteen-year-old schoolgirl from the country, on the cusp of discovering what it meant to be a woman, and her journal was published as a novel, under the pseudonym Willy. It soon became an all-time French best seller. Willy, was in fact, Colette's first husband, Henry Gauthier-Villars, who was a music critic and author.[48])

La Rotonde's Director saw something of a 'Claudine' in Gabrielle, with her wide mouth and long neck, and that mercurial expression, one moment shy the next fizzing to perform. He was not as impressed with her voice. But perform she did. Supported by her retinue of admirers from the garrison, she would rise with a shy smile and take centre stage. There she would launch into one of the two songs that she knew - 'Ko Ko Ri Ko' - an 1898 hit by Polaire from a revue at the Paris music hall, La Scala. Her second offering was greeted with much cheering and brought the house down - it was 'Qui qu'a vu Coco dans l'Trocadero', the story of a girl who lost her little dog at the Trocadero gardens, looking across to the Eiffel Tower.

The song ended with the words:

> *Coco at the Trocadero.*
> *Who has seen Coco?*
> *Oh, Coco,*
> *Who has seen Coco?*[49]

For an encore the young admirers called out 'Coco, Coco'. And Gabrielle had a new name.

The beautiful Adrienne also worked at La Rotonde - she had the job of passing the hat around. Pleased with her success, Coco started to think about her plans for a career in operetta. She needed more than the shabby surroundings of La Rotonde. She also needed to find a more respectable start for her career. Aunt Julia was unaware of the goings-on at Moulins, but Adrienne became increasingly worried.

At this time Coco's elder sister, Julia, became involved with a fairground trader and soon fell pregnant. History repeated itself. A son, André, was born and, although the father recognised the child, he would not marry Julia. The young man set up home with her and gave the little boy his name, Palasse.

Singing in the city

Vichy, a small city thirty miles away from Moulins, was famous for its Thermal Establishment where the wealthy middle classes came to 'take the waters', since it had been made fashionable by Napoleon III and his friends in 1860.[50] The focal point was the bandstand in Parc des Sources where afternoon concerts were held, amid the flowers and bright bunting. Coco and Adrienne decided to try their luck there for one season. It was the summer of 1905. Not everyone encouraged her to go: one of her admirers, a trainee officer in the infantry, Étienne Balsan, told her, 'You won't get anywhere, you don't have a voice and you sing like a trombone.' The apparently dismissive remark hid feelings stronger than friendship, however, as later events were to prove.

From a solid French upper middle-class family, whose background had been banking and textile manufacture for generations, Étienne was educated at a British public school. On his arrival in England, he had bought two horses and was soon to be seen at fox-hunting meets. He loved the social scene, to the extent that his father, disapproving of his way of life, summoned him back to Châteauroux where he enlisted in the African Light Cavalry.[51] He was remembered at Châteauroux by the workers in the family's factory who came out to watch him on race days, and place a bet on him.[52] Horses were his main interest, his life. His burning ambition was to breed them and, on his return from

Algiers, he managed to get transferred to the 10th Light Horse brigade at Moulins.

It was a fortuitous day for Coco Chanel. He saw something more than a café singer in Coco, so he told her he would finance the trip to Vichy. There was a spark between them: she a feisty young woman and he a warm-hearted young man.

Coco and Adrienne had to look smart and fashionable to have any hope of success, so they decided to sew themselves new outfits, and new hats to go to Vichy. There is a famous photograph of them at this time, the earliest known picture of Coco and her aunt, standing in the park at Vichy, a pair of elegant young women. It is one that fashion editors and Chanel *aficionados* alike have pored over for years. Because here are the seeds of the future, and indeed, compared with a portrait by society photographer, Cecil Beaton, of Chanel at fifty-five, the similarities in the cut of her jacket, with its neat fitted shoulders, small revers and cut away shape are apparent. Adrienne is sporting gilt buttons and contrasting collar and cuffs, all to be seen in the future Chanel look. Coco would never admit it in later years, but she could sew to perfection.

Vichy was not Moulins, and Coco needed all her determination to pursue her career and quest for improvement. A colourful, buzzing city, where returning soldiers from tours in Algeria came to refresh themselves, aristocratic ladies shopped in the elegant malls, and rich, over-indulged men sought rejuvenation in the invigorating waters. Foreign diplomats turned up with their retinues, and all of this, Coco took in on her afternoon walks.

They soon rented a small room and set to checking out the local venues where singers performed. There was more variety than in Moulins, and they were more up-market. Coco practiced her songs, dressed with care and set off to do the rounds. She knew she had no chance at the Grand Casino: too grand. There was the Eden Theatre, set in lovely gardens and where operettas were performed, but she needed general experience first, to learn the ropes, learn to dance, learn to perform.

Struggling to succeed

Coco decided to approach The Alcazar which specialised in variety shows and seemed an exciting place to work. She and Adrienne visited it and took in the atmosphere, the stage surrounded by tables, the lighting, the room for souvenir photographs, the authentic belly dancers and the Tunisian concert party. They had heard that it tried to emulate the Jardin de Paris, a fashionable nightspot on the Champs Elysées in Paris.[53]

This was the one, they decided, and they both got auditions - well a 'try-out' said the house pianist. Working in the cellar under the café where the auditions took place, he was used to these young girls with their dreams of stardom and he was not above using them for his deals with the wardrobe mistress. Girls with talent could hire a costume, pay for it themselves, and then he would put their names forward to the manager.

Finding her style was the next step for Coco. Would she would be a romantic, a comedy singer or would she be soulfull and aloof? The pianist put her through her paces, but it did not look hopeful. The voice that had soared in the Cathedral was not the voice of the variety stage. With sinking heart she tried another song, recalling the imitators of Polaire's songs that she had heard. She hit the right style. He told her it would be hard work, pulled no punches: her voice was too slight, too low, but... with her charm and her presence, and practice... well, he would give her a chance. She needed no second invitation.

Adrienne was not so lucky. Her heart was not really in it anyway, but it was a definite no. He sat at the piano and said she looked too much like a lady, too classy and as for her voice... well. There was nothing for it but to return to Moulins.

Hard work would never deter Coco, however, and she threw herself into it heart and soul. He became like a svengali to her, the house pianist. He decided her style would be that of a *gommeuse,* the style that was the rage of Paris at the moment, the style of

Polaire and Yvette Guilbert.[54] She had heard of Jeanne Bourgeois from the Île-de-France who, as Mistinguett, had made her debut singing at the Casino de Paris in 1895, and was now the toast of Paris. She had caused a sensation when she appeared in a short, black, low-cut, sequinned dress with a flared ruffled hem, a rose pinned on her breast and danced with the longest legs in the business. With her huge eyes, delicate features and generous mouth, she was beauty personified. She was as famous for her love affairs as her singing, and was to have a long relationship with Maurice Chevalier as well as torrid affairs with the future King Edward VII, King Alfonso XIII of Spain and an Indian prince. All the provincial music halls wanted their own 'Mistinguett', and Coco might fit the bill at The Alcazar.

They started work together; he adapting the Paris hit songs to suit her voice, she trying to master some dance steps, how to move with the rhythm, to feel the song, sing from her soul - she tried with all her heart. He was a hard taskmaster, he criticised her gestures - too stiff, her figure - too slight, her voice - too husky. She got her black sequinned gown: it would show up better in the footlights, but was constantly sewing and repairing it, because the sequins only needed a snag and they unravelled like a silk stocking. Paying for the wardrobe did not come cheap, neither did the singing lessons. Only with Étienne's support could she stay there - but stay she did.

And the little black dress? Well, it never left her, and its memory would be her inspiration twenty-five years later when she launched it from rue Cambon, and the women of the world would embrace it - until this day.

Firm bookings, however, were hard to come by: there was too much competition. Needing to supplement her finances, she looked around for a job and soon found one at the municipal baths, where she was hired as a water girl at the Grand Grille. Within sound of the band playing at the Grand Casino, she stood in a pit dressed in an all-white uniform, including little white boots and, solemnly taking a glass from the straw holder, she would fill it from the hot spring that poured forth below a crystal globe.[55] The crowd loved her, reaching down to take the health-giving drink from her, exchanging laughs and giving her compliments. The boots also were stored away in her subconscious mind, comfortable and practical, women would find them useful.

In the meantime, Adrienne had gone to live with Maud Mazuel near Souvigny. Maud might have been called a matchmaker: she filled her house (known locally as 'the château') with both the gentry and cavalry officers. It was where the provincial ladies gathered to meet the gentlemen, with not a wife to be seen.

Tea was served under the parasols in the garden, everyone relaxed on the chaises longues and chocolate cake was enjoyed amid the small talk. It was a meeting place: perhaps it would have been a salon in another class of society, but Maud was provincial and fun, and also a chaperone - there was no gossip about ladies seen in Maud's company. Coco went to join them, but Étienne was never among the officers who came to discuss horses. He said he found the ladies boring. Coco felt that she was just filling in time, and besides, Adrienne had a suitor, a land-owning aristocrat, who wished to include her in his party, going on a jaunt to Egypt to see the Sphinx, and cruise on the Nile. Coco was also invited, but refused to go, in spite of Maud's best efforts to persuade her.[56]

The days were kept bright by Étienne and his friends, who were frequent visitors and took her along to see the races. She was hooked on horses, and for the rest of her life would ride and attend the racetracks, watching the jockeys in their brilliant racing silks, eventually becoming an owner herself. As the season drew to its close and the visitors thinned out, the races were over, café-concerts began to close down, The Alcazar season ended as autumn turned to winter, and the cold winds blew down the forsaken boulevards. Coco had no work. There was nothing for it but to return to Moulins.

***

6

Étienne and Royallieu

Vichy, the lively spa town where Chanel finally realised she would never find fame as a singer

Royallieu: the grand name belied a long and varied history - from a fortified outpost of Paris - La Neuville - to a hunting lodge used by the Capet kings, it had become La Maison du Roy in the twelfth century after King Philippe le Bel stayed there, and from that, Royallieu.[57] Later, it became an abbey, with the Benedictine sisters of St Jean du Bois rebuilding it and making it a charming provincial manor house.[58]

Étienne had bought the property intending to 'do it up' as it was close to the stables and training ground at La Croix Saint-Ouen near Compiègne. The work was finished by the time he returned from Moulins. Situated to the north of Paris , it was only just over an hour by train from the Gare du Nord. When he asked Coco if she would like to come and live there, she was dizzy with pleasure. It was not an informed decision that she made, to go to Royallieu. Her heart was leading her head.

Speculation exists about her relationship with Étienne at this time. Were they lovers? We may never know. There were rumours throughout her lifetime that she had an illegal abortion as a young woman, and this had left her unable to have children, which she so desired when she later met Bendor, the second Duke of Westminster. Looking back in her last years, she recalled that Étienne had said, 'There's nothing to be frightened of... I only like old ladies.' ' I'll come with you,' she said, 'Just give me time to pack my case.' [59]

If she had simply been a social climber, it would have been a good move. The Balsans were a family of some substance who had lived with style and wealth since Étienne's grandfather bought the estate of Château du Parc at Châteauroux in the Indre valley in 1856. The estate was midway between Moulins and Tours, set amid parkland, and its textile factories were close by. The woollen factories had been founded in the 17th century by the Prince de Condé, in the reign of Louis XIV. They would become suppliers of blue cloth for British police uniforms until the Boer War in 1899.[60]

Étienne's parents, Auguste and Marie were both dead, his father dying in 1896 at their home at rue de la Baume, Paris, and his mother at Châteauroux in December 1902. Étienne therefore came into an inheritance, along with his two brothers and two sisters in 1903, at the age of twenty-five. He had little interest in the family business and left it to his two older brothers, Jacques and Robert, and his cousin Jean-Charles to run the family's banking and textile interests.[61] They were to be very successful and expanded the business, becoming defence contractors in World War 1, supplying the cloth used for military uniforms.[62]

Consuelo Vanderbilt, an American heiress (who married Étienne's older brother Jacques in 1921, after her divorce from Charles Spencer-Churchill, 9th Duke of Marlborough) described meeting this impressive family:

> *'On this my first visit the doors of the salon opened on a typical family scene. There were at least twenty people assembled in various groups - Jacques' brothers, sisters, cousins, his nephews and nieces. In a bergère near the hearth*

sat a lovely old lady dressed in black with a touch of lace. She was Madame Charles Balsan, Jacques' aunt and head of the family, who with masterful authority ensured the traditional discipline of the Catholic Church'.[63]

And Étienne himself, although not handsome, would have been considered 'a good catch' in his social circles. He was described by Edmonde Charles-Roux, author and a former editor of *Vogue* thus:

'Neither tall nor slender, with an unspectacular moustache and a round face, nothing military in his bearing, none of the audacities of dress so cherished by the horseman, not much distinction about him and no pretentiousness at all, he was assuredly less alluring and less elegant than they. But, wildly energetic, visibly openhanded, and a master at making and keeping friends.' [64]

An unexpected encounter

We have no record of Coco's ideas or wishes about the possibiity of a long-term relationship with Étienne. What is known is that, when Coco arrived at Royallieu, she found a former mistress already installed. Émilienne D'Alençon was born in Paris in 1869, the year that the Folies-Bergères, the first music hall in Paris, opened and she was thirty-seven when Coco moved in.[65] She had been a famous dancer at the Folies and as a young woman had married the well-known English jockey, Percy Woodland, who died in World War 1.[66]

Château de Royallieu, home of Étienne Balsan where Chanel lived for a time

She had been Étienne's mistress five years earlier and lived with him at his batchelor apartment on the boulevard Malesherbes in Paris, but by 1906 she was only interested in Alec Carter, a celebrated English trainer at the Chantilly racecourse, the main training area in France, he had become a jockey and his great success made him the idol of the race-goers. He was a small, slim, elegant man of immense personal charm and was well-remembered by all who knew him. Coco also found him fascinating.

A photograph of Émilienne at this time shows a rather plump woman wearing a pin-tucked shirtwaist with a tie and buttonhole carnation, a small, jaunty hat perched on her head. She had been born in a concierge's room on the rue des Martyrs, attended the Conservatoire and appeared at the age of fifteen at the Summer Circus.[67] In her earlier years at the Folies-Bergères she had been depicted in lithographed posters by Jules Cheret, where she exuded an air of simmering sensuality. It was rumoured that eight gentlemen of the Jockey Club, seeking her favours had formed a company to finance her living in style, and took their turn to be invited 'to tea'.[68] By the time she came to Royallieu, she had made her fortune and was looking for a life of ease and fun, joining in the practical jokes with Étienne's friends.

The house amazed Coco: it had three storeys, ivy-covered walls, turrets and long elegant windows. Its setting was in mature parkland with canopies of chestnut trees and old oaks looking across the finely kept lawns, with rose-beds bursting with colour and she had never seen such beauty. Inside, the house was luxurious, with the tiled corridor leading to the high staircase, where the portrait of abbess Gabrielle de Laubespine, who restored the house, hung. The cool decoration enhanced its modern bathrooms, elegant drawing rooms, and comfortable bedrooms.

This was horse-racing country, and there were stables, paddocks for exercise and grazing land, with stable lads and jockeys looking after their charges. The old hunting grounds of the fragrant forest of Compiègne with its oaks and beeches, and wide pathways to clearings for picnics, were close by. So in the summer of 1906, just before her twenty-third birthday, Coco moved in.

She was to claim years later that she could identify branches from the forest of Compiègne simply by their smell, so immured was she in the way of life there. And the beauty of the horses there was an enduring memory. [69]

Changing times, changing fashions

The period from 1895 until 1914 was known in France as La Belle Époque, or the 'beautiful era'. It was a time of peace and stability, and also a time of luxury living and extravagant clothes. New inventions enhanced life at all social levels, and there were new forms of art, with the development of the Impressionist School and the Art Nouveau movement. *Salon* music as well as the music halls, the risqué cancan, cabaret and cinema were popular. Yet life was not so carefree for all and socialist movements were beginning, together with a rise in working-class militancy.

In England, the Victorian era was in its last years, the Queen had celebrated her Golden Jubilee in 1887 and on her death in 1901, the charming, pleasure–loving, elegant Prince of Wales became King Edward V11. America at this time looked to Europe for the arts and fashion, and the wealthy made frequent trips to Paris where the 'father of haute couture', the Englishman Charles Worth, had established Maison Worth at 7 rue de la Paix in 1858.[70]

New York was America's principal city, where the Vanderbilts and others made up an elite society, and the world's first department store, Marshall Field's, opened in Chicago. Skyscrapers were built in New York and huge building developments took place. Ordinary women, at this time made up their own clothes from paper patterns, or had local dressmakers do this for them , and with the development of the department stores choice became wider. [71]

Clothes were beginning to change, the corseted look with leg-of-mutton sleeves was giving way to tailor-mades, with neat jackets,elegant dresses, starched blouses and soft flowing skirts. Charles Dana Gibson launched his illustrations of The Gibson Girl, in the 1890s, which epitomised the look and it found favour with college students and independent working women alike in America, and around the world.[72] Fashion was becoming big business and that arbiter of fashion and good taste, *Vogue*, was launched in 1892 in America, and bought by Condé Nast in 1909. He developed it into a worldwide fashion magazine whose influence was to stretch to all major cities around the globe into the 21st century.

Women such as Émilienne D'Alençon, as well as actresses, cabaret stars and courtesans, lived a life of luxury and pleasure while they could, relying on their 'protectors' from among the ranks of wealthy men, who often set them up in their own establishments with maids, and paid all their bills. The wives, if they knew, turned a blind eye: it was not unusual.

Coco had an absolute horror of being taken for such a woman. She eyed their fashions at the racetracks, where they paraded in ground-sweeping skirts, well-corseted with handspan waists and leg-of-mutton sleeves. Hats sat like overblown birds nests on their heads, abounding with flowers, feathers and veils, and requiring perfect posture. She

Émilienne D'Alençon, a former mistress of Étienne Balsan - she was one of the first to recognise Coco's millinery talents

was to say, 'How can a brain function under all that.' [73]

She felt out of her depth, this convent-educated girl was unaccustomed to the wealth and luxury that surrounded her, and to the type of rich, pleasure-seeking friends who visited Étienne. He spent most of his time at the training grounds and on the racetrack and, for the first few months, she did not leave the estate. Thirty years later he would say, 'She would lie in bed until noon, drinking coffee and milk and reading cheap novels. The laziest woman in the world.' But if they were going for an outing she was first to be up and ready. [74]

The horses were her joy, and Étienne began to give her riding lessons. Regardless of the weather she was there, practicing at all hours, with a steely ambition and determination to succeed. The grooms and stable lads became her friends and early mornings saw her at the training grounds, riding out with the apprentices. Later in the day, she would be sedately riding side-saddle with Étienne and his friends. Étienne believed she was a gifted horsewoman.

Charles Redfern, the London tailor who dressed Queen Alexandra, the consort of King Edward V11, had established a House in Paris, where he combined English tailoring with Parisian chic. This was the place to order your riding habit, but Coco could not afford to patronise him, instead she went to the tailor in the forest. The tailor had served in the 5th Dragoons, making his name as a craftsman and had opened his tailor's shop in a clearing in the forest. The forest was a way of passage for everything to do with the horse: men riding to hounds, gamekeepers, governesses with their charges going on picnics and young men driving dog-carts. The tailor was popular with the local grooms and huntsmen, making their riding breeches and hacking jackets. He did not usually make them for ladies. The day that Coco stood in the shop smiling, and holding out a pair of male jodphurs, that she wanted copied for herself was one he would never forget. It was all perfectly logical, she explained, she wished to ride astride and not be encumbered with a side-saddle skirt. So make them he did, and she became his regular customer, even keeping in touch years later, from rue Cambon. [75]

It caused quite a stir with Étienne's friends the first time they saw her ride astride - but she mastered it to perfection. (At the age of eighty-one, she could still describe the technique of having a good seat, in a rather earthy manner. 'To do it properly,' she said, 'there's one way and only one: you've got to imagine you're carrying a precious pair of balls [gesture] and under no circumstances can you put an ounce of weight on them. Good. You understand?' [76])

***

7

The love of her life

Autumn in Pau, beneath blue skies and the snow-capped Pyrenees, was idyllic, with its mild climate and Belle Époque charm. The town was a favourite resort with the English. Étienne and his friends went there each year for the racing and to play polo. It was here that Coco met her true love.

In 1908, Coco was twenty-five, an age when most women are thinking of enhancing their career or getting married and starting a family. She felt restless, the life of easy living was fun, but she needed to do more, to stretch her intellect and think of how to make her way in life. In that year, she met the man who she would never cease to love, or to mourn, and whose memory would be part of her to the end of her long life.

His name was Arthur Capel, and his friends called him 'Boy'. He had straight black hair, very beautiful blue eyes, a lightly tanned skin and sported a moustache. He was an Englishman and was born on 7 September 1881 at the Bedford Hotel, King's Road, Brighton, the watering-hole of the wealthy on the south-east coast of England. His parents, Arthur Joseph and Berthe Capel already had two daughters, Henriette and Edith. On Boy's birth certificate, his father is designated as a 'gentleman' and his mother was French, the former Berthe Lorin of Paris.[77]

His parents were wealthy, owning shipping companies which Boy would inherit. His father had followed the trade routes to China, where the development of Hong Kong in 1841 had seen trade burgeon under the aegis of Jardine, Mathieson and Co. (who took over when the East India Company lost its monopoly). Arthur Joseph Capel was part of the vast import and export business which was to flourish between South East Asia and America and Europe and, during the 1860s and 1870s, he regularly published *Arthur Capel & Co's tea circular*, which gave current prices and market reports.[78]

Boy was educated at the Catholic boarding school, Beaumont College, at Old Windsor in Berkshire, run by the Jesuits, and at Downside, the Abbey school near Bath where the Benedictine monks educated the sons of both noble and wealthy Catholic families. Consequently, he had grown into the perfect English gentleman. He was as well known on the polo lawns as in London's most sophisticated watering holes.[79] Boy Capel was no *dilettante:* he worked hard and he played hard. Inheriting interests in the coal industry in Newcastle and in South Wales, he had gone on to vastly increase his fortune. Not for him the life of ease and enjoyment. The work ethic was his lode star, but his charm and good looks made him a considerable hit with the ladies.

Despite his commitment to his businesses, he still found time to write and pursue his esoteric interests in things spiritual. Coco attributed this to the time he had spent in India and felt more than a pang of jealousy that this was an area of his life of which she knew nothing. Her fascination meant that she soon joined him in his beliefs. [80]

When he first met Coco, he was captivated and intrigued, and he kept coming back to Royallieu. An immediate spark sprang between them: she only had to look at him to know that his eyes held that rare quality, total understanding - it made her catch her breath - she felt as if she had come home. When Étienne would argue about her plans to improve her life, which he felt were unnecessary, it was Boy who would chip in with support. Eventually, Étienne suggested she develop her hobby of making hats. For some time, she had been making them for herself, and even Émilienne had taken to wearing some of her boaters outside. The gift for millinery was hers. She could take a simple shape from her raids on the Paris department stores, and turn it into an elegant, simple *chapeau* that became a society talking point.

The Capel family

Boy Capel's grandparents were John Capel and Mary Fitzgerald: his grandmother was born in 1809 in Waterford, Ireland, and his grandfather was born in Brompton, near Chatham in Kent, in 1810. The Capels had five children, two sons and three daughters. One of the sons, Thomas John, would become one of the luminaries in the Roman Catholic church, and the other, Arthur Joseph, would become a wealthy ship-owner, and Boy Capel's father.

When Arthur Joseph was born on 29 April 1847, the family were living at Leiston, near Aldeburgh in Suffolk, just two-and-a-half miles from the North Sea coast and ninety miles from London. John Capel worked for the Coastguard Service and was stationed at Hastings St Leonards in Sussex in 1851.[81]

By 1873 when Arthur Joseph married, his father is described as 'gentleman' or a man of private means.

Arthur 'Boy' Capel, the enduring love of Coco's life

Berthe Andrea Anna Eugénie Lorin was born in Paris and was attending the Convent of the Assumption girl's boarding school, run by the Sisters of the Order of the Assumption based in Kensington Square, London, when she met Arthur Capel. They married on 24 July 1873. Arthur was twenty-six years of age, and Berthe a girl of eighteen.

At the time of their marriage Arthur lived at Cedar Villa, Kensington, and was described as working for the Civil Service. Berthe lived close by at Scarsdale Villas. They married at the Catholic Church of Our Lady of Victories on Kensington High Street and the wedding ceremony was celebrated by Monsignor Thomas John Capel, Arthur's brother, and Father James Foley, the Parish Priest.

Cedar Villa was the home of Monsignor Capel, a handsome man with great energy, zeal and influence and whose main interest in life was education. In 1854 at the age of eighteen, he had become co-founder and Vice-Principal of St. Mary's Normal College in Hammersmith. During a time spent in Pau, in France, improving his delicate health in the bracing air of the Pyrennees, he founded a 'Mission' to English-speaking Catholics. His work was acknowledeged by the Pope and he was invited to give a series of controversial sermons in Rome which attracted much attention among American and English visitors.

A gifted public orator, he gave lectures at home and abroad, as well as writing on the moral issues of the day, including a response to Gladstone on his criticism of the Vatican. In 1873 he was named Domestic Prelate to Pope Pius 1X and in that year he founded the Catholic Public School in Kensington, which was intended to become the equivalent of Eton and Harrow, providing a Catholic education for the sons of the Catholic aristocracy.

By 1874 he established the Catholic University College in Abingdon House, Kensington supported by the Duke of Norfolk and others of the Catholic nobility. The venture failed some years later when Monsignor Capel resigned, and it fell foul to financial difficulties. Cedar Villa and its contents, including the altar, fittings and candlesticks from his private chapel were sold by auction in 1880 when he was declared bankrupt.[82]

Eventually he went to live in Florence and then to America, to become prelate in charge of the district of northern California where he died in 1911, at the age of seventy-five. Poignantly, among the artefacts in the sale was a marble bust of Monsignor Capel and in later years this apparently came into Boy Capel's possession, as he gave it to Coco and it remained on the mantel-piece of her dining-room in her private apartment at rue Cambon. 'He protects me,' she said.[83]

Arthur and Berthe set up house and their first daughter, Edith, was born in 1876, followed by Henriette in 1878 and Boy in 1881. By this time they were living at Old Stein Lion Mansion in Brighton and employed a nurse, Emily Higgins, to look after the children. The Lion Mansion was a luxurious hotel and a favourite of British Prime Minister William Gladstone who often spent holidays there.[84] At this time Arthur is described as a general merchant, meaning that he had diversified in his shipping business. Coco would describe Boy as having lived for many years in India, suggesting that his father worked for the Dutch East India Company.[85]

Hats at Malesherbes

160 boulevard Malesherbes was the address of Étienne's ground floor apartment in Paris, and this is where Coco started her first venture into the world of business in 1909. She was an immediate success, with Étienne's friends crowding in and bringing their actress friends. Boy sent his friends and racing society came to see this simply dressed young woman who was rewriting the fashion in millinery.

Coco never lacked sales skills: she could talk, demonstrate styles, advise on a look, but she did lack the technical expertise required to make more ambitious hats. Embellishing shapes would no longer do, she needed to know how to block and steam her creations. Her advisers said that the best person for the job was Lucienne Rabate, a young woman of twenty-three who worked at Maison Lewis. Lucienne agreed to come and also brought two of the best workers with her. By 1912 she was invited to work for Caroline Reboux, the top milliner in Paris, where she remained for forty years, becoming Director, and herself becoming known as the top milliner of the 1920s.[86]

Antoinette, Coco's youngest sister, was also employed to receive customers and look after the salon. She was a hard worker and would deliver the hats each day to the clients. As Coco still lived at Royallieu, it was Antoinette who slept on the shop premises each night. Space was at a premium as the clientele grew, and Antoinette had to move into a tiny apartment close by at 8 avenue du Parc Monceau, lent by one of the Royallieu set. Soon even more space was required for workrooms and, by February 1910, Coco realised that she would have to find more suitable premises.

Lucienne had left: trained as a professional in the rue de la Paix, the millinery centre of Paris, the Chanel sisters' establishment must have seemed amateurish to her and Coco did not like to take advice, however good it was. So they parted company. She was learning her craft, and she viewed mistakes as part of the learning experience. Believing in using her quick mind, together with a clear vision of the way ahead, she knew she had a future.

21 rue Cambon... Chanel Modes

Coco again approached Étienne about expanding her business, and again he would not take her seriously. It was a different story altogether with Boy: he was positively encouraging her to work, and it annoyed Étienne intensely. Why was Arthur Capel suddenly taking Coco's side on this issue? It soon became very clear that Boy was in love with Coco.

It was all done in a very civilised manner: the shop continued at rue Malesherbes, but Coco moved into Boy's apartment at avenue Gabriel and, near the end of 1910, he advanced her the money to buy a mezzanine on the Parisian street that she was to make known worldwide - 21 rue Cambon. The shop was known as Chanel Modes.[87]

Monsignor Thomas John Capel, Boy's uncle and a controversial figure in the 19th century Roman Catholic Church

Coco was elated: she now had her own boutique on rue Cambon and, with it, the opportunity to expand her dreams. Never a woman to rest on her laurels, she was soon planning and scheming to ensure the shop's success. Around this time her hat designs began appearing in the fashion magazines. In the October 1910 issue of *Comoedia Illustre,* Coco herself appeared, wearing her beautiful black velvet large brimmed hats, one trimmed with a simple spray of white feathers. These hats were a far cry from the huge monstrosities that women had worn, laden with flowers and fruit and covered in net and tulle, making it impossible to turn one's head. Instead they were fashioned in perfect proportion and beautifully crafted.

By March 1911, she made the front cover of the same magazine, when the actress Jeanne Dirys, who married designer Paul Iribe, was featured wearing another creation, this time a large black velvet with a cream crown and the amusing aigrette of feathers again.[88] This was chic, a plain simple design with a minimalist trim. The ladies loved it. Soon actresses were wearing her designs on stage and then modelling them for the fashion magazines. Gabrielle Dorziat, a friend from the Royallieu house parties, wore them with great élan, and was featured in *Les Modes* sporting Coco's latest creations.

With Coco and Boy still weekend guests at Royallieu, Étienne was becoming jealous, and he missed her. Coco was to say, 'Like every good Frenchman, like all men in general, Étienne Balsan began to love me again because I'd left him for someone else.' [89] The good times continued on Sundays, with amusements, riding in the forest and picnics. One Sunday, Coco decided to surprise Étienne by putting on a play of a country wedding. Costumes were made from cheap department store items, with Coco dressed as best man and Boy as mother of the bride. The actress Gabrielle Dorziat was maid of honour.[90]

Hurt by the situation with Boy and Coco, Étienne sailed for Argentina. When his brother Jacques asked Coco why she hadn't married him, the answer was blunt: Étienne was not the man she loved. [91]

But she was sure that she loved Boy Capel.

In later years, Coco was given, to voicing pithy, witty and wise maxims, which have been well quoted, but what she might have said at this point in her life was:

> 'Use the sights, sounds, experiences all around, distill their essence with original ideas and thoughts - and give birth to a new creation. The House of Chanel was built on this from the earliest times in my life - I used the costume of the nuns, the choirboys,the music-halls,the jockeys, the polo players, the jewelled Russians, the sailors, the English country look - everything. There may be nothing new in the universe or in the world of fashion, but I created something original from all of this.'

And she would have been right.

This was the beginning of the future, the time when dreams were about to come true.

***

Part Two

8

Dreams come true

By 1912, Coco had been running Chanel Modes for just over a year and it was a huge success. Meanwhile over in Scotland, William Linton was packing up and getting ready to move. It was a big step, not one he would undertake lightly, but he was now forty and his daughter Agnes was a bright ten-year-old. He had saved and planned for this day for years: if only Helen could be here to share it with him. He was going over to the English side of the Border, to the Eden Valley, to the city of Carlisle, the ancient Border City. At last, he would have his own company, his own tweed mill. It was a dream come true.

Located at the junction of three rivers - the Eden, the Caldew and the Petteril – Carlisle was in a particularly favoured spot for the development of a water-powered industry. It was aptly called 'the city of the waters.'[1] Of all the change that the city had seen in its long history, perhaps nothing affected the lives of its people as much as the Industrial Revolution. It brought social change, industrial development and, eventually, prosperity to its citizens – not least through its textile mills.

On a cold November day, William's destiny awaited him at a small mill a few miles north of Carlisle. Here, in the village of Warwick Bridge, he formed the partnership with Cranston Waddell that was the start of Linton Tweeds. He had already been to see the mill and discuss the terms of the partnership, and now looked forward to getting down to work, designing tweed.

The site at Warwick Bridge was a good choice as it boasted several useful amenities, lying between two small streams, the Cairn Beck and the Trout Beck, which converged downstream to become a minor tributary of the River Eden.

The mill itself had an interesting history and had played its part in the industrial development of Carlisle. Known as Langthwaite Mill, it was a former cotton mill built by three brothers, John, Richard and George Ferguson, who had leased Lowfield, a six-acre site from Philip Howard of nearby Corby Castle in November 1790. It had something of a chequered history and was inextricably linked with the fortunes of Carlisle's two major milling families, the Fergusons and the Dixons.

The growth of Cumbria's milling dynasties

The Ferguson brothers had been granted the right to build a mill, water wheel, and all the necessary mill races, sluices and weirs at Warwick Bridge. They were also given exclusive use of the Cairn Beck. In just over two years, the brothers had built the mill and a 700-yard mill race to harness the water from Cairn Beck. They also built warehouses and dye-houses. With 443 spindles, the mill was soon producing 800 lb of cotton yarn each week, a very good capacity.

Production had scarcely started when disaster struck. In the early hours of 8th August 1793, a fire broke out and destroyed the main building. Fortunately the property was insured and, undeterred, the Fergusons lost no time in rebuilding a larger mill (66 feet by 33 feet on the ground plan) with three storeys, as well as an attic. The improved mill was equipped with the latest water-powered mules (mechanised spinning wheels), which had become available by the 1790s. They were back in business, at the start of what would become an internationally renowned company.

Further improvements took place and, when John Ferguson died, his brothers continued in business there until 1809, when they leased the mill to their brother-in-law, Peter Dixon, and his sons for seven years. At this time, an inventory shows that the mill contained 1,064 spindles, which was more than double its original capacity.

Peter was married to their sister Mary and lived in the harbour town of Whitehaven, on the Cumbrian west coast, where he was in business as a linen draper and a dealer in fabrics. The town was an important port, only rivalled by Liverpool. It had been a major ship-building town since it built colliers to export coal to Ireland in the seventeenth century. At this time, Peter's father was the Customs Officer there and Peter imported flax from Hamburg and other overseas ports. Mary and Peter had ten children, and all their sons would work in cotton and develop their father's business interests. The firm, now known as Peter Dixon and Sons, flourished and would become one of the major employers in Carlisle.

Warwick Mill, near Carlisle, where William Linton worked in partnership with the Waddell family

Meanwhile, another branch of the family was developing a new textile factory at the Friggate Works at Damside, Carlisle, which later moved the short distance to Holme Head Works on the banks of the Caldew. This was Joseph, Robert Ferguson's son and Richard's grandson who, in 1824, was to become the founding father of a business that was to develop into Ferguson Brothers. The company played an important role in the industrialisation of Carlisle, and would, like Linton Tweeds, have links with Coco Chanel.

These were not only businessmen but men of vision, constantly looking for new methods of improving the fabric they produced. One of the earliest and important inventions Joseph made was the process of 'beetling' the cotton fabric, to give it a soft, silky finish. Before this the process had only been used on linen fabrics. Such new processes were important developments in the textile world and kept companies ahead of the game in world markets.

Politics, power and wealth

The Fergusons not only became the city's entrepreneurs, but took a very active part in its political life, with Joseph becoming Member of Parliament for Carlisle in 1852. This political interest was reflected in the trade name that Joseph's wife, Maria, chose for the new cottons: 'Silesias' was a Polish name chosen because of their sympathies with Poland, which was trying to avoid partition between the three great European powers, Germany, Austria and Russia. The 'Silesias' were immediately an enormous success, particularly in America. Later developments, such as new dyeing and finishing processes and the pioneering of Mercerising and Schreinering finishes, put the company in the forefront of cotton manufacturing in England, and they became known throughout the world for their quality cotton fabrics.[2]

The Fergusons' relatives, the Dixons, were also a family of ambitious men and, on taking over Langthwaite Mill, they set to work building and improving. Having obtained an extended lease, they added a new wing, built a reservoir and several cottages and improved the millraces. By 1832 they were no longer totally dependent on water: they had installed a steam engine, as well as the new Danforth Throstle spinning machines. The mill was a showpiece in the pretty, country village where it stood, and a source of pride to its workers.[3]

When Peter Dixon, senior, died in 1832 plans were already afoot to build a much larger mill in Carlisle, Shaddon Mills, to accommodate the expanding business. Shaddongate and Caldewgate were traditionally working class areas of Carlisle and the home of the handloom weavers, who would provide the work-force. As the railways developed, it became apparent that the Newcastle-Carlisle line would bypass Warwick Bridge and terminate in Carlisle, with a branch line to the Carlisle Canal ensuring a good distribution route to the sea for the cloth, and simplifying the import of raw cotton from Liverpool. The chosen site for the new mill was close to the basin of Carlisle Canal and had the benefit of water supplies from the Denton Holme mill race.[4]

With the completion of the new Shaddon Mill factory at Carlisle in 1836, the Dixon family decided to dispose of Langthwaite Mill but, as there were no takers, they kept it on (and its 300 workers) as an addition to the new mill.[5] Shaddon Mill was the largest cotton mill in England at that time, and the chimney, at 305 feet, was the highest in the kingdom. It is recognised today as one of the finest examples of early Victorian industrial architecture in existence. William Linton would come to know it well.

The mill owners became wealthy men and, like those in Hawick, soon acquired grand houses. In 1825 Peter Dixon, senior, bought Tullie House in Castle Street, Carlisle, a fine 17th-century building (which today houses the city's Museum and Art Gallery). His son, John Dixon, built a stately mansion at Knells, Houghton, a village on the outskirts of Carlisle.[6] Peter, junior, built a palatial sandstone Tudor-style mansion, Holme Eden, on the banks of the River Eden at Warwick Bridge which was completed by 1837. He had also built the nearby Holme Eden Church and vicarage by 1846 (Agnes Linton and the Geltsdale Kennels would stay here during World War 2). And in 1853, their cousin, Joseph Ferguson, acquired Morton Manor and estate on the western outskirts of the city, which had been built in 1807 by another family connection, the Forster family.

Like Warwick Bridge, the new mill was a spinning mill, turning raw cotton into yarn. Traditionally the Carlisle handloom weavers had operated as outworkers in their cottages, with whole families often congregating in one room to work. It was a hard life with long working hours for little pay. Sir Frederick Chance, Joseph Ferguson's grandson, writing on the occasion of Ferguson Brothers centenary in 1924, gives this description of the handloom weavers:

> 'Those were the days when handloom weaving was a thriving and popular occupation in Carlisle and the surrounding villages. The most familiar sounds to be heard within a radius of twenty miles or more around Carlisle were the whirr of the bobbin-wheel and the buzz and click of the shuttle.'[7]

The spinning mills supplied the weavers with the newly-spun cotton yarn from their warehouses: whole families would then work on weaving the 'cuts' or lengths required. The checked gingham cloth was 42 yards long and it would take a man six days, working for fourteen to sixteen hours a day, to complete a length. If he fell behind, he would often work through the night to deliver the woven cloth to Dixon's warehouse in Peter Street on Saturday morning, when payment was made. If he was working on Union Stripe cloth the length was sixty yards, taking even longer.

Often the weavers were working in a small room in their home, set aside for the loom, or some would group together and hire a ground-floor room in a tenement, where they would rent the looms from the mill owners and create a workshop.

Many of the weavers lived in squalid conditions, and worked in small badly-lit rooms, where the noise of the looms was unbearable. With extremely low pay and poor sanitary conditions, life was very hard. Children as young as eight became bobbin-mill operatives and worked on the loom by the time they were ten.[8]

Dixon's had a peak labour force of 8,000, of which 1,000 were employed in their factories, the rest as outworkers. Oddly, they did not install power-looms when they first built the new factory, as most of the cotton manufacturers in Lancashire were doing by this time. The power loom had been invented in 1785 by Edmund Cartwright and the steam-powered version was widely adopted by 1825,[9] but Dixon's were probably

Staff at Cumberland Mills (Warwick Mill), taken pre-1914

mindful of the economics of the employment situation in Carlisle and the ready availability of cheap outworkers.

Hard times get harder

By the mid-1860s the American Civil War prevented the import of raw cotton and cotton manufacturers in Britain were hit hard. The war was fought mainly over the issue of slavery, when the eleven 'Confederate' southern states wanted to break away from the 'Union' north, in order to continue the system of slavery, on which the cotton plantation economics relied.

Cotton was the mainstay of the Victorian industrial economy and in 1860 the port of Liverpool imported eighty percent of its cotton from the southern states of America. By 1862 President Abraham Lincoln's Unionist armies blockaded the port of New Orleans, effectively cutting off the southern states' exports of cotton to Britain. Without raw materials, the effect on British cotton manufacturing was disastrous. In Lancashire where the cotton mills employed a workforce of 500,000, half were laid off. Eventually new suppliers were found in India, Egypt and China and the industry began to recover.

Inevitably, international affairs impacted on the local scene in Carlisle. Looking to the future, however, Dixon's decided to modernise and introduced the factory system by building large weaving sheds across the yard from the factory and installing 600 power looms. At the Peter Street works over 200 power looms were installed, but it was really too late, and this time it was the handloom weavers who suffered. By 1871, all Dixon's weaving was done on power looms. As a result, many of the unemployed handloom weavers moved to Lancashire in search of jobs and better pay.

At the beginning of 1872 - the year William Linton was born - business was reported as good, but it seems that the cost of the new machinery (which ran into many thousands of pounds) was too much to sustain. By July the *Carlisle Journal* reported:

> *'We regret to learn that there is truth in the rumour that the old and highly respected cotton manufacturing firm of Peter Dixon & Sons... have felt themselves obliged to convene a meeting of their creditors with a view to liquidation.'*

The partners were declared bankrupt by their own petition, with debts of £66,500. The press reported that this had occurred 'not so much through losses in trade as from the depreciated value of the different properties, machinery etc, a new valuation having been recently made by a competent valuer.' [10]

The Dixons were not about to give up easily. The Mayor of Carlisle, John Irving, stepped in and, on 20 January 1873, they floated a joint stock company, Peter Dixon & Sons Ltd, and purchased Langthwaite Mill with all its equipment for £13,000. At the same time, the new company acquired Shaddon Mills at Carlisle and, although not using the mill at Warwick Bridge for the production of yarn, they used its dye and bleach works to finish work from the Carlisle factories. Ten years later, in 1883, the company ceased to trade and was sold to Robert Todd and Sons who were woollen yarn spinners.

The plight of Carlisle's workers would not improve for some time, despite the *Carlisle Patriot*'s bright comments at Christmas 1885:

> 'On Christmas forenoon the atmosphere was as balmy and the sky as blue as on an Easter day and the night was even more delightful – a brilliant sky and a clear and crisp air, yet genial.'

Life was not genial for the working classes, as the paper also reported that, before Christmas, a voluntary committee had been set up to look at the situation of providing some relief in each area of the city.

In Caldewgate, where the weavers lived, poverty was rife. Years before, their situation had provoked them to riot but now 300 families were helped to have a Christmas dinner. The committee estimated that if they were to provide help beyond the festive season, they would need to appeal for funds of £50 a week. Help was also given in the form of tickets which could be spent in the city's cocoa shops, and a clog fund was set up appealing for gifts of clogs and clothes from the better off.[11] While many of the mill owners provided some welfare and recreational facilities for their workers, this did not alleviate the underlying poverty.

Local competition for the Fergusons and Dixons

There were other major textile producers competing in the city at this time, most notably the Scottish firm of Alexander Morton & Co. of Darvel in Ayrshire and Stead McAlpin & Co.

The former expanded to Carlisle in 1900, setting up a factory at Murrell Hill. The company had an international reputation for making carpets and jacquard tapestry in its factory over the border in Scotland and was at the forefront of design, liaising with William Morris' company and becoming involved with the Arts and Crafts movement. The firm had humble beginnings, starting in Darvel in 1860, but by the 1890s had six hundred employees. The Carlisle operation became known as Morton Sundour Fabrics Ltd. The Mortons tried unsuccessfully to rent the two upper floors of Robert Todd's Shaddon Mills so they transferred their carpet, tapestry and chenille operations to the new premises. The invention of new dyes and dyeing methods with the development of non-fading fabrics, given the trade name 'Sundour', ensured their place in textile history. (The firm was eventually taken over by Courtaulds in 1965 and shut down to be replaced by Gleneden Textiles.) [12]

Stead McAlpin & Co. had started their print works in 1835 on the banks of the Caldew at Cummersdale, a village just outside Carlisle. They too became world famous for their luxury furnishing textiles, favoured by interior designers. They were initially printed by the old wood-block method, then on engraved copper rollers, until rotary screen printing took over in 1971. (The company was acquired by the John Lewis Partnership in 1965, who sold the lovely fabrics throughout their stores.[13] Since then it has had a chequered history but is still in production today.)

In the late-19th century, Carlisle was still a major textile town, but before long the golden age of cotton was in decline and King Cotton was giving way to wool.

Against this backdrop of well-established local mill dynasties, sharp competition, and rapid change, William Linton took his first tentative steps as an outsider trying to establish his own business in the Carlisle area.

***

9
The birth of Linton Tweeds

On 22 November 1912 the *Carlisle Journal* reported:

> 'This private company has just been registered with a capital of £8000 in £1 shares to carry on the business of woollen manufacturers, formerly carried on by Mr William Waddell, of Otterburn Mill and Mr Cranston Waddell of Warwick Bridge, as William Waddell and Sons. The mill, premises, machinery and cottages, the property of Messrs William and Cranston Waddell, are let on lease to the limited company. The subscribers are Messrs Cranston Waddell, Warwick Bridge, Carlisle, woollen manufacturer; William Linton, Warwick Road, Carlisle, manager; and A. G . Greaves, 2 St Nicholas Buildings, Newcastle-on- Tyne, agent. The number of directors is not to be less than two nor more than five. The first directors are Messrs Cranston Waddell, William Linton and A.G. Greaves (all permanent). The qualification is 100 shares.' [14]

On 12 December 1912, the *Carlisle Journal* further reported:

> 'The well-known business of William Waddell and Sons at Warwick Bridge, which was established 91 years ago has been formed into a private limited liability Company under the name of Waddell's Limited... The business will be under the management of Messrs Cranston Waddell and William Linton as joint managing directors.' [15]

The die was cast. William would have joint responsibility for the new venture. As a newcomer to the area, the challenge must have seemed daunting. Fortunately, Cranston Waddell, his new partner at Langthwaite Mill, had a strong family pedigree in the business on both sides of the border.

Love, ambition and hard work

In Scotland, the Waddells had a long history of woollen manufacture in the town of Jedburgh and by 1821 William, one of the younger family members, had leased Otterburn Mill in Northumberland.

William Waddell and his wife, Charlotte Ferrier, were an enterprising couple. When Charlotte was only seventeen they eloped to get married. This action by a feisty young woman caused great dismay in both families as she absconded from the fashionable 'School for Young Ladies' in George Square, Edinburgh. With a clear vision of their future, they took on Otterburn Mill in 1821. The terms of the 109-year lease were harsh and did not allow any major expansion. But they were young, ambitious and determined to make a success of the venture. They worked hard and, assisted by workers from the local community, built up a thriving cottage industry.

It was a mutually beneficial arrangement: they bought fleeces from the local farmers and produced the woollen yarn at the mill. The yarn was then supplied to the local handloom weavers who, working in their own cottages, made woollen cloth and blankets. The mill then washed and finished the cloth, ready for use. The business was secure with its solid local base providing jobs for the community and quality goods. [16]

William and Charlotte had eleven children and their son, William, was to follow his father into the business. William is remembered for developing the available colour range, and introducing many brilliantly coloured dyes from abroad, including Red Madder from Angola and Logwood from Honduras, a rich blue-black that turned green in differing lights. The importance of these new colours may be appreciated by looking at the journey William made to obtain them. He set out by horse and cart on a Monday morning to Kendal, to collect the dyes which had been shipped from overseas to the Port of Liverpool, before being sent by canal to Kendal. It was a journey of over a hundred miles, and he did not get back home until Saturday evening.

The third generation of the family continued its expansion of the business, and enhanced the Otterburn reputation for quality, durability and colour. By 1888 Langthwaite Mill at Warwick Bridge was sold to Messrs Waddell & Son of Otterburn, who set up a tweed manufacturing mill.[17] This was a partnership between William 111 and his sons, William 1V and Cranston who were based there. Another son, George continued the family business at Otterburn.

Setting up home in Carlisle

In Carlisle, William Linton set up home at 309 Warwick Road, a long leafy road going east from the city to the small town of Brampton. It was not far for young Agnes or Nessy as she was called in the family, to go to Botcherby Elementary School. Opened in 1900, this provided education for 200 mixed and infant pupils and was situated at the bottom of the hill leading to the small village of Botcherby, on the edge of Warwick Road, the road that took William to the mill at Warwick Bridge.[18]

William Linton was on his way.

By the early 1900s it was still a common sight for farmers and country people living in the Lake District to see a travelling salesman in pony and trap, trotting along in all weathers to sell his wares. William Linton decided to employ two such salesmen. They travelled in all seasons the length and breadth of Lakeland's green valleys and craggy mountain roads, with their cargo of woollen suit lengths for sale. Welcomed everywhere, when they reached the farms, they found the farmer's wife waiting to give them hot tea and a plate of home-cured ham, with crusty bread and pickles, and ready to sell her home-produced woollen yarn, for them to take back to the factory at Warwick Bridge. Life was good on the road.[19]

But William and Cranston were more ambitious than that: they had been partners for just over a year when they decided to expand the business and look further afield – they looked to America. Trade with Paris was drying up with the threat of war and the company could no longer rely on the European market. At a meeting of the Board of Director's on Friday, 22 May 1914, the Company Minutes state:

> 'The Director's discussed and agreed to the forthcoming visit of Mr Linton to the United States of America and it was felt that good business would result from his visit.'[20]

Not only the English trade was suffering: in the year before the outbreak of World War 1, the Scottish tweed industry was also facing hard times, mainly due to the vagaries of fashion.

Under a headline proclaiming *Tweeds Are Not Stylish*, *The New York Times* reported on 9 November 1913:

> 'The South Scotland tweed industry, which for two or three years has been very active, has quieted considerably the last three months. At a meeting of the Manufacturer's Corporation recently held in Galashiels it was said that the depression was due to some extent to the waste of capital caused by the Balkan war, but that the principal cause of loss of trade was the decree of fashion in favour of fine Saxony fabrics... [to the detriment] of cheviots. This gave worsted manufacturers an opportunity which they were strenuously improving, while the tweed manufacturers were facing an unpromising Winter business.'[21]

A new tariff on woollen goods brought in by America at the beginning of 1914 also led to uncertainty among British mill owners, as they worried that enforced higher prices for wool imported into America would hit their market.[22] The then American preference for the smoother worsted cloth and competition from cheaper English and European cloths were also a cause for concern.

Risking all to travel State-side

These were dangerous times: in August 1914 war broke out and, just after Christmas 1914, Zeppelins were bombarding the coast of England and the Royal Flying Corps were involved in 'dog-fights' with German pilots. The Germans were employing submarine warfare by 1915, and in Britain a quarter of ships were requisitioned for military use.

In May 1915 the *Lusitania,* carrying passengers, including Americans, and also carrying munitions was sunk.[23] President Woodrow Wilson of the United States was among those strongly protesting against this heinous act. Passenger ships were no longer safe. By April 1917 the President had declared that the United States was at war with Germany, as an Associated Power. The activity of German U-Boats increased, and in that month one ship in four leaving British ports would never return.[24]

War or no war, William's ambition over-rode all other considerations. President Woodrow Wilson would have understood this will to succeed: his own grandfather, the Reverend Thomas Woodrow, had left Carlisle to seek a new life in the United States in 1835.[25]

And the risk paid off: by 4th June 1915, at a Board meeting at which Mr C. Waddell, Mr W. Linton and Mr Grieves the Company Secretary were present, it was recorded that:

> *'The Secretary produced draft minutes for the year ended 30 April, 1915, which show a profit.. and this was considered very satisfactory considering that the expenses of two journeys to the United States of America were included.. and further that the Continental Autumn business was due to the war nil.'* [26]

For William to even cross the Atlantic at this time might be either foolhardy or brave, but it showed that he was ready to risk his life to ensure that the business stayed on top.

Sadly, the Waddell-Linton partnership was not destined to endure.

On 15 November 1917 Cranston Waddell died at his home, Eden Chester at Warwick Bridge, at the age of 59.[27] To the stirring strains of 'Rock of Ages' his funeral service was held at the local Primitive Methodist Church and he was interred at Holme Eden Churchyard, on the banks of the River Eden, amid masses of flowers. He had been an active participant in the church and local community and, in his address, the Rev. J. Tweddle described him as a tower of strength and as having taken a foremost position in life. He said that there was an air of reality about him and genuine sincerity and he was instrumental in building the Chapel at Corby, as well as travelling thousands of miles in the cause of lay preaching. William Linton was among the large number of mourners.[28]

The partnership had only lasted for five years, and now with Cranston's untimely death, he faced the future of developing the company alone. It was a task he proved more than equal to.

***

10
A life in fashion

While William Linton had been starting his first business in England in 1912, in Paris, Coco had never been so happy - she hugged it to herself. She spent her days working at rue Cambon and her nights in Boy's arms.

The business was developing well, as she began to attract clients from Boy's social circle. Boy had given up his other mistresses and devoted himself to her. He knew that she was intelligent as well as beautiful, with a bright, quick mind, and he wanted to see her develop it. Not just a successful businessman, he was also an intellectual, widely read, and he encouraged her to read books on politics, religion, history: all very different from the romantic novels of Pierre Decourcelle of her youth. She absorbed everything she read and heard like a sponge, but the longing for show-business was still in her blood, and when she heard of Isadora Duncan, she wanted to know more.[29]

Isadora's father had founded a school of decorative arts in San Francisco, involving the whole family. By 1898 they went to live in Greece to study the philosophies of the Ancient Greeks. Here, Isadora taught her free dance movements, while her brother Raymond and his wife Penelope started a commune outside Athens, producing handspun and handwoven rugs, which he designed. (Raymond eventually settled in Paris, founding a colony of fellow textile artists at Neuilly, outside Paris. He was invited to exhibit at the International Exhibition of Decorative Arts in Paris in 1925.[30])

In Paris, Isadora set up a school of dance based on her free-thinking Greek philosophies and, with Boy's encouragement, Coco went to take a look. She found Isadora greeting her clients with bared breasts, covered only by a flimsy peplum top, and the dance consisted of improvisation and high leaps. It was not for her. To Coco, respectability was all.[31]

Instead she went to the studio of Elise Toulemon in Montmartre. Toulemon used the professional name Caryathis and taught character dancing. She had a similar background to Coco, having been apprenticed with the House of Paquin as a seamstress before coming to the dance. She was married to the author Marcel Jouhandeau.

Montmartre was at the centre of the bohemian life of Paris, with artists such as Pablo Picasso, Maurice Utrillo and the poet Pierre Reverdy living close by. At the time, Coco was unaware of them and, in spite of her perseverance, she was no more successful with dance than with singing. It was time to concentrate on fashion.[32]

At Royallieu she met new friends on Sundays: Boy knew theatre people and they were invited to visit. The actresses took to Coco, and she was asked to make hats for them to wear both on and off stage. Gabrielle Dorziat, who was to become a well-known French actress, making sixty films in her career, was rehearsing Maupassant's *Bel Ami* and was to be dressed by the famous designer, Doucet. Coco wanted to make the hats, and make the hats she did: two plain straw hats, with a wide, turned up brim and no feathers. They were a triumph at the Vaudeville and much talked about in society.[33]

1913 saw Igor Stravinsky's *The Rite of Spring* performed for the first time at the new white marble and gilded Théâtre des Champs Elysées, and it caused a riot. Sergei Diaghilev, the great Russian impresario, had brought the Ballets Russes to Paris, and the star choreographer was Nijinsky. Both the music and the ballet totally shocked the audience, it was new, it was modern and it was discordant. There had been nothing like it before. Couture-clad Paris matrons stood up and protested, whistles were blown, wealthy gentlemen booed, and Diaghilev thundered out orders. The noise was such that the dancers could not hear the music. It would never be forgotten. Coco sat there with Caryathis and her two lovers - Coco had been invited to make up the numbers. She was totally amazed and amused at the scene. La Rotonde had never been like this.[34]

The great Italian professor of ballet and mime, Enrico Cecchetti, who had taught at the Mariinsky Theatre in St Petersburg and joined Diaghilev in 1911, commented: 'I think the whole thing has been done by four idiots. First: M. Stravinsky who wrote the music. Second: N. Roerich, who designed the scenery and costumes. Third: M.Nijinsky, who composed the dances. Fourth: M. Diaghilev who wasted his money on it.' [35]

Diaghilev first brought the Ballets Russes to Paris in 1909, and to London the following year, where the events were the talk of the town. The colourful spectacle exploded onto the stage like a fireworks display, with the music, decor and costumes all integral parts of the dance. The *Firebird* was produced that year and for the production of *Scheherazade* in 1910, Nijinsky, the principal dancer was painted black for his role as a slave.

The costumes were unlike anything seen before: instead of pale layers of tulle, they gleamed with the bright colours of the Orient, and flowed in soft fluid drapes. They influenced fashion, with harem pants, turbans, and richly embroidered silks and satins, becoming all the rage. In London, Selfridge's department store celebrated the influence of the Ballets Russes with a display of gowns by Paul Poiret, and marked the demise of the corset and the greater sexual freedom of the time with a Tango Ball on the roof garden![36]

Deauville – rest and retail therapy

Deauville, on the Côte Fleurie in western France, overlooked the English Channel and was a popular fashionable resort with the English, as well as the French. In 1911, for example, *The New York Times* published reports from London that Lady Marlborough (the former Consuelo Vanderbilt and the future Mrs Jacques Balsan) had rented the Château de la Baye for the month of August where she entertained some of her friends including Lady Kitty Somerset, Lady Essex and Mrs Rupert Evelyn Beckett. It noted that: 'Mrs Newhouse has also been recuperating in Deauville after the strain of a busy season.' [37]

Coco's decision to open a shop there in 1913, on the smart rue Gontaut Biron, proved an astute business move. Financed by Boy, it was well positioned within the orbit of these fashionable, wealthy women: close to the Normandy Hotel and the Casino. She had a white canopy fitted to shade it from the sun and on it was printed GABRIELLE CHANEL, in elegant black letters.[38]

She was soon the centre of attention, not just because of the shop, but because of her own simple, smart outfits and her constant band of escorts. Boy was often away looking after the fortunes of his coal-shipping fleet, and expanding his exports of coal. But when he was there, they were invited out and Coco was impressed by the welcome that the English lords and ladies gave her - it was the start of her love of all things English.

Adrienne came to visit, and they were photographed outside the shop looking elegant and happy. When Antoinette arrived from Paris to help, they both paraded the town wearing the hats, attracting much attention and admiration and - most importantly - improving Coco's sales.

Even at this happy time, family tragedy threw a shadow over her life when Julia, her older sister died, aged just twenty-nine, leaving her young son, André Palasse, an orphan. Coco and Boy decided to look after him, and he was sent to Beaumont College, Boy's old school in England. A photograph of Coco with her nephew at this time, shows a slim, dark-haired boy with a sensitive face.

Coco would later tell her friend Claude Baillén that when they saw a barge on the river Seine, André would say, 'Look, that's ours,' thinking it was one of Boy's coal boats. 'Not ours, Boy's,' Coco would answer. 'But he told me you're going to marry him!' [39]

Innovation + simplicity = success

Coco's quest was to be happily married and to have the security of financial independence - she was to achieve the second, but never the first.

As with many of her inspirations, when she started to make clothes the ideas came from the fabrics and styles that she saw in use in men's clothes all around her. Jersey, the inspiration for her first dresses, came from seeing her nephew's school uniform, and her gift was her ability to transform this into her own classic, elegant style. A man's sweater, picked up to keep warm when watching a polo match at Deauville, was cinched at the waist with a scarf and became the style of the jersey dress.[40]

Innovation was in her every thought, enhanced by practicality in her hands. Her friend, the actress Gabrielle Dorziat would recall the first jersey dress that Coco made for her: a long navy tailored sheath, with a matching long cardigan jacket and trimmed with a small rabbit fur collar from Jacques Heim, who was just starting up his furrier business. The design was timeless.[41] As Cecil Beaton would say: 'The age of elaborate ornamentation was over and an era of simplicity had begun. Chanel had literally pole-vaulted women's fashions from the nineteenth century into the twentieth.' [42]

CHEZ LA MARCHANDE DE FRIVOLITÉS A DEAUVILLE — RUE GONTAUT-BIRON

Chanel in her first Boutique at rue Gontaut-Biron, Deauville 1913, published in 'Femina' magazine

A stand-off between top Paris couturier Paul Poiret and his top client, the wealthy and influential Baroness de Rothschild, turned the wheel of Coco's fortunes. The Baroness had been banned from Poiret's salon, after insulting models sent to her home to show the collection when she purported to be too ill to attend his show. When she arrived at Chanel's, accompanied by her friends from high society, she also brought the actress, Cécile Sorel, who soon recognised Coco's individuality.[43]

Coco had long wanted to branch out into making dresses, but dresses that were totally different, with simple shapes, fluid lines and ease of movement - modern dresses. She had a *penchant* for simplicity, plainness almost, which was part of her psyche and born of the influences from her days in the convent.

She needed textiles and decided to innovate by using flannel and fine knit jersey, materials more common to men's clothing than to women's. The dresses were made with the bodice designed like a sailor blouse and the skirt falling away, merely skimming the body. Corsets were definitely not required, offering women the greater freedom of movement they wanted. Instead women welcomed the birth of the bra. Coco's dresses were a huge success, and she never looked back.

***

11
At war – and the only shop in town

The rumblings of war had been heard throughout Europe for some time and when it broke out in August 1914, Deauville emptied, the family villas were silent and the beaches deserted. But Coco stood firm, as Boy advised. He was right: the German invasion after the battle of Mons on the Belgian border, spread down to St. Quentin, north of Paris by 27 August. The aristocracy, with their châteaux under threat, fled back to their summer villas at Deauville, and the ladies found themselves without clothes, so they went to Chanel's, the only shop in town. Coco had to improvise, and quickly turned out the sailor blouse, a long straight skirt and a plain straw hat. The ladies loved it.[44]

When volunteers were needed at the local hospital, Coco found herself coming to the aid of these same ladies as they sought to help the sick and wounded, by adapting the hotel chambermaids' outfits into wearable nurses uniforms, and making them a neat cap. They were sewing all night, and Coco was furious with Adrienne, who refused to come and help. Adrienne, in the company of Maud, was prostrated with weeping, waiting news of her lover, Baron Maurice de Nexon, who was fighting at the Front. Coco had no patience, everyone was in the same boat she said, so Adrienne soon came to help.

The changes came swiftly. With the Germans just twenty miles outside Paris, the city was encircled with barbed wire and forty thousand civilians were digging trenches.[45] The Government moved to Bordeaux and when Coco heard that Royallieu had been taken over by German staff officers, she felt aggrieved.

As theatres closed, actors crowded to Deauville: in fact, the whole world seemed to have come to Deauville. Coco put chairs on the pavement under her white canopy so that the ladies could sit and chat and surmise what was happening. Rumour was rife, but when she heard that Sir John French and units from the British Expeditionary Force were joining the French Fifth Army from the battle of Mons, her heart leapt.[46] Lieutenant Arthur Capel was one of Sir John's liaison officers, having joined up on 15 August 1914.

By the middle of 1916 the size of the British Army had increased substantially. Men had responded to Lord Kitchener's recruitment call saying, 'Your Country Needs You' which was emblazoned on thousands of posters displayed in towns and villages of England. Although it was now fifty-seven divisions strong, it still did not compare in size with the French (who had ninety–five) or the Germans (who had one hundred and seventeen divisions on the western front).

As the French and British armies met at the Somme, it was thought that a united attack would prove successful. Thirteen British divisions started the attack, and went 'over the top' on 1 July 1916: it was a disaster. On that one day 19,000 men were killed and a further 57,000 were wounded: it was the worst day the British Army had ever known.[47]

Chanel-Biarritz opens for business

A holiday with Coco was what Boy needed before leaving for England, and to combine business opportunities with pleasure seemed a good idea. They decided on Biarritz.

Biarritz, on the south-west Atlantic coast of France, was originally a whaling port but by the 19th century it had become a playground for the rich. Its mild climate made it a fashionable resort with the Empress Eugénie, wife of Napoleon 111 who had an elegant home there. It became even more popular when King Edward V11, began taking annual holidays there from 1906, occupying a suite of rooms in the grand Hôtel du Palais, Empress Eugénie's former home. Here he could meet his mistress, Mrs Alice Keppel, who was staying nearby at the Villa Eugénie. Renowned for its relaxing atmosphere and good air, with its mixture of Atlantic salt and mountain Pyrénean pine, it was well placed to explore the Pyrénées and make excursions into Spain.[48]

Biarritz, the resort in southern France, where Chanel's shop attracted Spanish aristocracy as well as French customers

Coco wanted to expand by opening a couture house, and Boy was in total agreement. They found a place to rent - and it was magnificent. The Villa Larralde was a stone-built mini-castle with high stone walls and a cool inner courtyard. Its stone tower overlooked the street, and it had a prime location opposite the Casino on the road to the beach. Boy loaned her the money and Chanel-Biarritz was open for business.[49]

To open a new couture house in a country at war may seem as risky as William Linton's transatlantic trips, but business was business! The dresses came next. She needed seamstresses and Antoinette stepped into the gap bringing them from Paris, when Adrienne, who was going to see Baron de Nexon at the 25th Dragoons base, was slow to respond to her call. Coco was intensely annoyed, and let her know that 'from now on your later is too late.' [50]

Marie-Louise Deray was twenty-one years old when she went to work for Coco, in 1915. She was from Bordeaux and looking for a job in couture, when she heard of the boutique opening in Biarritz. She stayed with Coco for ten years, eventually moving to rue Cambon. As an old lady, she recalled to Pierre Galante, writer and editor of *Paris-Match*:

> *'Mademoiselle Chanel was not there. There was her sister, Antoinette Chanel and another lady. I was hired and I became one of the mainstays of the firm. We immediately enjoyed a great success. Soon I had about sixty women working under me. In the beginning we worked only in jersey. No-one before her had ever dared make dresses out of this type of wool fabric. For us it represented a real tour de force, for jerseys were badly woven in those days. The 'diagonals' went any which way, and work had to be started over several times - especially since Mademoiselle demanded perfection!... But what she made was sensational, of unparalleled simplicity and chic.*

> *'She chose everything: laces, ornaments, colours. She always chose the most beautiful tones among all the different pastel shades... Our workrooms were like*

44

fairyland, a veritable rainbow. We sold a great deal to Spain - San Sebastian, Bilbao, Madrid - wherever there were elegant women and money.

'Soon she sent me to Paris. She had just moved into 31 rue Cambon. I was in charge of a workshop where sixty people worked on clothes for Spain alone. The entire court ordered from me. These ladies bought dresses by the dozen - in Paris it was wartime and one did not always have enough to eat.

'During the war, she herself wore large jersey coats, quite long and of a school-girl simplicity. She was extraordinarily chic.' [51]

By September 1915. at thirty-two years old, Gabrielle was truly on her way - and she would never look back. Biarritz was no chance choice. Close to neutral Spain, from here she could attract new customers, and access to those hard-to-find fabrics and materials. By December she knew she was a hit: the Spanish ladies loved the elegant new clothes and orders came from wealthy aristocratic women - even the Spanish court sent in orders. Employing sixty workers, she was running at full capacity. The dresses were of couture standard and at couture prices: it was what the ladies expected to pay.

The headquarters of her blossoming empire remained at rue Cambon in Paris and, as Boy was there, she hurried back, leaving Antoinette in charge at Biarrritz. Coco was a quick learner and it seemed to come naturally to her: business sense, the organisation, the logistics of being in sole charge of her expanding empire. The workshops in Paris were expanded to accommodate the increasing Spanish orders, and 1916 saw her employing three hundred workers. [52]

War meant that textiles were in short supply and, looking for fabric for her new Paris designs, she visited many manufacturers. When she called on Jacques Rodier, all he had was a machine-knitted wool fabric, called jersey - but she immediately saw its possibilities. He was extremely surprised, as he had developed it before the war to make sporting men's underwear. Unpopular, with its rather rough texture and the boring colour beige, he had all the stock left on his hands, and no-one wanted it. [53]

Coco was not deterred: she used jersey in the Deauville shop with great success and now decided to buy his complete stock, and even wanted more. Rodier was not keen to use his scarce raw materials on what he regarded as a flop, but when he saw the clothes she made of it, and was wearing herself, he agreed. Later, the company developed other types of jersey, as well as kasha (a fine fabric woven from cashmere wool) and long continued to supply the House of Chanel. [54]

The cloth almost dictated the cut of the garment. It was difficult to sew, so Coco made a loose redingote jacket, but done in three-quarter length, and cut in a smooth princess line with a flat collar so that it fell smoothly over the above-the-ankle length skirt. There was no ornamentation and the *ensemble* relied on its elegant clean line. It was new, it was a success, it was jersey. [55]

Poverty deluxe – the first collection

1916 has been designated as the year of her first true collection. The look was what the top couturier Paul Poiret called *la pauvreté de luxe* or poverty deluxe, with sable linings hidden inside top-coats, or fur used on collars, cuffs and hemlines. The evening dresses were of filmy fabrics in soft slim styles and were easy to wear, giving a youth-enhancing look. Shorter pleated skirts were teamed with plain long jersey cardigans, often embellished with discreet embroidery or lined with silk, and the total look gave women a new freedom in dress. [56]

There was also a more mundane reason for the restrained use of material and embellishments: the shortages caused by the war. Not just society women were influenced by the new styles; ordinary women were stepping into men's shoes and working in the fields, driving ambulances and public transport vehicles, toiling in the munitions factories of France and the United Kingdom, and nursing the wounded.

They found emancipation in the freedom of the new unstructured and corsetless fashions.

Coco's success was helped by the fact that Paul Poiret had closed his business and joined the French army, working in the quartermaster corps and redesigning army overcoats to save time and cloth.[57] The void he left helped Coco to expand her business. In addition Jean Patou, who might have been a rival in creating modern clothes, sold his entire 1914 collection to an American buyer, and was drafted into military service becoming a captain in the Zouaves.[58] Coco again took full advantage of the situation.

Independence suited her, her former shyness had given way to a glowing confidence. Her bank account was suddenly very healthy and her first thought was to repay Boy, and feel truly independent. His surprise at her financial success was only surpassed by his disappointment that she no longer depended on him.

America now gave Coco her first international publicity, although she may not have been aware of it. 1916, the year that Condé Naste began to publish French *Vogue,* saw Chanel's chemise dress featured in *Harper's Bazaar* in America. Its plain, simple style bore no resemblance to anything seen before. It was from the Biarritz collection and its economical style, with a deep vee neckline, long narrow sleeves, figure skimming outline, with no waist and embellished only with a matching long scarf on the hips, made it truly different. It was worn with a plain broad-brimmed hat trimmed with a sliver of sable. The sketch was captioned 'Chanel's charming chemise dress.'[59] She had to wait until 1920 to get her first publicity from the French press.

The war affected the supply of many things and, in France and Britain, the textile industry was working flat out to keep the armies of Europe in uniforms, wool supplies were requisitioned, even dyestuffs were in short supply, as the imported chemical colourings from Germany became unavailable.[60]

***

12
Boy's own war

As the war continued, France became a bloody battlefield, with great loss of life on all sides. This was the war of armies of men crouching in a sea of muddy trenches, and going 'over the top' to face heavy artillary fire, of 'dog-fights' between flyers, and burning aircraft screaming to the ground.

Boy Capel was one of those lucky individuals who always seemed to fall on his feet. He resigned his commission with the Intelligence Service in London on 3 March 1916, citing as his reason his extensive business contracts in supplying coal and coke to French companies, some of whom made armaments. It was thought that this would necessarily involve him in French political affairs.[61]

A meeting with Georges Clemenceau led to his secondment onto the Franco-English War Coal Commission. Clemenceau, a trained doctor, had been Premier of France from 1906 to 1909, and survived a stormy political career. After spending some years in America as a journalist, he started his own newspapers in France, attacking Germany and championing the cause of military preparedness in his own country. His newspaper, *L'Homme libre* criticised the French government before the outbreak of World War 1, for defeatism.

Boy's new job would take him back and forth between London and Paris, negotiating at the highest levels. He saw this as a step forward to his higher aspirations. In the United Kingdom, the coal mines had been nationalised for the duration of the war, using the rich supplies but without any modernising investment.[62] Coco was delighted to be able to spend time with him in Paris.

Throughout 1916, Boy had been writing a book in his spare time, reflecting his optimistic

Boy Capel's letter of resignation from his commission in the Intelligence Service

outlook on the outcome of the war, and his great confidence in the future. Called *Reflections on Victory and a Project for the Federation of Governments,* in it he made a case for the creation of a federation of the British Empire and the Allies, inviting neutral countries to join with the aim of bringing a lasting peace to all nations. It would operate without exacting revenge on the Germans (a policy he viewed as storing up trouble for the future). In time, those enemies who desired peace would be invited to join the federation. The book was published in London by Werner Laurie in 1917. It was a strange time to publish such ideas and he caused great comment among his fellow polo players and business associates. The London *Times Literary Supplement* reviewed the book in the 10 May issue, and sniffily commented, 'The book would gain in cogency if more attention were paid to the practical working out of the proposed scheme.' [63] But the idea was a fore-runner of the eventual League of Nations and United Nations, and had Clemenceau's support in his vision of the future.

Taking care of business

In November 1917 Clemenceau again became Premier and formed a coalition cabinet in which he was also Minister of War. At this point, Boy went to see him and put his shipping fleet at the Premier's disposal for the service of France, and undertook to keep the French factories supplied with coal.[64] Clemenceau accepted and Boy's stock soared in London, where he began to move in government circles. Clemenceau proved himself to be a dynamic Premier, raising the sagging morale of France, persuading the Allies to agree to a unified command, and vigorously pursuing the war until the 1918 victory.

(After victory, he led the French delegation at the Paris Peace Conference, and insisted on Germany's disarmament. His harsh demands were at odds with the idealistic proposals of American President Woodrow Wilson, and the moderating influence came from British Prime Minister David Lloyd George. [65])

Boy's friends could not understand his friendship with Clemenceau. But Boy was open-minded and politically astute: he could see that Clemenceau's predictions were about to be realised, as Europe plunged deeper into war.

He was already looking to expand his coal export business into the French colonies, and was talking about using Casablanca as a foothold for exports into North Africa. As the war dragged on, his shipping fleet became invaluable to the war effort. Already a partner in Lloyds bank, he intended to be well-placed and have the right friends to ensure his success, and courted bankers, industrialists and press magnates to achieve it.[66]

His was no small-time company. Sunderland on the north-east coast of England was by now the greatest shipbuilding town in the world, and it was here that Boy commissioned the firm of Robert Thompson & Sons to build the *S.S. Capelcastle*, [67] a 360 foot steel built steamer of 3,874 gross tonnage, [68] which was launched on the river Wear in 1917 resplendent in her war-time camouflage of 'dazzle' paint.

In 1917 also, Boy dissolved his two companies Arthur Capel & Co. (London) and Arthur Capel & Co. (South Wales) and launched his new company Arthur Capel & Co. Ltd. His Welsh company had operated out of Newport in Monmouthshire, and he appears to have been consolidating his coal and shipping interests at this time.

His steamship, the 822 ton *Arthur Capel,* built at La Seyne in Provence in 1911, was leased to Leroux and Heuzey in Rouen, Normandy, a long- established French shipping company whose origins were part of a company previously noted for transporting British coal to Paris. The fate of the *Arthur Capel* is noteworthy, as it was torpedoed on 14 January 1918 by U-boat 80 under the command of Captain Max Viebeg and sunk fourteen miles north-west of Barfleur off Normandy.[69] It was on its way from Rouen to Barry in South Wales, the largest coal-exporting port in the world at this time, where the vast production of the Rhonda Valley coal-mines was exported worldwide.[70]

These were the hazards of war, but Boy retained a successful company which operated throughout the war and went from strength to strength afterwards. By now he was a member of the British Military Mission, and with his knowledge of France, his bi-lingual abilities in speaking the language and his contacts with French politicians and businessmen, he was well suited to the job.

Enter Major General Spears

During World War 1 the Head of the British Military Mission to the French War Office in Paris was Major General Sir Edward Louis Spears. Born in Passy, near the Bois de Boulogne in Paris in 1886, of Anglo-Irish parents, he was gazetted in 1906 to the 8th Royal Irish Hussars and in 1910 to the 11th Hussars. By 1911 he was working for Colonel G.M.W. Macdonogh, chief of the War Office intelligence department, MO5. His skill in foreign languages meant that he could work as a translator, and soon he was working on a new project, the compilation of an Anglo-French codebook. Here he met Captain Anthony Henley, with whom he became friends, and it was in Henley's drawing room that he first met Winston Churchill. Henley was also a business partner of Boy Capel.[71]

By 1914 with the outbreak of war, he was serving as a Captain in France, and was appointed liaison officer between the British Commander–in-Chief of the British Expeditionary Force, Sir John French, and his opposite number, General Charles Lanrezac of the French Fifth Army. A friend of Winston Churchill since 1915, Spears was regarded as a brilliant liaison officer between the French and British forces. Boy Capel was to work under his command.[72]

SS Capelcastle, one of Boy Capel's merchant fleet built in Sunderland, in wartime camouflage of 'dazzle' paint

The role of the liaison officer was not an easy one, and the letters of Edward Spears indicate the difficulties he had experienced since 1914 in taking news and reports between the French generals and the British commanders. In a time without modern communications it meant dangerous travelling at night out to the Front in all weather conditions, reporting back orders, information on artillery, troop movements and tactics, as well as smoothing relations between commanders who frequently did not agree or even respect each other. Only later in the war did the army provide field telephones and wireless equipment.[73]

The British Miltary Mission to Paris, headed by Spears – by now given the rank of Major - and reporting to the War Office in London, was set up in 1917. It operated from his office in boulevard des Invalides and his staff were both English and French.[74]

A particularly well-informed man

At the time that Boy was living with Coco at 138 rue Malesherbes, he was increasingly involved in the politics of the war, and Coco was certainly aware of these events. It is likely that the influences of these years, remained with her and fuelled her own efforts at peace-making during World War 2.

As an example, in a letter marked 'PERSONAL & SECRET', Major-General Spears wrote with some spirit and indignation, to the Director of Military Intelligence in London, on 1 November 1917:

> *'I saw Capel today, he told me that Clementel had obtained 3,000,000 tons of tonnage over and above the tonnage already placed at the disposal of the French by the British. This tonnage was obtained under pretext that the French Government was unable to import sufficient wheat into France and that the country would otherwise starve. Now, to provide these three millions tonnage, the British Government has had to take the decision of stopping the cotton trade of England and the French have not stopped any of their ordinary lines of shipping.*

> *'Capel thinks this is absolutely scandalous; Monet the French representative in London, prepares the ground for Clementel who comes over carrying reams of*

statistics, which have been prepared for him, according to Capel, by men who know absolutely nothing about the question, and these statistics are accepted in London as absolutely bona fide.

'We make this great sacrifice and are only laughed at for doing so. Our trade, notably to the East will certainly fall to pieces as the French lines are carrying on their commerce absolutely unfettered by any restrictions and are being amalgamated in such a way that the individual British competitors will be absolutely unable to deal with them after the war.

'I venture to think the matter is really most serious and imposes the absolute necessity of having some really able representative in Paris who will be able to advise on the shipping questions. It really is too silly that we should ruin ourselves, possibly to the extent of not being able to pay for the war, just because we have not the material to contend against any sentimental twaddle put up by Monet & Co. in London.

'Everything that is said by these people is taken as Gospel truth just because we have absolutely no system of control.

'Capel is particularly well informed on this subject as his own partner, who is a Frenchman, is greatly instrumental in having these deals put through.

'I understand that there is a big deal on just now on the part of the French with a view to buy Japanese ships.' [75]

Once again the British cotton trade was at the mercy of war. At this time Spears (who announced the changed spelling of his name from Spiers to Spears in the *London Gazette* on 3 September 1918)[76] was waiting to marry the beautiful and wealthy American novelist May Borden of Chicago. She was in the process of finalising her divorce from her first husband, a former missionary in India, Douglas Turner.[77]

Spears and May Borden-Turner had first met in 1916 when she financed and ran a hundred-bed field hospital at Bray-sur-Somme, for the French army. She recalled him turning up at her hospital with his Alsatian dog, Rex. He recalled being covered in mud and astonished to find women working so near the front lines. She gave him tea. They were to meet again in 1917, and became lovers, eventually marrying at the British Consulate in Paris on 30 March 1918. May was awarded the Croix de Guerre by the French for her work in the field hospital.

On 21 December 1917, Boy wrote to Colonel Hankey, the Cabinet Secretary in the War Office in London, with a covering letter from Spears to Sir Maurice Hankey, Secretary to Major General Sir G Macdonogh , the Director of Military Intelligence.

Boy wrote:

138, Boulevard Malesherbes

21st December 1917

Dear Colonel Hankey,

I had a private conversation with M. Clemenceau last night.

In these private conversations, M. Clemenceau no doubt speaks more freely than he does on official occasions.

I am anxious therefore, to convey to you the strong preoccupations which appear to be weighing on M. Clemenceau's mind.

He is convinced that the enemy will, as soon as they can, put in a big attack at the point of junction of the British and French lines, accompanied by demonstrations in other parts of the line.

The German object being to separate the French and British Armies.

I gather that his opinion is based partly on information received and partly on the conviction that if the Germans succeed in separating the French Army from the British Army it will mean the defeat of France and England.

He estimates that it will take 275,000 men ten weeks to put the French lines in a moderate condition of safety, that is:-

First , second and third line trenches and wire, but without dugouts or gun emplacements.

In order to do this , he is going to call up the older classes from the farms and factories.

This is all he can do as far as his own lines are concerned.

Now, he is greatly preoccupied by the reports he has received, to the effect:-

> *That our defence lines are in a worse state than his.*

> *That very little work is being done on them.*

> *That the liaison between the two artilleries at the point of junction is bad.*

He asked me if I could not do something about it and suggested that I should go to London to see Lord Milner. I understand, however, that Lord Milner will be here very shortly; also that it is obvious that a matter of this importance should go through the proper channels.

I am, therefore, taking this letter to Spiers, with the request that he will treat it as the result of a private conversation, but leaving him free to take such steps as he considers proper.

If, as I have no doubt , the reports received by Mr Clemenceau regarding the safety of our lines are exaggerated , I should be glad to have the opportunity of allaying his anxiety on the subject.

After my interview, Captain Amery, who had a message from Mr Lloyd George for Mr Clemenceau, was called in and Mr Clemenceau repeated to him part of what he had said to me and he will no doubt report direct to Lord Milner.

Yours sincerely

ARTHUR CAPEL

P.S ……. There is no doubt a labour shortage on the front, complicated by the difficulty of transporting labour from England. Can I help by raising a few labour battalions from the Foreign element in France? [78]

In his covering letter, Spears states that he knows the contents of Arthur Capel's letter to be accurate, except that M. Clemenceau now had information that the enemies attack would not take place in the near future.

He goes on to report that Clemenceau thought that the British were not taking their fair share of the burden, in extending the line of battle. In order to take the heat out of this argument he proposes: 'give the French full credit for having until recently, borne the main burden of war, but to point out to them that our hopes lie in the future, and that the Army which will have to bear the brunt of this fighting next year should be given the chance of resting, reforming and training the men it will have to engage.' [79]

This army was, of course, the British.

Clemenceau held a grudge against Prime Minister Lloyd George because of his apparant rudeness to him over an issue of Italian coal, and when the British Ambassador, Lord Bertie of Thame, enquired whether the French government would come to London for the next meeting of the Inter-Allied Council, Clemenceau was disinclined to do so.[80] (The

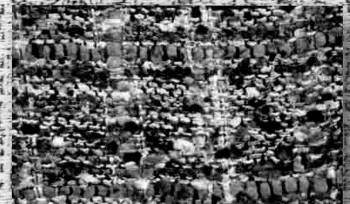
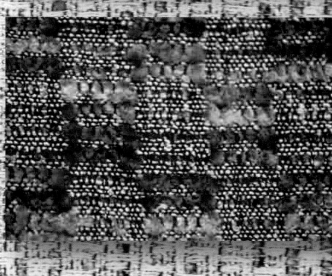

Foreign Secretary, Arthur Balfour was to say of Colonel Hankey:'without Hankey we should have lost the war.' [81])

On the French side of the war effort, one of Boy's opposite numbers on the front line was a man who was to play no small part in saving the French couture industry during World War 2. Lucien Lelong, an intelligence officer in the French military attachment to the British Army in World War 1. He had begun to make his mark in revitalising his parents Parisian couture house before the war, and now reported on the movement of German troops to a British colonel.[82]

Ambition trumps love

Coco and Boy had both made the most of the business opportunities the war presented to them: he with the expansion of his shipping business and Coco in the world of fashion. They were a vibrant couple: both had ambition, the will to succeed, were prepared to work hard, and they really should have married.

But besides wealth, Boy wanted power and position, and that meant a good marriage. How could he marry a young woman brought up in an orphanage, with no elite family background, no position in society and whose parents were market traders? He was not snobbish, he admired her talents, but it would not do, it would be social suicide. Perhaps these were his thoughts. Yet, he really could not do without her, needed to bounce his ideas off her, needed her warmth and wit - in fact, he loved her. But ambition was to prove more powerful than love.

Rumours were abounding in Paris, as he was seen in the company of other women, women who were socially acceptable, from high society and fine families. Coco eventually heard about it, and even though he was always there, helping her, advising her and loving her, she knew that it was over. There would be no marriage out of this love-match. She knew that she should break with him, make a fresh start. It was not possible for her, and instead she settled to be where she would never again bc in her lifetime - on the sidelines.[83]

Bitterness engulfed her, but she smiled and carried on with her work, work that would give her independence, never having to rely on anyone else. She was his equal, in talent and business acumen, and would build an empire, such as he would have only dreamt about. But Boy would never see it.

13
An enduring friendship, a broken heart

Boy and Coco were starting to drift apart, although each still loved the other, Boy spent more time away and Coco began going out into society. She knew that Boy's ambitions meant that he was looking to marry into the aristocracy, and she started to build her own life. There was only so much she could take.

Her friend, the actress Cécile Sorel invited her to a dinner party on 30 May 1917, and there she met the woman who was to become her greatest friend for the next thirty years - Misia Sert.

Born in St Petersburg in 1872, Misia, a talented pianist, would be a notable figure in Parisian artistic and musical circles until her death in 1950. Her father, Cyprien Godebski, was a well-known Polish sculptor, and her Russian mother died when she was born.

Renoir loved her, Diaghilev relied on her, Ravel dedicated *La Valse* to her and Caruso sang for her, and in her colourful life she was a friend and patron of avant-garde artists, musicians and poets.

She was to marry three times, firstly as a young, fifteen-year-old girl to Thadée Natanson, the co-founder of the arts magazine *La revue blanche.* A wealthy man, he provided her with luxurious country houses to entertain her prestigious friends. Alfred Edwards, a newspaper tycoon, and editor of *Le Matin,* came into Misia's life in an extraordinary way. In her Memoirs she recounts his pursuit of her, when she was shopping in antique shops on boulevard Haussmann, and he suddenly called out:

'At last! I've got you! And now I won't let you go!' [84]

Edwards was besotted with Misia, arranging business deals with her husband, and eventually sending him to Koloschvar (now part of Romania) as Director-General of his coalmines.

Thadée saw it as a business opportunity, but it was not successful and he eventually needed bailing out. Misia embarked on a train journey to meet Thadée, and found Edwards had followed her. The threesome appear to have made the novel agreement that if Edwards bailed out Thadée, Misia would become his mistress. She did eventually marry Alfred Edwards, a much older man, and lived in great style, with her own yacht, until one day Alfred saw the beautiful young actress, Genevieve Lantelme, and he was off in pursuit again. The affair dragged on and Misia lived in luxury until the final break came.

Misia Sert, by Renoir - she was Chanel's closest friend

Misia said, 'My life with Edwards had reached its end, and my third marriage was to be, in fact, the first; for it was the only one that rang true in my heart.' [85]

Jose-Maria Sert was a Spanish artist who did work for the Ballets Russes, and was well known in the Palais des Nations in Geneva, specialising in designing and executing large-scale murals. Sert had forgone the opportunity to inherit the centuries-old family weaving business in Barcelona, where his family supplied carpets and fabrics to the stores of Catalonia. He had a brilliant mind, and took a degree in Humanities before going to Paris, as a student of art. On meeting Misia, he invited her to join him on a tour of Rome, he was colourful, enthusiastic and well informed about all they saw. Misia was smitten.

He had the rare gift of making all of life interesting, and of their trips in pursuit of culture, Misia was to say, 'Never did I have with Sert the harassing experience of the "visit to the museum" which usually leaves you with a mind stuffed with a catalogue of old faded glories, a body more weary than from climbing mountains, and a sad heart. I walked out of all these innumerable monuments as though we were leaving the studio of a friend to which he had taken me to see some favourite works.' [86] A rare gift indeed.

Sert soon gained commissions from the United States, Latin America, England and Spain, and he and Misia married.

Near the end of her life, in the 1940s, Misia dictated her memoirs to her friend and companion Boulos Ristelheuber - including a chapter on Coco - but it was never published, nor was there any mention made of Chanel by name in the book, she was only described as a 'great friend.' This was because Chanel objected to anyone else writing her story - she was going to write her memoirs herself. Misia was hurt by this denial, and angrily told her friend, 'But they're already written, all you have to do is publish your account books.' [87]

That unpublished chapter is now available and this is how Misia describes their first meeting in 1917:

> 'At table my attention was immediately drawn to a very dark-haired young woman. Despite the fact that she did not say a word, she radiated a charm I found irresistible. She made me think of Madame du Barry. Therefore I arranged to sit next to her after dinner. During the exchange of banalities appropriate to a first meeting in a salon, I learned that she was called Mademoiselle Chanel, and had a milliner's shop in the rue Cambon.

> 'She seemed to me gifted with infinite grace and when, as we were saying goodnight, I admired her ravishing fur-trimmed, red velvet coat, she took it off at once and put it on my shoulders, saying with charming spontaneity that she would be only too happy to give it to me. Obviously I could not accept it. But her gesture had been so pretty that I found her completely bewitching and thought of nothing but her.. The next day I could hardly wait to go to see her in the rue Cambon.. .that same evening Sert and I went to dine with her at her apartment on the quai de Tokyo. There in the midst of countless Coromandel screens, we found Boy Capel, who represented important British interests in Paris.' [88]

Over the next few years, Coco was to draw on the strength of that friendship, as her own life threatened to fall apart.

Boy decides to marry

Back in London, Boy's friend, Laura Lovat had introduced him to her sister, Diana Wyndham, and before long they announced their engagement. Diana was a member of the aristocratic Lister family, the youngest daughter of the 4th Lord Ribblesdale and his wife, Charty, formerly Charlotte Tennant. She was born in May 1893 at Ascot but her childhood was spent at Gisburne Park, ancestral home of the Ribblesdales, in Lancashire. The millionaire industrialist Sir Charles Tennant was her grandfather, her uncle was Lord Glenconner, and her mother's sister, Margot Tennant, was married to the Liberal Prime Minister, Herbert Henry Asquith.

In 1913, Diana married Percy Wyndham, of the famous family, whose house 'Clouds' in Wiltshire hosted the meetings of the 'Souls', a group of aristocrats, including Diana's mother and aunts, who met to discuss common intellectual interests. Percy's father, the Rt Hon. George Wyndham had married Lady Sibell Grosvenor in 1887, three years after the death of her husband, Earl Grosvenor. From her first marriage she had two daughters and a son, Bendor, who was to become 2nd Duke of Westminster and feature largely in Coco's life in the future.[89]

Percy was in the Coldstream Guards and, on the outbreak of war, he went to France with the British Expeditionary Force. He was killed in action on 14 September 1914, leading his men at Soupir, near Soissons. He and Diana had been married for seventeen months.

Bendor, who had been at the scene, wrote to Diana's father, Lord Ribblesdale, 'I went to his grave, he was buried in the wood where he fell... My thoughts are with dear little Diana, and with my mother, whom I hardly dare write to.' [90]

As a young widow, Diana threw herself into work. She trained as a nurse, qualifying to Voluntary Aid Detachment status and went to France, working as a nurse and driver in the hospital unit organised by Millicent, Duchess of Sutherland and other aristocratic ladies in the ambulance corps. A year later her brother, Charles Lister, also died fighting in France.[91]

At a field hospital near the front, Boy Capel visited Diana. She must have seemed like the answer to his search for the perfect wife, as she could not have had better connections. Diana was part of the social group of young aristocrats who kept London buzzing, whether lunching at the Ritz or dancing at the Alhambra. The set included the young Prince of Wales and Prince Albert (later King George VI). She was a tall, beautiful, sweet-tempered young woman, with courage and great strength of character. As Boy was a Roman Catholic, she converted to his faith.

Success and bitterness in Biarritz

Boy did not know how to tell Coco of his impending marriage, but she knew something was in the air. In the months before his wedding, Boy went back to Coco in Biarritz and found her radiant and financially independent. Furthermore , she had bought the Villa Larralde, paying 300,000 francs cash. With its hydrangea-filled courtyard and couture dresses, it was an absolute success.

His greatest fear in telling Coco of his forthcoming marriage was that he would lose her. By March 1918 he was given the rank of temporary Captain attached to Brigadier-General Spears office in Paris for special duty, and by May 1918, he was appointed Political Assistant Secretary to the British Section of the Supreme Inter-allied War Council at Versailles,[92] and on his frequent trips to Paris, he was her constant companion.[93]

His priority was to get her out of his apartment, and he suggested that she find somewhere in the suburbs, where they could be more discreet. She took an apartment that Misia was letting out on behalf of the previous tenant: a ground floor on the Quai de Tokio, overlooking the Seine on one side and the Trocadero on the other. She liked what she saw, and it would inspire her future ideas on decor. The entrance had walls lined with mirrors beneath a black lacquered ceiling, the light was dim as the windows had been covered with opaque silk, and standing guard over this opulent look was a large Buddha. The cupboards held a collection of kimonos. Here she spent her last happy days with Boy. [94]

The war was not going well. The Germans had a new weapon, Big Bertha, a long-range cannon, trained on Paris. The ladies taking refuge in the Ritz needed night wear they could be seen in, seeking shelter in the cellar of the great hotel. Coco made some scarlet pyjamas for them which they wore like a badge of courage.

At this point in the war the British Embassy in Paris was a hive of social and political activity, a meeting place where diplomats, French high society, politicians, and members of the Intelligence Service had dinner and exchanged the latest news on the progress of the war. The British Ambassador in 1918 was the fifty-three-year old, 17th Earl of Derby, who had been Director-General of Recruiting in London in 1915 and had a reputation for shrewdness and intrigue, dressed up in a 'John Bull' presentation.[95]

Lord Derby had become Secretary of State for War at the end of 1916 when David Lloyd George became Prime Minister, but by the end of 1917, amid political machinations, his future in that post was under threat. By April 1918 he was appointed Ambassador to France but with the added duty of being Head of Britain's War Mission and, as such, had power to discuss matters relating to the war with the French government on behalf of the War Cabinet in London.[96]

Derby became an important player on the French political scene, as well as in diplomatic affairs. He knew Boy Capel well, as part of the Military Mission, and valued his friendship and opinions. Boy was a frequent guest at the Ambassador's luncheons and dinners and very much at home in this tightly knit inner circle. Throughout that summer Boy worked hard on his war work, liaising with Clemenceau, attending meetings and reporting to Spears, at the same time he was running his shipping company, arranging his wedding with Diana and making his explanations to Coco.

Lady Diana Westmorland, Boy Capel's wife, drawn by John Singer Sargent

On Saturday 3 August, Lord Derby wrote in his diary, 'Much amused to hear that the Capel-Wyndham marriage has still not come off though he telegraphed to me to say he was going to be married on Wednesday. Spiers thought they were being married that day but I shall only believe it when I know the ceremony has actually taken place.'[97]

In fact, the marriage had taken place that day, many miles away, in a Scottish castle.

Coco was devastated, even though she had known it would happen.

'I could have married Boy Capel,' she murmured. ' I was destined for him. We were made for each other.'[98]

A society wedding

Diana's sister, Laura, was just two years older than her, both had been pretty, much admired children and were nick-named 'The Dolls', and they were to remain close for the rest of their lives. Laura and Diana finished their education in Munich, before being launched into London society. Laura met Simon, 16th Lord Lovat of Clan Fraser, and married him in 1910, at the Jesuit Church in Farm Street, London, having become a Roman Catholic. Margot Asquith, her aunt, gave the wedding reception at No.10 Downing Street.[99]

Simon's home was Beaufort Castle, in Inverness-shire, a vast red sandstone house which looked down on the river Beauly and across the moors and woodlands. He was twenty years older than the eighteen-year old Laura, and had raised an army regiment, the Lovat Scouts, to fight in the Boer War: they were to become the forerunners of the Commandos. Simon Lovat was also a frequent visitor to the British Embassy in Paris, and a friend and confidante of Lord Derby.

Laura and Simon offered the use of the private chapel at Beaufort Castle for Diana and Boy's marriage. Here on 3 August 1918, amid the peace and rolling beauty of the Scottish hills, a world away from the conflict in France, they wed. Diana was twenty-five years old and Boy was thirty–seven, twelve years older. Their marriage

57

certificate shows that Boy's parents, Arthur Joseph and Berthe Capel (née Lorin) were both dead and that, at the time of the marriage, Boy was living at 88 Avenue Du Bois, Paris and Diana was living at Lyegrove in Badminton, Gloucestershire.[100] This was the beautiful house that she rented from Lord Beaufort, after Percy Wyndham died, and which she later bought from him. Diana's father, Lord Ribblesdale was alive, but her mother, Charlotte was dead.

Was Boy in love with Diana - or was it more a match of convenience, a match which gave him that final social acceptance, an aristocratic connection? He certainly did not forget Coco, and had no intention of giving her up. That was non-negotiable.

The honeymoon was short as by the following Saturday, 10 August, they were back in France, picking up Lord Derby's dinner guests at Le Havre and driving them to Paris. The Capels were very much part of the Parisian social scene that summer and the next day Sunday, 11 August , Lord Derby with his son and daughter-in-law went to luncheon at Versailles,and his diary notes that the Capels were there.

Diana seems to have talked very freely to him, confiding that the delay in their marriage had been due to her own uncertainties. Derby felt she sounded very happy and that she would soon smooth down Boy's 'rough edges'.

She converted to Roman Catholicism to marry Boy - a significant change but one she made with some understanding of the commitment involved because of her sister's earlier marriage to Lord Lovat.[101]

On 17 August - two days before Coco's thirty-fifth birthday - the Capels were guests at an Embassy dinner, where fellow guests included Edward, Prince of Wales (later the Duke of Windsor) and the Italian Ambassador. It was a happy evening as, 'some of them danced afterwards to the gramophone. I never saw anybody enjoy himself more than the Prince of Wales did.. I must say he is a real good boy.' [102]

Boy seemed in a rundown state of health that August and, by the 22nd, Lord Derby was writing in his diary:

> 'Capel is an invaluable connecting link with Clemenceau but I am very anxious about his health. He is very neurasthenic and I am certain he himself thinks he is going off his head which is very far from being the case. Though he talks quite freely with me they tell me when he is alone at home he sits for hours without saying a word and you cannot get him to buckle down to any work. I am sending him away for a fortnight's holiday.' [103]

Was he unsure of his feelings? Was Coco on his mind? It is impossible to know, but it seems that the vibrant, vital Boy was feeling the strain of his multi-faceted lifestyle.

Julian Fane, Diana's son from her third marriage to Vere Fane, 14th Earl of Westmorland, writing of his mother's life, says that she rarely mentioned Boy Capel, only to recall that he could be very witty and amusing, and to remark that Coco refused to return some furniture that he had lent her.[104] We do not known whether Diana knew of his other liaison, but family sources later noted that she and Boy were incompatible.[105] Whatever the truth, Diana still bought Chanel fashions from rue Cambon for years afterwards.

At last the end of this appalling war was in sight, and Coco needed all her courage when she heard the details of Boy's marriage. It should have killed the love that she felt for him, but it didn't. It only increased the bitter pain she felt.

A villa seemed the answer, a flower-filled garden, somewhere to rest after work, somewhere for Boy to visit her. So she rented La Milanaise at St Cloud, where amid the lilacs and roses she had a view of Paris. The festivities marking the end of the war left her unmoved, her pain was too great.[106]

Peace becomes a reality

The fragrant forest of Compiègne was the place where, in a railway carriage at Rethondes and after being given seventy-two hours to refuse or accept the terms, the German delegates signed the armistice at five o'clock in the morning. It came into effect at eleven o'clock - it was 11 November 1918.[107]

Coco and Boy would know the place well.

The Great War was over, and it left behind a world devasted by the death toll, the Allied Powers had lost more than five million men killed in action, and the Central Powers had lost three and a half million. The effects of the war were to be felt for decades afterwards.[108]

President Woodrow Wilson had not wished the United States to enter the war, but had done so in April 1917, hoping to shorten it, and to give him a voice at the Peace Conference. On 8 January 1918, he proposed a peace programme, the Fourteen Points, setting out the aims for world peace, and leading the way for prosperity.[109]

On his way to the Paris Peace Conference at Versailles, the President visited England for discussions with Prime Minister David Lloyd George, arriving on 26 December 1918, and amid cheering crowds, travelled by coach with King George V and Queen Mary to Buckingham Palace. On Sunday 29 December, he made a 'pilgrimage of the heart' to Carlisle to visit his mother's home town to see the site of his grandfather's church in Annetwell Street, and to visit Cavendish House, on Warwick Road, built by his grandfather. He then went to Lowther Street Congregational Church, which had replaced the Annetwell Street Church where he gave an impromptu address. This is part of what he said:

> 'And so it is from quiet places like this all over the world that the forces accumulate which presently will overpower any attempt to accomplish evil on a great scale. It is like the little rivulets that gather into the river, and the river into the sea, and there goes out from communities like this the streams that fertilise the conscience of men; and it is the conscience of the world that we are trying now to place on the throne which others tried to usurp.' [110]

In Carlisle, in spite of pouring rain a crowd cheered the President and Mrs Wilson, as they arrived at the Citadel Railway Station and went to the Crown and Mitre Hotel where they attended a reception to meet local people. A photograph was taken of the occasion and, today, it proudly hangs framed in the foyer. William Linton may well have watched the whole event.

In Paris, Coco designed a dress for the Hon. Mrs Sylvia Henley to wear at the Paris Peace Conference celebrations. By a strange twist of fate it was Sylvia, the second daughter of Lord Sheffield, who during 1915 and 1916 was the chief correspondent to Prime Minister, Herbert Asquith, much to the chagrin of his wife, Margot Asquith. Margot was Diana Lister Wyndham's aunt. Her husband became Brigadier-General Anthony Henley and died in 1925.[111] (In 1971, Sylvia Henley loaned the Chanel dress to Cecil Beaton who was organising a couture exhibition at the Victoria and Albert Museum, London.)

***

14

New beginnings and sad endings

1919 was a seminal year. Within the previous eighteen years the seeds of the future of the Twentieth Century had been sown. The young men of the United Kingdom, France and Germany had given their lives on the bloody battlefields of Europe, and a period of enormous social and technological change was beginning.

The world would never be the same again.

Coco was to declare that 1919 was the year when she woke up famous. The war years had seen the birth of a new era in fashion and she was now a major player in designing the new look of the fashionable, modern woman.

It was also the year that William Linton established his company in a new location. Cranston Waddell's death in November 1917 meant that William Linton was again reviewing his business interests. He changed the name of the company to 'Linton's Cumberland Homespuns Ltd' to reflect his new status.

On 14th October 1919, the *Carlisle Journal* reported the sale of Warwick Bridge Woollen Mills the previous evening, at an auction in the Victoria Hotel, Carlisle. Cranston Waddell's executors had put the property up for sale. The premises were described as freehold, with twenty cottages, land and water rights, and the site had an area of 6.5 acres. It was a substantial and attractive proposition.

Attendance at the sale was good, and at the outset the auctioneer pointed out that the machinery was a valuable asset, having increased in value by 100% since its installation. The turbine was capable of turning out 70 horse power. With excitement in the air, bidding started at £3,000 for the whole property, and ended satisfactorily for Mr William Waddell who purchased it on behalf of Otterburn Mills Ltd. Northumberland, for the sum of £6,350. The mill continued to produce tweed under the name 'Otterburn Textiles' and was managed by William Waddell 1V.[112]

The wheel had turned full circle, and Linton's Cumberland Homespuns was in search of a new home.

Shaddon Mill and a permanent home

Seven years had elapsed since William Linton had journeyed over the border to Carlisle, and now with his own mill in the city, he looked to developing tweed production on his own. There were reports that all was not well between William and the Waddell family by this time. Perhaps they felt that, after learning the business of running a tweed mill at Warwick Bridge, he was about to set up in direct competition within a short distance of their mill.[113]

William looked for premises in Carlisle and soon found the ideal location, it was within the Shaddon Mills complex – the old weaving sheds at Dixon's Mill. This was also an inspired choice of location, as he now had immediate access to the woollen yarn he needed, it was on hand, just across the yard, at Todd's mill.[114]

Shaddon Mill, with its high chimney, had been spinning wool since the factory was taken over from the Dixon family by Robert Todd and Sons in 1882. The Industrial Revolution had ended the practice of home–based handloom weaving, and mechanisation took over. The building was regarded as quite a phenomenom when it was built in 1835, with its chimney completed in 1836. A national newspaper described it thus:

> *'An immense chimney has recently been built in Carlisle. It is one of the highest buildings in England, being 306 feet high and, for the purpose in which it is being used , it is believed to be one of the highest buildings in the world. The entire work was executed by a native of Carlisle, a builder called Mr Richard Wright.*

The erection of the chimney was carried out from the inside and materials were taken up in boxes.' [115]

Richard Wright was a well-known local builder and had the distinction of being Sam Bough's uncle, as in 1815 he had married Sarah Walker, the sister of Sam's mother, Lucy. Sam Bough was to become Carlisle's most intriguing and successful artist, with his work still being sought world-wide today.[116]

A well-known Carlisle legend has it that on completion of the chimney, Dick Wright and some friends climbed to the top to drink a toast, and threw their empty glasses over the side. The glasses falling onto a passing hay-cart, were not shattered and one was preserved in the Managing Director's office.[117]

In August 1919, photographs show William at his new home, Hill House at Great Corby, surrounded by members of his family, it is a happy group and his dreams and ambitions were being realised. But in Paris, in spite of her huge success, Coco was far from happy, as Boy, although now married was still involved in her life.

Two weddings and a funeral

1919 saw Boy return to Coco. It was as though, now married, he was more aware of what he had thrown away. His younger sister, Bertha, entered an arranged marriage on 4th January, to Herman Alfred Michelham. Three days later on the death of his father, Lord Herbert Stern Michelham, Herman inherited the title and Bertha became Lady Michelham. The circumstances of Bertha's marriage are somewhat bizarre, as Geraldine, the wife of Lord Herbert, had encouraged her to marry Herman with the promise of a marriage settlement. Herman was only nineteen, while Bertha was thirty-six.

In June 1920 the *New York Times* was reporting on the decision of the High Court in London, that the deed signed by Lord Michelham just before his death, to provide an annual income for Bertha of £20,000 per year was invalid, due to medical evidence that he did not understand what he was signing. His wife Geraldine was reported to have guided his hand to make the signature.

Dixon's Chimney and Shaddon Mill, Carlisle - still a famous landmark

Herbert Stern, the first Baron Michelham of Hellingly, was raised to the peerage in 1905. He had been born in 1851 into a wealthy Jewish banking family. His father, Baron Hermann de Stern, and uncle Viscount David de Stern had founded the firm of Stern Brothers in 1844 in London. They were prominent in Portuguese finance and had been awarded the patents of nobility by the Portugese government in 1869. Herbert, a multi-millionaire, became a notable philanthropist.

It was a year of marriages, as on 11th November, exactly one year after the armistice, Coco's sister, Antoinette married Oscar Fleming, a Canadian serving in the Royal Air Force, who was training at Brighton. The wedding took place in Paris, with Coco making the wedding dress and Boy Capel and Adrienne's lover, Baron Maurice de Nexon, acting as witnesses. Antoinette and Oscar went back to Canada to live with his family at Windsor, Ontario, and soon, as Oscar went to Toronto to study law, Antoinette found herself alone and unhappy. Coco and Adrienne wrote numerous letters to Antoinette to keep up her spirits and Coco appointed her Canadian agent for the House of Chanel, urging her to take her dresses to show buyers in the department stores. Nothing came of it as the fashions were too different for the local taste, and she asked Coco for a ticket home.

In the meantime, Coco asked the Flemings if they would play host to a young Argentinian who wished to visit Canada before returning home. They agreed and soon Antoinette embarked on a flirtation with him, as he taught them the latest dances. When he returned to Argentina, it was not long before the flirty Antoinette followed him and broke Oscar's heart. The marriage had lasted less than a year. Some time later, when he got news that Antoinette had died, his father had the Royal Bank of Canada undertake an inquiry. This confirmed that she had died while touring South America representing Chanel. Coco was devastated as now she was the only one of the three sisters left.[118]

In the 1919 New Year's Honours list, Boy had been awarded a Civil Commander of the British Empire (CBE) for his work at the Supreme War Council in Versailles. He was back and forward between England and France that year. Work on the Peace Treaty had been on-going for months since the armistice and on 28 June 1919 the Signing of the Peace took place in the Hall of Mirrors at Versailles. All the heads of state with their secretaries, advisers and interpreters were present bringing to an end the years of conflict.[119]

Boy's visits continued, and Coco must have felt exasperated with him as he told her how unhappy he was. Diana was pregnant, but his regrets at his marriage were frequently discussed. On 13 January, from his home at 138 Boulevard Malesherbes, Boy made his Last Will and Testament. This was probably due to the fact that he was about to become a father and wished to put his affairs in order. The Will was short and concise.

Julian Fane, describes how Diana returned to England when she became pregnant. She moved into Boy's house at 6 Cheyne Walk, a fashionable street once the haunt of writers and artists, such as Henry James, T. S. Eliot, J.M.W. Turner, Whistler and Rossetti, close to the Embankment Gardens, Chelsea. Here she awaited the birth of their first child. The move may have been due to her fragile health and her wish to be close to her sister, Laura during this period. Diana and Boy's first daughter, Anne was born in April 1919 and, with his work at Versailles over, Boy relinquished his commission on 22 May when he was home at Cheyne Walk. Diana remained in London for some months after that.[120] Her uncle, Lord Lovat, asked Georges Clemenceau to act as godfather at the christening. Agreeing to this, he sent a delegate to England to act as proxy.[121]

An untimely and devastating death

By October 1919, Diana was again pregnant but Boy was unaware of this, and never saw their second daughter June, who was born in June 1920. By then Boy had been dead for six months.

The last time Coco saw him, he said he was driving to Cannes on the Riviera, supposedly to spend Christmas with his wife, and his sister. Speculation exists that Boy was going to seek a divorce from Diana, in order to marry Coco, but Julian Fane refutes this, knowing as he does the family background.[122]

Some of the Royallieu group were together when the shocking news broke in Paris. Boy had set out with Mansfield, his chauffeur, to drive down to Cannes. On the road between St Raphael and Cannes a burst tyre caused a terrible crash. Mansfield was seriously injured, but Boy was dead. It was 22 December 1919.

His friend, Leon de Laborde, set out in the middle of the night to St Cloud to see Coco and break the terrible news. Joseph Leclerc, her faithful butler, knowing the ordeal that faced her was loathe to wake her, but Laborde insisted. She had to know, now. Coco came down with short tousled hair and in white satin pyjamas, and - as he struggled to find the words, speaking of an accident - the butler said, 'There is no need for that, sir, Mademoiselle has understood,'[123]

Mademoiselle understood very well, and was so stricken with grief that she could not speak, her face twisted, she was crying with dry eyes, as Leon would recall. It was breaking dawn when they set off, and they drove late into the night. Coco sitting motionless in the back of the car. On reaching Cannes, Coco refused to stay in an hotel and eventually at three o'clock in the morning, Leon found Boy's sister Bertha who put them up in her suite of rooms. Coco was even more devastated when it emerged that Boy's body, burnt beyond recognition, had been sealed in its coffin that night. She would never see him again.

In London, Diana Capel was to receive news of Boy's death in an even more devastating way. Duff Cooper, one of her friends and a high flyer in political and social circles, recorded the events in his diary.

On 23 December 1919, for example, Diana Capel phoned him, having returned to London from Paris the previous day. She told him that Boy was heading for the South of France where she planned to join him in two weeks. As she was lunching with Vera, Lady Rosslyn, she invited Duff Cooper to join them, which he did. After lunch, he and Diana drove to a bookshop before meeting up again with Lady Rosslyn at Asprey's. Forgetful, she left her book in the taxi and when Duff Cooper took it back he was surprised to see both of them still on the pavement. He noted there was a look of horror on Lady Rosslyn's face but thought no more of it.[124]

The next day, he read in the *Daily Express* that Boy had been killed in a motoring accident in the South of France. Suddenly that look of horror made sense.[125]

On Christmas Eve, at 2.30 in the afternoon, Boy was buried at the nearby town of Fréjus with full military honours, but Coco was not there. Instead, driven by Bertha's chauffeur, she went alone to the scene of the accident. The remains of the mangled car, where Boy's life had been prematurely snuffed out, were still there, and Coco had gone round it, feeling what was left of the burnt metal, caressing it with her hands, as if touching the car that he had last touched, would somehow bring him close. Then she sat on a milestone, with her head down, and cried horribly for hours. The chauffeur reported this back to Bertha.[126]

Boy's death was recorded in the Register of the Mayor of Fréjus on 23 December 1919, but not registered in the United Kingdom until 4 July 1928, when it was registered by C.H. Thomas, Acting British Vice-Consul,for the district of Toulon (Var), after sanction had been obtained from the Secretary of State. Boy was thirty-eight years old.[127]

On Christmas Day in America, *The New York Times* headlined:

'BRITISH DIPLOMAT KILLED

Arthur Capel, Friend of Lloyd George, Victim of Motor Accident.

NICE, December, 24.- Arthur Capel, who during the war was Political Secretary to the Inter-Allied War Committee, was killed last night in an automobile accident while he was on his way from Paris to Monte Carlo. A tire on his car blew out, ditching the machine. Mr. Capel was a close friend of Premier Lloyd George.' [128]

In London, on 29 December 1919, *The Times* reported:

'Captain Capel's death is a great blow to his many friends in Paris. He was probably one of the best-known Englishmen living in France where he had important coal interests. During the war, he did excellent liaison work both officially and unofficially, and was a great favourite with Clemenceau. He was a thorough sportsman and at the same time a lover of books.' [129]

By February 1920 *The Times* was reporting on Boy's Will, which simply said:

'The following sums are to be paid free of taxes, £40000 (forty thousand pounds) to Yvonne Viggiano C'tesse de Beauchamp, £40000 (forty thousand) to Gabrielle Chanel, 46 Quai de Tokio, Paris, £20000 to my sister Henriette, (twenty thousand), £20000 to my sister Edith (twenty thousand). The balance of my estate is to be held in trust for my wife Diana & after her death for our child. The Trustees are to be Lord Ribblesdale & Lord Lovat. The Executors of this will are Evelyn Toulmin of Lloyds Bank & the Duc de Guiche – Paris Jan 13 1919 – ARTHUR CAPEL – Witnesses –CARLOTTA ROBINSON – MAY ROBINSON.' [130]

Out of a fortune of more than £700,000, including a personal estate of more than £300,000, his bequests to a young widowed Italian countess, and to Coco Chanel must have raised some eyebrows.

It appears that Boy and Diana's marriage had been foundering during 1919, and she was not about to spend Christmas with him that year. It was a cruel coincidence that she had left France on the day that he died. Harry, the 5th Earl of Rosslyn and his third wife Vera were friends of Boy and Diana, Harry was a Director of the collieries at Dysart in Fife and so also involved in the coal industry. He was in France on the day Boy died and it was he who had telegraphed the news from St Raphael. Duff Cooper would again record in his diary on 21 January 1920:

'After dinner I had a long talk with Lady Rosslyn whom I found charming. She told me how terrible it had been for her that day breaking the news to Diana . How Diana had arrived full of spirits and tried to drag her into Asprey's to choose a Christmas present for me, how she had to restrain her and get her away and tell her. It must have been ghastly. She told me also how impossible Diana's relations with Capel were becoming, how he had entirely ceased to live with her and hardly ever spoke to her. That he confessed she had got on his nerves and he could hardly bear her presence.' [131]

Boy Capel's children from his marriage, Anne and June

As Boy had not been aware of the conception of his second daughter, he had made no provision for her in his will. Diana had to institute legal proceedings to ensure that June was awarded a share of her father's estate. [132]

Diana Capel returned to England and lived at Lyegrove, Gloucestershire. In 1923 she married Lt-Cdr Vere Anthony Francis St Clair Fane, 14th Earl of Westmorland and had two sons, David Anthony Thomas Fane, 15th Earl of Westmorland, born 31 March 1924, and Hon. Julian Charles Fane, born 25 May 1927, and a daughter Lady Rose Fane, born 4 January 1931. [133]

(In 2005, by a strange twist of fate, French war veterans searching for graves of Allied troops who perished in World War 2 came upon a sandstone memorial cross, covered in brambles and ivy, which had lain undiscovered for years. It was erected on the roadside at the site of the crash, at the village of Le Muy, on the road to Cannes. Today, the monument stands with distorted railings, tarnished by time, in the middle of what is now the busy commercial zone of Puget-sur-Argens.[134] Passing motorists will not be aware of the tragedy and heartache that underlies the simple inscription, in French, which Coco had inscribed. It reads:

'In memory of Captain Arthur Capel of the British Army. Legion of Honour.

Died in an accident on this spot. 22 December 1919.

Mons Star. CBE.' [135]

It was a sad but telling memorial and Coco had kept this loving gesture private in her lifetime.)

***

15
A footnote to grief – and mysteries galore

Diana and Coco were not alone in grieving Boy's untimely death. Edith Capel, his elder sister could not accept that he had died and over the ensuing years grief seems to have affected the balance of her mind. British War Office records show how she kept telephoning, writing and turning up on the doorstep at the offices in Whitehall, in search of the truth about Boy's military career and death. Throughout the 1920s and even until 1938, when the file was closed, she kept up a sporadic stream of questions which the men in grey suits never answered to her satisfaction. In fact, they stone-walled her, abiding by the regulations. Although today we can see the copies of the few simple letters that Boy had written that might have assuaged her disbelief, she was refused them, and over the years her paranoia became wilder.

Edith believed that Boy had not been killed outright in the crash, and had been taken by motor ambulance to a convent at St Raphael, and had not died until Christmas Eve, 24 December. She was obsessed with knowing whether he had been given the Last Sacraments of the Catholic Church by the local priest.

She also told the War Office that Madame Clemenceau had arranged Boy's military funeral and that Lord Derby had attended or was represented at a Memorial Service in Paris at a later date, and that Boy was a personal friend of Lord Allenby.[136]

Money seems to have been on her mind also. Although she had been left £20,000 in Boy's will, she was questioning that he had received no pay while on military service, requesting certified copies of the letters in which he had voluntarily given up his pay. She demanded confirmation of his whereabouts on certain dates in 1919, including one when he had signed his will in Paris, as she questioned his whereabouts at this time. With her excited talk of her brother dying 'under peculiar circumstances' and of an 'International Gang', the urbane civil servants politely refused her requests.

By 1925, when it is noted that she was divorcing her husband, Captain Hope, and had custody of their two small daughters, who were subsequently taken away from her by appeal, she was saying that General Peyton had given instructions to let her have copies of the letters. It was to no avail, the letters could not be given and as Boy had resigned his commission on 22 May 1919, there were no military records of his death.[137]

Edith appears to have given up until 20 February 1935 when she sent a typed letter, quoting Sir John French having mentioned Arthur Capel in despatches, together with a list of questions about his military service. She enquires if it is the same person as her brother, as, 'He has been missing since 1920.'[138]

The War Office internal draft memo noted, 'She says he was not in the army before July 1915, he was at the front with the French and tried to transfer to the British Army. There were reasons why folk would want to get rid of her brother. Miss Capel is apparently strained mentally over the death of her brother, she believes it possible he is still alive.'

The reply to Edith on 14 March 1935 was kind but firm. They gave her details of the dates of Captain Arthur Capel's service in the army, and that he was mentioned in despatches on 22 June 1915 in the London Gazette, and had been awarded the Legion d'Honneur-Chevalier on 10 October 1918.

Of his death it said: 'I am to state that a report was received in this Department that the above-mentioned officer was killed as a result of an accident on 22 December, 1919, but as he had already relinquished his commission, no detailed report on the circumstances of his death was rendered to the Department.'[139]

It was their final word.

Edith's final contact was on 21 September 1938, when she telephoned and asked for a copy of the reply they had sent her in 1935. They sent it to her, and on 29 November 1938 closed the file, with the note, 'No Further Minutes must be Placed in This File.'[140]

We do not know the reasons behind Edith's persistence in her pursuit of the War Office. Had her eccentric sister Bertha not told her the details of Boy's death that she knew so well. We do not know whether she had any contact with Coco, or with her sister Henriette. Or was it all just another part of the never to be resolved mysteries of the Capel family?

The mysteries had surrounded Boy since the day he was born. He was born in a hotel and his birth was not registered until the day after his second birthday, when his mother had obtained the authority of the Registrar General to register him in the Sub-district of The Palace, Brighton. Rumour surrounded him as a young man, when it was variously stated that his real father was a Portuguese businessman or a French banker. In truth, of course, his father was the businessman and ship-owner Joseph Capel.

Even in death, sanction had to be obtained from the Secretary of State to register his death with the British Vice-Consulate at Toulon on 4 July 1928. Whatever the truth, we know that he was a talented man who, had he lived, might have been one of the shining stars of his generation.

Years later, Coco was talking to her friend, Franco Zeffirelli, the Italian film and theatre director, and she sadly remarked, 'You never stop loving the people you've loved. Even if they betray you, it's not true that love turns into hatred, it turns into resentment, into anger. But the love you had lingers for ever not because of the person – no, it's because of yourself, because of that moment in your life. Whoever the person was doesn't really matter, that moment is always there.'[141]

***

16
The House of Chanel - a couturière at last

31 rue Cambon, Paris, was the address that would be the home of the House of Chanel from 1919 for all of Gabrielle's lifetime and beyond, right up to the present day. It was the same year that William Linton moved his business, now known as Linton's Cumberland Homespuns, to Shaddon Mills in Carlisle, and it could be said that both she and William had a fresh, but permanent start that year. It was one of the last things that she and Boy had done together, when three months before his death, she moved from number 21 where she had been registered as a milliner since 1910, to number 31 where she became registered as a couturière.

If 1919 had seen both a beginning and an end in Coco's life, 1920 was a catalyst and she began by making changes. Her escape from the numbing pain of Boy's death was to throw herself into her work. At the beginning of 1920, she gave up the lease on La Milanaise and bought a villa named Bel Respiro, at Garches, in the western suburbs of Paris, with a beautiful garden and surrounded by woodland. Joseph and Marie Leclerc, her butler and housekeeper, together with their daughter, moved there with her. Her two Alsatian dogs, their five puppies, and the two little terriers, Pita and Poppée (Boy's last present to her) completed her household. She had the villa elegantly decorated in cream stucco, with its shutters lacquered in black, her favourite colour palette.[142] The house became her bolt-hole, her haven, her retreat, and here she looked for solace, which she tried to find in the arms of other men.

At the age of thirty-six she aimed to revolutionise women's fashion and her success was evident in the two Parisian fashion magazines *Femina* and *Minerva,* which soon showed

31 rue Cambon, headquarters of the House of Chanel

page after page of Chanel models.[143] The fashion writers filled their columns with descriptions of her latest offerings and innovations. It was a profound but simple look: a black tulle dress, a white satin sheath covered with an embroidered and beaded cloak, a red chenille dress, the matching jumper suit, jersey sports suits, a long black silk fringed dress and all cut in the simple, pared-down,elegant, easy to wear style which became her *motif*.

Rival designers in the world of couture

In Paris, fashion had been long been dominated by men: ever since the Englishman Charles Worth started the world's first couture house, Worth et Bobergh, at 7 rue de la Paix in 1858. Jacques Doucet was the last great name of the old world of Paris fashion, known as a designer who espoused good taste in the gossamer-light materials he used, dressing women in the frills and ruffles so beloved of the Belle Époque. He inherited the long-established family business, Doucet Lingerie, which made fine lace lingerie, linens and made-to-measure shirts for high society, turning it into a couture house in 1875.

His clients included the actresses Sarah Bernhardt, Réjane and Cécile Sorel, who would wear the new styles, which other women would then want to emulate. Near the end of his career in 1924, Doucet was showing long tunic-style dresses, drop-waisted dresses and coats with matching linings and evening gowns with handkerchief hemlines.[144] In addition, his intense interest in the arts led him to become a great collector, and he established two libraries of works by contemporary writers, assisted by Pierre Reverdy, the poet, and Louis Aragon and André Breton. These were left to the French nation on his death in 1929.[145]

Paul Poiret worked for Doucet as a draughtsman when a young man, completed his training at Worth, and went on to establish his own couture house, Maison Paul Poiret in rue Pasquier in 1906. Poiret was born in 1879, the son of a cloth merchant in Les Halles, and became prominent in the early years of the new century, with his innovatory ideas. His sheath dresses and tunic styles led to women discarding their corsets and hourglass figures in favour of less rigid undergarments. He introduced the first suspender belts, flesh-coloured stockings and the modern brassiere to enhance a looser, less constricted mode of dress.

With the first visit to Paris of the Ballets Russes in 1909, Poiret showed the oriental look using the brilliant colours inspired by the exotic sets designed by Leon Bakst and others for Diaghilev's ballet. This was followed in 1911 by fashion parades in all the European capitals and by the first culotte skirts. By 1913 he had introduced harem trousers and the lampshade tunic, and was using Liberty-type silks with oriental embroidery or wood block prints designed by the artist Raoul Dufy.[146]

The first couturier to introduce a house perfume, named *Rosine* after his eldest daughter, he founded a decorative arts studio 'Atelier Martine'. His wife Denise Boulet modelled his high-waisted styles, and he created a beautiful garden with fountains at his House at avenue d'Antin - the setting for an exotic fancy-dress ball, the celebrated Thousand and Two Nights on 24 June 1911.[147]

The couture houses may have been dominated by men, but women were beginning to take the opportunity to open their own fashion houses, after centuries of working as unseen seamstresses.

The first woman to found a couture house in Paris was Jeanne Beckers who, with her husband Isidore Jacobs, opened The House of Paquin in 1891. They became known as Monsieur and Madame Paquin and by 1900 she was appointed President of the Fashion Section of the Paris Exposition. She would go on to use outside designers, such as Paul Iribe. The house closed in 1956.[148]

Jeanne Lanvin had been a seamstress before setting up as a milliner in a small apartment in 1890, and later opened her couture house. With her design for a chemise dress in 1914 she was one of the first minimalists. She died in 1946, after which her daughter Countess Jean de Polignac directed the house.

Another designer, Madeleine Vionnet had trained as a seamstress at an early age, and in 1898 went to London to work for the dressmaker Kate Reilly. On her return to Paris in 1900 she joined Callot Soeurs – the four sisters who had set up their couture house in 1895 - and went on to join Doucet in 1907. After gaining this wide experience she opened her own couture house in 1912, and became famous for her use of the bias-cut, diagonal seaming and draping in her designs. Madame Vionnet made an enormous technical contribution to haute couture, and retired in 1939.[149]

The Spanish textile and dress designer, Mariano Fortuny settled in Paris and became famous for his invention of fine, pleated silk which he patented in 1909. He used it in the Delphos cylindrical, form-fitting gown which, made in silk, rippled with colour. The style is still seen today. He died in 1949, famed for his unique mastery of dyes and textile printing and his use of colour and texture in his designs.

Perhaps the designer closest to the simple, sporting style which would signify Chanel was Jean Patou. After working in his uncle's fur business, he opened Maison Parry in Paris in 1912. Such was his success that he sold his complete 1914 collection to an American buyer. After serving in WW1 he set up the House of Patou in 1919 and was immediately successful. He became known for his sporting wear, with wearable pleated skirts and sleeveless cardigans and dressed the tennis star Suzanne Lenglen, winner of the Wimbledon women's championship from 1919 to 1926. He died in 1936, but his family kept the house open and Karl Lagerfeld eventually became one of its designers.[150]

Since 1858 when Worth opened his couture house, Paris fashion had forged ahead. The industry was backed by textile factories producing silks and satins and by thousands of small craft workshops producing everything from buttons and braid to feathers and flowers. It made Paris the centre of the couture world. It was into this milieu that Coco stepped in 1919 at the age of thirty-six and - always ready to do battle - she set out to make her competitors look out-moded. She succeeded beyond her wildest dreams.

**

17
The Roaring Twenties

They have been called 'The Dancing Years', ' Les Années Folles' and 'The Jazz Age', and the Twenties were certainly all of these things. Following WW1, with prosperity and freedom in the air, society looked for pleasure and found it in the new dances such as the Charleston, new fashions in bobbed hair and short skirts, popular music and films of the day. People wanted to shake off the memories of the horror and loss of the Great War and sought new distractions. [151]

Many of the new trends in America soon found their way to Britain and to Europe. These were the years of Cole Porter, Al Jolson, Charlie Chaplin and Louis Armstrong. In Paris, Josephine Baker with her exotic image, had emerged from the obscurity of St Louis on the Mississipi river to be the toast of Paris, and the highest paid entertainer in Europe when she opened in *La Revue Nègre* at the Théâtre des Champs Elysées.[152]

Elsa Maxwell, the well-known American hostess and party-giver, was living in Europe in the Twenties and organised events for high society and royalty. Together with fashion designer Captain Edward Molyneux, she opened a nightclub, Les Acacias, in Paris and Molyneux hired Clifton Webb and Jenny Dolly, one of the famous Dolly sisters, as cabaret dancers. The audience gasped when Jenny appeared wearing the spectacular costume he had designed. It had an eighteen-feet-long cloak of white chiffon and feathers, covered in five thousand real gardenias and the train carried by two little black boys, dressed as Nubian slaves. They opened a further nightclub, Le Jardin de Ma Soeur, where Josephine Baker and Leonora and Maurice Hughes entertained.[153]

In her memoirs *I Married the World*, Elsa Maxwell recalled that the huge success and publicity of the nightclubs caused a boom for Molyneux's fashion house, which he had opened in Paris on being demobbed from his Regiment after the war (where he had served with distinction and won the Military Cross).[154] At the age of twenty-eight he became a huge success and the newspapers reported the story that the British Ambassador, Lord Derby had attended his opening show, making history by being the first ambassador 'to visit a dressmaker's salon on exhibition day.' [155]

In 1927, the first talking, singing movie, *The Jazz Singer*, was released by Warner Brothers and caused a stir when its star Al Jolson started singing 'Blue Skies' on screen. Film became an affordable major source of entertainment for people at all levels of society, and Hollywood a source of inspiration to ordinary women seeking the world of beauty and fashion.[156]

Pleasure was not all: since the war, women were looking for a new place in society. There had been some improvements to women's working conditions as more stepped in to take over men's work, but they were paid less and had often worked in dangerous conditions in the munitions factories. At Enfield in London and in Gretna in Scotland skilled women worked a fifty-three hour week for a wage of two or three pounds.[157] Dangerous it may have been, but life would never be the same again for women, they had tasted the freedom of earning their own living.

Votes for (most) women

In the United States women, apart from Native American women, won full voting rights in 1920, and the struggles of the Suffragette movement brought full voting rights to women in England in 1928. The women of France would not achieve this until 1944. Women were playing an increasingly active part in the quest for equal rights and social reform, and the Fabian Society founded in 1884 had many women members. The Fabians promoted idealistic values of building a society which took responsibility for social justice for all, to be achieved by education and debate.

Women were also accessing higher education as well as taking their place in the world of work. New sexual freedoms emerged from the work of Doctor Marie Stopes and her controversial teachings on contraception, while women acquired new rights in divorce and child custody. By 1930, in Britain, The Women's League of Health and Beauty was formed to promote exercise and sport for women, and to establish beauty and good health as an ideal to be pursued.

More developments were seen in the world of medical science: radium had been discovered in 1903 by Pierre and Marie Curie, and was followed by insulin in 1922 and penicillin in 1928. Charles Lindbergh made the first solo flight across the Atlantic and Britain saw its first Labour government under Ramsay MacDonald in 1924. In literature, F. Scott Fitzgerald wrote *The Great Gatsby,* D.H. Lawrence wrote *Women in Love,* and T.S. Eliot and Ezra Pound were writing *modern* poetry.[158] In America, the voting influence of the Women's Temperance League helped bring about the establishment of Prohibition.[159]

The 1920s may have been the years of the bright young things, progressive thinking and artistic and scientific development, but they were also a time of economic hardship for most people. This time of change and development did not improve the life of ordinary working class people. Poverty, dole queues and hunger marches were the lot of many. Women lived in grinding poverty, trying to bring up small children on little money and in poor housing conditions. Men struggled to provide for their families, working long hours, often in harsh conditions. The imbalance between the social and welfare conditions of the rich and poor had never been so marked, and these years saw the rise of socialism and the trade unions. Such was the level of discontent that in 1926, workers in Britain held a General Strike. This was an awakening, both to government and to the middle and upper classes, as the plight of ordinary working people became the focus of national attention. Black Friday, 24 October 1929, saw the crash of the Stock Exchange.

***

18

Linton's grow at home and abroad

William Linton's company was catering for the luxury market of dressing society women, but his mill workers in Carlisle were not finding life so easy. The company was going from strength to strength but the war had meant a shortage of skilled workers as men were called up into the Armed Forces. To counteract this William had been forced to bring in skilled men from outside the area.

In 1914 he had offered the job of loom tuner to Samuel Cavers, a man from Derrymore, Northern Ireland, who moved with his wife, Christine, and family to Carlisle. A loom tuner in the Irish tweed industry, Samuel saw better prospects at Linton's and he was eventually joined there by his second daughter Annabella when she left school in 1920. Apart from the period when she was conscripted to work at the Air Ministry during World War 2, she spent the rest of her working life at Linton Tweeds working as a darner. Miss Cavers retired at the age of 65 in 1971, and went on to celebrate her 100th birthday in 2006, becoming one of the longest living family links with Linton's, from the early days of the company to the 21st century.[160]

1920 was a difficult year for local businesses in Carlisle, and a review of the business year published in the *Carlisle Journal* on 4 January 1921, reported that Linton's Cumberland Homespuns, although doing well in the early part of the year, were now feeling the slump in trade. However, even though the outlook was uncertain, the fall in wool prices meant that there was likely to be a greater demand for their goods going forward.

> 'Mr Linton pointed out that the Government are still holding wool to the value of sixty million sterling, and that there is still a large quantity in the hands of farmers, who are holding on for higher prices. As an instance , however, of the drop in prices, the firm have recently purchased a large consignment of wool from Scotch blackfaced sheep at 10d a pound, though 1s 4d a pound was refused for the same wool four months ago. Mr Linton claims that with the present slump in the wool market , it is possible to standardise the price the public should be called upon to pay for the finished material, and that a reduction of 50 per cent in the cost is possible under existing conditions.' [161]

William felt sufficient confidence in the situation to open a retail shop in Citadel Row, a pretty, narrow cobbled street in Carlisle town centre, where he could display the beautifully woven earth-coloured tweeds so in demand for men's suits. A week later he was advertising all his wares in the local paper. [162]

For a time he continued expanding into the retail business and by 1925, he had a shop at West Street, Wigton, a small market town eleven miles from Carlisle, and one in Cockermouth, a market town thirty miles to the west of Carlisle. He was also encouraged by the orders for the Spring season he had received from major stores in the West End of London, where the tweeds were extremely popular.

Transatlantic travels – again

William began his transatlantic journeys to America again, and the minutes of the Director's Meeting on 23 July 1921 record, 'there is no doubt that had the Managing Director not proceeded to the U.S.A. and obtained considerable orders it would have scarcely been possible to keep the mill open... the prospects of business for the current year in this country were not very bright and there appeared to be a likely market in U.S.A. It was decided that this market should be cultivated and that the Managing Director make another journey there next month...' [163]

In those days before international air travel, the great shipping lines advertised in local provincial newspapers, such as the *Carlisle Journal,* where in 1921 the Cunard Line were promoting their monthly sailings from Southampton and Liverpool to Cherbourg and New York, and William became a regular customer.[164]

America - put your glad rags on!

The trips to America came at a time when New York City's Garment District was booming. Although he was selling Linton tweed to the upper end of the market, to top-class designers and manufacturers, William would be well aware of the huge growth potential in the American ready-to-wear business, at all levels.

The industry in New York had developed from the days when the slave masters on the Southern plantations bought simple, low-quality clothes for the slaves from the New York manufacturers. By the 1850s, the influx of German, Russian and Central European immigrants, many of them Jewish and experienced in business and garment manufacture, made New York the centre of American ready-to-wear clothing production.[165] The popularising of the sewing machine by Isaac Merritt Singer at this time also made it possible to produce clothes of reasonable cost quickly, and the garment industry expanded further. In the 1860s, the American Civil War meant the manufacture of thousands of military uniforms, for both the Union and the Confederacy.

WOOLLEN MANUFACTURERS
ESTABLISHED 1821.

ORNA · VERUM

Our registered Trade Mark is our guarantee of excellence.

LINTON'S CUMBERLAND HOMESPUNS, LTD.,
(formerly WADDELL'S, Ltd)..

CITADEL ROW,
CARLISLE,

In our warehouse stock on view, at Citadel Row, we have a very attractive range of men's suiting materials, in all weights and qualities.

We specially recommend our Cumberland Frieze at 17s. 6d. per yard, 56in. wide, for extra hard wear and especially suitable for working men's trousering.

We also hold a nice stock of Homespun material for sports suits at 12s. 6d. per yard, double width.

Come and see for yourselves, and if unable to call write us for patterns.

Special discount allowed to the trade.

From then on the industry developed apace. The sewing workshops, the sellers of buttons, braid, lace and fancy goods, the fabric shops with glowing silks, satins and every type of material and trimming imaginable, the hat shops with their steaming blocks - all were conglomerated in the Garment District. This noisy, colourful milieu was located in one square mile, between Fifth and Ninth Avenues, from 34th to 42nd Street, in the borough of Manhattan. It made New York City the clothing manufacturing capital of America. There was a buzz of excitement in the air, and fashion was in the making!

Top dressmakers had always catered for the elite and high society women who patronised their shops on Fifth Avenue, but many more set up shop in their homes in tenement buildings, using paper patterns and selling their garments from there. They made affordable dresses and tailored suits for women of slender means. At the end of the nineteenth century, the growth of department stores had a major impact on the livelihoods of independent dressmakers, as the stores often provided their own in-house dressmaking service. This was the era of new stores such as Bonwit Teller, Macy's, Stern, Lord and Taylor, and others. Catalogue shopping became popular, with catalogues from companies such as Sear Roebuck and Montgomery Ward providing a wide choice of garments of every description.

Advert for William's new business in Carlisle, Linton's Cumberland Homespuns, January 1921

The beginning of the twentieth century saw the development of tenement 'sweat shops', where the clothing manufacturers designed the clothes and provided the cloth and materials, which were then handed over to contractors. The contractor would have a workshop equipped with sewing machines and workers who were paid by piece work, based on the number of garments that the whole group produced. The workers were usually low-paid female immigrants and were often exploited. When the garments were finished, they were returned to the manufacturer who marketed the clothes.

As technology developed, with patterns, cutting machines and improved sewing machines it was possible to produce more sophisticated designs, and by 1910 demand for stylish, reasonably priced clothes had leapt ahead. In that year, 70% of America's women's clothing, and 40% of men's was produced in New York.[166]

Styles were changing and, by the 1920s, designs such as Chanel's little black dress, 'A Ford named Chanel' as American *Vogue* described it, became simpler to make, with clean cut lines and less material.

By the 1920s, the garment worker's unions were extremely powerful: there were political differences and bitter strikes. Before long the industry was infiltrated by gangsters and the mob influenced everything from the unions to the trucking industry who transported the goods. Over the next decades this situation got worse. The head of the Amalgamated Clothing Workers of America was a Lithuanian immigrant named Sidney Hillman, and he would become one of the leaders of industrial and political reform.

England's sweatshops

Not only in America were women working in poor conditions and for low pay. In the years before the turn of the twentieth century, fashion meant exploitation for those women who spent their days sewing in cramped factories and workshops, working long hours for little pay. From London to Leeds, Manchester to Macclesfield, the small workshops and larger factories of the tailoring and garment trade hummed with activity to supply the increasing demand for cheap but fashionable clothing.

Sweatshops developed because of the soaring demand for fashionable clothes by men and women who had come into the cities from the countryside, with the explosion of the industrial revolution. At the same time the development of machinery and sewing machines meant that clothes and textiles could be more speedily produced. Many of the workshops were opened by Jewish refugees who had fled their homelands in eastern Europe, due to persecution and settled in London. In 1901 there were more than 1300 Jewish workshops producing garments.[107]

While the tailoring trade was a largely male domain, women would be employed making skirts and blouses, many with finely sewn tucks and ruffles, lace insertions and embroidery. Many of the women did 'outwork' in their own homes, which conveniently fitted in with their family duties and the care of their children. As in America, large London department stores, such as Swan and Edgar and Liberty, had their own workrooms, employing women to make up models and do alterations.

And so it was that the 'Roaring Twenties' with their social change, pleasure and fun, medical advancement, technological change and outright *joie de vivre*, exploded on the post-war scene like the phoenix arising from the ashes.

Industrial strife was not an issue back in Carlisle and William Linton had returned from his 1921 trip to America with enough orders to keep the mill going for the coming year. He also looked forward to his daughter Nessy joining him in the business, as he knew she would be an asset at the mill and on trips to meet clients in Paris and America. The future looked rosy.

***

19

Nessy, Norah and the deerhounds

William's only daughter, Agnes, or Nessy as she was known to family and friends, was making plans to work with her father in the business. A bright, dark-haired, vivacious young woman, with a winning smile, she was later to become a celebrated breeder of deerhounds, exporting them internationally.

Since her mother's death, Nessy had been brought up by her Linton aunt, who lived with the family at Hill House. She attended the County High School for Girls, in Lismore Place, Carlisle, from the Spring term of 1914, and gained her Oxford School Certificate with Honours in July 1920.[168] The school had been opened by the Duke of Devonshire in 1909, and accommodated three hundred pupils.

In September 1920, at the age of eighteen, Nessy travelled to Gloucestershire where she was enrolled at Cheltenham Ladies' College, a prestigious college for the daughters of aristocratic and wealthy families. Here she met a fellow student, Norah Hartley who was to become a life long friend, and a fellow breeder of deerhounds.

Nessy left the College in July 1922 at the same time as Norah, who went on to gain a degree in English Language and Literature at St Hilda's College, Oxford in July 1925. This was a time when the Oxford colleges were just opening up to women, who had only been allowed to matriculate as members of the University since 1920. There were many restrictions on women undergraduates, especially in their contact with male undergraduates, and they had to be chaperoned if going to tea in a men's college.[169] Norah was among the first to graduate.

Agnes 'Nessy' Linton at Hill House in 1921

Nessy, her first love being textile design and with her sights set on entering the family business, gained entrance to the Scottish College of Textiles, over the border in Galashiels. It is thought that she was the first female student to attend there.

Norah was the sister of L. P. Hartley, the distinguished modern novelist, whose work includes *The Shrimp and the Anemone, The Hireling* and *The Go-Between*. She was brought up with her brother, Leslie, and sister, Enid, at the family home of Fletton Tower, Peterborough, where she eventually set up the Rotherwood Kennels, and devoted her life to breeding her beautiful deerhounds. The Hartleys had moved to Fletton Tower in 1900 and Norah was born there on 17 September 1903.[170]

Her father Harry was a solicitor and prominent in the local community where he played an active part in local business and political affairs. His wife, Bessie Thompson, was the daughter of a farmer in the Fen country, around the Crowland area. Both families were Wesleyan Methodists with strong ties and involvement in local public service. Their eldest child, Enid, would continue this tradition of public service, devoting her life to serving the local community with her work in education and social work. She received the MBE in 1949.

Harry had invested in the Fletton brick manufacturing industry and, when it was discovered that the clay on part of the estate had special properties, it proved a sound investment and brought wealth to the family.[171]

Fletton Tower was a large Gothic building and over the years it had seen a number of changes, with parts of the estate being sold off. By the time the Hartleys moved in 'The rooms were spacious and elegant, their doors carved with linen-fold and other Tudor-type panels. The hall had a curved painted ceiling. The windows overlooked well-kept lawns and gardens. From the drawing-room a distant view of Peterborough cathedral could be seen, and the huge dining-room featured a window over the fireplace.' [172] The Hartley's made it into a beautiful home filled with antiques, paintings, china and textiles. In the holidays, Nessy was a frequent visitor and Norah made the reverse journey up to Cumberland many times in her lifetime.

An idyllic summer

The summer of 1922 was idyllic, and Nessy captured photos of Norah, Enid and her friends, on trips they made to Stratford-on-Avon, Warwick Castle, the Border country (including Abbotsford, home of Sir Walter Scott, Melrose and Dryburgh Abbeys) and the Lake District, visiting Derwentwater and Bassenthwaite in August. They are pictured driving along the country roads in a bright yellow open-topped Citroën C 5CV: young, well-educated women, just starting out to make their mark on the world. William was with them when they visited Warwick Castle, with its peacocks strutting on the lawns - and Nessy recorded it all on her Box Brownie camera. (The photos remain, a reminder of those glorious halcyon days, neatly annotated and numbered in her albums, in the safe-keeping of the Deerhound Club Library.)

It seemed a never-ending summer; its lazy, hazy days spent visiting historic monuments, boating on the lake, sightseeing with family and friends. This was the dawn of the Twenties and, in the aftermath of the the war, life suddenly seemed to be fizzing. It was great to be young. There was only one thing missing: young men. The cruel war had decimated the young male population, who gave their lives selflessly in the pursuit of peace, and now the women of Britain would feel that loss for years.

In their different ways, Nessy and Norah did make their mark on the world, and they remained friends until Nessy's death nearly sixty years later.

After coming down from Oxford, Norah decided that she wanted to breed deerhounds. She describes how this came about in the book that she wrote in 1955, *The Deerhound* – still a valuable reference work to all who breed and love deerhounds today.

> 'For a variety of reasons, I began with an absolutely open mind, having no knowledge of nor bias towards any breed whatsoever. I liked big dogs and wanted to be able to hold my dog's collar without stooping. I wanted one with graceful lines and a lithe active movement. I didn't want one that was heavy enough to pull me over... I wanted a breed with a pleasant disposition, one that was affectionate, trusting and to be trusted, not suspicious, nervous or aggressive' [173]

Her father supported her ambition and in 1925 they went together to the Kennel Club Show at the Alexandra Palace, London. From that day until her death in 1995, deerhounds were Norah's life.

She describes the amusing trip that she made from Oxford to Bridge Sollers, a village near Hereford, to Miss Richmond's kennels to buy her first deerhound, an eight month old bitch puppy called Little Bizi. The price was fifteen guineas. On their return to Oxford, Little Bizi was in boarding kennels for the night and broke from her collar when the kennel owner tied her to the back of his bicycle, leaving her trotting along behind. After a night in the police cells, Little Bizi was returned to her distracted owner. When registered as Silver Cloud, she became the first deerhound in the Rotherwood Kennels. [174]

Years later Norah recalled:

> 'When I bought Silver Cloud in the Autumn of 1925 she was a gangling eight months puppy and my sister and Nessy dubbed her Tutankhamen's couch because her shelly resembled (or so they said) that piece of furniture... A year later I asked Nessy what she would like for a birthday or Christmas present (I forget which it was) and she said a bit sheepishly that if she could win her family round it would be a deerhound, please.

Hill House, Great Corby
- home of William Linton
and his family

Nessy and the first Geltsdale deerhound,
Brutus of Bridge Sollers and Norah Hartley's
Silver Cloud

William Linton,
Norah and Enid
Hartley at Warwick
Castle, 1922

Norah Hartley

Linton family at Hill
House, 1919

Hill House kennels,
home of the Geltsdales
until 1938

'Nessy's home was already furnished with a collie and the question was would Laddie tolerate another male. On no account would a bitch even be considered, it would be too difficult with Laddie and of course there could be no question of ever doing anything so dreadful as breeding. In any case Nessy was working full-time in her father's tweed mill and to Mr Linton this was the aim and object of life. It would just not have occurred to him that anything else could be of equal interest or importance. But he was very fond of Nessy and if she wanted a deerhound he would make no objection, always provided that her work at the mill didn't suffer.

'Nessy's Aunt, who was the family's housekeeper, had doubts of quite a different kind. She loved all animals and was perfectly prepared to welcome another dog, but what would poor Laddie feel? Wouldn't he feel that his nose was put out of joint? How could she make him feel that he was just as important as ever and that the newcomer would not steal the limelight?'

A deerhound at the mill!

In March 1927, on her return from a business trip to America, Nessy picked up her first deerhound, Brutus of Bridge Sollers, in London. Norah had got him from Margaret Richmond at Bridge Sollers kennel, and he was soon ensconced at Hill House.

Norah wrote: 'With much trepidation Nessy asked her father whether she might take Brutus to the mill. "If not I shan't see very much of the dog." There was a long pause - Brutus's fate trembled in the balance, for a "no" would have been final, it could not have been questioned. Finally, "I don't see why not if he behaves himself".'

It was a grudging permission, but Brutus never gave any reason for Wiliam to change his mind. Indeed, the day came when Brutus was shown off to favoured customers, not by Nessy, but by Mr Linton himself. [175]

As it turned out, William was so taken with Brutus of Bridge Sollers that he commissioned a portrait of him to be painted by Cecil Charles Windsor Aldin, the famous illustrator of Anna Sewell's book *Black Beauty*, as a gift for Nessy. The portrait is now in the possession of The Kennel Club , London, left to them by Norah Hartley.

So began Nessy's life-long love of deerhounds. On that March morning she had no thought of establishing a kennel and Brutus was kept as a pet, not a show dog. The charm of this ancient breed was soon apparent, kennels were built behind the house on the hill, and in 1929 Nessy bought Jock of Geltsdale and made him a champion in 1934. Her first champion was Dramatic of Ross, who gained her title in 1930. During the 1930s the Geltsdale Kennels went from strength to strength, and it was considered remarkable that Nessy had established one of the most prestigious kennels of the breed in a very short time. For the rest of her life Nessy would work hard, balancing her efforts and talents between her joint loves, deerhounds and tweeds.

✳✳✳

20
The young designers

The beauty and quality of his tweeds made William want to see them used in international fashion. Throughout the Twenties he developed the company, with progressive ideas and his belief in quality goods. It was all a far cry from the days of the travelling salesmen. A stong domestic clientele of major West End stores in London, was complemented in the United States by such prestigious department stores as Bloomingdales and Bergdorf Goodman. (Bloomingdales was one of the first department stores to have a fashion boutique, where designers could show a selection of their clothes to a wider clientele.[176]) American women took Linton Tweeds and the Chanel look to their hearts, appreciating the luxurious soft wool, tonal colours and elegant wearable designs.

William also started to widen his links with a new breed of young British designers, who were gradually establishing their own international niche. They were contacts that have benefitted Linton's business ever since.

The British already had a strong foothold in the Parisian couture scene. Charles Worth started it all back in 1845, and went from being a fabric salesman at Swan & Edgar, the London department store, to becoming the favourite designer of the French Empress Eugénie. He became known as *the father of couture*.[177]

John Redfern followed. After establishing a successful tailoring business on the Isle of Wight, where he would design sports clothes for the yachting ladies at Cowes, he opened salons in London and Paris in 1881. He then set up branches in Edinburgh and New

York, and his son Ernest managed the shops in London and New York. Charles Poynter looked after the couture house in Paris, where he continued to make Redfern's *trotteur* suit for ladies. The *trotteur* or walking suit had been successfully introduced in the 1890s, and had a smart braid-trimmed jacket, buttoned down the front. Made of serge or wool, it was worn with an ankle-length skirt, flaring at the back, to give freedom of walking.[178]

Before World War 1, the 'court dressmakers' with their links to the British monarchy were powerful in British fashion, providing for the aristocratic way of life of the upper classes. Based in London's West End, they specialised in making copies of Paris designs for their clients attending Royal Ascot, balls and charity events in the London season, and for débutantes being presented at court. Many of Britain's talented young designers felt that unless they opened a Paris house, they would not succeed: everyone wanted clothes from *Paris.*

But the end of the war saw a gradual change to all that, with the decline of the 'court dressmakers' and an upsurge in the development of the British fashion houses, based in London. This was a turning point for British fashion, as small couture houses were established and the young designers set to work.

Norman Hartnell, for example, opened his house at 10 Bruton Street in 1923, but only when he showed his collection in Paris four years later were his clothes truly accepted by society women. Prior to that, he would relate, clients came into his salon, choose a dress, and then enquire if it was by Patou or Lelong: on learning that it was not, they changed their mind and left without it. 'I suffered from the unforgivable disadvantage of being English in England,' he wrote in exasperation.[179]

The House of Lachasse became known for its tweed suits and sportswear when the owner, businessman Fred Shingleton, opened it in 1928 as the sportswear offshoot of his company Gray & Paulette Ltd in Mayfair. The clothes were in the elegant casual style of Coco Chanel, using British wool and tweed, as she did. It was said that Lachasse was so named to suit the tastes of British women who craved French labels in their clothes!

The first designer at Lachasse was a talented young Dubliner, Digby Morton, who would go on to become one of the mainstays of the early British fashion scene. Morton became famed for his tailored tweed suits for women and revolutionised their design to a degree previously unknown in British women's tailoring. Using his native Irish tweed, his suits were no longer the type seen on the grouse moors of country estates:now they could be worn at the Ritz bar by fashionable women. In later years, Hardy Amies acknowledged that Morton achieved this new look in tweeds by his intricate cutting technique and placing seams to give a more decorative line when he wrote: 'such clothes have become so much a part of the fashion picture in all parts of the world during more than the last fifty years that it is hard to realize how much they owe to Morton's original ideas.'[180] (In 1934 Digby Morton left Lachasse to establish his own couture house, paving the way for Hardy Amies to join them.)

These new town-and-country clothes were an instant hit when Morton showed his first collection in 1929, the year of the Wall Street crash. American and other overseas buyers deserted the Paris fashion houses and looked to London for lower prices and the excitement of a new couture style. Morton used innovatory colour mixes, such as duck-egg blue and pale lime green with chocolate brown and bought printed silks from Rodier for jacket linings and blouses, making the tweed suit a fashion statement.[181]

Parisian designers fought back, looking to expand their markets by setting up couture houses in London. Chanel was among them, opening up in Beauchamp Place in a house belonging to the Duke of Westminster.[182]

***

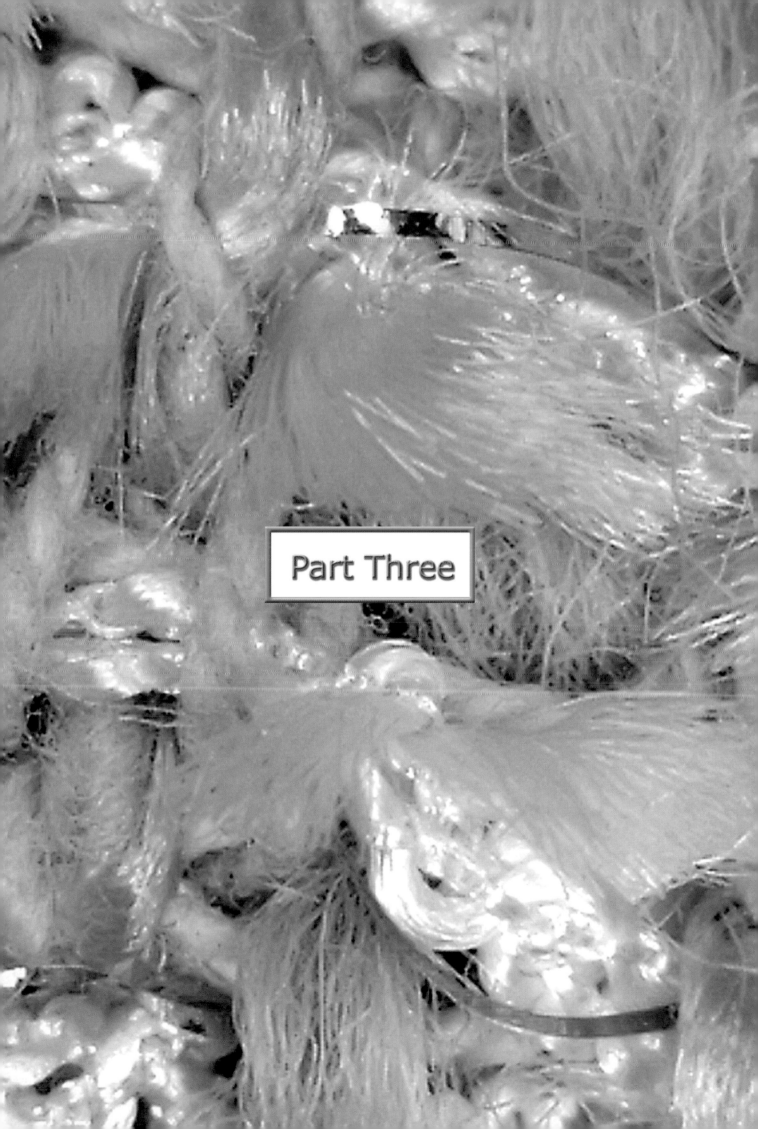

Part Three

21
Friends, lovers and businessmen

In Paris, Misia and José Sert kept a close eye on Coco after her move to Bel Respiro in early 1920. Misia was concerned that her friend was not getting over Boy's death and even quizzed Joseph about it when she visited. Coco worked hard at rue Cambon during the week, but weekends could be lonely. She was invited to all of Misia's gatherings, silently listening and watching, as guests were enchanted by their hostess.

The *avant garde* life in Paris blossomed in the Twenties as dancers, musicians, artists and poets met at the cabaret café, Le Boeuf sur le Toit, or 'The Ox on the Roof', at 28 rue Boissy-d'Anglas, to gossip on the events of the day. Jean Cocteau and Pablo and Olga Picasso were among those who crammed the tiny floor to dance to the jazz piano played by Jean Wiener.[1] Here the dancers of the Ballets Russes met and José Sert introduced Misia to Serge Diaghilev. With the return to Paris of Igor Stravinsky, there were plans afoot to present the ballet, *Pulcinella,* with sets by Picasso and choreography by Massine.[2]

Misia decided that Coco needed a holiday, a complete break from dresses, and proposed a trip to Venice with her and José. He proved the perfect guide and implanted in Coco a love for Venice that she would never lose. Coco began to recover, at least outwardly, and took great interest in everything she saw. She was later to say that the Serts had saved her.[3] In Venice, they happened to meet Diaghilev lunching with the Grand Duchess Marie Pavlovna, who had sponsored his productions at the Imperial Theatre. On joining their table, the talk turned to forthcoming productions for the Ballets Russes programme in Paris, and the impossible costs of presenting them. Diaghilev said that Massine was rehearsing a new production of *The Rite of Spring* but costs were prohibitive. As Dame Margot Fonteyn would describe him: 'Diaghilev had the heart and courage of a gambler - he loved the excitement and risk of being an impresario of the arts, and Paris was his natural element.'[4]

Coco was impressed by Diaghilev's imagination and style and decided she would help - but in secret. On returning to Paris, she visited him and handed him a cheque to cover the costs, the one condition she imposed was that he never told anyone - ever. Serge was overcome at this grand gesture from a woman he didn't really know, but he did tell someone - Boris Kochno. Kochno joined Diaghilev as his private secretary but was also a gifted poet who, from 1925, composed ballet scenario's and worked with Diaghilev on the artistic direction of the Ballets Russes until the impresario's death.[5] (Kochno became a friend of Coco, but only in 1971, the year of her death, did he reveal her generosity to the world.)

Stravinsky – an affair of the heart

Coco was making great strides in her business, and began once more to embrace her love of life, in society and in the arms of her lovers. She filled Bel Respiro up with her friends, particularly those impecunious Russians. Igor Stravinsky was one of them. She recalled seeing him at that first memorable performance of *The Rite of Spring* in 1913: he had made a deep impression on her. Igor was a small bespectacled man, with a rich vibrant personality, and talked as passionately about his music as Coco did about her dresses.

Born in St Petersburg in 1882 he had studied with Rimsky-Korsakov, and was also influenced by composers such as Tchaikovsky, Borodin and Debussy. His work was a new development in Western music, with its rhythmic energy and driving pulsations.

Igor, his wife Catherine, their two children and members of his extended family, had left Russia in 1910, as the harsh Russian climate affected Catherine's delicate health. Returning only in the summer months to their country home in south-west Russia, they spent the winters in Switzerland and on the French Riviera. It was a nomadic existence and two further children were born in Switzerland.

Stravinsky had a five-year contract with Diaghilev for performances of *The Firebird* [6] and was working on new ballets, including *Petrushka* and *The Rite of Spring* which would have their first performances in Paris. With the outbreak of World War 1, the family remained in Switzerland and, when the Russian Revolution broke in 1917, Igor lost everything: his home, his money, his personal belongings. With such a large family to support and an uncertain financial future these were lean years when he relied not only on his music, but on the patronage of his friends.[7] He would not see his native land again for forty-eight years.[8]

In June 1920 Igor decided to make the family home in France, where he was nearer to developments in art and music. By this time he was working with Picasso and Diaghilev and had completed the ballet *Pulcinella* which opened at the Paris Opera in May. Together with members of their extended family, they set up home in the Breton port of Carantec and spent the summer enjoying picnics, boating and shrimping.

In the autumn, with Igor composing and in need of a quiet place to do so, he went apartment hunting in Paris. Here he met Coco, who invited him and his family to move into Bel Respiro, her lovely house at Garches. This gave him the space and peace to work

Igor Stravinsky, the gifted composer, who stayed at Chanel's house, Bel Respiro, and had a brief affair with her

at his piano, and she loved the sound of the music resonating around her cool elegant rooms. The house and grounds were extensive, with a cedar tree in the park, and luxurious pinky-beige furnishings and objets d'art. The children played in the first-floor games room and in the gardens with Coco's three dogs, two wolf-hounds and a frisky fox terrier. Catherine was soon organising tutors to attend to the children's education, and she and Igor would often visit art exhibitions in Paris.

There was a drawback to this enviable lifestyle: Igor was of a flirtatious nature, and Coco at the height of her beauty and elegance. Soon the inevitable happened – a brief affair ensued.[9]

The Stravinskys and the others stayed through the winter and the New Year of 1921 brought a turning point for Coco and the House of Chanel. With Catherine and four children to consider, the family moved from Bel Respiro in March 1921[10] and settled in the south of France. (Catherine died in March 1939, just before the outbreak of war. In 1940 Igor was invited to America to give a series of lectures at Harvard University, where he was joined by his mistress Vera Sudeykina, and they married one year after Catherine's death. On the brink of his brilliant international career, Igor now settled in America. He died in New York on 6 April 1971 aged eighty-eight, just three months after Coco herself died.[11])

Igor was to write: 'Do we not, in truth, ask the impossible of music when we expect it to express feelings, to translate dramatic situations, even to imitate nature?'[12]

Prince Dmitri – in love with an exile

By early 1921 Coco was in Biarritz, combining business with pleasure, when she met up with some of her old friends from her Royallieu days. Marthe Davelli and Gabrielle Dorziat were there and, at a party, Coco was introduced to Prince Dmitri, another Russian exile. Theirs was an instant attraction. Eight years younger than her, Dmitri appreciated her style, her wit, her commonsense, and - hidden beneath that - her kindness. Coco appreciated his charm, his courtly elegance and his shy and reticent manner. Since coming to Paris from London, he was living in a small two-roomed apartment near his sister Marie and her husband. Like Marie, he was looking for employment and had been offered a post with a champagne-producing company in Reims, where he became a Director.[13]

Prince Dmitri and his sister, the Grand Duchess Marie, had been virtually abandoned by their father when their twenty-one year old mother, Alexandra, died in 1891 giving birth to Prince Dmitri. On his remarriage to Princess Paley, their father, Grand Duke Paul, lived in exile in Paris and his children remained in Moscow, where they were brought up by their uncle, the Tsar's brother, Grand Duke Serge, who was Governor-General of Moscow.[14]

Marie was born in 1890 and, when she was seventeen, she was betrothed to the homosexual Prince William of Sweden. In spite of her protests and her father's disapproval, the Tsar had agreed to this arranged marriage. The marriage did not last and Marie fled Sweden, forced to leave behind her son Lennart.

Prince Dmitri was a tall, graceful, fair-skinned young man who, before being exiled in Persia for the part he played in Rasputin's murder, had served with the Horse Guards regiment and enjoyed a full social life. When diplomat Sir Charles and Lady Marling were recalled to England at the end of 1918, Dmitri accompanied them. In 1919, by now an officer in the British Army, he went with them to Paris, then to his father's house at Boulogne. Finding that the house was empty and his father in prison in Russia, he returned to London, living at the Ritz Hotel on the capital he had made from the sale of his palace in Petrograd, as St Petersburg was now called.

Marie remarried after her divorce from Prince William and with her husband, Serge Putiatin, escaped from Russia to Romania, from where they travelled to London to see Dmitri in 1919.[15] She described that bittersweet meeting: 'Dmitri had not only grown more mature physically he had developed mentally as well, and for me this change was both extremely gratifying and in a way heartbreaking. Nobody had had an easier, a more brilliant debut in life than he... unusually good looks, coupled with charm, and he had been the recognised favourite of the Tsar... there was no young prince in Europe more socially conspicuous than he ... He walked a golden path, petted and féted by everyone.'[16]

After hearing of their father's murder in Moscow in 1919 and realising that they

Prince Dmitri, the exiled Russian who won Chanel's heart

might be in exile for a long time, Marie looked for ways to support them. Her business instincts were to bring her to Chanel.

Dmitri came to stay at Bel Respiro, and he and Coco began a love affair. His quiet loving kindness helped to heal Coco, and she regained some of the old confidence that she had lost with Boy's death.

They talked far into the night, he describing a glorious Russia that was gone forever, and she telling him of her life, the pain and the joy. There was no need for any pretence here, and she became the one great love of Dmitri's life.

Bel Respiro was the meeting place for the Russians that year, along with the Stravinsky family, Dmitri, and his manservant, the six-feet-six Piotr, the visitors included Count Kutuzov, his wife and two daughters. Count Kutuzov was to become one of her main business associates for the next fifteen years.[17]

Coco and Dmitri took a two-month long holiday at a villa at Molleau, near Arcachon on the Côte d'Argent, the golden Atlantic coastline in south-west France. They spent their time swimming, and strolling in the sunshine, and in total isolation. On her return to rue Cambon Coco, who was always alive to innovations she could adapt into her designs, fell under the Russian influence of Prince Dmitri and the influx of high society ladies, who had emigrated to Paris to escape the aftermath of the Russian revolution. She decided to use those influences in her work.

***

22
Threads of gold

'*There was something decidedly stimulating to the imagination about the great warehouses where I bought my reels of China silk, wound up on large wooden spools. Heavy bales of raw silk stood around the floor, just as they had come from the Orient, with Chinese lettering on the coverings. The shelves were laden with the richest and most varied assortment of embroidery silks, all of which were of an exquisite quality. The place was flamboyant with colour; it was like moving through an enormous paint box. I loved fingering the silks and assembling and contrasting the shades.*' [18]

This description of a visit to a silk warehouse by Grand Duchess Marie encapsulates the exotic and sensual appeal of embroidery. Embroidery was not new to fashion: this extravagant form of enhancement of textiles had its roots in the Middle Ages, when church garments were richly embroidered in Byzantine style. In the following centuries it became not just a form of adornment, but an indication of social rank and wealth. Coats and dresses sparkling with jewels and gold and silver thread, were worn in court circles and in high society. By the Twentieth century the Ballets Russes, with lavishly embroidered costumes in brilliant colours was a further influence. There was a resurgence in the specialist workshops and by 1909 there were three thousand operating in Paris,[19] producing fine needlework, embellished with exclusive designs in silk, metallic threads and jewel encrusted.

Paris had many skilled craftspeople who excelled at producing work for the couturiers. One of the best known houses was Maison Michonet, founded in 1858 and producing work for European royalty and the early couture houses of Charles Worth and Jacques Doucet.

In 1924, Albert Lesage bought Maison Michonet, renaming it The House of Lesage. When he married Marie-Louise Favot, who worked as a milliner for Madame Vionnet, he was given an exclusive contract with Vionnet as a wedding present. The House of Lesage became one of France's most prestigious ateliers, and they have supplied the couture designers with breathtaking embroidery ever since. Albert's son, François, carried on the business, when Albert died in 1949, supplying all the major couture houses, including Chanel, Schiaparelli, Dior, Yves Saint Laurent and Lacroix.[20]

Another famous embroidery house was La Maison Lallement: working between 1898 and 1950, it supplied the couture houses with hand and machine embroidery. Skilled workmanship was also used on accessories, such as bags, gloves and belts. The designer Ugo Lo Monaco specialised in making lace, artificial flowers and hand-painted feathers, as embellishments for dress, bags, hats and shoes.[21]

Coco found herself taking another route with her requirements for embroidery: her lifestyle informed her business life, and it took the form of Prince Dmitri's sister, Marie.

A woman of enterprise

Dmitri's sister was an enterprising woman, and in London she had begun to support herself, her husband and his parents, by using the skills she had in knitting and sewing, to make sweaters and dresses. She sold these to ladies' dress shops, but realised this was not enough to make them financially independent. The move to Paris brought her greater success and enabled her to start her own company.

In the autumn of 1921 she met Coco, and was very impressed: 'It was the firmness of her jaw , the determined carriage of her neck that struck you. You were swept off your feet by the fierce vitality she exhaled, the quality of which was inspiring and infectious. Mlle. Chanel was an innovator and a revolutionary in her particular line.' [22]

Marie used to visit Coco in the private studio at the top of 31 rue Cambon. 'She was then at the height of her creative ability. Every day some new and original idea came to her and was launched forth, to be eagerly snatched up both by those who could afford its expensive first edition and by others who had to be satisfied with a reproduction by a copyist.' [23]

One day Marie witnessed an argument between Coco and Madame Bataille, who did embroidery for the House. A crimson crêpe de Chine blouse, machine embroidered in Chinese silk was the source of contention. Its price, Madame Bataille insisted, had to be six hundred francs due to the high cost of materials. Too expensive, declared Coco, and Madame Bataille retreated.

Marie, taking advantage of the situation, offered to make them for four hundred and fifty francs even though, in answer to Mademoiselle's smiling question, she had to admit she knew nothing of machine embroidery. Marie recalled, 'Why had I not thought of this before?... I had training for it acquired many years ago at Stockholm Art School. I ran out into the street and took a taxi to the Singer sewing machine company. On the way I was summoning up from my memory the principles of composition as applied to textiles.' [24]

After eventually locating the right type of machine, Marie undertook a month's training, disguising her identity from the other girls. In the evenings she excitedly made plans with her husband and Prince and Princess Putiatin, her parents-in-law, for the new embroidery factory, deciding on the name 'Kitmir', the name of a dog in Persian mythology. She decided on a wholesale business, selling to

Grand Duchess Marie, Dmitri's sister, who introduced Chanel to Russian embroidery

84

trade, and employing Russian girls. After finding a workroom on rue François 1er and training two girls she was ready to start. Her first client would be the House of Chanel.

This was the beginning of Chanel's look for 1922 - the Slavic look - and the designs had to be ready for the spring collection being shown on 5 February 1922. After matching silks, getting the designs ready and approved, the material was cut, the designs stencilled onto it, and then the painstaking embroidery done. The cutting was done at Chanel and the rest of the work at Kitmir. There were blouses, tunics and coats: one of the favourites was a grey tunic embroidered in shades of grey, with dashes of red. This was soon being sported at the Ritz by a lady of fashion.[25]

Marie continued to supply Chanel and the partnership proved highly profitable:

> 'For several years to come I watched Chanel's creative genius express itself through her fingers. She never designed on paper and would make a dress either according to an idea which was already in her head , or as she proceeded. I can still see her sitting on her tabouret, generally beside the mantelpiece with a log fire burning in the grate. The room was overheated. She would be dressed in a simple sport suit, a dark skirt and a sweater, with the sleeves pushed up above her elbows... The fitter standing beside her handed her the pins. No one spoke except Chanel, who kept up a steady flow of monologue. Sometimes she would be giving instructions or explaining some new detail, sometimes she would criticize and undo the work that had already been done. The old fitter would listen to all in silence, her face inpenetrable except perhaps for her eyes, which at times would soften or again throw off a spark of anger... I had never yet met with a person whose every word was obeyed and whose authority had been established by her own self out of nothing. For the first time I began to reflect upon the power of personality and to realise its importance.'[26]

The nearer it got to the day of a collection, the more nervous Coco became, but that pressure drove her to prduce some of her best creations. The day before the show there would be the final 'dress rehearsal' when she and senior personnel would look at each dress, determining how it would be presented and in what order. Sometimes a model would be discarded as not up to standard, or needing alteration, or even completely remade. No detail escaped her notice until, at last, she asked for the tray of flowers and jewels to choose suitable accessories for the model. The watchful saleswomen, sat in rows, casting an experienced eye over the creations, giving little smiles of admiration or a whispered aside to their neighbour, on an outfit's qualities. Chanel watched with pure concentration.

Marie attended the first show of her embroideries, sitting at the top of the mirrored staircase above the salon with Coco and her friends. The foreign buyers, largely American, were there in the first few days by invitation only, anxious to place their orders and receive early delivery, to remain ahead of their competitors. They represented the major stores, the most important being invited to the first day. Marie described the scene:

> 'At three o'clock exactly the models began to parade. I was choking with excitement. When the first dress appeared which had my embroidery on it I almost cried out loud. The parading of the models lasted till nearly six o'clock but long before then Chanel's experienced eye had detected the attention attracted by the embroideries. She told me so, but I dared not believe it until I had a tangible proof... The saleswomen, their arms full of the new dresses, were rushing backwards and forwards between the customers and the model room. Over and over again I heard the buyers demand the embroideries. They were interested in the originality of the designs and the novelty of the treatment. There could be no doubt any longer, this was success.'[27]

* * *

23
Scent of a woman, patron of the arts

Roses in the snow is how you might describe it, but it is no floral scent. The idea of perfume was another inspiration that Dmitri discussed with Coco. With the arrival of huge numbers of Russian émigrés fleeing the effects of the Revolution and the Communist state, Parisian fashion was finding inspiration in their rich culture. The Russian court was renowned for its passion for perfume, and the Tsars had even employed their own perfumer, Edouard Beaux. Prince Dmitri introduced Coco to his son, Ernest Beaux,who had worked for the Rallet Perfumery in Russia from 1889 to 1914 before coming to France to be a perfumer in Cannes.[28]

Many myths and legends surround the birth of Chanel No.5 in 1920, but the Chanel Archives show that in his laboratories at Grasse, Ernest Beaux produced two sets of sample perfumes for Coco, numbered 1 to 5 and 20 to 24, each with slight variations. It is said that she first chose No.22, before deciding, a few months later, on No.5 as her couture perfume.[29]

One absolute certainty is that Chanel No.5 was unique. Until then, perfumes relied on a floral or plant extract base, which meant that they were overpowering when first used but had little staying power. All that changed, as Ernest Beaux, either by accident or design, used large quantities of a synthetic substance, aldehyde crystals, that stabilised the perfume, giving it a lasting, sparkling quality, and lightened the heady flower scent, producing a cool sensuality. It was a complete innovation. With its eighty ingredients, and its notes of jasmine de Grasse, rose de mai, lily of the valley, orris root, neroli and vanilla, and its woody base notes of cedar and sandalwood, it is like no other perfume in the world. And it is impossible to name any one note. The scent bottle was also an innovation, a simple and elegant square flacon, labelled black and white, holding its golden liquid, and called simply No.5. It was an abstract creation and timeless yet it made history and Coco became a multi-millionare.

'I wanted to give women a perfume that was artificial,' she claimed, 'exactly in the way that a dress is artificial, that is, man-made. I'm an artisan in dressmaking... I don't want the smell of rose or lily of the valley. I want a perfume that is a composition.' [30]

Coco used the clever ploy of spraying the perfume in the salon when her wealthy clients came for fittings, and gave small bottles as gifts to her best customers. When asked what it was she would say, 'You want to buy some? I don't sell perfumes, I just happened to stumble on it in Grasse, in a little perfume shop whose name I don't even remember. I just thought it would make an original gift for my friends.' [31]

Meanwhile, she was despatching telegrams to Beaux in Grasse, urging him to step up production. When her customers next asked about the perfume, she would say, 'Really, you think I should have some made and sell it? You like *my* perfume that much? Maybe you're right.' [32]

When Beaux had his supplies complete, she announced that she was receiving a shipment the next day.

Her friend Lady Abdy was to recall that the spectacular success was due to Coco's energy:

> *'Her egocentricity was extreme, her energy fierce. When she decided on something, she followed her idea to the end. In order to bring it off and succeed she brought everything into play.' [33]*

Never one for half measures, Chanel wanted to learn as much as she could about perfumes - and sought advice from anyone who had something to offer. But she also took the precaution of poaching the best chemist in Grasse from his employers.

No.5 was a hit with the new liberated woman of the Twenties, with her short cropped hairstyle, playing sports, smoking, wearing trousers by day and elegant cocktail gowns in the evening and dancing the night away in the fashionable cabaret clubs. No.5 was the prototype of modern perfumes.[34]

Jacques Polge, the present top perfumer at Chanel, has said, 'People often ask me what makes a beautiful perfume. To which I reply, it's the perfume which the woman you love is wearing.' [35] He is only the third perfumer or 'nose' at Chanel since the House launched No.5, on 5 May 1921. Ernest Beaux was followed by Henri Robert who created No.19, the last perfume that Coco was to see produced.

(Chanel is the last couture house with its own 'nose' and its own laboratories, at Neuilly, outside Paris, where the raw materials are received from Grasse and all over the world, and new creations are made.[36] Today, there are many more fragrances and aftershaves in the Chanel stable, including some which are recreations of old formulas.[37] Such is its popular appeal, that when Channel 5, Britain's new terrestrial TV station was launched in 1996, Chanel secured the inaugural advertising slot for Chanel No. 5.[38])

Enter the Wertheimer brothers

Chanel No.5 was first sold at Galeries Lafayette, the ten storey department store at 40 boulevard Haussmann in Paris. In 1893 Theophile Bader and his cousin, Alphonse Kahn, had opened a small haberdasher's shop on rue La Fayette. By 1903 they had bought the whole building and by 1908 had expanded even further. With its beautiful glass and steel dome, and its *Art Nouveau* staircase built in 1912, the store is classified as an historic monument. The store was popular with Parisian women and visitors alike, with its many departments, selling everything from perfume to fashion. It was the perfect outlet for No.5. Coco knew the shop well, as she had bought straw boaters there when she started her millinery creations, back in her Royallieu days.

Soon the store needed larger quantities of the perfume than Ernest Beaux could produce at his Grasse laboratory. Bader suggested that Coco meet the two brothers who owned Les Parfumeries Bourjois, Pierre and Paul Wertheimer. The brothers were of Jewish-German descent and their ancestor, Ernest Wertheimer, had bought Bourjois when it was theatrical make-up company in 1870.

They were rich men who viewed Chanel's new company, Les Parfums Chanel, as a lucrative investment. In 1924, Coco agreed to a partnership whereby she owned 10% of the perfume company, Theophile Bader owned 20% and the Wertheimer brothers held the remaining 70%, and manufacturing and marketing the perfume was handed over to them. It was an agreement that Coco would later spend years disputing.[39]

The Wertheimers lived well, with race horses and art collections. Pierre was a leading race-horse owner and won the 1954 Epsom Derby with Lavandin. He also owned a forty-one metre luxury yacht, named Mathilde after his mother and built for him by Witsen and Vis in Holland.[40] Pierre died in 1965 aged 77, and was succeeded in the business by his son Jacques. (Today, Pierre's grandsons, Alain and Gerard own 100% of the company, but continue to keep a tight control on its privacy. They have branched out into non-Chanel brands and acquired Holland & Holland, the British gunsmiths, as well as interests in lingerie, leather goods and saddle brands. They appeared in Forbes World's Richest People list as having a net worth of $7.5 billion in 2010.)[41]

Crazy love - a poet of genius

'If you wrote your poems on separate sheets and signed each one as your painter friends sign their pictures, regardless of what snobbery has to do with it, you would be as rich as they are,' Coco said to her poet friend and lover Pierre Reverdy.[42]

In the floor-to-ceiling bookcases that graced her lavish rue Cambon apartment sat dozens of beautifully bound, priceless, personally-dedicated, first editions: the collection constituted the whole of Pierre Reverdy's published work, including a copy of the 1922 edition of *Cravates de chanvre*, illustrated with original watercolours by Picasso. [43] The inscriptions were tender, loving words, which Reverdy would write to her from 1921 until his death.

Pierre Reverdy was born on 13 September 1889, in Narbonne in southern France. His father was a wine-grower and descended from a family of master-craftsmen, woodcarvers and stonemasons. Pierre was described as a 'a Mediterranean from head to toe, his hair black and thick, his skin swarthy... he was a reticent man full of strange modesty.' [44]

In October 1910, he moved to Paris and became part of the company of writers and artists who lived in the primitive conditions of the famous Bateau–Lavoir in Montmartre. Formerly an old piano factory, the Bateau–Lavoir (so named because of its resemblance to the laundry boats that used to travel the River Seine) was home and meeting place to many famous names of the future. Here Reverdy met writers such as Guillaume Apollinaire, Louis Aragon, Max Jacob, André Breton and artists including Pablo Picasso, Henri Matisse and Georges Braque were his companions. For the next sixteen years he was part of this bohemian community, dedicating his life to his writing. He was regarded as an inspiration for the development of surrealism in art, and in 1917 he founded *Nord-Sud,* a journal carrying many Dadaist and surrealist contributions. It continued to be published until 1918, with Misia Sert as one of its main patrons.

By 1920 Picasso, his great friend, had brought him to Misia's apartment in the Hotel Meurice where she held court and entertained the best minds and talents of Paris. There, in rooms filled with Venetian glass, fans, blue irridescent butterflies and baroque statues, Reverdy met Coco. [45]

She was fascinated by him and they began an affair which lasted until 1924, although she remained his friend for the rest of his life. He moved into her house at 29 rue du Faubourg St. Honoré. It seemed almost like a platonic friendship: sharing literary quotations, he expounding on the meaning of poetry and directing her reading, and she writing aphorisms for his approval, and supporting his genius. It was far more. In 1921 Paul Morand sent them a copy of his book, *Tendres Stocks,* inscribed with a dedication to them both. Coco kept it on her bookshelves alongside Reverdy's works.

He converted to Catholicism in 1926, under the influence of his friend, the poet Max Jacob. Moving to a cottage near St Peter's Abbey at Solesmes, outside Paris, with his wife Henriette, he became part of monastic life. [46] Perhaps at last, he had found the spiritual solace he sought and which Coco understood. Their affair was over, but towards the end of her life she recalled: 'Give up one's soul for God – I like that expression... What remains of us is what we've thought and loved in life. The life one leads is unimportant. The life one dreams, that's the great existence, because one goes on with it after death.' [47]

Reverdy continued writing, producing several collections of work. He came back to Paris in 1927 and Coco tried to rekindle their affair after her split with another lover, Bendor, Duke of Westminster, in 1930. Her friend, Iya, Lady Abdy, would later say that she was only trying to make the Duke of Westminster jealous after his engagement to Loelia Ponsonby. Bendor's comment was that Coco was crazy to be involved with a man of deep faith. [48]

Pierre died at Solesmes in 1960: Coco would never forget him and continued to extol his genius until the end of her life. She considered he was never given the true place he deserved in the world of French literature. Georges Auric, the gifted musician and composer, reflected: 'She conserved an immeasurable esteem for Reverdy until the end of her life. She always spoke of him with warmth and admiration. I believe him to be the only person she had always admired, perhaps because he escaped her.' [49]

A friend in need

Another of Coco's friends from this time was Jean Cocteau who was born in 1889 in Maison-Lafitte, a small town near Paris. He became a poet, novelist, dramatist, designer, boxing manager and film-maker. As a young man he was the *enfant terrible* of Parisian society. By the time he died in 1963, he had a long, distinguished career behind him, and a raft of honours to his name: he received the Legion of Honour, was made a member of the Academie Française in 1955, and was internationally honoured by many Associations and Academies in his lifetime. Described by his friends and acquaintances of the social milieu of his day, as charming, original and multi-talented, with the gift of brilliant conversation, he published his first book of poetry at the age of nineteen.

Gifted he may have been, but not everyone felt the same about him, as it was thought that he introduced his young friends into the dangers of opium. The Cumbrian–born artist Winifred Nicholson, grand-daughter of the painter George Howard, 9th Earl of Carlisle, wrote harshly to Frosca Munster, the lover of the young English artist, Christopher Wood, warning her to steer clear of Cocteau's influence. Wood, a friend of Cocteau and a protégé of Winifred and her husband Ben Nicholson, had committed suicide in 1930 at the age of twenty-nine. 'The fact is that those of his young friends who have liked him have killed themselves - this is quite sufficient in itself to tell one that he is one of those who have let themselves become a channel for sin.'[50]

Diaghilev, who nicknamed him Jeanchik, challenged him to write, with the words: 'Astound me! I'll wait for you to astound me.'[51] The resultant work was *Parade* which opened in 1917, with Diaghilev as producer, music by Eric Satie and sets by Picasso. It inspired the poet Guillaume Apollinaire to coin the word 'Surrealism,' meaning super-realism, to describe it.[52]

Cocteau later wrote: 'It was when I knew Stravinsky, and later, when I knew Picasso, that I understood that rebellion is indispensable in art, and that the creator always rebels against something if only instinctively – in other words, that the spirit of creation is the highest form of the spirit of contradiction.'[53] Coco had an almost love-hate relationship over the years: she had known him since her first introduction into the artistic life of Paris, as Paul Morand noted in his diary on 30 May 1917:

Still going strong after 90 years - Chanel No. 5

'Cocteau tells of a preposterous dinner party at Cécile Sorel's the day before yesterday. The Berthelots were there, Sert and Misia, Coco Chanel who is definitely becoming quite a personage.' [54]

Cocteau was a visitor to her villa in Garches, where she moved after Boy's death, along with all the others of the *avant garde* with whom she sought to fill her life. His friend, the young poet, Raymond Radiguet was regarded as a great literary talent and Cocteau sought to promote him within his artistic circle, even arranging the publication of his novel, *The Devil in the Flesh* by Grasset, which won the *'Nouveau Monde'* literary prize. Both Cocteau and Radiguet were addicted to opium and Coco, having them as house-guests at Faubourg-Saint-Honoré, often helped out by paying for Radiguet's medical bills and Cocteau's detoxification at the Thermes Urbains, a clinic at 15 rue Chateaubriand.[55] In December 1923, Coco accompanied the grief-stricken Cocteau to visit Radiguet who was dying of typhoid: Coco paid for the funeral.

She helped other friends afflicted by drugs, including Al Brown, the world –champion boxer, who wished to regain his crown. Preferring to keep her charitable acts secret, she yelled at Cocteau, 'Everybody is going to take me for a Sister of Charity' when he talked about her generosity to the Ballets Russes, to the company gathered at the Boeuf sur le Toit.[56]

Costumes by design

When the affair with Pierre Reverdy was over, Coco looked to her artistic friends for her next challenge. The Théatre de Montmartre had just been acquired by Charles Dullin who had changed its name to the Atelier. It became a meeting place for students, intellectuals and artists. Jean Cocteau had given the ancient Greek play *Antigone* by Sophocles a new treatment and Chanel was invited to do the costumes. Cocteau said: 'To costume my princesses I wanted Mlle Chanel, because she is our leading dressmaker and I cannot imagine Oedipus's daughter's patronizing a "little dressmaker"... I chose some heavy Scotch woollens, and Mlle Chanel's designs were so masterly, so instinctively right, that an article in the *Correspondent* praised them for being historically accurate. Between us, they were admirably inaccurate.' [57]

Pablo Picasso designed the sets using a restrained colour palette with neutral shades of brown and light beige, highlighted with splashes of red. Honegger composed the music. The play, which opened on 20 December 1922, was well received and Coco's first foray into the world of theatre design was a great success. The fashion photographers were present; Man Ray made an acclaimed portait of the Greek actress Genica Athanasiou, who played the title role; and Frank Crowninshield, editor of French *Vogue*, published drawings of the costumes by George Lepape. Coco found herself the centre of acclaim, with *Vogue* declaring, 'these woollen robes in neutral tones giving an impression of garments of antiquity rediscovered after centuries.' [58]

This was the beginning of many years of designing for the theatre by Coco, as Cocteau always wanted her to design for his productions. *Le Train Bleu* came next, telling the contemporary tale of a journey to a fashionable beach resort on the Riviera on the famous, luxurious Blue Train, with its rich, upholstered carriages.

By the 1920s resort life had become fashionable, with sun-bathing and swimming the new vogue. Coco helped by making gaining a suntan the latest craze. The sporting life was on the increase, with golf and tennis favourite pastimes. The fashions of the day reflected this and, when Diaghilev and Cocteau conceived the operetta, a story of the *fast* world of pretty young women and gigolos, they wanted to convey this modern look. Diaghilev commissioned Darius Milhaud to write the score: a feat achieved in twenty days. Sets were by the sculptor Henri Laurent, a friend of Pierre Reverdy, depicting where the idle rich disported themselves among beach cabins and bright parasols. Bronislava Nijinska, the sister of the famous Nijinsky, was invited to choreograph Cocteau's ballet. Picasso had agreed that his painting of *The Giants*, a powerful depiction of two women running, wearing white tunics whose torn shoulders exposed bare breasts, could be used as a model for the stage curtains. He was overwhelmed when he saw the finished set, and signed a dedication to Diaghilev on it.[59]

Coco designed the costumes and dressed the four principal dancers in contemporary fashions. Anton Dolin played ' le beau gosse'– the 'beautiful brat', and the Golf Player played by Leon Woizikovsky was attired in similar dress to the Prince of Wales, a keen player and sartorial sophisticate on the golf course. Lydia Sokolova, the former British dancer Hilda Munnings, played the role of Perlouse, and Nijinska herself danced the role of the Tennis Player, dressed in white with raquet in hand. The bathers wore the knitted swimming costumes of the day with their thigh-length leggings; they were all real clothes, not costumes.

After gruelling rehearsals, where Coco's costumes were taken apart and refitted, and the choreography was revised and rehearsed, the curtain eventually rose on 13 June 1924 in the Théâtre des Champs–Elysées. It was the most modern ballet that Paris had ever seen. The international audience of the great and the good gave it a magnificent ovation, with Anton Dolin the show-stopper. Afterwards the company went back to Misia's to savour their success.

Coco continued to design for the theatre: in 1926 for Cocteau's *Orphée,* a one-act tragedy and in 1929 for Stravinsky's ballet *Apollo Musagetes* at the Théatre Sarah Bernhardt. Throughout her life she would continue to design for ballet, film and stage. French *Vogue* was to quote her as saying: 'Costume designers work with a pencil: that's Art. Fashion designers work with scissors and pins: that's a news item.' [60]

During these years Chanel was regarded as the leader of fashion and was making an impact on all levels of society, Elsa Maxwell again records:

> *'The undisputed arbiter of fashion then was Gabrielle Chanel, a woman of exquisite taste and a flair for exploitation. Her prestige was so towering that deviating from her styles was tantamount to professional suicide. Her creations, displayed by Gabrielle, the most famous fashion model of all time, dominated the field. Social leaders throughout the world made appointments with her months in advance. Her annual line was awaited with the breathless anticipation that attends the drawing of the lucky numbers in a lottery. Rivals who guessed Chanel's trend correctly – or got reports of it from spies who infiltrated her workrooms – were 'in'. Those with inventories that did not conform to the mode she was featuring faced ruin.' [61]*

***

24
Baubles, bangles, and Bendor

1924 saw the launch of Coco's jewellery workshop, managed by the elegant Comte Étienne de Beaumont, who undertook the production of some of the most original, classy and elegant pieces of work ever seen. They were all fake, but they looked real. The Gripoix workshops in Paris were the manufacturers: they had previously made *Pâte de verre* jewellery for Paul Poiret and had developed a technique of treating molten glass until it took on the white and creamy patina of pearls, which could be used for buttons as well as jewellery. Beautiful enamelling, made by laying down layers of enamel and lacquer onto the base metal achieved an almost translucent effect. [62]

The workshop was like Aladdin's cave, with rich Byzantine crosses, pretty floral sprays and glittering peacocks. There were brooches, bangles, necklaces and ear-rings, in every colour of semi-precious stone, all of great magnificence – and all of them *fakes.*

Coco had an amazing collection of real jewels herself - much of it was from Grand Duke Dmitri -

precious pieces of Romanov family jewellery brought out of Russia. Boy had first given her pearls, including a sautoir of pearls from Cartier, which she still wore many years later.[63]

After weekends away, she would book several compartments on the Train Bleu for her guests to return to Paris. She carried her fabulous collection of jewels in an old canvas sausage-bag. Once, when they all crowded into her compartment for an *aperitif* and Bettina Ballard was about to sit on it, Coco cried out, 'My jewels - my jewels - don't sit on them.' The reason for the bedraggled bag, she explained, was that she had once left an elegant jewel case, containing a fortune in jewels at Monte Carlo station. It had cost her a large sum to retrieve it from the Monaco authorities: hence the old canvas bag, which always stayed at her side.[64]

Bettina Ballard recollected: 'She opened it that night in the Train Bleu and, to my rather naive eyes, it was an Ali Baba scene. The train was hurtling into the night so violently that the jewels jumped on the table – a great jumble of strings and strings of real pearls, necklaces of mixed rubies, emeralds, diamonds and pearls... '[65]

The woman who owned this luxuriously rich collection was to say: 'Jewels aren't meant to give people a rich look, they're made to give an air of elegance, or adornment, which isn't the same thing.'[66]

Fulco Santo Stefano della Cerda, Duke of Verdura, a Sicilian born in 1898, was a major force in the design of Chanel's jewellery. He was responsible for one of her most photographed and celebrated designs: the bracelets in white enamel, set with magnificent precious stones in the form of a Maltese cross which glowed like a stained glass window.[67] As with her clothes, Coco was her own best model and was frequently seen wearing a bracelet on each wrist. Cole Porter and his wife, Linda, were admirers of Verdura's work and would commission special jewellery, including cigarette cases which Linda gave to Cole on the opening of each new show.[68] By 1934 Verdura had moved to America where he eventually set up his own business in New York.

Coco herself designed much of the jewellery, seated on the sofa in her salon, working on a low Chinese table. Here she would work a ball of soft plastic into a flattened base for her creations. Little boxes and bowls held all manner of stones, some precious, others imitation. She would select these for best effect and embed them in the plastic, irrespective of their value - for her the impact was everything. [69]

Not just the concept of the jewellery was new: it was the whole new way of wearing jewels. No longer kept for evening wear and then consigned to be locked in the safe, ropes of fake pearls were now thrown casually over a sweater, brilliant brooches pinned to a hat and bracelets that looked like blood-red rubies worn on both wrists. It was fun, it was elegant and the fashion world loved it.

Bendor, Duke of Westminster

'I'm not one of those women who belong to several men. I'm sure it was Boy who sent Westminster to me.' [70]

The harbour at Monte Carlo sparkled in the sunshine, under the azure blue skies, as the Duke of Westminster's yacht, *The Flying Cloud,* sailed into port. It was Christmas 1923, the fourth anniversary of Boy's death, and Coco was spending the holidays with her friend, Vera Arkwright Bate, at the Hôtel de Paris, relaxing in the resort's sunshine. Vera, born in London in 1885, was rumoured to be the illegitimate daughter of seventeen-year-old Adolphus Charles, Duke of Teck, who became 1st Marquis of Cambridge on renouncing his German titles in 1917. Her mother, Rosa Baring of the banking family, was married to Captain Frank Wigsell Arkwright at the time, but divorced him and married Colonel George Fitzgeorge, son of the 2nd Duke of Cambridge, a few months after Vera's birth. (King George V, sensitive to German connotations in the names of members of the Royal Family at a time of war, changed the name of the Royal House to Windsor and invited those relatives who resided in England to adopt British surnames.)[71]

Adolphus, tall, blonde and handsome, was Queen Mary's brother and married Lady Margaret Grosvenor, the 21-year-old daughter of the 1st Duke of Westminster in 1894 at Eaton Hall, Cheshire. Vera was accepted in royal circles, being a close friend of Edward, Prince of Wales, and his brothers, and was also close to the Westminster family. During World War 1 she had nursed in France and then, with her friend Clementine Churchill, had set up a canteen for women munition workers in London. She married an American officer, Fred Bate, whom she met in Paris in 1919, where they now lived.[72] Well known in society and accepted in aristocratic circles, Vera was a beautiful, statuesque woman, and had been working for Coco, wearing and showing her clothes to great advantage at social functions. Greatly admired, women wanted to know where they could buy the clothes, and Vera would casually respond, 'This? Oh, at Chanel.' She also provided an entrée for Chanel into English society.

Hugh Richard Arthur Grosvenor, 2nd Duke of Westminster, was the head of the Grosvenor family and had inherited the title from his grandfather in 1899. Eaton Hall near Chester in Cheshire, the family seat since the 15th century and surrounded by an estate of 11,000 acres, had been rebuilt several times.[73]

The Duke was the richest man in England, owning Belgravia and Mayfair estates in London, a member of the Conservative party and a friend of Winston Churchill. He was reputed to have been nicknamed Bendor after a Derby winning racehorse owned by his grandfather - *Bend'or*. Born in 1879, four years older than Chanel, his father, Earl Grosvenor, had died when he was four and he was brought up by his grandfather, the 1st Duke of Westminster, and his mother Lady Sibell Grosvenor, daughter of the 9th Earl of Scarborough. On his mother's remarriage to George Wyndham, a future Member of Parliament, Bendor gained a step-father.

In 1899, at the age of twenty, Bendor inherited the title and estate. By 1925 he had been married and divorced twice; had two daughters, and a son, his heir, who died of appendicitis when he was just four years old. Bendor, or Benny as he was known to family and close friends, was tall, debonair, blue-eyed, with fair to reddish hair and excelled at sports.[74]

Always something of a ladies' man, Bendor saw Vera, an old friend and family connection, dining with Coco at the Hôtel de Paris one night and joined their table. An invitation followed to join him for dinner on board *The Flying Cloud* the next evening. Prince Dmitri was visiting them, so he too was invited along. A four-masted schooner, at 203 feet long one of the largest private yachts in the world, the yacht was luxurious and had been built for the Duke at Leghorn that year. His architect and personal

Chanel with Bendor, 2nd Duke of Westminster, at the Grand National, March 1925

assistant, Detmar Blow, had decorated it in the style of a small country house with carved oak, and a four poster bed hung with embroidered Florentine silk curtains in the stateroom.[75]

Earlier that year Winston Churchill had been a guest on the yacht as it sailed for France, and had stayed at Bendor's hunting lodge at Mimizan, playing polo and tennis. Now at Christmas, Bendor was cruising without his second wife, Violet.[76] That evening, he hired a gypsy orchestra to serenade the ladies and they went on to a nightclub afterwards. Bendor was fascinated by Coco, as she was so very different from the usual society women he met. The fact that she worked, and very successfully, and had made a fortune from that work was something totally new to him. He was also struck by her vivacious beauty and her wit. All his initial attempts to woo her came to nothing: Coco had a full and independent life and was not looking for love with an English Duke.

Bendor, however, had no intention of giving up and pursued Mademoiselle Chanel relentlessly. He overwhelmed her with letters and gifts, having three messengers going back and forth across the Channel. There were baskets of fruit from his own greenhouses, orchids and gardenias, even salmon flown from his estate in Scotland. A huge uncut emerald was in a jewel case found in the bottom of a crate of fresh vegatables. Then one day Joseph opened the door to a delivery man hiding his face with a large bunch of flowers - Bendor had come in person.[77]

A few days later, Joseph again answered the door to a young fairhaired Englishman asking for Vera Bate. As she was out, he was asked to wait in the butler's pantry. On her return, Joseph asked the young man who to say was calling: 'the Prince of Wales' was the reply. The Prince and Bendor called at rue Cambon a few nights later to see Coco, and she was delighted when he made himself comfortable and asked her to call him David.[78] Years later she was to reminisce to a friend, 'Out of my three chaps, the Prince of Wales, Dmitri of Russia and the Duke of Westminster, I chose the one who protected me best.' [79]

By 1925 - and with Bendor now divorced from Violet – Coco agreed to accompany him to Bayonne to embark on a cruise. She later said, 'He had a yacht, and that's the best thing for running away to start a love affair. The first time you're clumsy, the second you quarrel a bit, and if it doesn't go well, the third time you can stop at a port.' [80] From then until it ended in 1930, when Bendor announced his engagement to the Honourable Loelia Ponsonby, the lives of the English Duke and the French couturier were totally linked.[81]

Coco started travelling with him, from his house at Mimizan in the Landes,which had been built after World War I for boar hunting, to the château in Normandy, to his estate in Scotland where she learnt to fish for salmon. The Scottish estate, Lochmore, was described as a granite, turreted lodge, standing on a hill looking out over the beautiful wild Sutherland countryside.[82] She often visited England where she would attend social events with him; they were seen together strolling on the turf at the Grand National and she became a frequent visitor to Eaton Hall. When she visited his mother, Lady Sibell, would say to her, 'Darling, marry Benny. The first years are the best.' [83]

It was a passionate affair and caused much speculation in the press and in society that they would marry. Bendor wanted a son and heir, but as Coco was forty-six years old, time was not on their side and, in later life, she revealed that she had indeed consulted doctors with the hope of becoming pregnant. If this had happened she, no doubt, would have married him, but it was not to be.

Other reports indicate that she would never have given up either her couture house or the friends that she surrounded herself with - the artists, writers and dancers that were an essential part of her Parisian world. Bendor, with his Victorian upbringing would never fit into this *milieu*. She did not wish to be an English duchess quite enough to give it all up. When asked about marrying the Duke of Westminster Coco is famously quoted as saying, 'There are many Duchesses of Westminster, there is only one Coco Chanel.' - but she later denied having said this.

La Pausa – a haven by the sea

In 1928, Coco bought some land on the hillside of Roquebrune, above Cap Martin and here she built her lovely house, La Pausa. It was surrounded by fields of hyacinth, lavender and mimosa, giving a glorious scent and it had magnificent views of the sea. It is an area whose legend today has become well-known due to the book *The Da Vinci Code*, for its name, La Pausa, commemorates the flight of Mary Magdalene to Roquebrune when she sailed, with other of Jesus' disciples, from Jerusalem after the crucifixion. Seeing a beautiful garden of olive trees , she paused to rest, and a chapel was built there, adjacent to the property that Coco bought. Coco paid 1.8 million francs for the property, and although it was assumed that Bendor had bought it for her, the deeds were in her name and the money came from her own company.[84]

The house was built by a young architect, Robert Streitz, who was invited on board *The Flying Cloud* in Monte Carlo bay to discuss the project. It was to have a high standard of luxury and privacy, with the two-bedroomed guest suites reached by private foyers, and Coco's suite in a separate wing, along with a suite for Bendor. As it turned out, he used it very little.[85]

Streitz recalled that Coco said: 'I want very much to have a large stone staircase in the entrance hall. I remember from my childhood the immense staircase, with its steps worn from use, in the orphanage at Aubazine. We used to call it the monk's staircase. That's what I want.' [86]

It seems strange that Coco made this request to Streitz, given that she spent a lifetime hiding the fact that she had lived in the orphanage at Aubazine. Perhaps she thought the architect would never discuss it, and he only did so, many years later after her death, to describe the architecture of La Pausa. (But in 1973, Emery Reeves, Winston Churchill's literary agent, who bought La Pausa from Coco in 1953, told the author, Pierre Galante, that Robert Streitz went to Aubazine to take photographs of the staircase, in order to replicate it at La Pausa.)[87]

Coco was involved in all aspects of the building, travelling down once a month on the Train Bleu to Monte Carlo, with a taxi at her disposal for the period of her stay. Streitz described intelligence and generosity as the two main characteristics he saw in her personality.

The house had large low-ceilinged rooms, sparsely but elegantly furnished with simple pieces of Spanish and Provençal furniture, and with large beige chamois leather sofas. The effect was simple and elegant, with the shades of beige colour scheme giving a spacious airy feel to the rooms. The garden was planted in equally simple manner, with large clumps of lavender and rosemary, amid the centuries-old olive trees.[88]

Roderick Cameron, one of her

Roquebrune, where Chanel built her hillside retreat, La Pausa neighbours, described Coco at this time:

> *'I remember her at La Pausa sitting on the floor of her terrace hugging her knees. Our conversation escapes me, but not her presence which was tomboyish, but alluringly feminine - the nose slightly tilted, the eyes dark and lively, and the mouth mobile and curled up at the corners... She wore trousers and a sweater and a great deal of jewellery, wide ivory bracelets encrusted with a Maltese cross of rubies, and rows of pearls strung with seed pearls instead of knots in between each bead. Wound in with these were blobs of emeralds joined together with heavy gold links... I think the secret of Chanel's great success as a couturier was that she never designed anything that she could not wear herself... Added to this was an unerring eye for colour and an innate sense of quality. Much of her jewellery was identical to that which she sold in her mirrored boutique on the rue Cambon in Paris, the only difference being that hers was real!'* [89]

The affair ends

By 1928, Coco was aware that Bendor was not being faithful to her. In December 1929, he met Loelia Ponsonby in London and spent the first evening with her, fox-trotting at the Café de Paris. Loelia Ponsonby was well known in society and royal circles as her father, Sir Frederick Ponsonby, later Lord Sysonby, was Head of the Royal Household in the service of King George V, having been Private Secretary to Queen Victoria, and lived at St James Palace.

Bendor was to court her in the same way as he had Coco, with surprise gifts of fabulous jewels, posies of wild flowers, and a round of social engagements and trips on his yachts. They spent time together at Bourdon House in London and at Eaton Hall. At Christmas 1930 he sent her a sapphire engagement ring from Monte Carlo and asked her father for her hand in marriage, She was the third of his four wives and the marriage lasted just five years, with no children. [90]

Perhaps one of the more bizarre twists of the engagement period was when Bendor took Loelia to stay at the Hotel Lotti in Paris, and said they were going to visit an old friend of his, Mademoiselle Chanel. Years later Loelia described the event:

> *'Mademoiselle Chanel was at the height of her fame, her quiet, neat, uncomplicated clothes being considered the epitome of all that was most chic. Small , dark and simian, Coco Chanel was the personification of her own fashions. She was wearing a dark blue suit and a white blouse with very light stockings (light stockings were one of her credos). Described in this way she sounds as if she looked like a high-school girl, but actually the effect was one of extreme sophistication.*
>
> *'She had more or less invented costume jewellery, specializing in most attractive ropes of imitation pearls, clasped at intervals with bunches of rubies and emeralds. When I saw her she was hung with every sort of necklace and bracelet, which rattled as she moved. Her sitting-room was luxurious and lavish and she sat in a large armchair, a pair of tall Coromandel screens, now to be seen in her Paris showroom, making an effective backcloth. I perched, rather at a disadvantage, on a stool at her feet feeling that I was being looked over to see whether I was a suitable bride for her old admirer - and I very much doubted whether I, or my tweed suit, passed the test.'* [91]

The years with Bendor gave Coco innumerable ideas for new fashions and she created new styles based on what she observed: navy–blue pea jackets, striped nautical sweaters, sports clothes, neat fitted riding jackets and tweed coats and suits. When Coco met Bendor, she not only started a love affair with the Duke of Westminster, but a love affair with all things English.

∗∗∗

25
Captain Molyneux and an historic meeting

If there was one designer who epitomized 'all things English' in these years it was William Linton's great friend, Captain Edward Molyneux.

Edward Molyneux was born in London of Irish parentage in 1891. He too, like Boy Capel, was educated at Beaumont College and he had studied art. He earned his living sketching designs for magazines and advertisements, and when the fashion house of Lucile set up a sketching competition, he won first prize, and was engaged as a designer in its London salon.

Lucile, the professional name of Lucy, Lady Duff-Gordon, was a colourful and inventive designer who by 1912 had established fashion houses at 23 Hanover Square, London and in New York and Paris. She was famous for her ability to produce elegant, wearable, un-corseted clothes in shimmering, soft, sweet-pea colours, as well as for her designs for the stage. She became the first British designer to win an international reputation, and she was to say: 'I loosed upon a startled London, a London of flannel underclothes, woollen stockings and voluminous petticoats, a cascade of chiffons, of draperies as lovely of those of Ancient Greece and draped skirts which opened to reveal slender legs... I showed the world that a woman's leg can be a thing of beauty.' [92] She was also among the first to introduce the tea gown as a fashion item, and used live mannequins to show her clothes. Elinor Glyn, the sensational author of *Three Weeks* and one of the first female Directors in Hollywood, was her sister. Lucile and her husband were to be survivors of the Titanic disaster.[93]

Before the outbreak of the 1914-1918 War, Toni, as Molyneux was known to his friends, travelled with her to her salons in Paris, New York and Chicago. Lucy said of him: 'He had been brought to me while he was still in his teens, a pale, delicate boy with a passion for drawing and a still greater love of beautiful colours... before long I realised that here was someone who had more than mere talent, he had a genius for designing clothes.' [94]

At the start of the war, he joined the 9th Battalion, Duke of Wellington's (West Riding) Regiment, serving as a Captain and had a distinguished career, winning the Military Cross but losing the sight of an eye.[95] Lucile was in America for the duration of the war and, whenever Toni Molyneux had leave from the Front, he would give her support, both in America and in the salon in Hanover Square. Fabrics were scarce, but his neat elegant designs made of barathea or serge were seen as a new 'modern' look, and new younger clients began to patronise Lucile's salon.[96]

Lucile lost control of her business in 1918, blaming those she had left in charge in London. She did, however, heap praise on Molyneux for his efforts on her behalf. It did not last, and by 1919 came the parting of the ways when she issued an ultimatum to him to design in the Lucile mode, or work elsewhere. He chose to leave and found backers to set up his own salon, where his simple, chic designs were perfectly in tune with the Jazz Age.[97]

Captain Molyneux is described as being 'noticably good-looking', with fair hair and a gracefully elegant slender figure. He became a very rich man with a yacht, an Hispano Suiza car and a villa in Monte Carlo where he entertained Noel Coward and the Cole Porters among others.[98]

Between 1925 and 1932 he established branches in Monte Carlo, Biarritz, Cannes and by 1930 had opened a house in London, under the direction of his sister, Kathleen. It is likely that during these years he met Coco Chanel, who by 1925 was a friend of the Duke of Westminster and was moving in the same social circles.

Coco Chanel discovers Linton Tweed

William Linton was always in tune with the modern world, and in the 1920s he was almost unique among tweedmakers in his use of brightly coloured yarns to produce brilliantly coloured tweeds. The vibrant, singing colours were sought after by fashionable women of the Jazz Age, and Paris soon became his marketplace.[99]

On visits to the Lake District in Cumbria, Edward Molyneux and William Linton went shooting, and by 1928 Edward had introduced William to Coco Chanel. Since her liaison with Bendor, Coco had rekindled her admiration for the English look, which she had first felt when she was with Boy Capel. In particular, she admired English textiles, and under Bendor's influence she had come to admire the qualities of English tweeds. It was a fortuitous meeting and an historic day, as in 1928 Chanel used Linton Tweed for the first time in her couture collection, and it has been used in every collection since, until the present day – more than eighty years.

In 1932 Molyneux opened a salon in London and Sir Hardy Amies recalled:

> 'The shop was like a grand private house, and at 48 Grosvenor Street you were greeted by the butler. Molyneux settled into a suite at Claridges, the walls hung with pictures from his collection. He himself was a painter of no inconsiderable talent. I was given the freedom of his house and often attended his fittings. He was carrying on supplying to his favourite stores in the U.S.A. Princess Marina of Kent was his favourite customer.

> "I remove everything that is not necessary," he said. "Plainness is all." But he paid great attention to cut, finish and above all proportion. Molyneux loved English tweeds...'[100]

Captain Molyneux was based in London until the end of World War 2 when he returned to Paris, closing his House in 1950. Sir Hardy Amies had no doubts about his importance to the world of haute couture:

> 'He was, without question, the most talented designer of clothes that Britain has ever produced. He was also, of course, a couturier of the highest order. He had great influence on me. He showed me how the sobriety of English style could become international chic.'[101]

Molyneux's style soon attracted other young designers who were keen to learn from him. When he was first starting out, Pierre Balmain, the talented couturier, worked at Molyneux's elegant salon at 5 rue Royale, Paris, which he established in 1922. He described his first meeting with Molyneux in 1934, when as an architectural student bent on working in fashion, he went for an interview:

> 'Captain Molyneux was standing in front of a blazing fire in a room with high windows, pearl-grey satin walls and mirror-covered pilasters. On the mirrored mantlepiece stood a rare Khmer head. He read the letter and glanced through my drawings. Then, with an English accent which amused me, he asked a few questions about my architectural studies. None of my designs interested him, he said, but he would see me again the following week when he had more time.'

He was making Princess Marina's wedding dress and was off to London that day. A week later Balmain was taken on.[102]

Charles Creed at Linton Tweeds

Charles Creed was another talented young designer, whose family had been in the tailoring business for generations. In the late 1920s William Linton took him on as a trainee at the Carlisle mill. The Creeds were an old-established firm of tailors working in London since the 18th century. Henry Creed (the elder) was born in England and opened a branch of his business on the place de l'Opera in Paris in 1850. His son, Henry was born in Paris in 1863, and followed his father into the family business. Specialising in tailored suits, which were popular in the 1900s, women patronised his salon looking for elegant daywear. The suits, with basque jackets and full skirts flaring from the hips, were made of Linton tweed, and he claimed to be the first to use tweed in the making of women's suits.[103]

Henry, a friend of William Linton, was well-known in the Royal courts of Europe. A men's tailor of the highest rank, he often travelled across Europe, to Spain, Italy, Austria and Russia to his famous clients, taking along twenty 'hands' to assist him in his work. His son, Charles recounted the story of one such visit, to the Duke of Alba, in Spain:

The fashion designer, Captain Edward Molyneux, who introduced William Linton to Coco Chanel in 1928

> 'Most of my father's clients were men, but this was soon to be changed, through the Duke of Alba. While he was being fitted for a suit… the Duke, surveying himself in the glass with considerable complacency, said: "Creed, in this I shall outshine the Duchess – you must make her a suit too, in the same tweed." My father, who much admired the Duchess's figure, readily undertook to do so… When the ducal couple appeared in public wearing matching suits they caused quite a buzz in the world of fashion – and the tailor–made for women became the thing.'
> [104]

Charles was born in 1909 and would continue the family tradition. Although born in Paris, his parents sent him back to England to be educated at Stowe. After this, at the age of seventeen, he studied tailoring and art in Vienna and, on his return to England, William Linton took him on at the mill in Carlisle, to learn the craft of weaving. Following his time at Linton's, he spent a period with the New York department store Bergdorf Goodman. By the 1930s, now well qualified in his craft, he joined the family business in Paris.[105]

He opened his own London fashion house after the war and married Pat Cunningham, a fashion editor at *Vogue,* in 1948. He is described as one of the movers and shakers of British fashion in the 1940s, and in 1946, *Vogue* would say of him, 'He was pre-destined to design exquisite clothes. Like any artist he seeks perfection, in his case it is tailored perfection.'[106]

In 1961, Charles Creed published his autobiography, *Maid To Measure,* and in his own inimitable style gives a vivid description of working with William Linton, and of his apprenticeship at the mill, more than thirty years earlier:

> 'Mr Linton , the head of the firm was an old friend of my father and insisted that I should stay with him and his daughter, Agnes, at their house outside Carlisle. Though he was very rich , they lived very simply, almost austerely. I shivered all through the winter. Mr Linton did not seem to feel the cold. He was a remarkable old boy with a great, bald, pear-shaped head, a red face and a distinctly gross figure: a prosperous, self-indulgent butcher or publican one would have guessed him to be from his appearance, gruff voice and broad Scots accent. He was, in

fact, a genius in the designing and weaving of tweeds – the greatest artist in the world, I would say, in colour combination in this material.

'He was an enormously robust and active man with a huge zest for food and drink. He travelled all over the world selling his unique and exquisite creations - and though his own home was somewhat Spartan, he invariably stayed at the best hotels and entertained lavishly – with champagne flowing like a river in spate. My father too, who, like Schiaparelli and Coco Chanel, was a good customer of his, told me that Mr Linton never made a note of any orders given him: he would suggest, over copious drinks, modifications in colour and design – and my father would agree to them, for they were always strikingly original. But, he said he was often doubtful whether Mr Linton would next morning recall a word of the conversation and only conducted it in a 'Let's hope something comes out of it' spirit. Something always did come out of it: the very thing my father had visualized, down to the last glowing tone or subtle nuance.' [107]

Nessy was too busy breeding deerhounds to pay much attention to Charles and did not therefore become the object of his flirtatious eye. In addition, he was engrossed in his work at the mill, determined to learn all he could, in order to merit a place in his father's company, the House of Creed, in Paris.

'At the mills I was put to work with the chief designer, Mr Jamieson, a rather dour-looking Scot with a fine sense of humour and infinite patience. He made his first designs on a hand loom working with extraordinary speed and skill. I never achieved his dexterity but I learned to set up the loom for the weaving of a pattern – a fascinating and complicated business. This taught me the feel of a material and a knowledge of the actual structure, which is important in its handling and use: without it, indeed, it is difficult to gauge a material's possibilities.'

In his leisure time he found little to do, but spent it in William's company and found himself introduced into the pleasures of whisky drinking.

While Nessy would drive William and Charles to the mill in Carlisle each morning, they returned to the house at Great Corby in the evening by train. Charles described what happened when they alighted from the train:

'On the short road from the station to the Linton home there were four pubs, each of which had to be visited: it took hours to get home. Mr Linton was generous in the extreme and obviously loved standing the locals drinks, as much as he loved his whisky. At first, while he was buying round after round and carrying on conversation in a genial roar, I used to hang about in the background, embarrassed and bored. Later when I began to take a glass or two myself, some of the quieter customers took pity on me and taught me to play dominoes - a very great art. I learned to play well and to respect the cunning old folk who were my teachers.' [108]

William proved a genial host, determined to show his old friend's son a good time and at weekends they all went on long car drives, touring in Scotland, where William introduced Charles to the game of golf, which remained his favourite sport.

'He was known at every golf-club and every pub within a radius of two hundred miles and was welcomed wherever he went with enthusiasm: it was generally accepted that Mr Linton was a 'guid mon' as well as a rare card – and I certainly found him to be so. He did his best to keep me interested and amused and when touring companies (fifth-rate ones, they seemed to me) visited Carlisle he never failed to give me an evening out at the theatre – where he was received rather as if he were royalty.' [109]

A question of colour

Charles readily acknowledged his debt of gratitude to William: 'Through Mr Linton, I developed an eye for colour – for which I have always been grateful to him, as it contributed greatly to the simple pleasure I find in just looking around me. Often when I was walking across the moors with Mr Linton, the old man would pick up a leaf or flower or a sprig of some small herb and say "Lovely isn't it? I must see if we can dye to and use that colour".' [110]

Colour is of major importance to the tweedmaker. He must be well versed in its properties, in the dyes that go to make it, and in the myriad possibilities it can produce. He must be aware of which colours will contrast and complement each other and the effects of light and reflection to produce the right mix for his fabric.

The mix in tweed is extremely important and consideration has to be given to the final

'look' required. It is a delicate process as 'in order to produce a sparkling and lively mixture, the original colours must be brilliant, but at the same time must not be divided too minutely for the eye to see them seperately – otherwise the result is dull, for one colour cancels out the other.' [111]

William Linton appears to have been one of those designers who had a natural affinity with the colours of the natural world and demonstrated his gift in his tweed.

Charles, who had been used to the excitement of Paris and Vienna where he had lived a full and flirtatious social life, as the son of a well-known and rich man, no doubt found life in Cumberland very different, but he recognised the role it played in his development:

> 'The eight months I spent in Carlisle were the steadiest I had ever spent, but I enjoyed them. The Lintons were kind, the mill-folk friendly and all of them had a pride in their work which they communicated to me. Before I left, it happened that some interesting American buyers visited the mills. Mr Linton introduced me to them - and they were later most helpful to me when I went to New York. My time "up North" had certainly not been wasted: even my father conceded this, on my return to Paris – and it seemed possible, at least, that he might find a small place for me in the business.' [112]

On returning to Paris and to the House of Creed, Charles was expected to learn the business from the bottom up. He was assigned to the stockroom, where he was responsible for all the woollen materials arriving from the

A youthful Charles Creed outside the Hôtel Normandie, Deauville, 1927

mills, supplying yardages to the cutters and booking in and out materials from manufacturers on a 'sale or return' basis. The lure of Paris proved too much for the would-be designer. Charles soon began slipping out in the afternoons to the *thé dansant,* where he met Andrew Goodman, of Bergdorf Goodman, New York, who was working as an apprentice at the House of Patou.

The outcome was that, in late 1929, Charles travelled to New York with Andrew's father and was given a position in Bergdorf Goodman, where he planned to study the American clothing industry. He then went to work for the Seventh Avenue firm of A. Beller, who were wholesale designers and manufacturers, and where he learned the art of designing simplicity of line, which was imperative in keeping down the costs in wholesale manufacture. A chance meeting with Philip Mangone, the head of a vast wholesale manufacturing empire in the United States, who remembered meeting him at Linton Tweeds when he had visited Carlisle, produced a job offer. For the next three years, Charles worked as a dress designer for Mangone's firm, Rufflo, and remembered it as 'the best possible opportunity of studying the vast technical set-up of mass-producing garments, which is of the utmost importance in the American market.' [113]

William Linton's network among designers, fashion houses, manufacturers and retail outlets had become very sophisticated. He was now a well-known and respected figure, not only in the world of couture, but in the rag *trade* in general.

***

26
That Italian artist... and Hollywood calls

It was a feud from day one with the woman who Chanel saw as her main rival in these years. She was an Italian designer and her name was Elsa Schiaparelli. Coco never spoke her name but referred to her as 'that Italian artist who's making clothes'.

William and Agnes Linton knew Elsa well, for she loved working with tweeds. Coco was not the only one who was enamoured of British textiles, for Elsa too had fallen for them. Coco may have tolerated the copyists of her fashions in the interests of business, but such beneficence did not extend to her rival. Indeed, she may have felt that Elsa was her *doppelgänger,* a force waiting to invade her very spirit. Elsa showed her first collection in 1929, and by the 1930s she was following Chanel's lead and making trips to the United Kingdom, in search of beautiful cloths in exciting weaves and colours. As well as her visits to Linton Tweed in Carlisle, she went to the weaving factories in the far north of Scotland and to Ireland, always seeking new and unusual fabrics, which would then appear in her collections as quirky, brilliantly-coloured creations.[114]

Schiap - pronounced Skap - the name by which Elsa became known in Paris, was born in Rome in 1890. Her first visit to Paris was made in 1913 *en route* to London and she was both awestruck and impressed by these two very different, but magical cities. In London she met her future husband, Comte William de Wendt de Kerlor, who was lecturing on theosophy. They married in 1914 and lived in Nice, but by 1919 travelled to New York where Elsa was intrigued by the modernity and forward-thinking social mores, which made Europe appear outmoded.

When her marriage hit the rocks, after her husband's affair with Isadora Duncan, and with her small daughter, Yvonne - known as Gogo - to support, Elsa was facing financial difficulties. For three years she tried a variety of employment, doing translations, selling gowns from some of the Paris fashion houses, but always keeping an involvement with the new artistic movements, particularly the Surrealists. In Paris she began to mix with many of the same group of people as Chanel and got to know the famous designer Paul Poiret.

In 1925 she opened a small fashion house - Maison Lambal near Place Vendôme - and went on in 1927 to produce her first black and white *trompe-l'oeil* sweater, which featured a bow-knot on the front as part of the knitted design. From then on, she never looked back, as she became famed for giving the colour 'Shocking Pink' to the world, and for her use of the work of artists such as Salvador Dali, in her creations. Her hats were notable for their witty originality. (Today, perhaps only talented milliner Philip Treacy comes close to her muse, with his skill in blending elements of surrealism and abstract art.)[115]

Elsa Schiaparelli, Coco's Italian rival

Goldwyn days

Since Coco's break-up with the Duke of Westminster, Misia had spent more time in her friend's company and they were on holiday in Monte Carlo when Prince Dmitri introduced them to the Hollywood legend, Samuel Goldwyn.[116]

Samuel Goldwyn was a larger-than-life character born in the Warsaw ghetto into a Polish–Jewish family in 1879. After a brief spell living in Birmingham, England he emigrated to the United States in 1898. When he arrived in New York he found work in the city's colourful garment industry and soon became vice-president of sales in his company.

But his great interest was the movies, and he soon went into business with his brother-in-law, Jesse L. Lasky, a vaudeville performer, and with theatre-owner Adolph Zukor. They were ambitious men and soon produced their first film, directed by the young Cecil B. De Mille. These were the fledgling days of the film industry and the company became Paramount Pictures, but by then Goldwyn had fallen out with his partners. By 1916 he set up the Goldwyn Company, famous for its trademark 'Leo the Lion': this company was to become Metro-Goldwyn–Mayer but again, by this time, Goldwyn had moved on. He started the Samuel Goldwyn Studio in Hollywood, and during the next thirty-five years built a formidable reputation as a film-maker of excellence. The films during the 1930s were released through United Artists, and he was responsible for discovering many famous stars, including Gary Cooper.[117]

By 1931, the 'talkies' were becoming well-established and Goldwyn, a film genius who believed in quality and showmanship, recognised the universal appeal of Chanel's designs. He planned to persuade Coco to come to Hollywood twice a year to design for the leading ladies in his movies: the clothes would be seen all over the world, wherever the films were screened. Not only that, he wanted his stars to wear Chanel both off the screen as well as on. There was much scepticism in the American newspapers over the idea: movie stars such as Bebe Daniels, Gloria Swanson, Mary Pickford or Ina Claire were not likely to give up their favourite styles, dress shops and lavish fol-de-rols, to wear Chanel's simple styles.

After hesitating for a long time, Coco finally agreed. Perhaps it was the offer of the million-dollar contract, or perhaps it was the notion that she could sell her models to the American ready-to-wear manufacturers, who would produce 'copies' at girl-next-door prices. In either case the publicity value would be immense. Samuel Goldwyn was interviewed by Laura Mount in *Colliers* in April 1932 and was clearly bullish about his idea: 'I tell you it will start a new era in the movies... Women will go to our movies for two reasons: one to see the pictures and the stars; two to see the latest in clothes.' [118] In the same article Coco gave her take on the deal:

> 'But it will be so interesting, so amusing! To design clothes that will be seen in every small village in the world, in every city, in every country! That is fascinating, stimulating. I shall work day and night to make it succeed.'

Ready to take up the new challenge, Coco sailed for America aboard the *S.S. Europe* on 4 March 1931. She was accompanied by Misia, as well as dress cutters, seamstresses and press secretaries.[119] In New York, Goldwyn had arranged press interviews and receptions and treated Coco in true Hollywood style – journalists stared in awe at the sight of the special, white-painted train that took her to California, and reported on Chanel's lifestyle with incredulity. Here were champagne, Paris models and the famous French wit, when Chanel gave interviews. Hollywood was agog as the reports preceded her arrival. In New York they were joined by Maurice Sachs, who went with them to Hollywood. The stars were out to welcome her, standing on the platform at Los Angeles station, with Greta Garbo waiting to greet her.

Gloria Swanson was one of the stars that Coco was to dress for the film *Tonight or Never* and, after being measured at the studio, she went to Paris and visited rue Cambon every day for fittings with Coco. During this time Gloria became pregnant by her lover Michael Farmer but wanted to keep this private from the studio, as she was in the process of divorcing her husband. Writing in her autobiography in 1981, she described her fitting:

> 'Coco Chanel, tiny and fierce, approaching fifty, wearing a hat as she always did at work, glared furiously at me when I had trouble squeezing into one of the gowns she had measured me for six weeks earlier. It was black satin to the floor, cut on the bias, a great work of art in the eyes of both of us. I said I would try it with a girdle, but when I stepped before her again she snorted with contempt and said anyone a block away could see the line where the girdle ended halfway down my thigh.

> '"Take off the girdle and lose five pounds," she snapped briskly,"You have no right to fluctuate in the middle of fittings. Come back tomorrow and we'll finish the evening coat with the sable collar. Five pounds!" She cried again, unable to restrain herself. "No less!"' [120]

After further arguments with the suspicious Coco, Gloria asked the House of Chanel's corset-maker to make her a series of surgical corsets to disguise her condition until the picture was completed. By mid–August she travelled back to Hollywood with a trunk of Chanel oufits, and a stack of sturdy elastic panties.[121] Gloria Swanson became a firm friend of Coco and visited rue Cambon many times over the years.

The film was a great success for Gloria Swanson, and Chanel's gowns were much praised. The Hollywood stars, however, did not wish to wear the same designer's styles in all their films, not even Chanel's. She regarded her contract as ended and, while Sam Goldwyn may have lost money on it, he had gained a vast amount of publicity.

Coco had now achieved success on the international stage and, before leaving for France, did the social rounds in New York, meeting with Carmel Snow of *Harper's Bazaar* and Margaret Case of *Vogue,* both of whom gave Coco high praise in their magazines. She also took the opportunity to familiarise herself with the structure of the American fashion industry, from large stores like Macy's and Bloomingdales with their departments where Paris models were reproduced to Klein's in Union Square in downtown New York. Here Coco shuddered at the sight of copies of her clothes on sale for a few dollars.[122]

She had already moved into producing textiles herself, opening a factory at Asnières-sur-Seine in 1928, where she produced her own exclusive designs of silk-enriched wool and cotton jersey fabrics. Known as Tricot Chanel, the factory gave her exclusivity in her designs and control over production. As she expanded into producing new printed silk fabrics and other woven fabrics , the factory's name was changed to Tissus Chanel.[123]

But the fashion and luxury trades were hit particularly hard by the depression that followed the 1929 Wall Street crash and many of the couture houses were promoting their ready-to-wear lines, with even Chanel cutting her prices by half in 1932.[124]

***

Gloria Swanson, in a still from 'Tonight or Never,'
wearing a specially designed dress by Chanel

27
The Coco-Carlisle connection develops

Once Coco started using Linton Tweeds in her collections in 1928, the relationship was established and Linton Tweeds continued to supply her: their fabrics were appearing in every one of her elegant shows in the mirrored salon in rue Cambon, Paris, with orders coming in every year for the lovely tweeds. Carlisle's links with Coco Chanel had developed apace as she looked for other enterprising suppliers.

Among them were Ferguson Brothers Ltd the long-established, cotton-manufacturing firm, founded by Joseph Ferguson in 1824.[125] By 1929 Ferguson's had become an international company with offices in London, Manchester, Glasgow and Bristol, and agencies throughout the world. The highlight of that year was when their exhibit in London was visited by the Duchess of York (who later became Queen Elizabeth, the Queen Mother). She complimented Mr R.C. Chance on their beautiful productions and purchased a dress length of a red and white voile made in Carlisle at their Holme Head factory.[126] It was patronage that would endure, as time would tell.

They also established their own Coco connection – for in 1931 *Vogue* was reporting on Chanel's spring collection where she included thirty-five cotton evening dresses made from Ferguson Brothers fabric. Fergusons had invited her to come to London and design a range of dresses to launch their new range of cotton textiles as fashion fabrics.[127]

Always ready to embrace new opportunities Coco accepted. Although her affair with the Duke of Westminster had ended in 1930 on his marriage, they remained friends and she was still an *aficionado* of British fabrics. The well-cut evening dresses had a charming simplicity and were made from cotton piqué, lace, spotted muslin, organdie, lawn and net, fabrics which were not traditionally used for evening wear. As *Vogue* reported: 'These young and fresh looking dresses with their billowing skirts were the most popular evening dresses of the year with English debutantes, and with their fathers who paid the bills.' [128] Following the success of the collection, by December 1931 Ferguson's opened a Paris office in agreement with R.D. Fermo.

In May 1932, Coco was back in London again and she produced a charity show, to benefit the War Service Legion which was founded in 1918 by Lady Londonderry and Lady Titchfield.[129] Coco suggested showing the collection at 39 Grosvenor Square, one of the several London houses that the Duke of Westminster had put at her disposal. She made one hundred and thirty outfits, using British materials and all the outfits were modelled by society ladies, rather than professional models with race gowns in fine materials including organdie, muslin, lace, lawn, net and piqué: an immediate hit with fashionable society women. The artist Drian, sketched Lady Pamela Smith (who became the wife of Lord Hartwell, the millionaire newspaper proprietor) wearing a white cotton piqué race gown, trimmed with a flower garland of the same material and with floating hem and sleeves scallop-edged to give movement and Coco was photographed with her and other society women at the rehearsal for the show.[130]

The *Daily Mail* reported on 14 May: 'The exhibition of models of Mademoiselle Chanel the French dressmaker at 39 Grosvenor Square has now been opened more than a week. Since May 6, the collection has attracted between five and six hundred people daily and manufacturers have come from all over the country to see it. Many women have brought their dressmakers with them, for Mlle Chanel has allowed the collection to be copied although the dresses are not for sale.'

All of London's high society went to see it, with Duchesses in abundance. This was another instance of Coco's famous credo of 'poverty deluxe' and evidence of how she had the knack of always hitting the right note on what women desired. Coco's connection with Ferguson Brothers would continue as she was invited to design a range of materials for them, which proved very successful.

But despite the public success of the relationship, the prolonged depression in the cotton trade was still being felt and in 1932 the Directors and officials were taking a ten per cent cut in salary.[131] Ferguson's further consolidated their links with Coco as she began to design textiles for them. In January 1933 the local press were reporting:

> *Messrs Ferguson Brothers Ltd are again exhibiting at the British Industries Fair. They have a large stand in a prominent position which enables them to give a most effective show of their latest productions in dress goods... On the opening day the Ferguson stand was visited by H.R.H. the Duchess of York, to whom Mr Robert Chance was presented. The Duchess congratulated him on the excellence of the display from Holme Head works and ordered dress lengths of Ferguson voile and Ferguson Rosemary crepe.*

> *'On Wednesday the Ferguson stand was visited by Her Majesty the Queen[Mary], the Princess Royal and the Prince of Wales[later the Duke of Windsor] accompanied by Lord Derby. Mr R.C. Chance, the Director in charge had the honour of being presented to Her Majesty, who expressed interest and pleasure in the Ferguson collaboration with Mademoiselle Chanel, the eminent French fashion expert. Her Majesty was pleased to select a dress length of a quality named Fersyl in a Chanel design, and also a length of Carloya, another artificial silk quality and a daintily printed checked cotton fabric... The textile exhibition is specially good this year and there is an impressive display by most if not all of the eminent firms. All ladies who have the opportunity of being in London before it closes... should make a point of visiting this section and seeing what successful efforts have been made to cater for their requirements in wool, cotton and artificial silk goods.'*[132]

Linton Tweeds probably also exhibited at these London exhibitions, as they did at others, but no record appears to have survived.

Chanel, Lady Pamela Smith and fashion models in London, 1932

In February 1933, Harvey Nichols store in London's Knightsbridge was advertising ready-to-wear elegant Chanel jumpers - 'You simply must have at least one of these Jumpers...the latest creations of Mademoiselle Chanel, the famous Parisian couturier, but actually made in Scotland.' Prices were reasonable a 59s 6d. (about £105 today).[133] The jumpers were described as smart enough to wear into late afternoon, sporting design features such as puff sleeves, shoulder capelets and fitted waists with tie necklines.

In subsequent years there were reports of the Duchess of York buying fine cottons from Fergusons for dresses for her young daughters, Princess Elizabeth and Princess Margaret Rose, and of Queen Mary buying lingerie designs in a fabric named Fergoneen, which was being used by the House of Paquin and other leading Paris dressmakers. The local newspaper reported: 'Her Majesty said that she was very pleased to hear that the Haute Couture Houses of Paris were buying British goods and she thought it was highly creditable to Messrs Ferguson Brothers that they should be able to supply their demands.' [134]

The Carlisle textile manufacturers would continue to have strong links with supplying the Royal family and with the Parisian couture houses into the future.

By strange coincidence, Carlisle's new Member of Parliament, elected on the National Conservative ticket in October 1931, was Major General Edward Louis Spears, Boy Capel's old friend. His home at this time was in Berkshire, but on his visits to Carlisle he stayed with George Howard, 11th Earl of Carlisle, and his wife Bridget at Naworth Castle, just outside Carlisle.[135] He supported Ramsay Macdonald's National government, and in a speech in Carlisle advocated equal pay for men and women. He also championed the cause of the dispossessed, taking up the case of a vagrant, one Thomas Parker, who had been picked up by the police and died in prison.

In the House of Commons, Spears said:

> *'This man's crime was his extreme poverty. I say to myself, "This man Parker was an ex-soldier, just as I am. He may have been a better soldier than I was for all I know. In any case, he volunteered to go to war, whereas I was sent. He did his duty, he was honest and, but for the mercy of God, it is Louis Spears, not Thomas Parker, who might have been standing in the dock." '* [136]

He was also to intervene in the case of Flying Officer Fitzpatrick, who was taken into custody by the police and beaten up, for no apparent reason. He obtained a personal apology from the Commissioner of the Metropolitan Police, Lord Trenchard, and on 5 August 1933, the *Cumberland News* reported that a parliamentary commentator had stated that because of these two interventions, 'in the last session General Spears was the member who had most strengthened his position.' [137]

It was perhaps a symbol of his common humanity and his feeling for his fellow servicemen that he should introduce a private members bill to amend the Vagrancy Act so that it would not be a crime to sleep out with 'no visible means of subsistence.' [138] In these days before the Welfare State, he was highlighting the plight of men who, on returning from the war suffering from shell-shock or injuries that prevented them from working, became homeless and desperate.

At the next election in October 1935, with Stanley Baldwin as Prime Minister, he was re-elected amid disruptive meetings in Carlisle. He won with a majority of 2,635 votes over his Labour and Liberal rivals, and stated that he would rather represent Carlisle than 'all the wealth and fashion of Mayfair.' [139] He continued representing the Border City in Parliament until 1945,when he was defeated by the Labour candidate, Edgar Grierson.

***

28
Paul Iribe – Coco's new love

Colette loved St Tropez: she had bought a little house there in 1926, La Treille Muscate, named after the old muscat vine that crept around the water-well. She was there in 1933, working on her short novel, Le Chat, and writing to the love of her life, her future husband, Maurice Goudeket, in Paris. Telling him of the wonderful moonlight, the sea, the bathing, the brilliant pink lilies, the pale blue of the plumbago and how much she missed him. 'And you're not here!' [140]

Writer of tender words she may have been, but she was also a perceptive observer of her fellow Tropezians. The gossip that summer was of Coco – and the demon, Paul Iribe!

When Misia Sert broke the news to Colette that their affair might end in marriage, she soon passed the rumour on to her friend, Marguerite Moreno, with the pithy comment: 'Aren't you horrified – for her?' [141]

Paul Iribarnegaray was born in Angoulême of Basque parents in 1883, the same year as Coco. With his black hair, thick-set physique and biting wit he was something of a prodigy. His father was a writer for Le Temps, and the young Paul was apprenticed to a typesetter in the printshop of the paper. This was not his choice of vocation as all he wanted to do was draw. His first drawings were published in the celebrated satirical review L'Assiette au Beurre when he was only seventeen. After two years he left this job and, at the age of eighteen, enrolled on the architecture course at the École Nationale Supérieure des Beaux Arts. He became one of the most celebrated caricaturists of his generation with a style reminiscent of Aubrey Beardsley. [142]

By 1906 he had founded his own weekly political newspaper Le Témoin. He took on a fellow illustrator, the young Jean Cocteau, whose Parisian style and sophistication he admired. The newspaper was published for four years before closing, but it had attracted a certain readership. The famous couturier, Paul Poiret invited Iribe to become fashion illustrator and make drawings of the gowns in his collection, which were published in 1908 in a glamorous (and now collectable) promotional book, Les Robes de Paul Poiret racontees par Paul Iribe. The book, with its clean, crisp drawings, depicting the stylish outline and witty details of the gowns became widely influential both in terms of fashion and illustrative style. [143] When copies were sent to the crowned heads of Europe, all of whom received it graciously, Queen Alexandra of England had her lady–in-waiting return it to Poiret with a letter requesting that no further offerings be sent. [144]

Iribe, a gifted and multi-talented man was described by Paul Poiret in his memoirs thus:

> 'He was an extremely odd chap, a Basque plump as a capon, and reminding one both of a seminarist and of a printer's reader. In the seventeenth century he would have been a Court abbé. He wore gold spectacles, and a wide open collar around which was tied rather loosely a scarf... He spoke in a very low voice, as if mysterious and gave some of his words a special significance by separating their syllables... he would say, "It is - ad-mir-able." Altogether a charming and remarkable personality.' [145]

With his skills as a technician from his days in the print-shop and his talent for illustration, he went into partnership with Jean Cocteau in 1914 and started a new journalistic venture, an illustrated magazine aimed at the Parisian luxury market. It was called Le Mot and was to have a short lifespan, folding after just one year due to the war. Pierre Galante tells of Iribe in Deauville during the war, where the back of Chanel's shop had become a meeting place for volunteer nurses. Poiret had turned his delivery vans into a fleet of ambulances, and Iribe, his designer, was driving Misia, magnificently swathed in a nurse's uniform designed for her by Poiret. [146] This did not deter him and, in the aftermath of the war, he played a full role in the life of the Twenties, becoming one of the foremost designers of the decade. His prolific skills saw him designing furniture, receiving commissions from connoisseurs such as Jacques Doucet and Robert de Rothschild; rich fabrics were made for Bianchini-Ferier, producers of silk and crêpe-georgette; and jewels for Lalique, always with his ideas of luxury to the fore. He became a contributor to *Vogue* and *Femina*, and designed advertisements for the couturiers, Paquin and Callot Soeurs.

Notoriety followed his lifestyle, as his name became synonymous with great luxury in design, great feats as a lover of women and a need for wealth. He was said to have married Jeanne Dirys, a well-known star of silent films and the vaudeville. All Colette's friends in Paris turned out to see the opening of her 1921 film *L'Equipe,* directed by Francis Carco. Whenever Iribe was short of money, she took on the role of model, being photographed with luxury goods, advertising ermine capes and sumptuous coupé cars. While Iribe was away, Jane fell ill and Colette wrote to Francis Carco about how useless she felt in the face of her serious illness. Jane died in 1922, but by this time Iribe had gone to America where he had met and married Maybelle Hogan, a beautiful and wealthy heiress, in 1919.

The Ten Commandments... and after

Doing the rounds of Hollywood, he met Cecil B. De Mille who found his skills and knowledge of couture, architecture, furniture and costume design impressive. De Mille had once told Howard Greer, an earlier designer, 'I want clothes that will make people gasp when they see them. I don't want to see any clothes anybody could possibly buy in a store.' [147] In Iribe he had found someone to match his ambition.

At Paramount, Iribe was taken on to research the background for a number of films, most notably *Changing Husbands* and *Manslaughter*, which starred Leatrice Joy. The beautiful, fluid costumes he designed for her caused a sensation and Iribe was promoted to Artistic Director over designers who had worked with De Mille for many years, including the gifted Mitchell Leisen. Iribe did not have the skills of De Mille in getting his own way while pacifying bruised egos. Mitchell Leisen and Iribe were constantly at loggerheads with the result that Leisen refused to have anything to do with the next big picture, *The Ten Commandments*. Leatrice Joy again headed the cast of this Hollywood extravaganza, with its profusion of gold and glitter, temples, gods and divinities, all set beneath the inscrutable gaze of a huge sphinx.

Iribe's costumes and sets may have owed more to the Twenties than to the Bible, but they were a visual triumph. The film was produced and directed by De Mille, and brought the Bible to life in a way never before portrayed on screen – it was a smash-hit at the box-office. The next biblical epic was *King of Kings*, which saw Leisen as head of the costume department, and Iribe as Artistic Director. Filming hit a crisis when De Mille found that Iribe had made no arrangements for the Crucifixion scene, Iribe's days in Hollywood were numbered, and Leisen was back on the job.[148]

Back in Paris, Maybelle set him up in an elegant shop on the rue du Faubourg-Sainte-Honoré, where he turned his talents to interior design, as well as supplying furniture, rugs and jewels to fashionable Parisians. His most notable commission, was for Spinelly, a friend of Colette and a famous musical revue singer. Poiret, whose interior design company, Chez Martine, had been established in 1912, had decorated her studio, and Iribe was invited to decorate her bedroom and dining room, with the last word in luxury. Her palatial home, described as 'a mixture of Hindu temple, Greek palace, Persian corner and nightclub loggia,' was the scene of Iribe's artistic muse.[149]

He designed an enormous brass bed for her, with a gold signature at its foot and set on a raised platform, with walls of willow-green and low Chinese lacquer tables. The whole thing caused much gossip. [150]

Photography was his next ambition and, as usual, he threw himself into taking his talent to the highest point of success. His photomontages were entered in a Hollywood publicity competion in 1931, where out of fifty well-known European photographers he came second, beating Hoyningen-Huene. But although he could easily make money, he could just as easily lose it, and frequently had to sell his possessions, his luxury car and yacht, even his house. Maybelle stood by him throughout, and she obtained commissions for him to design jewels from Cartier and also from Chanel. Maybelle , who had been his rock, was losing patience with his extravagance and his affairs. She feared for the financial security of their two children and by early 1933, under pressure from her family, she left their home on avenue Rodin and returned to America with the children.[151]

Paul Iribe, the Basque designer-artist, who became Chanel's lover

Coco's friends all agreed that she loved him, perhaps her first real love since Boy Capel. As with Boy, she involved him in her business affairs, and when she became embroiled in her long-running business disputes with the perfume company, it was Iribe to whom she gave power of attorney on 12 September 1933, and had him attend a Board meeting in her place. She bank-rolled a publishing house, the Chanel Éditions, and he started publication again of the political *Le Temoin.* Coco featured in his illustrations of Marianne, symbol of France.

Theirs was a passionate affair, but full of crises, Serge Lifar would recall; 'He dominated her and she couldn't stand that. Soon she began to hate him as much as she loved him.' [152]

But, love him she did. Despite the gossip of her friends, this was a man of intelligence, sophisicated wit and creative gifts, and that is what attracted Coco to him. He was there for her, they shared a glance and understood each other, no need for words. He was proud of her achievements and she of his – they were well matched to each other.

Diamonds in the sky

The first two weeks of November 1932, saw an exhibition displayed at Coco's house that was the talk of Paris. It was diamonds, diamonds all the way. Wax models with ruby lips, curling eyelashes and short, black-slicked hair were to be seen being carried into Coco's grand house at 29 rue du Faubourg-Sainte-Honoré. Here they were draped in long evening gowns and furs, set on black marble plinths covered in glass cases, with security wired to the local police station.

The *Bijoux de diamants crées par Chanel* exhibition, with its shooting stars and constellations, glittered from the wax dolls and reflected in the décor of shimmering crystal and mirrored glass screens like diamonds in the night sky. Nothing quite like these designs had been seen before. Instead of designing in her usual semi-precious and fake stones, the International Guild of Diamond Merchants had invited her to create an exhibition of real jewellery, in aid of children's charities.

It was Paul Iribe who worked with Coco to produce jewels that were unusual, simple and modern. There were hair bands shaped like the crescent moon and stars, a tiara that hung over the forehead, like a fringe, and necklaces that followed the contours of the neck, resting there without closing. There were necklace-collars with bows, diadems of long delicate ribbons of diamonds, sunburst brooches and sparkling coiled rings. None of the pieces had any visible clasps; many were adaptable into different variations. Although this was a time of economic depression, following the Wall Street crash of 1929, the exhibition travelled to America, enabling thousands to see it and raising funds for the charities.

Chanel herself would say: 'My jewellery never stands in isolation from the idea of women and their dress. And because dresses change, so does my jewellery.' [153]

***

29
Princess Marina's wedding

Captain Edward Molyneux was considering his designs. He had just received confirmation from the Royal Household that Princess Marina wanted him to make her wedding dress, and on 12 September 1934 the Princess and her mother, Princess Nicholas, visited his fashion house in Paris to order the bridal gown and honeymoon outfits. The Princess had previously patronised Jean Patou's couture house and planned to ask him to make her wedding dress, but Prince George, who took a great interest in her clothes and once told a friend, 'I always discuss with Marina what dress and jewels I advise her to wear,' [154] advised her that she should use an English designer. She chose Captain Molyneux whom she had met socially. [155]

For her wedding gown, Captain Molyneux designed a simple elegant sheath style dress, with draped neckline and medieval sleeves but made from a sumptuous, shimmering, silver lamé tissue embodying an English rose design in the weave. The only stipulations had been that some dresses had to be made of English material and that as many Russian refugees as possible should be employed in making the trousseau. This reflected the interests of the Princess and her mother, who had set up a home and school in Paris in 1924, the 'Home for Russian Children,' to help children of refugees from the Russian revolution whose aristocratic parents had to leave them home-alone as they looked for work. [156]

The Captain telephoned his old friend Wiliam Linton in Carlisle and explained his ideas: he wanted to do something totally new for these special dresses and suits. He had an idea for a new shade of blue - could William help? William could: he and his designers looked at the myriad shades of blues, peacocks, aquatones, turquoises and greens and decided to mix something special for this royal commission, a subtle shade of deep greeny-turquoise. [157] It was woven into a soft tweed and sent to the Captain for approval by Princess Marina. It was accepted and the colour was known ever after as 'Marina blue', and the cloth as 'Marina tweed.' [158]

When the newsreels were shown, and the wedding photographs appeared, William and the staff at Linton were justly proud. The trousseau aroused world-wide interest: it was one of the smallest any Royal bride had chosen but, as the practical and unassuming Princess said: 'Fashion changes so suddenly that I do not want to buy too many clothes.' [159]

Princess Marina was the youngest daughter of Prince and Princess Nicholas of Greece and was born in Athens in 1906. Her mother, born the Grand Duchess Helen Vladimirovna was a cousin of the Czar of Russia and also a cousin of Prince Dmitri. The Greek royal family had been deposed in 1917 and forced to live in exile in Switzerland. After a brief return to Greece in 1920, political unrest forced them to leave in 1922 and they made their home in Paris.

Princess Marina married Prince George, Duke of Kent, after a whirlwind courtship. The Prince, one of the most handsome men in the Royal Family, was born in 1902, the fourth son of King George V and Queen Mary. The marriage ceremony took place at Westminster Abbey on 29 November 1934, and was the first Royal wedding in history to be broadcast. Afterwards the couple returned to Buckingham Palace, where the one-thousand-year-old Greek Orthodox wedding ceremony was celebrated in the private chapel, by Dr Strinopoulos Germanos, the Greek Archbishop in London.

The Princess was a noted beauty known for her smart and chic style of dress which favoured classical, slim, elegant designs. She became known for her simple neat suits and her jaunty 'pork pie' pillbox style hats, worn with a jewelled pin and two small feathers on the side. Captain Molyneux described her as ranking with the Empress Eugénie among the world's outstanding leaders of fashion. [160] As a leader of fashion and a woman whose style was much copied, she also had a social conscience, and in the hard times of depression and unemployment of the 1930s she would strive to popularise British fashion and textiles. When the cotton industry was suffering she ordered cotton summer dresses, which then became the rage with fashionable women who previously would not have worn what was regarded as a humble fabric. Her use of Nottingham lace and British tweeds was also widely copied.[161]

Such was her impact on British fashion at this time that when, in 1938, King George VI announced the appointment of the Duke of Kent as Governor-General of the Commonwealth of Australia, there was dismay in the fashion and textile industries. The British *Sunday Express* led the protests with a front-page lead story saying, 'It is feared - and openly said - that the absence of the Duchess from Britain will have an adverse effect on the whole fashion industry... The Duchess has made fashion history. She has given London the leadership that belonged to Paris and fashion houses fear that... in her absence London will lose that lead again.'[162]

Princess Marina at her wedding in 1934 - the inspiration for William Linton's Marina tweed

The arrangements for the move went ahead with the Princess ordering clothes from Molyneux to take with her. Government House in Canberra was refurbished with textiles and colour schemes chosen by the Duke himself with oatmeal silk tweed curtains, pale blue satin-covered sofas and chairs and white Grecian rugs.[163] By July 1939 everything was ready to be shipped out but in September war broke out and the Duke's appointment was postponed: he was back in the Royal Navy.

Cecil Beaton who was to become Princess Marina's friend in later years, thought highly of her:

> *'Those who had the good fortune to meet her on her arrival in England could see the cool classical features in a perfect oval head held high on a straight column of neck, the topaz eyes, the slightly tilted smile, the apricot complexion, and the nut brown cap of flat silken curls...'* [164]

With her informal, friendly style she became one of the most popular members of the Royal Family, and in some ways was a forerunner of the style of Diana, Princess of Wales. The Kents had three children, Prince Edward, Princess Alexandra, and Prince Michael, but the Princess was widowed in 1942 when Prince George, serving as an Air-Commodore in the Royal Air Force, was tragically killed in an air accident flying over Scotland. Princess Marina had waved him off as he drove to Invergordon, where he boarded a Sunderland flying boat for a secret tour of inspection in Iceland. Taking off down the Cromarty Firth before turning north for Iceland, the plane crashed in a mass of buckled metal amid the heather on the Scottish hillside.[165]

When she heard the news, Beaton recalled that 'for hours on end she remained speechless and motionless as she stared out of the window.' [166] (Princess Marina died in 1968 from an inoperable brain tumour.)

*** * ***

30
A time of upheaval

It started with a riot. On 6 February 1934 forty thousand demonstrators crowded the Place de la Concorde. By the time it was over, a cleaning lady at the Crillon Hotel was dead and there were fifty people seriously injured. The riot spilled over into rue Faubourg, outside Coco's house. Gendarmes and mounted police were out in force, and sharp-shooters were in the trees: a bus was burning at the foot of the Obelisk.

Nothing like it had been seen on the streets of Paris since the days of the Commune. The aims of the booted young men of the Fascist movement were to overthrow the government by driving out President Daladier from the Elysée Palace and setting up a provisional government. Right-wing movements in Paris had been partly financed by Italy and Germany, where the rise of fascism was at its height. They did not succeed.[167]

Spring of that year saw Coco deciding to give up her lease on the house at rue Faubourg: she told Joseph Leclerc, her long-time major-domo, of her decision. She was cutting back and dismissed all the servants, except for her maid.[168] Perhaps also she was preparing to marry Paul. She moved into a suite in the Ritz Hotel across the street from the House of Chanel on rue Cambon and, with her Coromandel screens and her antiques, she set up a lavish home. She would never again own her own home in Paris, preferring to keep only her suite at the Ritz. She also had a suite of sitting rooms at the House. La Pausa became her main retreat that summer: with Iribe waiting for his divorce from Maybelle, he joined her amid the peace of the olive trees and assumed the role of master of the house. She was happy to let him.[169]

Politically, it was an unsettling time, Hitler was reinstating compulsory military service and flouting the Treaty of Versailles by re-arming Germany. The host of English on the Riviera talked of nothing else.

Tragedy loomed in 1935 when, on a summer afternoon at La Pausa, Iribe and other friends were warming up and chatting on the tennis court. Coco came out to join them and, as he turned to look at her, he fell to the ground. He had suffered a massive heart attack. He died in a clinic in Menton a few days later without regaining consciousness.[170] He was fifty-two years old. Misia came running to her again: as with Boy, it seemed that only she could understand the depths of despair that the silent Coco felt.

A sit-down on Mademoiselle's dresses

A strike at Chanel's – impossible! But that day dawned in 1936. Election Day was 26 April and the heavens opened. There were those who hoped that the torrential downpour would deter the voters, and the polling booths would be empty. Instead 85 per cent of the voters of France braved the rain and cast their votes. It was a victory for the *Front Populaire,* the left-wing coalition of Socialists, Radicals and Communists; heralding a period of disbelief and fear for the wealthy aristocrats and rich bourgeoisie, with money being moved to foreign bank accounts and a run on gold. The workers celebrated a new era of working-class rights, waving banners and singing *The Internationale.* It was the culmination of a year of almost daily protests by working men: they needed jobs, not unemployment benefit.[171]

Leon Blum was the socialist head of the coalition, the first Jewish premier in France, but could not take up post until the outgoing National Assembly left office at the end of May. The workers wanted immediate action on the social and welfare reforms that they had been promised, and began a series of strikes affecting the aircraft and auto-mobile industries. The strikes spread through all areas of services and industry – even to the bakers. Coco had maintained a cool head throughout and kept the doors of her couture house wide open, awaiting her clients. She was amazed when the strikes spread to the textile industries, to her suppliers of jersey, silk, lace – everything.

Like the true autocrat that she was, she believed in the total power of the boss: worker's rights? – unbelievable!

Her disbelief was even greater on 6 June when she walked out of the Ritz onto rue Cambon and was there faced with the sight of her workers, the seamstresses, the vendeuses, standing on the pavement outside her House, with a strikers' collection box and waving to the press. She turned round and went back into the Ritz, to plan her response.

Later in the morning, a delegation of her workers found courage to go to the impressive front entrance of the Ritz in place Vendôme, past the distinguished, gold-braided doorman, into the elegant foyer, and requested to see Mademoiselle. Not a chance. Mademoiselle sent word to them that she did not know what *workroom delegates* were, but she would meet her *workers* in her office when she arrived at rue Cambon. To the consternation of her maid, Eugénie, Mademoiselle intended to confront her wayward workers wearing her best chic navy suit and her longest rope of real pearls, which were worth a small fortune. But she was humiliated: her workers would not allow her into her House. She would never forget it. In spite of all arguments, this woman who employed four thousand workers, had to turn haughtily away.[172]

The new Premier had taken up office the previous day and had called an historic meeting - the first ever to take place in France - between representatives from industry's management and delegates from the largest labour union federation in France, the CGT. The meeting took place in Blum's office in Hotel Matignon on rue de Varenne.

Worker power at Chanel

Coco called in her lawyer, René de Chambrun, for talks and his advice was to play it cool – use moderation. This did little to assuage Coco's angst at the thought of a sit-down on her dresses: it was sacrilege!

The workers of the couture industry were notoriously low-paid, as were many other workers in this decade of depression and wide social divisions: these were the hungry Thirties. The House of Chanel, was in fact, known in the industry as a well-run establishment noted for its high standards of management. Coco headed design while a team of managers organised the manufacturing and sales side. For years she had rented the property next to the Duke of Westminster's at Mimizan, using it as a retreat for any of the women workers in need of rest and recuperation. She paid wages that were higher than at Schiaparelli's. She did not understand it.

Premier Blum was successful in his talks with the delegates and, by the early hours of the next morning, a number of agreements had been reached, destined to improve the lives of ordinary men and women, and their social and work conditions. It was an historic day for France. For the first time, the Matignon Agreements ensured that there would be workers' rights. The strikers agreed to go back to work and there would be no reprisals. They would gain wage inceases ranging from 7 to 15 per cent, two weeks' paid annual holiday, a forty–hour working week, the right to collective bargaining, and the right to have trades unions. As well as this, the Bank of France and the railways were nationalised and the price of grain controlled. The troubles continued as employers said they were being forced into the new agreements, and the unions struggled to control their members.[173] In the month that followed President Blum taking office, the Ministry of Labour counted 12,142 strikes taking place.[174]

At the House of Chanel negotiations dragged on. Coco's first response was to say 'no' to all demands, regardless of the Matignon Agreements. 'No' to workers' rights, paid holidays, contracts of employment and regular working hours. It was stalemate and she sacked three hundred workers.[175]

The tension rose as her workers saw strikes gradually being settled around them: change was in the air. Gabrielle, never one to take the easy option, offered to turn the whole business into a workers' cooperative, with herself as manager. They refused.

With her lawyers and the Wertheimers advising settlement, and the knowledge that the Autumn/Winter collection would not be possible if they did not settle by the end of July, she had little choice. Besides, Schiaparelli with her much smaller workforce was waiting for her to fail. The House of Chanel had to get back to work. So she settled – but she would never forget the humiliation.

As work got back to normal an exhibition, 'La Foire d'Échantillons de l'industrie legère de France,' had been organised by the French light industries, under the patronage of M. Edouard Herriot, a minister of state. The trade fair travelled to Moscow with the aim of showing the best that the French manufacturers had to offer. Those exhibiting included Chanel, Coty and Guerlain perfumes, textiles

Film star Virginia Cherrill, wearing a Hardy Amies creation in Linton Tweed, with her husband the 9th Earl of Jersey, 1937

by Bianchini, Coudurier and Colcombert, Perrin couture gloves, Courvoisier brandy, champagne by Pommery and Roederer, and the top department stores, such as Samaritaine were represented. Elsa Schiaparelli was invited to attend by her textile supplier Colcombert, and Cecil Beaton went along to photograph the event.[176]

***

31
Celebrations and the end of an era

> *'I went on a tour of the tweed mills in Cumberland. At first, tweeds I was shown seemed no different from those in London: then suddenly something caught my eye in a pile of scraps of old material lying abandoned in the corner.*

> *'It was a soft tweed made in a mixture of dark plum sprinkled with specks of vivid cerise and then criss-crossed with a fairly large overcheck in emerald green. I know it sounds awful, but the tweed glowed. I can describe it in no other way. I made it up into a little jacket and had a skirt made of the tweed without the green overcheck.'* [177]

This is how Sir Hardy Amies describes one of his visits to Linton Tweeds in Carlisle when he worked as designer for the House of Lachasse in London.

> *'I remember we called the model "Panic". We always rather enjoyed naming the models... "Panic" was shown in the spring collection of 1937 - the year of the Coronation of George VI.'*

It became his first full page in *Vogue* in April 1937.[178]

The abdication of King Edward V111 on 11 December 1936 ended a period of uncertainty and upheaval for the royal family and the country. King Edward's Coronation had been set to take place on 12 May 1937 and, when his brother Bertie succeeded him, it was thought advisable to keep the ceremony on the same date. King George V1 and Queen Elizabeth were crowned in Westminster Abbey amid the fanfare of trumpets and the representatives of governments. Afterwards they drove in the pouring rain through streets thronged with joyful crowds, and appeared on the balcony of Buckingham Palace, together with the two small princesses, Elizabeth and Margaret - a united family waving to the people.[179] Similar joyful scenes were taking place across the land, including Carlisle, with street parties overflowing and union jacks flying.

Textiles were also in the news in Carlisle that year. On Saturday 29 May, the Earl of Carlisle was opening the Exhibition of Carlisle and District Textile Manufacturers. The Exhibition was organised by the Cumberland Textile Society, under the Presidency of Mr W. Ian Brown: it was not a trade exhibition, but intended to show the variety and quality of local textile products. It sought to increase the public's knowledge of the industry, on which by now the prosperity of the area largely depended. There were exhibits from ten local firms, as well as the Technical and Art Schools, and fabrics of all types from the eighteenth century until the present day were on display.[180]

1937 was a year of exhibitions. In Paris there were three International Exhibitions between the two world wars: in 1925, the Exposition des Arts Décoratifs; in 1931, the Exposition Internationale Coloniale, which Britain did not attend; and in 1937, the Exposition Internationale des Arts et Techniques dans la Vie Moderne. The Blum government had decided that the theme of the 1937 Expo would be the interaction of art and science in the modern world, and there were pavilions with scientific and technological themes, such as aeronautics,as well as those on the arts and modern living.

Twenty-five-thousand workers were employed on the site and, in spite of Leon Blum's attempts to convince them that to finish on time would be a victory for the workers against fascism, it did not happen. When the Expo was inaugurated on Labour Day, 1 May, many of the pavilions were not ready and it would be 24 May before it opened. It was a setback for the Popular Front, who counted on it to revive the economy. By August all the pavilions were open and, over the months, thirty-four-million people arrived from all over the world to make their way round the huge park.

It had all the fun of the fair, with the aromatic smell of food from dozens of countries wafting from the stalls, with chefs in tall white hats competing with waiters offering fine wines. A vast area at the foot of the Eiffel Tower held the national pavilions where countries displayed their exhibits. Perhaps the most striking was the fifty-four-metre high German pavilion topped by a huge eagle, standing opposite the Soviet building with its great statue of industrial workers, and which dwarfed other countries' buildings, including Great Britain's. The Spanish pavilion was designed by José Luis Sert and Picasso was invited to paint a mural. The Spanish Civil War was raging and, when the Basque town of Guernica was destroyed by Spanish rebels aided by Nazi German allies four days before the official Exhibition opened, he painted his poignant mural *Guernica.* It was a remarkable achievement, as three photographs from the 1 May issue of *Paris Soir* were all he had as reference.[181]

Coco designed a beautiful Baccarat crystal plate, depicting her scissors on a ribbon cutting through cloth, and had it displayed with the inscription ' I used these scissors to cut all that was superfluous in the creations of others.' [182] She attended the opening gala event and the chic parties that surrounded the Fair. She was frequently seen holding court, surrounded by photographers and journalists. Arriving on the arm of Christian Bérard, wearing a dress which was a delicate froth of organdy and appeared weightless, with a diadem of flowers in her hair, she was the centre of attention.

Carlisle's contribution

An air of excitement abounded in Carlisle among the business community and in artistic circles. For the British pavilion, the Council for Art and Industry had taken as its theme the particular contribution Britain had made to the current civilisation of Western Europe, looking to the ideas expressed behind such words as *le weekend*, *le tennis*, *le five o'-clock*, which the French had taken as their own. The organisers had decided on sport, clothes, the weekend cottage, books and posters and the life of British children to depict British goods, as well as a way of life.

Six firms from Carlisle and district were invited to exhibit. These were: tweeds as shown by Linton's Cumberland Homespuns and Cumberland Mills Ltd of Warwick Bridge; Woollen fabrics by James Waddell & Son, Heads Nook; rugs by Alexander Morton &

Miss Kidd, Nessy and McMullen, the chauffeur, with the Geltsdales, 1938

Sons; and rayon and cotton fabric by Morton Sundour Fabrics Ltd. The work of Keswick School of Industrial Art was represented by a metal tray.

The pavilion had every sporting item from a golf ball to a thirty-five-foot motor yacht moored alongside in the Seine. The clothes featured the tweeds and tartans, cottons and silks as worn by the British at leisure. A three-roomed weekend cottage was furnished to the last detail and pioneering children's toys, furniture and clothes were all on display. There was one unifying principle for these exhibits: the ideal of modern industrial art, that whatever is made should be 'good in design and workmanship, fit for its purpose and capable of providing a background for a good life.'

The *Carlisle Journal* opined that to study the Exhibition catalogue was as good as a holiday, but suggested, 'Better still, to pack it in a British suitcase and clothed in British garments for *le sport*, to make across the Channel and see for oneself.' [183]

A number of the worthies of Carlisle did just that.

July saw William Linton taking his staff on the annual work's outing to Scotland, and it earned a paragraph in the local paper. The extent of this long but enjoyable day is worth recording. The *Carlisle Journal* reported:

> *'The party numbering about 100, left Carlisle on the 5.16 a.m. train and arrived in Perth at 10 o'clock. Three of Alexander's luxury coaches were awaiting to convey the party for a 125 miles tour of Perthshire, through continuous magnificent scenery. The route was via Methven, Sma' Glen, Amulree, Ballinluig, to Pitlochry, where lunch was taken at Scotland's Hotel. Proceeding after lunch via Pass of Killiecrankie, Coshieville, to Kenmore for a sail up Loch Tay, to Killin and return here again, the everchanging scenery was beautiful. Tea was served on the boat. Rejoining the coaches, the route was via Aberfeldy, Ballinluig, Dunkeld, Bankfoot to Perth in time to catch the 9.10 p.m. train, arriving at Carlisle at 1.50 a.m., Sunday. Breakfast and dinner were served on the train.*
>
> *'Nearing Carlisle, Mr D. Elliot, on behalf of the employees thanked Mr Linton for so generously providing an excellent day's outing. Mr Linton in reply said his greatest pleasure was in seeing everyone so happy. The company then sang "Will Ye No Come Back Again" and "For He's a Jolly Good Fellow" thus bringing to an end a very enjoyable day.'* [184]

Such were work's outings seventy years ago!

That summer also saw the opening of a bowling green and bower behind Hill House in the village of Great Corby where William lived. The previous summer he had bought a plot of land from a local farmer, had the bowling green constructed and presented it to the village. He became the first President of the club when it opened in 1937.

William's business affairs took all of his energies and, although a benefactor to the village and to the Church of Scotland, he did not seek public office as other businessmen in Carlisle had. All in all, 1937 had been a good year and William must have felt content as Christmas approached to know that the twenty-fifth anniversary of the start of his company had just passed, with his future business assured and his products in demand world-wide.

The end of an era for Linton's

William had not been feeling well for some time and his health had been causing concern to Nessy and his sister. It was a great shock to his family when, on Friday, 7 January 1938, he died suddenly at Hill House from a heart attack. He was sixty-five years old. His brother Robert came to Carlisle from Ross Gardens, Edinburgh and took charge of the arrangements. William's body was taken back across the Border and he was buried at Wilton Cemetery, Hawick, beside his beloved Helen. A large grey granite Celtic cross stands as memorial to this couple, so long separated, at last reunited.

The *Carlisle Journal* published his obituary on 11 January saying of him:

> 'He was his own designer and his homespuns met with great success. They were in great demand by Society ladies in Paris and New York, as well as in London. At the time of the marriage of Princess Marina to the Duke of Kent, Mr Linton designed a beautiful cloth which was selected for her honeymoon. The cloth became very popular and was known as the Marina tweed. He also executed orders for dress cloths for members of the Royal family.' [185]

The same obituary was repeated in the *Hawick News*, recalling this adopted local man who had gone from his early beginnings at the firm of Greenwood Watt & Co. to owning the company which supplied best quality tweed to the fashion houses of the world.[186]

His links to Hawick were still there as his sister, Mary H Linton, was teaching at Hawick High School, where she had been since before 1912.

The Times of London recorded his death, and the dog world too felt his loss and paid tribute to him. He had always taken great interest in his daughter's well-known kennels. On 14 January *Our Dogs* reported:

> 'Those in Deerhound circles who are more closely associated with Miss Linton have ever held great admiration for the courage with which she has filled the dual role of son and daughter. Since the day upon which she graduated from Oxford [sic] she has quietly shouldered a man's burden holding the eminent position of joint managing director in a famous business. For someone only just out of their 'teens to make a signal success in such a capacity was an achievement which the heart of the senior partner must have treasured with intense pride... By strange coincidence Mr Linton's favourite among her 'Geltsdale' Deerhounds died on the same day and Ch. Stag o' the Pentlands is no more.' [187]

In a further report *Our Dogs* wrote:

> 'All sympathy will go out to Miss Linton, of Deerhound note, on the death of her father, a gentleman of international fame as a designer and manufacturer of homespun tweeds. The deceased gentleman designed the tweed for the Duchess of Kent's dress and other members of the Royal Family.' [188]

... from the scrapbooks of the Deerhound Club

J. G. Clemitson, another famous breeder, wrote:

'In the course of business Mr Linton travelled much abroad and crossed the Atlantic on his way to and from the U.S.A. and Canada nearly a hundred times , so becoming a well-known personality on American liners. His activities took him frequently to the Continent. He was so highly thought of that his advice was sought and acted upon by such celebrities as Schiaparelli, Molyneux, Bernard and others... Miss Linton who is a Director of the firm has been associated with her father in the business for many years, having the creative gift, and has herself enjoyed many notable successes in designing... Mr Linton was a man of genial and generous disposition.' [189]

Coco's swan song

The years 1937 and 1938 found Coco as busy as ever, as she was still designing for the theatre, ballet and film, still attending social events. But her friends sensed that all was not well with her.

William and Helen Linton's memorial at Wilton Cemetery, Hawick

The strike of 1936 had unsettled her and she seemed engulfed in a sense of strain and tension, but she was still producing innovative fashion. In 1937, for example, Jean Cocteau's *Oedipus Rex* was staged featuring the young Jean Marais as the chorus, clad in a minimalist costume of wrapped strips of cloth by Chanel.[190] In her 1937/38 collection she had turned to romanticism showing dresses for the hourglass figure and the traditional influences of folk dress. White muslin and cotton dresses sported striped sashes and black ribbons. There were gypsy style dresses with flounces, and evening dresses of lace and crystal pleats with the look of the music hall. There was tonality with shades of light and dark, crisp tailoring, dramatic important jewels and perky hats, no more than headbands.

Diana Vreeland recalled Chanel visiting Moscow in the Thirties and when she went there herself years later and saw the rich peasant dresses in the Historical Museum, she described her reaction: 'These were Chanel's clothes of the thirties – the big skirts, the small jackets, the headresses.' [191] One of the most enduring and dramatic designs in the 1937/38 collection was the black sequinned trouser suit that Coco designed for Diana Vreeland herself. This would become one of the most enduring looks of the twentieth century, the very essence of 'smart casual': it has appeared on the catwalks in its different guises until today.[192]

Her final collection in 1939 was the most poignant. Coco showed designs in the patriotic *tricolore* colours of red white and blue.

Two strong women, two hard decisions

Wiliam's early death had a huge impact on Linton Tweeds. Agnes, although she had been joint Managing Director for many years and was well versed in the ways of the couture and the textile world, suddenly found herself at the age of thirty-five in sole charge of this internationally recognised company and carrying the responsibility for the hundred workers employed there. She proved more than equal to the task. On the other side of the channel, Coco was considering her own options if war should come - both of these strong women had to make hard decisions, and while Agnes carried on, Coco found another way out.

***

Part Four

32

A state of war

Janet Flanner, the famous Paris correspondent for *The New Yorker,* wrote in a 1939 'Letter from Paris':

> *'Herr Hitler's chances of winning the big fight have declined in the past week. France and England, after at first acting as if they would fight for anything and then as if they wouldn't fight at all, have finally made it apparent that they will fight for only a few things, but for them will fight to the death. In the last war against Germany, America came in late, but now all Germans angrily believe (whether Americans are pleased to or not) that America would be the first to pour its money, if not its men, into an anti-Nazi ideological war... If Germany is willing to risk Germany in order to destroy England, there will be war. Otherwise there will be this thing we now call peace.'* [1]

The legacy of World War 1 and the harsh treatment of the Germans with the Treaty of Versailles made World War 2 almost inevitable. The situation that Boy Capel had feared when he wrote his book in 1917 was now reality.

The 1920s had seen the Weimar Republic face a severe economic downturn. The situation was so bad by 1923 that the German mark was devalued and the crisis that followed led to the rise of Nazism. With nationalism on the increase the stage was set for Adolf Hitler's rise to power, the overthrow of the Weimar Republic and the emergence of the Third Reich. The French too, had not forgotten the great loss of men in their armies at Verdun on their eastern boundaries. There had been a huge bombardment with Big Bertha guns capable of firing shells weighing a ton, with the German advance reaching the outskirts of Paris. Marshall Phillipe Pétain had emerged as the hero of the war in defending the honour of France, and both the French and the English regarded it as 'the war to end all wars'.

It was to prove a pious hope.

The 1930s were a time of economic depression, and eastern and central Europe saw an increase in communism and fascism. By 1938, Germany was making territorial claims on the Sudetenland in Czechoslovakia, and the European leaders including French Prime Minister, Edouard Daladier, together with British Prime Minister, Neville Chamberlain, went to Munich to sue for peace. After many negotiations and false hopes, and without the participation of the Czechoslovaks, the Munich Agreement was reached on 29 September, permitting German annexation of the Sudetanland. It was a policy of appeasement to Hitler, and Chamberlain then sought a peace treaty between the United Kingdom and Germany to which Hitler agreed. Returning home to a hero's welcome Chamberlain was pictured, waving a piece of paper - the agreement with Hitler - at the airport, and declaring, 'Peace for our time '. It was to be a short-lived sentiment.

Hitler's aggression became a desire for world domination by the Germans and he invaded Poland on 1 September 1939. Britain and its Dominions (Australia, New Zealand, Canada, South Africa, India and the colonies) declared war on Germany on 3 September, with France following. The appeasement policy had only served to buy time for Britain to produce armaments and build aircraft - and perhaps that was the best that Chamberlain had hoped for.[2]

Coco quits

With war now declared, and France expecting the worst, Coco considered her options. She had thought long and hard about it in the preceding months, and now the decision was made. It caused uproar in the Parisian fashion trade and became the gossip of the pavement cafés and drawing rooms alike. It was impossible, unbelievable, it could not be true - Chanel had announced that she was closing the House of Chanel. Her entire workforce was laid off and only the boutique selling her perfume would remain open. Her latest collection shown in the spring of 1939 had been patriotic: long gypsy dresses, white with embellishments in red, white and blue - the colours of the *tricolore.* Now she said, 'This is no time for fashion.'[3]

Amid the general outrage, she appeared impervious to all pleas for her to reconsider. The Trade Union Association and the government, anxious about the loss of jobs of four thousand workers, as well as the effect on the small suppliers who made the jewels, braid, buttons and trimmings, tried to change her mind but without success. Many ploys were tried. Would she stay for the sake of her employees? No. For the customers then? No. For the prestige of Paris? No. To raise funds for the fighting forces? No. Nothing succeeded: neither appealing to her sense of patriotism nor flattery made any difference.

She was adamant, she was closing she said, 'Come what may.'[4]

In the fashion trade, her name was vilified and she was branded a deserter. It made no difference, she shrugged it all off with *hauteur.* The question, almost impossible to resolve, is 'why?' She who had sailed through World War 1 with Boy at her side, had shown no fear, and had in fact used the situation to expand her business interests and develop her elegant style. Now, at fifty-six-years old and in her prime as an international couturier, she was giving it all up or, some might have said, throwing it all away. Did she feel that perversity that is sometimes seen in the gifted - when the last prize is within reach, suddenly, at that moment, it no longer looks attractive, and they walk away? There is nothing more of interest or left to achieve.

She later said, 'I had the feeling that we had reached the end of an era. And that no one would ever make dresses again.'[5]

What might have been?

Ironically, there was a final collection that had been created but it was never shown. Perhaps if it had been, it would have been Coco Chanel who would have been credited with creating the New Look and not Christian Dior, who shocked the post-war fashion world in 1947. In an historic photograph by Horst, Coco is shown looking pensively into the future, as model Muriel Maxwell displays a black silk velvet suit, sporting a white frilled ruff collar and frilled cuffs. The design was dubbed the 'Watteau suit' after the women depicted in the paintings of Jean-Antoine Watteau in the early eighteenth century. With its nipped-in waist, peplum jacket and smooth full flared skirt it might almost be the birth of the New Look although, in Coco's elegant hands, it would never have become the exaggerated style of Dior. The photo was published in American *Vogue* on 15 September 1939 just as war in Europe had been declared. It is a sad picture and with it hangs the question of what might have been if world events had taken a different turn?

(Fifty years later the look was the inspiration for another great designer. As Alice Mackrell notes in her book, *Coco Chanel*: 'When Karl Lagerfeld showed his collection for Chanel in July 1989 it was dubbed a modern version of Dior's New Look. Lagerfeld replied: "But it wasn't the New Look. It was inspired by Coco Chanel's 1939 collection that was never shown. She got there first and I've got the documents to prove it." ')[6]

Coco wrote to her brothers, Lucien and Alphonse, virtually separating herself from them and ending the financial support she had always given them. Only Julia's son, André Palasse, would continue to receive her support. She was an immensely wealthy woman, yet she seemed bedevilled by a belief that now she had closed her couture house, she would be short of money. To Lucien she wrote as though she had lost everything and was bankrupt: her business was at an end; she was heading for poverty; and he could no longer rely on her.[7]

Lucien responded by offering her his savings. She never saw him again as he died in March 1941 from a heart attack. Alphonse took a different view: he realised that it would change his lifestyle, the end of the allowances, free cars, the trips to Paris - but, *c'est la vie* - he wrote and said, 'My Gaby, you're in the drink. Had to happen.' [8] And he went on happily running his café-tobacco shop. He too would die without seeing his sister again.

It was a strange time. There was an uneasy feeling: with the declaration of war, people in Britain and France had expected bombs to start falling. For a moment in time, it was as though the war was suspended, hanging in the air, a nine-month lull which was called *the phoney war* in England, and the *drôle de guerre* by the French. The *couture* was in a depleted state, as many of the men working in it were mobilised but, in spite of this, the beginning of 1940 saw them preparing the spring collections. They had simply all asked for their leave during those weeks: the *couture* staff, the tailors, photographers, artists and fashion journalists had returned to their work to ensure that the houses could have their show. The shows were called, *Les Collections des Permissionnaires* or the Collections of Men on Leave,[9] and were a great success in spite of the bitter cold winter conditions, fuel shortages and burst pipes. Some American buyers made their way to Paris that year and, in spite of the dangers of travel and French red tape, managed to buy the clothes to send back stateside.

Paris enjoyed a cloudless spring that year, the chestnut trees blossomed in the Champs Elysées, many of the cinemas, theatres and cabarets were still open and Parisians strolled along the boulevards soaking up the spring sunshine, drank coffee at the café-terraces and did not worry too much about the war.

This false sense of security was soon shattered, as on 10 May 1940 Hitler launched an attack on northern and eastern France, with the German armies sweeping in from the Netherlands and Belgium. On the same day, Winston Churchill became Prime Minister of Great Britain. Thousands of refugees from Belgium, Holland and Luxembourg poured into France, and with the German Panzer tanks seeming unstoppable, the British and French armies were forced back to the sea at Dunkirk. With a three-day lull in the fighting, and aided by a French rearguard action at Lille, the British organised a massive evacuation of the beaches at Dunkirk, with a flotilla of large and small boats, and by 3 June 227,000 British troops and 110,000 French troops had been saved.

South to safety

The way was open for the Germans to take Paris, and the French government fled on 10 June to Vichy. Paris saw an exodus in those days before the Germans arrived. All those who could, the famous, the wealthy and those who were not, all had but one thought - to leave before the tanks arrived. They travelled south to the furthest corners of France. Even the Duke and Duchess of Windsor were among those picnicking at the roadside *en route*. Edna Woolman Chase describes what happened to the *Vogue* office:

> *'Tommy Kernan rode alone. He had left Paris at six o'clock in the evening of June 11, heading for Bordeaux, but, though alone in the car, he was not unaccompanied. Loaded in beside him were the Vogue ledgers and all the liquid cash of Les Éditions Condé Nast. When it grew dark he pulled over to the side of the road and slept in a field with the money under him.'* [10]

He was heading for a château, La Valade, which the office had rented in anticipation of providing a refuge for the staff.

Coco was among those who fled south by car, she went to Corbères, near Pau in the Pyrenees, where in earlier times she had holidayed with Boy.[11] Before the war she had bought a château, through Étienne Balsan for her nephew André Palasse and it was here that she stayed.[12] Étienne was still there, now married and still with his beloved horses. Coco was among friends.

***

33

France divided

By 14 June, and without a shot being fired, the Germans rolled into Paris and the swastika replaced the *tricolore* flying on the Hôtel de Ville. Under blue skies and in the brilliant summer sunshine the people of France continued their exodus, with millions heading south to escape the German armies.[13]

It was a dangerous journey, as columns of families, piled into cars, some on bicycles or on foot, pushing prams and handcarts, some in horse drawn farm carts containing as many of their personal treasures and family heirlooms as they could carry. With clothes and food packed up and rolling along the crowded roads, they faced the terror of being strafed by German planes and the uncertain prospect of finding food and shelter in the overflowing towns and villages of the south. Many were women alone with children and grandparents, worrying about husbands and teenage sons, serving in the French army who were trying to no avail to hold the advancing Germans at bay. Many young French soldiers had been taken prisoners and others, separated from their regiments, wandered the countryside seeking food and shelter mixed in with the mass of refugees. It was a scene of total chaos.

The French government seemed paralysed by defeatism and was loathe to fight back. Paul Reynaud, the French Prime Minister, appointed the eighty-four-year old Marshall Pétain as his Deputy. By 17 June, Reynaud resigned and the aged Pétain became Prime Minister, announcing that he intended to seek an armistice with the Germans. By doing so he hoped to preserve a national government for France and end the fighting - it was seen as the realistic thing to do, but the decision split France in two. The Vichy government ruled in name only, as the northern two-thirds of the country over which it presided, the Occupied Zone, was subservient to 'the rights of the occupying power'.[14]

Humiliation at Compiègne

Hitler chose the forest of Compiègne and the railway carriage used to witness Germany's defeat in 1918 for his humiliation of the French when signing the armistice on 22 June 1940. By agreeing the armistice, Hitler knew that the French were effectively out of the war and that the way was left clear for the invasion of Britain. By July those who had fled began making their way back to their homes and a kind of normality returned, as the German soldiers were seen to behave correctly and were friendly towards the population. The Occupation brought rich pickings for the Germans as northern France contained 67 per cent of the country's population with 25 million people, more than 75 per cent of her industry, 66 per cent of cultivated land, 70 per cent of her potatoes, milk, butter and meat and 97 per cent of fishing, in other words, the cream of this beautiful country.[15] The smaller, unoccupied Southern Zone, or 'free zone' with a population of 14 million people[16] with its wine and fruit-growing regions was regarded as less important, but a demarcation line was set up which required a *laissez-passer* to cross, and remained in effect until February 1943.[17]

Harsh terms were exacted, with France having to pay the Reich for the cost of being occupied. By the end of the war, this had amounted to nearly sixty per cent of her national income.[18] This was the 'Occupation', which began one of the worst periods in the history of France, which would see thousands of its citizens meet death in Nazi concentration camps, engulf the country in a mesh of suspicion and collaboration and set Frenchman against Frenchman.

Not all Frenchmen agreed with the Armistice. General Charles De Gaulle fled to England where, with the agreement of Winston Churchill and the British Government, he took charge of the French armies evacuated at Dunkirk and set up the Free French resistance movement. Regarded as a traitor by the Vichy Government, he was sentenced to death in his absence.

Coco's old friend, Winston Churchill, refused to capitulate to Hitler or to negotiate with him, even when defeat by the Germans seemed a possibility. In his first speech as Prime Minister he said, 'I have nothing to offer but blood, toil, tears and sweat.' In Paris, the Germans paraded with a military band down the Champs Élysées every morning, and in London, the Blitz started. As the bombs began to fall that September, many of London's landmarks were hit including St. Paul's Cathedral, Westminster Abbey and Euston Station.

The American President, Franklin D. Roosevelt, although he had turned down Reynaud's appeal for help before he fell from power, now agreed to the 'lend-lease' scheme. In December 1941, when the Japanese bombed the American navy at Pearl Harbour in Hawaii, America entered the war.

Back to Paris and a new lover

Those who had fled in the vast exodus began slowly to return to Paris. So too did Coco, where she found that the Germans had taken over many of the rooms at the Ritz Hotel for their officers. As a long-standing resident, who had for years stepped out of the back door of the Ritz and crossed the road to her couture house on rue Cambon, she was well-known as an important, influential and wealthy woman. The Germans allowed her to keep her rooms and she moved back into her suite, which would be her home for the duration of the war.

It was hardly the best time to start a romantic affair, but among the Germans in Paris was a tall, handsome, blonde, blue-eyed officer named Hans Gunther von Dincklage, who was nicknamed 'Spatz' or 'Sparrow' by his friends. Born in Hanover on 15 December 1896, he was the son of a German father and an aristocratic English mother. He had first come to Paris in 1928 and in 1935 had divorced his wife, Maximilienne, when it became known that she was of Jewish ancestry.[19]

Between the wars he was a member of the international 'smart set' and Coco may have known him then. He was regarded as a playboy and had many flirtations and conquests among society ladies. In 1933 he described himself as an attaché at the German embassy in Paris and was accepted into the drawing rooms of high society. Now he was part of the entourage of Ribbentrop, the Minister for Foreign Affairs of the Third Reich.[20]

Coco, alone and bored, with no salon to run, was soon having a love affair with Spatz and regarded him as more English than German. Her thinking must have been unclear on the true position of Spatz, or she may have been unaware of all his activities. Never a woman to take heed of others opinions and always a rebel, she apparently gave no thought to the damage she would do to her good name by consorting with the enemy.

Pierre Galante, later the editor of *Paris Match,* described Spatz as working as a spearhead of the Fifth Column clandestinely undermining the government and spreading defeatist propaganda among the French. Counter-espionage services found that he was an important *Abwehr* agent, part of the German military intelligence.[21]

Keeping a low profile, he and Coco went out little during the war. Coco spent her time making stage costumes for Jean Cocteau's theatre productions and sending parcels of warm clothing to soldiers in her friend Jean Marais' squadron, keeping up a war-time correspondence with him as he fought in the Free French Forces.[22]

She also tried to regain control of her perfume business from the Wertheimers. As Jews they were barred from owning a business in France and had moved to the United States, temporarily selling their interests in Chanel Perfumes to a Frenchman, Félix Amiot, the aviation pioneer.[23] Coco's attempts failed as Amiot held the Wertheimers' seventy percent share in the company, but she continued her legal battles with the Wertheimers for many years to come.

***

34
Couture keeps going – at a price

Paris was in a state of shock and the couture houses were in flux. Chanel had closed leaving only her boutique open to sell No.5 perfume and accessories. Others now had to make that same hard decision. As it turned out some closed, some remained open. Elsa Schiaparelli, wondering whether the importance of the couture business as propaganda for France was understood at this time, described the events of her last collection:

> 'From six hundred employees we came down to one hundred and fifty… some of the midinettes had to walk twelve miles to work. We built up a collection in three weeks hoping for some response. This was the 'cash and carry' collection with huge pockets everywhere so that a woman obliged to leave home in a hurry or to go on duty without a bag could pack all that was necessary to her… There was… the woollen boiler suit that one could fold on a chair next to one's bed so that one could put it on quickly in the event of an air-raid driving one down to the cellar.' [24]

She also recalled a scarf that was printed with the apt words: 'Monday - no meat. Tuesday - no alcohol. Wednesday – no butter. Thursday – no fish. Friday - no meat. Saturday – no alcohol... but Sunday – *toujours l'amour.*' [25]

As the Germans advanced, a fearful Schiaparelli telephoned Lucien Lelong to ask what the *couture* might do. Where could they go? They had discussions with Edward Molyneux, who suggested that they should share his premises in Biarritz and keep their three houses going, shipping the clothes they made to New York. At Bordeaux they met many of the other designers, including Piguet, Balenciaga, Patou and Heim, and together held a meeting in Madame Lanvin's office. As the meeting ended, word came through that the French government had agreed the armistice, and Occupation would be the order of the day. [26]

William Linton's old friend, Edward Molyneux left that night on the last boat from Bordeaux to England, Charles Creed became a liaison officer between the French and British armies, and Lucien Lelong returned to Paris to save the *couture*. The American Mainbocher, who had designed the Duchess of Windsor's wedding outfit, and Charles James returned to New York, while Schiaparelli left for a lecture tour of New York, but kept her Paris house open. Piguet was on military duty in Switzerland and Jacques Heim, who was Jewish and a Gaullist, went into hiding as he was under German surveillance and forbidden to do business. It was as though the *couture* was scattering to the winds. [27]

The spirit of the fashion world would never be extinguished, however. When she finally arrived in New York, a journalist asked Schiaparelli about the brooch, shaped like a bird, which she wore on her coat. 'It is a phoenix,' she said, 'a bird which, after being burned, rises again from the ashes and grows in full beauty. It is the symbol of France.' [28]

Berlin eyes the couture business

Hitler had set his sights on the lucrative couture business and planned to move it to Berlin, for him the cultural capital of the world. In his vision of the New European Order, he saw Berlin and Vienna as the new centres of fashion, reincarnating their glory days of the late-nineteenth century and bringing about the demise of the powerful French fashion industry. By August 1940, the Germans had informed Lucien Lelong, President of the *Chambre Syndicale de la Couture* of their plans to move all the designers and fashion houses to Berlin, together with the supporting skilled workers. The offices of the *Chambre Syndicale* were ransacked and its archives together with its client list, including all files on American buyers, were seized and taken to Berlin.[29] The plan was to open a training college in Berlin where young German women would be taught the crafts by the French professionals.[30]

Lelong recalled, 'One of the first things the Germans did was break into the syndicate offices and seize all documents pertaining to the French export trade. I told them that *la couture* was not a transportable industry, such as bricklaying.'[31] Lelong's reply to the Germans was brave in view of the dangerous times, and he wrote: 'You can impose what you will by force, but "Paris" *haute couture* is not transferable, either *en bloc* or bit by bit.'[32]

In 1940 Lelong was fifty-one-years old and came from a family who had long owned a small couture house and a textile company. At the age of twenty-four, after studying at the *Haute Études des Commerciales* in Paris, he designed his first collection, due to be shown in 1914. This was postponed as he was drafted into military service, but at the end of the war he started his own couture house. Producing beautifully crafted elegant clothes in luxurious textiles, he introduced a ready-to-wear collection in 1934, and had a number of young designers such as Pierre Balmain, Hubert de Givenchy and Christian Dior working for him.

Just before the outbreak of war in 1939, he had shown full-skirted, nipped-waist designs, which would return in the 'New Look' created by Dior in 1947.[33] He was a man well respected in the fashion world, running a first-class salon and elegant society women and wealthy foreign clients flocked to his house at 16 avenue Matignon. At ease in the highest circles, he had been married to a beautiful model, the Russian Princess Natalie Paley, half sister to Coco's former lover Prince Dmitri, who famously modeled his elegant, sculptural designs and frequently graced the pages of *Vogue*.

Lelong had been President of the *Chambre Syndicale* since 1937 and knew that it would be disastrous for Paris and France if the *couture* was lost to Germany. The *couture* was part of Parisian life and the industry had built up since the time of Louis XIV now employing over one hundred and twelve thousand skilled workers.[34] 'Couture is an industry whose importance goes far beyond its physical end product,' he would say.[35]

Lelong saves the couture for Paris

His determination to save the *couture* was fired by his knowledge that not only the jobs of thousands of workers depended on it, but also that it was vital to the French economy, now and in the future. National pride was at stake in holding on to the most prestigious fashion industry in the world and the skills built up over generations. Whole families were employed, not only in the fashion houses, but in the hundreds of specialist ateliers across France where the fine embroidery, lace, trimmings, fur, jewels and all that went into keeping the Parisian fashion industry at the top of the tree were crafted. It could not be allowed to falter and he knew that he had to convince the Germans that its demise would not be practicable. He would argue that Berlin did not have the skilled workers necessary, that only Paris had the expertise and skills that an industry such as this could not be moved *en masse,* and no other country could take over the dominance of Paris. He knew he had to succeed.

When Lelong went to Berlin in November 1940 with the support of the *Chambre Syndicale*, he found the Germans determined to set up the *couture* industry in Berlin. Thanks to his steadfastness and diplomatic persuasion, after long negotiations a compromise was reached: the archives were returned and it was agreed that the *couture* would remain in Paris, where it would operate under German rules. The terms were harsh and the designers found that they would have to serve a Nazi-approved, Franco-German clientele, with exports forbidden and suffer severe fabric rationing, with each fashion house only allowed to produce forty models, instead of the usual one hundred and fifty, for each collection.

In 1941 Lelong reopened his own house, while the Germans issued textile cards, comprising a points system, to each fashion house. The scarcity of textiles made it impossible to create a collection. The textile industry was decimated as eighty percent of French fabrics were taken by the German authorities for their own war effort; the Vichy government took seventeen percent to clothe its police and military, leaving the population of France with three percent of all production to clothe the nation.[36]

Lelong again had difficult negotiations with the Germans and succeeded in gaining exemptions for twelve houses. However, ninety-two houses stayed open, including Paquin, Pierre Balmain, Worth, Nina Ricci, Lanvin, Lelong, Marcel Rochas, Jacques Fath and Balenciaga. Madame Grès defiantly presented a collection in the colours of the French flag and was temporarily closed down by the Germans. The German Command, realising the scale of the *couture*, held more negotiations eventually leading to their allowing sixty houses to stay open. The customers at the couture houses were now likely to be the wives of German officers, or their girlfriends and mistresses, as well as those made rich by black-marketeering. Shortages began to bite as the Germans sent quantities of luxury goods back to Germany. France was being plundered. Those who stayed had to face the day-to-day fact that the Nazis were using everything that was French for their own purposes.

Without Lelong's courage and skill in negotiating it might have been a very different story for the *couture*. He said, 'Over a period of four years, we had fourteen official conferences with the Germans... at four of them they announced that *la couture* was to be entirely suppressed, and each time we avoided the catastrophe.' [37] The war was not only being fought on the battlefields: Lelong had saved twelve thousand textile workers from being deported into German war industries.

After the war, he published a report on the industry, the *'Lelong Report on French*

Lucien Lelong who saved French couture from relocation to Berlin during World War 2

Fashion from July 1940 to August 1944.' In it he wrote:

> *'It does not lie within the power of any nation to take away from Paris the creative genius of fashion, which, in the city where it belongs, is not only a spontaneous outburst of talent but the result of a tradition maintained by a body of specialist male and female workers employed in a number of different crafts.'* [38]

In the meantime, French women upheld their chic reputation as best they could.

Lisa Deharne, a poet and hostess of a Surrealist salon, wrote in *Les Lettres Françaises*:

> *'Yes, Parisian women, true Parisian women, were supremely elegant for four years, with the elegance of a racehorse and not of a horse pulling a hearse. With a tear in their eye but a smile on their lips, beautiful, well made-up, incredibly discreet and insolent in their impeccable suits, yes, they exasperated the Germans. The beauty of their hair, their complexion, their teeth, their slimness contrasting with the fat hideousness of those trouts wrapped in grey, [the German servicewomen], yes that got on the Germans' nerves. These Parisian women were part of the Resistance.'* [39]

But it was the ingenuity of the industry and of Frenchwomen themselves that kept up this spirit, as supplies and shortages of cloth became acute and they were driven to look for substitutes. Thick wooden soles were used on shoes; viscose for clothes was made from wood-pulp: with rayon and man-made fibres they were the only materials available. Restrictions on cloth, brought in from 1940, meant that a coat was allowed four metres and a blouse one metre: styles became skimpy with shorter skirts, but they were worn with humour and chic. Hats became not just a fashion statement but a symbol of defiance, as women used anything and everything to create bright wacky concoctions, aimed at cocking a snoot at German eyes. [40]

Edna Woolman Chase tells of the tensions in Paris in the first days of the war, and of the style upheld by the editor of French *Vogue*, Bettina Ballard:

> *'On September 5th came the first air-raid alert. Sick with dread, Bettina and her faithful maid Marcelle gathered up gas-masks, warm blankets, flashlights and money and descended to the cellar. Attired in Chanel jersey slacks, a Creed tweed jacket, a yellow scarf, a red knitted turban, woollen socks and bead sandals, she dazzled the blinking eyes of the other tenants of the apartment building, who, wrapped in old dressing gowns and shawls, sat in their cellar chairs shamed by such splendour.'* [41]

Times get tougher

Life became harsher as the war progressed. Jews had to register and were barred from work in the professions or public service and by 1942 had to wear the yellow star on their clothing. The persecution and harassment got worse as they became treated as outcasts from society. The Vichy government was hand in hand with the German Reich as the policy of internment began, followed by deportation as thousands of men, women and children were herded onto trains headed for concentration camps in Poland and Germany and to almost certain death. An atmosphere of fear reigned among people, with the population split between those who favoured the Vichy government, and those who supported the resistance movement, while those in hiding lived in fear of being denounced.

Ginette Spanier, the elegant and vivacious woman who was to become *Directrice* of Pierre Balmain's couture house, spent the war on the run in the southern unoccupied zone. Her husband, Doctor Paul-Émile Seidmann, had his licence to practice medicine taken away by the Germans because he was a French Jew. She would describe how they spent these years hiding with families who were sympathetic, and yet faced death if they had been found harbouring them. The Gestapo was everywhere, and there were French people who were willing to collaborate and denounce their neighbours. [42]

Coco's old friend from the days of the Ballets Russes, Serge Lifar described his own experiences. Since the end of the Ballets Russes he had been employed at the Paris Opera, as *maître de ballet,* choreographer and star dancer until the outbreak of war in 1939. During the period of the war, he remained in France, taking on a secret liaison job, and trying to protect the artistic world from the Germans. He had a certain influence with the Vichy government by passing himself off as a German agent, and Pierre Laval, the Prime Minister, on a visit to Paris, said to him, 'Above all, in so far as your influence reaches protect the Auvergnats, Chanel and all the others. Watch over them.' [43]

Lifar recounted that he spent long evenings talking with Coco, when she would sing, accompanying herself on the piano, and he was impressed with her musical ability. Sometimes she would read aloud from the French classics, and from the works of her favourite poet and former lover, Pierre Reverdy.[44]

***

35
Coco and the spymasters

Of all the bizarre twists of fate in Coco's life, the affair code-named *Modellhut* or Model Hat is perhaps the strangest. It began in 1943, when the fantastic notion was born in Coco's head that she could hasten the end of the war and bring about a negotiated peace - if only she could talk to her old friend, Winston Churchill.

That August she had turned sixty, perhaps a time in a woman's life when she takes stock. Ever the idealist with her feet on the ground, she decided that the war had gone on too long - she wanted it to end. She wanted to see peace, to save lives and a way of life, and any problem only required common-sense and application to sort it out. This was her belief.

Julia's son, André Palasse, had been taken prisoner by the Germans and sent to a P.O.W. camp in Germany. Coco was concerned to see her favourite nephew set free as his health was declining. At the beginning of the Occupation she had been introduced to a German Cavalry Captain, Rittmeister Theodor Mömm, by her lover, Spatz. As Spatz had not been able to gain André's freedom, he had called in his old friend, to see what influence he could use. Mömm had a background that induced Coco to trust him. Of German origin, he had been born in Belgium where his father managed a dye factory used by Manchester cotton manufacturers. His family had worked in textiles for five generations, and had returned to Germany in 1914 at the outbreak of war. Dr Mömm was now in Paris in charge of the French textile industry, which was under German administration.[45]

Knowing of her interest in all things equestrian, he told Coco that he was a cousin of a famous show-jumper who had won World Cups in 1935-36, and who Coco had so admired. These credentials impressed her and she sought his help in the matter of André. Mömm was able to obtain his release by re-opening Tissus Chanel, a small textile mill near St Quentin in northern France, which he testified was owned by Coco and which the German authorities agreed that André should manage.[46]

Dr Mömm, therefore, was her choice to act as liaison with the German High Command in arranging for her to meet with Winston Churchill. He could scarcely conceal his surprise when she broached the matter, and told him of her scheme. He knew her as a talented, vital woman who had built up her fashion and perfume empire through her originality and hard work. But to meet with Churchill and change the course of the war - that was something else.

Chanel's biographer, Edmonde Charles-Roux, described how Mömm listened to her impassioned voice a she acted out her imaginary conversation with her old friend. To her, it was as normal as if she had been talking to him at Roquebrune, when she visited with the Duke of Westminster. Pacing the floor of her drawing room at rue Cambon she declared:

> 'You foretold blood and tears and your prediction has already been fulfilled. But that won't give you a name in history, Winston. Now you must spare human lives and end the war. By holding out a hand to peace you will show your strength. That is you mission.'

The stupefied Mömm felt that he could see Churchill, wreathed in cigar smoke, growling, 'You're right, Coco, you're right.' [47]

Thirty years later, Theodor Mömm would say, 'The force of a unique personality.' [48]

This could be important or it could be a fiasco, Mömm had no doubt. Coco was asking him to obtain permission for her to make a return trip to Madrid, to meet Sir Samuel Hoare, the British Ambassador, whom she believed would arrange for her to meet Churchill and put forward her ideas for Anglo-German talks, which would be held in total secrecy.

The German High Command was not known for its benevolence towards French *couturières*, not even Mademoiselle Chanel. If he took this to Berlin, Dr Mömm knew he had to protect himself as such ideas in times of war could be construed as treason. Considering his position, he decided to make his first approach to the Foreign Affairs Ministry where a Secretary of State, Baron Steengracht von Moyland, agreed to see him. The Baron, suspicious of Chanel's motives and connections, was not impressed. Mömm was politely told that no action would be taken and that the plan was 'not to be pursued.' [49]

That Mömm did not give up at this point, is testament to Coco's powers of persuasion. On reviewing his options, he decided to approach, somewhat reluctantly, the Reich Central Security Office, which came under the authority of Hitler's most trusted officer, Heinrich Himmler. This was a dark maze of departments dealing with counter-espionage and the supervision of foreign intelligence. Mömm counted himself fortunate when Walter Schellenberg, the Head of AMT VI, the Foreign Intelligence Service, agreed to see him.

Walter Schellenberg was the youngest of Hitler's SS officers, and in 1943 was thirty-three years old, known as a handsome, charming man with polished manners. He had graduated from Bonn University where he studied law, and was working with a judge who advised the penniless student to join the Nazi Party to further his career. In May 1933, at the age of twenty-three he joined the SS and was given a series of assignments to prove his ability.

By 1940, he had been given the task of compiling a list of over two thousand prominent Britons who were to be arrested after a successful invasion of Britain. He was also to arrange numerous plots of subterfuge and intelligence gathering including a plot to kidnap the Duke and Duchess of Windsor, who had fled France at the invasion and who were in Lisbon *en route* to the Bahamas, where the Duke was appointed Governor for the duration of the war.[50] The Nazis hoped that the Duke, with his pro-German sympathies, would be a quisling King when they defeated Britain. It seems unlikely that the Duke would have acted against the interests of Britain: he may have been foolish and naive in his understanding of Hitler, but he was not a traitor.[51] Schellenberg failed as the plot turned into a fiasco and the Duke and Duchess sailed for the Bahamas.

Despite this setback, Schellenberg was viewed as a gifted and highly intelligent man by the German High Command. His superiors soon recognised that he could be used as a spy and his meteoric rise began. By the time Mömm visited him on Coco's mission, he was Hitler's top spy-master. What Mömm had to relate caught his interest. He had his own ideas about a negotiated separate peace with the Western Allies, leaving the way clear to pursue the war on the eastern front against Russia, and Communism and his boss, Heinrich Himmler, was not unsympathetic to this thinking. In Britain, too, there were supporters of these ideas. At the beginning of the war, there were those in the British aristocracy who had some sympathy with the Nazis. Even the elderly Queen Mary, at this time, was known to lean towards the compromise peace solution, much to the annoyance of Churchill.[52]

In the context of what was going on at this time, Coco's scheme was not as mad as it might appear. The Allies' Casablanca Conference had taken place in January 1943 and there was no compromise in the terms that Churchill and Roosevelt announced. In short, there would be no negotiations, only acceptance of unconditional surrender by the Germans. While this was a cause for joy among the majority it did not meet with universal approval. There were supporters of the Vichy government who would have supported a negotiated peace and, in England, there was a minority, including the Duke of Westminster, who wished to stop the bombing and save Europe. We may never know whether the Duke of Westminster was an influence behind Coco's plans, but she certainly held similar views to his and other members of the British aristocracy on how to bring

Walter Schellenberg, the German SS officer, Chanel's wartime German connection

peace to Europe. Churchill was not about to give credence to his old friend's arguments - the war had been bloody, lives had been lost and Hitler had to be knocked out of the arena. There could be no compromise.[53]

The plot thickens

Schellenberg agreed with Coco's requests, and Mömm returned to France to tell her that she could set off for Madrid to meet Sir Samuel Hoare immediately. A shock awaited him. Coco announced that she could not travel alone to Madrid: she never travelled alone, and she wished to take a companion. Mömm assumed that she was going to say Spatz would accompany her, but no, she wished to take her old friend, Vera Bate Lombardi, who had been married to Fred Bate, European Manager for NBC, and a friend of the Duke and Duchess of Windsor [54] but who was now married to an Italian colonel and living in Rome. There was nothing for it, Mömm thought, but to return to Schellenberg and ask for further permission.

At this point, Coco was practicing deceit in order to get her own way: she knew that she needed Vera along or Churchill might not see her. He was unlikely to refuse a request from Vera, with her connections to the British Royal Family but she had to find a way to get Vera to agree to accompany her without divulging the real reason for the trip.

Commonsense went out of the window and it may have been Spatz who was the perpetrator. On 29 October 1943, a tall German officer turned up on Vera's doorstep at 31 via Barnaba Oriani carrying a huge bouquet of red roses from Coco. Vera's husband was in hiding from the German occupiers in the Frascati hills, and Vera was living anxiously, alone. The officer delivered the roses together with a letter from Coco, asking her to join Coco in Paris, where she was going to reopen her fashion house. Vera turned down the invitation as she wished to stay in Rome. On the morning of 11 November, Vera found herself arrested and taken to Mantellate, the women's prison.

Meanwhile, Mömm was talking to an increasingly annoyed Schellenberg in Berlin, and on giving him the name of Coco's preferred travelling companion, Schellenberg asked his Rome unit to investigate her. The report came back straightaway: Vera had been in prison for two weeks on the orders of the Gestapo, on a charge of supposed espionage. Schellenberg was furious at this turn of events and ordered Vera's release, to be personally undertaken by the top SS colonel in Rome. She was to be treated as the society lady she was and escorted to Paris to meet Coco. By this time Vera was sure that something sinister was about to happen to her and she refused to go. Word came back from Schellenberg: he was sorry, but he

Vera Bate with Chanel in Scotland, 1925. Vera was Chanel's introduction to English high society

must insist and, if she did not go to Paris, she would be returned to prison.[55]

In a further bizarre twist, Vera was told that an old friend and notable society figure in Rome, would accompany her to Milan, to take a flight to Paris. This was the German Prince Eddie Bismarck, and although not in the German forces, he would be wearing an SS uniform. Vera again refused but, after mulling it over all night, saw that she had no option and decided that she would agree to go to work in Paris: perhaps Coco would explain these strange events.

But events got even stranger. Eventually Vera arrived in Paris and found Coco waiting for her at the Ritz. No, Coco told her, she was not re-opening in Paris, but in Madrid, and she wanted Vera to come to Spain with her. Fashion was on the move.[56]

Neither woman was being honest with the other. Coco was making plans to see Sir Samuel Hoare, the British ambassador in Madrid, to arrange a meeting with Churchill, and Vera, in spite of appearing to go along with Coco's plans, was in fact planning to see the same ambassador. Her idea was to gain his support for her to return to the part of Italy held by the Allies, where she hoped to be reunited with Berto, her husband. The farce deepened when each, unknown to the other, visited Sir Samuel, Coco seeing him and Vera seeing his Intelligence Officer. As they were leaving they met face-to face in the embassy hallway. There was nothing for it but to admit the truth. Coco told Vera that the ambassador was going to pass her message to Churchill, but there is no record of the meeting or the message in the British archives.[57]

Coco brought doubts to Sir Samuel's mind when he discovered what Vera had told of the coercion she had suffered. Coco had not mentioned her companion at all and it made the ambassador suspicious. After several days, word came from London that Churchill was ill: Clement Atlee made the announcement in the House of Commons on

16 December 1943. He had been near collapse, and his illness meant he was unable to see either his War Cabinet or the Chiefs of Staff, all his meetings were cancelled, and real concern was felt about his health.

Eventually, Winston went to Marrakech to convalesce, and Coco knew that her moment had passed. She returned in disappointment to Paris. Vera stayed in Madrid and earned her living by painting equestrian scenes on screens. Suspicion still hung over her and the British would not allow her to return to Italy until six months after Rome was liberated, in July 1944.

Coco wrote Vera a stern letter of reproof for what she saw as her betrayal, and then she took off to Berlin to see Schellenberg. It is interesting that in her letter to Vera she would say, 'My English friends cannot blame me, at any rate, or find the least thing wrong in what I have done. That is enough for me.' [58]

In spite of information given in British Foreign Office files inadvertently de-classified in 1972 that she was privy to secrets embarrassing to the government and the Royal Family, the true facts of these bizarre events are probably still hidden. Speculation exists that Coco knew too much: about the Windsors and about the fact that Churchill broke his own rules by paying the Germans to protect their house in Paris.[59]

What did Schellenberg and Coco talk about when they met? Was she merely reporting her failure, a fact that he would have already been fully informed of, or were there other conclusions to be drawn? All that is certain, is that it would be to her he would look to for help in his hour of need after the war. And Coco was the woman courageous enough to offer just that.[60]

This has been the accepted version of events, but it is interesting to note that there may have been other explanations. Writing in 1965, Serge Lifar mentions that he had helped Coco at a time when she had assisted her friend, Vera Bate Lombardi to escape to Spain. The grateful Mrs Bate Lombardi had related her escape on Allied radio and mentioned Chanel's name. Lifar reports that Coco was not disturbed.[61]

And Pierre Galante, to whom Coco granted interviews towards the end of her life, recorded that, at the end of 1942, the BBC credited Coco with helping Vera Bate Lombardi to leave Italy. She also, at the request of her architect Robert Streitz, who built La Pausa and who was a member of the Resistance, helped his friend Professor Serge Voronov who was being held by the Nazis.[62]

***

36
Meanwhile, back at Linton's...

While Coco was living a life of high drama in Europe, in Carlisle Nessy was coming to terms with her father's unexpected death and getting to grips with her new responsibilities: running a tweed mill and a kennel in a country preoccupied with war. Her father's premature death at the age of sixty-five must have come as a great shock to Nessy. She had worked in the business since leaving Cheltenham Ladies' College and training in Textile Design at the Scottish College of Textiles in Galashiels: by 1938 at the age of thirty-five there was little that she did not know about the company's operation.

She was her father's sole heir, having being named in the will he made in October 1925, and receiving £50,000 at his death (about £1.8million at today's value), making her a wealthy woman. Nessy also had other considerations to think of. Since receiving her first deerhound as a gift from her friend Norah Hartley, she had set up the Geltsdale Kennels behind the house at Great Corby, and was by now a well known breeder and

Linton's buy in their yarns from suppliers all over the world or use their own twisting machines to produce unique fancy yarns. In the dyehouse, they can dye yarns to any colour specification, as well as piece-dyeing whole fabrics. The warp of the fabric is produced on a warp mill or vertical Hergeth mill and the warp beams are then loaded into the loom for the fabric to be woven. The fabric then goes through a variety of finishing processes - darning, washing, spinning and drying, before being closely scrutinised for quality. Fabrics are then press finished for a smooth effect or steam finished to provide a fluffy texture. A final quality control check ensures that the fabrics are to the required standard before they are packed, ready to send to customers.

George Arnott Linton, father of George Stirling Linton who became Managing Director of Linton's when William died

exporter of championship dogs. A family conference took place, no doubt with advice from William's brother, her uncle, Robert Linton, known as Uncle Bob.

The Linton brothers had always been close and Bob, four years younger than William, had started his working life at the age of fourteen as an apprentice clerk in Selkirk. Together with Margaret Horsburgh, he was witness at William's marriage to Helen Horsburgh in 1898. Bob joined Edinburgh Corporation in 1896, and by 1901 was a Law Clerk there. He married Helen Beattie Oliver of Selkirk in 1905, and became a qualified solicitor spending forty-three years working in the Town Clerk's office in Edinburgh. During the 1930s he was one of four Depute Town Clerks, working under the Town Clerk, Sir Andrew Grierson. A man of wide professional experience, he specialised in Parliamentary work and was an authority on municipal law. He was associated in the work of consolidating the local Acts of Parliament, and by 1939 was working with the Town Clerk, Mr David Robertson on the preparation of two Draft Bills in connection with the Forth Road Bridge and negotiations for the extension of the city of Edinburgh, which were suspended due to the war.[63] Uncle Bob, and his two daughters, had always been close to William and Nessy, spending holidays at Hill House, Great Corby, as Nessy's family photos of 1922 show.

Another of William's brothers, John, was chief designer at George Roberts & Co. in Selkirk. He became famous for inventing a new type of men's suiting, used in Savile Row, London, by top class tailors. It was named 'crammed lined silk' and had a band of twenty threads of multi-coloured silk woven into the woollen cloth, giving it a distinctive sheen.[64]

After William's death, the company needed a tweed designer and the family decided that George Stirling Linton, who had studied textile design at the Scottish College of Textiles in Galashiels [65] and was working as a tweed designer, would come to Carlisle and run the business with Nessy. George was the son of George Arnott Linton, William's cousin, who was also a tweed designer at George Robert's Forest Mill in Selkirk. George Jnr had carried on the family tradition by studying textile design, attending the College from 1933 to 1936 where he gained bronze and silver medals in weaving, finishing and design as well as the diploma in Woollen and Worsted Manufacture.[66] However, it would not be long before George was called up for war service and joined the Royal Air Force, based in Canada. It left Nessy on her own again facing the problems of running the mill in wartime.

Margaret Linton, George Stirling Linton's mother

During the war George became a pilot, training at the American Army Air Forces Advanced Flying School and, along with other Royal Air Force personnel, graduated and received his Diploma at the United States Army's Southeast Air Corps Training Centre at Maxwell Field, Montgomery, Alabama on 3 July 1942.[67] The arrangement for British pilots to receive training at American bases was part of the Lend-Lease Act which the United States Congress passed on 11 March 1941. With the fall of France and the retreat of the British Expeditionary Force from Dunkirk in 1940, Britain was fighting for its very survival and the Royal Air Force had only prevented the invasion of the British Isles by holding air supremacy against the German Wehrmacht. The

United States, although not yet in the war, helped the British by setting up pilot training programmes and the first 750 cadets arrived at Maxwell Field in the autumn of 1941. In all, 4370 British pilots graduated and qualified for combat duty in the Royal Air Force.[68] George Linton was eventually based in Canada.

World War 2 had a major impact on textile manufacturers, with Government restrictions on exports and the demands on production for the war effort. In truth, Nessy was taking over the reins of the company at a very difficult time. On 30 June 1939 *The Carlisle Journal* gave a review of the industries of Carlisle and Cumberland, under the title 'Progressive Cumberland', and outlined the achievements of the Carlisle textile firms, noting with some pride that Morton Sundour Fabrics had supplied soft furnishings for the new Cunard-White Star liner, *Mauretania,* which had made her maiden voyage to New York the previous week. It also commented on the success of Linton's Cumberland Homespuns and R. Todd & Sons 'who occupy the great building known as Shaddon Mills, hard by Dixon's Chimney, which forms such a landmark for miles around.'[69]

Nessy's war effort

This optimism would change into concern as the year unfolded: a difficult time for Nessy as events which would affect the business began to bite. The British government introduced constraints on textile manufacturers from 1939. The four main ones were Price Control, Yarn Rationing, Export Allocations and Clothing Rationing by coupons. These constraints were to remain in use until the early post-war period. Further restrictions were imposed by the balance between Utility Quotas, Export locations and ordinary 'free' Home Trade.[70]

It was a difficult year on a more personal level too. With property prices low in Cumbria, Nessy decided to move to a more spacious house, an elegant country property, Geltsdale House on Plains Road, Wetheral.[71] It was an imposing stone-built gabled property built in the 1880s by Christopher Ling, a future mayor of Carlisle, and well known for its beautiful views and pleasant location. There was an adjacent Lodge to house McMullen the chauffeur, surrounded by a low stone wall and black iron railings, clipped yew trees graced the garden, and the honey-coloured, dressed-stone walls were part-covered with ivy.

The house was set in a village not far from Great Corby and Nessy held a house warming party for her friends. The deerhounds were soon settled in their new home. Great Corby and Wetheral are linked by a picturesque railway viaduct which spans the green valley of the River Eden. Until recent times the villages were also linked by a ferryboat service

George Stirling Linton, pilot in the RAF during World War 2

George Stirling Linton's pilot's diploma from Maxwell Field airbase, Alabama, 1942

Geltsdale House, Wetheral - Nessy's home at the beginning of World War 2 until it was taken over by the Air Ministry in 1941

and the ferryman's cottage still stands on the river bank at Corby. The spire of Holme Eden church, where Nessy later stayed in the vicarage, lifts among the trees of this beautiful area of woodland and meadow, overlooking the silver ribbon of the Eden.[72] It was in the churchyard here that Cranston Waddell was buried.

The beautiful pastoral scenery of Cumbria would soon become the home and safe haven of thousands of children. The outbreak of war meant that children were evacuated from cities such as London and Newcastle, which were under threat of air-raids and devastation from bombing by German aircraft, and sent to safe places like Cumbria. This government policy was meant to save lives and give respite from the ravages of war. In all, some three and a half million women and children were part of one of the largest social upheavals ever seen in Britain.[73]

Susan Goodman, in her evocative book *Children of War,* describes the events when the children who had been signed up for evacuation by their parents had to leave.

> *The signal to begin the evacuation was given over the radio on the evening of 31 August, and early the following morning the children, clutching suitcases and sandwiches and perhaps a sibling by the hand, left home for their assigned meeting places in school yards. Their teachers were waiting with lists and banners and labels, and as the sun rose across the country the exodus began. Few parents had the time or opportunity, to say goodbye before the children were off, marching to the buses that took them either directly out of the towns or to main-line railway stations to catch the special trains painstakingly laid on for the evacuation.'* [74]

Cumbria was fortunate because it did not suffer the blitz of German bombing in the way that other areas of the country did. Nevertheless it played a full part in the war effort.

The first sign of the start of hostilities was the arrival of 37,000 evacuees, mainly from the north-east of England.[75]

Before long Carlisle's local newspaper was reporting on the human crisis which resulted from the threat of the coming war. On Friday 1 September 1939, Carlisle received four thousand evacuees, at London Road railway station, and in the following days the surrounding Border Rural Area received over seven thousand evacuees from the city of Newcastle-upon-Tyne. They were mainly school-age children, but were followed by pregnant women, small children and people with physical disabilities and had left home- with little more than a quick hug and a whispered 'keep your pecker up'. The city had made detailed plans for their reception and a survey in Carlisle had shown that there were voluntary offers of accommodation for over seven thousand people.[76]

The children were met off the trains, each clutching their suitcase, gas mask and luggage label with their name on it, and taken to de-training centres. The centre for Brampton area was in the Tweed Mill, where these brave, bewildered children were met by the local ladies and checked in, before being driven to their new homes. Nessy had several of the young evacuees at Geltsdale House, and they immediately fell in love with the deerhounds.

The duration of the war was a difficult time for many of the larger breeds of dogs, particularly if there were not large numbers of them. Deerhounds were in this category and Nessy was one of sixteen breeders who determined to keep the strength of the breed intact. In spite of her busy life at the mill and all her other activities helping in the war effort, the Geltsdales (as they had become known) were producing new litters of puppies. As a further precaution against possible loss of the breed under the threat of invasion, a famous American sculptress Mrs A. H. Huntingdon, who was a deerhound enthusiast, visited Britain and took back a team of the finest dogs for safe-keeping in America until the end of the war. All Dog Shows were suspended for the duration, as Britain concentrated on war work.[77]

Another loss for Nessy

Nessy was engrossed in her work but would soon be even more alone as she suddenly found herself without the support of Uncle Bob, when he died of a heart attack in Edinburgh on 14th November 1939 at the age of sixty-three. He had been a widower for some years, and had been ill in 1937 and planned to retire, but the then Town Clerk, David Robertson, made a special request for him to return to give the Town Council the benefit of his experience and knowledge.[78]

In less than two years Nessy had lost both of her stalwart supporters and would have to go forward into the difficult war years alone.

She threw herself into her work and by September 1940 she was reporting to *Our Dogs* magazine that 'Miss Kidd, the kennel manageress, was busy getting the cellars ready as air-raid shelters for both the children and the dogs. By now, each child had "claimed" a deerhound to take home, and one small boy continually asked, "Please, Miss Linton when will 'Boy' be back?" A dog who had gone to a new owner, and whose ways had claimed all of this small fellow's affection. "Boy" stood thirty-four inches at shoulder; his admirer had seen five summers, so they must have looked an oddly assorted pair going about together.'[79]

The deerhounds caused Nessy some anxious times, especially when one of them decided to go 'walk-about'. When Ch. Diana of Geltsdale disappeared into a factory yard near the railway, all were out searching for her. Eventually going into a sports club with disused gardens and then on to the house, Nessy found herself looking through a window onto a vista of camp beds. The military had taken over the house, and there was Diana stretched out asleep on one of the beds. Surprised soldiers appeared from all sides and it became clear that they were of the same mind as the small evacuees: they wanted to keep Diana. She had been well-fed they assured Nessy, and was basking in the attention. One soldier plaintively said, 'You're not surely going to take her away after all the trouble we have had in getting her here.' In the end, she was carried bodily out of the window and led away. 'Miss Linton's hounds have always been much-travelled folk, accustomed to accept the homage of strangers, so Diana's outing was just a little diversion to lift the tedium of war-time conditions.' [80]

The advent of the evacuees was not without problems on both sides. Many came from inner-city slum backgrounds and cleanliness and manners were not their *forte*. There were sad stories also of children being badly treated and given little affection. On the whole, however, everyone survived the experience with good humour.

On a visit to Carlisle to see his young citizens, the Lord Mayor of Newcastle, Alderman W. R. Wallace would say, 'Nothing will do this old town of Carlisle so much good as to see the Newcastle children smiling in the streets – let them see you do it, and let them know that you come from Newcastle simply because you are smiling. It isn't at all like Newcastle there today, there are no boys and girls there, and we want you back. But while you are here, remember that you represent a great city. I only hope that Carlisle will not be disappointed when you go back home.' [81]

War! Are we at war?

The citizens of Carlisle were not without their own brand of humour. On asking a man for his views on the present conflict, a local reporter received the sarcastic reply, 'War! Are we at war? Good Heavens, I thought it was the Army's annual manoeuvres.' But this was followed by the wistful comment, 'It is the queerest war ever. Poland has been wiped out and we don't seem to have been able to do anything about it.' [82]

Carlisle was not the only place in Cumbria to play host to the children. Many other towns were also helping and Keswick, in the northern Lake District, became home to students from Roedean Public School in Brighton and to students from St Katherine's Teacher Training College in Liverpool. [83]

It must have seemed as if the whole world was on the move. The North–East coast of England was being particularly hard-hit as the German bombers tried to wipe out the shipyards and destroy coal supplies on the River Tyne. On 30 August 1940, Miss W. S. Walker was writing to *Dog World* magazine:

> *'We had to leave our house at Seaton very suddenly, as it got decidedly "warm" in that quarter, so in twenty-four hours we had packed and come to Wetheral, as we had heard what a good hotel there was there. We had a hectic journey across England; my mother, myself, two Dachshunds, and a Dandie, plus piles of luggage in the first car, followed by my sister, the Deerhounds, another Dandie, and more luggage in the second. However, we arrived somehow, and there we settled down until we could find a house. Miss Linton, we can never sufficiently thank for her kindness to us. She took Fruggie, Petunia and the two Dachshunds, and for the last fortnight my two show Cairns as well! I tremble to think what would have happened but for her generosity, as the hotel would only take two dogs. My mother has just bought this place (Caldew House, Dalston, Cumberland), and it is really a lovely place for dogs, We have two lots of stabling, a big coach-house, a large garage and a big paddock for the dogs to roam in at will, so they are in clover.'*

The editor said, 'It is good news to hear that they are so well settled with their dogs, and looking forward to "after the war" with shows to go to. Not a single complaint after having all one's roots torn up. Surely this is the kind of thing that is an example indeed in these days, when the Nazis are trying to shake people's nerves and break our resolution to carry on this war until Hitler's schemes are in the dust.' [84]

By 1941 Nessy was on the move again as her house was taken over by the Air Ministry and became known as RAF Wetheral, part of Maintenance Command 50 Wing. On 21 November 1941 *Our Dogs* reported on a cheery letter received from Miss Linton on more upheaval for the Geltsdales, who were now housed at Holme Eden Vicarage, under the care of Miss Kidd. McMullen, the chauffeur was allowed to live on in the lodge at Geltsdale House, and when he was off duty he would go across to Holme Eden to walk his favourite dog, Jason of Geltsdale.[85]

Cumbria's war

Cumbrians may have escaped any significant bombing, but the wheels of war still turned as, amid the small towns and rural villages, the silver lakes and misty mountains, from the industrial west coast to the gentle green slopes of the Eden valley, they did their bit. Royal Air Force stations sprang up along the Solway Plain, from Silloth to Crosby. At Kingstown, an RAF aircraft maintenance unit, 14MU, was built. A large stores depot, it spread along the north of the county as far as Longtown. The Army also arrived in force. Hadrian's Camp was built to house three thousand soldiers and the nine-hole golf course at Durranhill became a smaller camp with the old clubhouse acting as the officer's mess.[86]

Carlisle Castle was at full stretch and huts were built in the adjoining Bitts Park to take the overflow of service personnel. In 1940, the Home Guard was raised to defend the area from invasion: these were older, often retired, men who undertook local security duties, such as checking that all black-out blinds were closed on windows, and were prepared to defend local communities in the event of invasion. People joked about the image of 'Dad's Army', but these men were the only local defence at that time and served with bravery. Paratroopers were seen as the main threat and pill boxes to defend the roads into Carlisle were built. The civilian population was at the centre of this hive of activity. *The Cumberland News,* reporting on a talk given by David Hay to the Friends of Tullie House, described it thus:

> 'The ARP wardens, the nurses, particularly the VAD's at Fusehill, which was partly turned over to be a military hospital; the Women's Land Army on the farms and training at Newton Rigg [Agricultural College]; the auxiliary fire service, many of whom went to Liverpool to help in the blitz, as did many of the Civil Defence. The ambulances in the city were driven by women and the WVS carried out a multitude of jobs.

> 'Then there were the canteens which sprang up in Carlisle. The YMCA's John Peel hut, TocH, the Salvation Army, the Citizen's League and the Catholic Women's League served not only the troops stationed locally, but also many passing through in convoys and troop trains.

> 'The youth organisations were all involved in the war effort – the Air Training Corps, the Army Cadet Force, the Scouts and Guides and the Boy's Brigade.'[87]

On May 25 1940, the *Cumberland News* reported that:

> 'The organization of the Local Defence Volunteers is progressing smoothly and rapidly and in a few days the patrols will all be on the look-out for Nazi parachutists who might attempt to land in this county.'[88]

By 8 March 1941, Major-General Spears, Boy Capel's old boss, now Member of Parliament for Carlisle, inspected Carlisle City Home Guard at Carlisle Castle. It was the first time that the battalion had paraded with rifles and bayonets.

Cumbrians also took part in the salvage efforts of War Weapons Week; the money–raising events held to pay for arms and equipment; allotment holders were Digging for Victory, and everyone, even babies, held gas masks. Identity cards and ration books were the order of the day as women joined any queue available to buy food for their families. German and Italian prisoners of war were held at camps in the county, the largest at Moota in the west. Local factories were all involved in war work, making everything from submarine nets to aircraft wings.[89]

Perhaps one of the most ambitious and inspired schemes was the 'Carlisle Spitfire Fund' launched by the Mayor, where £5000 was raised to buy a Spitfire aircraft for the RAF. Everyone was involved, from children selling apples to the Workington United Steel Company orchestra giving a concert in the Lonsdale cinema. The most appealing sight must have been the two children who took their pet lambs to join the collectors, and money flowed into the boxes strapped to their sides. The *Carlisle Journal* wrote: 'Their mute appeal met with a ready response from the shopping public.' Eventually £5500 was sent to Lord Beaverbrook, who in his thanks to the Mayor said, 'their Spitfire shall certainly be called 'City of Carlisle.'[90]

They took the upheavals in their stride without fuss. Throughout all this activity Nessy kept Linton Tweeds going and stayed in touch with her network of suppliers and designers. Todd's mill began spinning khaki yarn as Linton's, like many other companies, were told what they had to produce: utility cloth for the home market and khaki cloth for the military. A far cry from the soft, glowing tweeds, but playing their part in keeping the country going.

✳✳✳

37
Fashion under siege

The war meant that the fashion industries of Europe and America were operating in a vacuum as Paris was isolated from the rest of the world. During these years, the American manufacturers were left without their twice-yearly trips to the Paris collections. In the 1930s it had been standard practice for the couture houses in London and Paris to sell models to buyers from the American and Canadian department stores. These took the form of *toiles,* copies of models made of a cheap material such as calico, which were bought legitimately each season. The *toiles* were the basis of the garments made for sale at more reasonable prices, and they were an important source of income to the couture houses.[91]

The American fashion industry believed that Paris-led fashion was dead, and looked to its own designers to develop new styles and designs for the domestic fashion industry. The designers rose to the challenge in spite of shortages of textiles. Manufacturers, their workforce depleted by men serving in the armed forces and obligated to supply cloth for the armed services, did their best to meet demand, in spite of the Regulation L.85 restrictions imposed on women's clothing in 1943.

The war created a boost to the fashion industry, as Mainbocher and Charles James were now back in New York, and two designers who had worked for the successful ready-to-wear designer Hattie Carnegie (well-known for adapting French fashions for the American market) now started out on their own.

Norman Norell had been at Paramount Pictures where he designed for stars such as Gloria Swanson, and worked in costume design on Broadway, before joining Hattie Carnegie in 1928. In 1941 he went into partnership with Anthony Traina forming Traina-Norell where he designed chemise dresses, fur trench coats, empire-line dresses and his famous sequined-covered sheath dresses – using unrationed sequins.

Claire McCardell also came to prominence during the war years. She too had designed for Hattie Carnegie but, in 1940, returned to Townley Frocks where she had worked until 1938. Here she began to design sports clothes and practical, wearable clothing that suited women's lifestyles. She brought in innovatory ideas such as the wraparound dress and capezio pumps (or 'ballerinas' as they became known in the UK) which would become an American favourite. (She died in 1958 having become one of the most influential American designers.[92])

Both of these designers would take the American fashion industry to new heights during this period of isolation from the influence of Paris: American ready-to-wear never looked back.

British designers fight back

While in occupied France the fashion and textile industries were being squeezed by the Germans, in Britain the situation was different but no less difficult, and the constraints on manufacturers were also felt by the fashion houses. Edward Molyneux, now back in London, played a major role in the war effort of promoting British fashion to American buyers and *Harper's Bazaar* estimated in January 1941 that British exports of models, fabric and trimmings to American buyers totalled £500,000 - in today's value over £14million - largely due to his efforts.[93] It was Molyneux's links with Paris and French style that gave him such *cachet* in the eyes of discerning Americans, as store buyers in San Francisco, Chicago and New York cabled their appreciation of his work, and his efforts enhanced London's position on the global fashion scene.

The British Board of Trade was trying to juggle many balls, keeping them all in the air at the same time: it was not an easy task. In 1942 they requested that the ten major couture houses in the UK should form the Incorporated Society of London Fashion Designers (INCSOC). Before the war, the major houses had been part of the Fashion Group of Great Britain, but this had gone into decline.

The founder of INCSOC was Harry Yoxall, the managing editor of London *Vogue,* and its purpose was to promote British fashion by sending collections abroad. With the fall of France, designers such as Edward Molyneux and Charles Creed were refugees in London. Harry Yoxall gave a cocktail party, inviting them and the London designers, together with leading resident American buying agents, to meet and try to get the society off the ground.

Although brought into being to assist the war effort, INCSOC was to play an important role in the development of the British fashion and textile industries. It is worth quoting from their first annual report, those early, idealistic aims:

'a) *To maintain and develop the reputation of London as a centre of fashion*

b) *To collaborate with groups of fabric and other manufacturers, and with companies, firms and individuals, with a view to increasing the prestige of British Fashions, and promoting the sales of British Fashions in home and overseas markets.*

c) *To assist fashion designers by protecting their original designs; enabling them to exchange information to their mutual advantage, arranging dates for their respective showings; fostering the professional and trade interests of persons engaged in creating British fashions; developing the standards of skilled workmanship and representing the views of government and trade bodies to the press.'* [94]

Lofty aims indeed and perhaps a typically British version of the influential *Chambre Syndicale de la Couture Parisienne* founded in Paris in 1868, which looked to protect the interests of the fashion houses and to save the designers from plagiarism. Unauthorised copying had always been a problem, both for the couture and fabric designers and most went to great lengths to protect their designs. Chanel, unlike most women, to whom copying of their personal style or originality is anathema, had a relaxed view. She knew that she could not prevent it and so took it as a compliment. It meant that her look was seen everywhere, on the streets, the sidewalks and the boulevards. It meant success, but nevertheless the industry went to great lengths to prevent it.[95]

Hopes were high when, in order to raise foreign revenue for the war effort, the INCSOC designers sent a collection of designer clothes to South America, together with eighteen beautiful models to show them. They were promoting London as a centre of fashion, hoping to fill the gap left by the Parisian couture for the duration of the war. It might seem strange that it took a world war to bring about coordination and cooperation in the British fashion and textile manufacturing industries, but the importance of this development, seen as a no-brainer today, cannot be over-emphasised. This is what Harry Yoxall wrote to Edna Woolman Chase of American *Vogue*:

> *'I am trying to assist as a kind of midhusband at the birth of an Incorporated Society of British Designers, but it is a pretty hard function, as all the limbs, so to speak, are kicking in different directions.'* [96]

He despaired of the British couture houses ever achieving a joint marketing strategy, given the problems he had experienced with the South American collection.

The group was initially chaired by Edward Molyneux, followed by Norman Hartnell, and had presidents such as Lady Rothermere and Lady Pamela Berry. (Over the years, it also had royal patronage from Queen Elizabeth, the Queen Mother, Princess Margaret and Princess Marina.) It was the beginning of a period of professionalism in the British fashion industry.

Writing in his memoirs, *A Fashion of Life*, Harry Yoxall recalled, 'When the war came, our export effort was next in importance to the war effort itself. British wool textiles had a world-wide reputation, but except for tailor–mades and cashmere sweaters our fashions commanded no international respect. However, the government now wanted us to export models as well as yardage, and silks and cottons, as well as wool.' [97]

Hardy Amies joined the group even though at this time he was a serving soldier, having left Lachasse on his call-up to military service. The bombs might be falling over London, but with indomitable British spirit, the fashion houses were still producing collections. By now, Hardy was an officer in the Intelligence Corps, and was posted to the Canadian Corps. Later, making use of his gift of languages, he served as British liaison officer to the Belgian Section of the Special Operations Executive (SOE), training agents in sabotage and parachuting them into Belgium. The Board of Trade requested that he be given six weeks' leave to help take a collection to South Africa. [98]

Foreign revenue was key to the successful operation of the war, as weapons and supplies not produced at home had to be imported and paid for in cash. The government sought to raise revenue by a number of means. Those industries whose production was not required for the war effort were to make export drives. The Wool Textile Industry had already efficiently procured sufficient cloth for uniforms of the Armed Forces, and in March 1940, a body was set up, The Export Group for the Wool Textile Industry, to ensure that exports were directed to those countries who would be paid in sterling for war materials - in other words, the United States. [99] By March 1941, the American Congress brought in the Lend-Lease Act which meant that immediate hard cash was not required to pay for weapons and war materials.

The American Wool Textile Industry began to see this increase of export trade as an unfair advantage to Britain, to the detriment of its own textile manufacturers. Assurances were given that there would be no deleterious effects on American production, as many British textile workers were transferred to the munitions and aircraft producing industries. In its Annual Report for 1942/43, the Export Group noted that by 1943 the British textile industry was greatly reduced, with production priorities being cloth for the Armed Forces and the coupon controlled home trade. As export allocations were diminished, no allocation could be made for the United States or South American countries, thus assuaging the fears of the American textile manufacturers. [100]

Make do and mend

Clothes rationing was introduced on 1 June 1941, and whereas today the double C symbol is recognized world-wide as meaning Coco Chanel, in 1941 Britain, the logo CC41 stood for the Utility scheme introduced to ration clothing. The CC stood for 'Civilian Clothing' and '41' the year of introduction. Its designer, Reginald Shipp, was instructed to shape the double C in such a way that the public would not recognise the letters, the symbol becoming known as 'the cheeses'.[101]

The Board of Trade, under Sir Laurence Watkinson was looking at ways to control consumer spending and, by issuing clothing coupons and designating each garment with an allotted number of coupons, women's ability to buy clothes was greatly reduced. Only twenty coupons were allocated in 1941, and this was increased to sixty for 1942, but shortages meant a reduction to forty by 1943, with forty-eight in 1944. With a coat requiring fourteen, a blouse five, and a woollen dress eleven, women who did not have a large pre-war wardrobe found themselves having to 'make do and mend'.[102] The Board of Trade even issued a booklet advising women how to do this in 1943, and set up the 'Make Do and Mend Campaign'. In his introduction to the booklet, Hugh Dalton, President of the Board of Trade said: 'I would like to thank you all for

'Make do and mend' - one of the Board of Trade wartime booklets, encouraging people to make the most of scarce resources

the way in which you have accepted clothes rationing. You know how it has saved much-needed shipping space, manpower and materials, and so assisted the war effort. The Board of Trade Make Do and Mend campaign is intended to help you get the last possible ounce of wear out of your clothes.' [103] The booklet makes interesting and amusing reading today. One piece of advice on giving new life to old woollies, suggests:

'An Old Tweed Cardigan or Jacket - You can brighten up a tweed jacket that has worn sleeves by putting in knitted sleeves in a contrasting colour, or in one of the colours of the cloth.' [104]

Some of the advice was basic, but some would need a skilled dressmaker to undertake it, but the message was – use everything - waste nothing - and try to have fun doing it.

A further restriction affecting both textile producers and garment-makers was the Civilian Clothing Order, which introduced Utility clothes in 1942. The fashion designers in INCSOC were asked to develop a collection of thirty-two garments from which the prototypes for production would be chosen. The designers, who included Hardy Amies, Victor Stiebel, Charles Creed, Norman Hartnell and Digby Morton, each designed four specified basic outfits - a coat, suit, afternoon dress and cotton overall dress. The originals were given to the Victoria and Albert Museum, London, and the suits show a simplicity of line that Chanel might have approved. The clothes went into mass production and strict guidelines were laid down for manufacturers making them. They had to bear the Utility symbol and restrictions were set on how much material could be used, including just three buttons per jacket, with no trimmings or decoration. Cut, therefore was all-important.[105]

In America too, restrictions began to bite as, by the summer of 1942, rationing and price control were introduced. President Roosevelt spoke to the nation informing Americans that the restrictions were necessary to ensure fair supplies for everyone, due to wartime shortages. Large supplies of cotton and wool were needed to provide the US Army with millions of flannel shirts, coats and trousers, and because of this the War Production Board brought out a 'Victory' suit for civilians, sporting narrower lapels and cuffless trousers. The efforts to save cloth were similar to those instituted in Britain: pleated skirts were out as a new shorter plain style was designed, and the one piece bathing suit gave way to the smaller bikini.

As in Britain, women accepted these restrictions as part of the war effort, even donating their old girdles as part of a national drive to save rubber. This was in short supply due to the Japanese attacks on the rubber producing countries of Malaya and Indonesia: the effect was to cause strict rationing of car tyres and petrol supplies. A national appeal was made for rubber items to be handed in, anything from old garden hoses to rubber raincoats. Mrs Meta Kirkland of Santa Ana, California, even sent a package to the White House with a letter saying, 'Today I am mailing you my old rubber girdle I have cut and torn into strips… I hope I may claim the privilege of being the first to donate personal wearing apparel for the good cause.' [106] The women of America, along with those in Britain and France were doing their bit to win the war – and with humour.

Deerhounds in the movies

In spite of all the restrictions and difficulties of wartime production at the Mill, 1943 brought an interesting diversion to Norah Hartley and to Nessy. Hollywood came looking to make film stars of her deerhounds. Well, perhaps not quite Hollywood, but rather Denham Studios in Buckinghamshire, England. Michael Powell and Emeric Pressburger planned to make a film described as a 'simple moral tale set in the wild Scottish Highlands, it follows the journey of a headstrong young woman forced by her encounter with this magical, mythical world and its exotic customs to revise her materialistic priorities.' [107] Strong sentiments in time of war. Pam Cook's critique of the film analysed its emotional depth and beauty and she described falling under its spell. 'Magically, it changes lives, inspires new directions in those who see it; a simple love story, it draws us into the dark, dangerous waters of sexual desire and death; like myth, it works on unconscious levels.' [108]

The film *I Know Where I'm Going* – its title taken from an old Irish folk song – starred Wendy Hiller, Pamela Brown and Roger Livesey. Part of it was filmed on location on the beautiful, wild and windswept Isle of Mull in Western Scotland. Other notable stars who appeared were Valentine Dyall, Finlay Currie, and a very young Petula Clark. During the austerity of the war years, Nessy and Norah embarked on this light-hearted venture with gusto. On 7 December 1945, A. Bruce writing in *Dog World* reported:

> *'A most interesting and exciting letter from Miss Hartley. Nearly two years ago Michael Powell asked if she would have some of her hounds filmed. Of course, she agreed, but finding nine hounds were needed, enlisted the help of Miss Linton. Some of the scenes were on the Island of Mull and Miss Linton's chauffeur McMullen (loaned from the RAF) took Jason and Juniper there. After that he and Miss Hartley went to Denham, where they braved the cold for three weeks, keeping three Rotherwoods and six Geltsdales in trim and persuading them to walk on and off the set, to climb stairs and hardest of all to remain on the set without either of their friends. But all of this was done at last, and "I Know Where I'm Going" is to be seen at the Odeon in Leicester Square.'*

'I Know Where I'm going', a wartime film shot on the Isle of Mull featured the Geltsdale deerhounds, seen here with Pamela Brown, 1945

A further report gives the names of the deerhound 'stars': 'The Rotherwood hounds taking part are Bracken, Locksley, Bevis and Tara. There are also Jason, Juniper, Avala and Gilia of Geltsdale, while Veronica of Enterkine also plays a small part. These hounds are of the highest breeding and learning their parts in the short space of three weeks.' [109]

(In the deerhound world the film was regarded as a triumph. Such is the long-lasting power of the film that it was listed in *The Daily Telegraph*'s 'Must Have Movies' feature on films available on DVD in recent years.[110])

∗∗∗

38
Paris is liberated

In the last days of the war, Serge Lifar describes going back to the Hôtel de Castille in Paris, where he was living. A German army car was outside and, when he saw the manageress, Madame Rene Walpen, signalling him not to enter, he ran through the dark streets to 31 rue Cambon, where the old janitor locked the door behind him, as he breathed, 'No, it's not death even this time.' [111] Coco, her maid Germaine, and Leon, her butler looked after him, and he watched the liberation of Paris from here.

With the Allies pressing forward to Paris, and amid street fighting by Resistance forces, the Germans signed the surrender. The Germans left, the tanks rolling out of the Tuileries, and firemen hoisting the French flag onto buildings. It was Friday 25 August 1944 and, amid brilliant sunshine, crowds were gathering, as they saw American Sherman tanks, jeeps and trucks driven by French soldiers entering the streets of Paris. There were scenes of wild jubilation, children were hoisted onto shoulders, excited girls climbed onto tanks to kiss the soldiers and give them flowers. It was a sight never to be forgotten.

On 26 August, to the pealing of the city's bells, General Charles De Gaulle entered Paris and made a triumphant walk down the Champs-Elysées and across the Place de la Concorde. At the Hôtel de Ville he made a rousing and emotional speech: 'Paris... Paris outraged, Paris broken, Paris martyred, but Paris liberated!' [112] There was rejoicing in the streets as the whole of Paris crowded to celebrate their liberty. The next day, with the Germans still north of Paris, over a million people were on the streets to celebrate victory.

Settling old scores

Despite the celebrations, for some it was a dangerous time, with retribution in the air. Serge recalled: 'I had nothing to fear in Coco Chanel's house where I was lodged and fed. It was the only house in Paris that received me and maybe saved my life, for I was an undesirable everywhere. A sort of living corpse.' [113]

There may have been dancing in the streets of Paris but, after the Liberation, feelings ran high, as the many factions who had co-existed throughout the Occupation began to look for scapegoats. It was pay-back time. *The Forces Françaises de l'Interieur*, the FFI or *les fifis* as they were called, worked under the Communist-dominated National Council of the Resistance and had been prominent in the last days before the Liberation. Many were now prepared to take the law into their own hands, and not all of them had been resistance workers. Some of those who had supported Vichy now quickly changed sides and became members of the FFI. To the shock of Allied soldiers who were liberating towns and villages as they advanced from Normandy, they found women, accused of sleeping with the enemy, whose heads had been shaved. The fate of others was even more degrading. This was the start of the *Épuration Sauvage* or the unofficial purge, whereby rough justice was meted out to those deemed to have collaborated with the Germans.

Even Lucien Lelong had called for a purge within the fashion industry of those, mainly textile manufacturers, who had helped German ambitions. This was short-lived because the industry was too important to the French economy for it to be blighted in any way.

At eight o'clock in the morning, two weeks after General De Gaulle's march down the Champs Elysées, Coco was confronted by two men in her room at the Ritz. Coco stared coldly at the two youths, wearing FFI armbands and with revolvers in their belts, who demanded that she accompany them, by order of *Le Comité d'Épuration*. Without a further word, she picked up her bag and gloves and walked out of the Ritz with her head held high. The contempt she felt for *les fifis* was shown in her conversations with Marcel Haedrich years later: 'Those Parisians of the Liberation with their shirtsleeves rolled up. Four days earlier, when they were with the Germans they didn't have their sleeves rolled up.' [114]

'Do you know this gentleman?' they asked her, referring to Spatz.

'Of course, I've known him for twenty years.'

Within a few hours she was back at the Ritz. It was rumoured that she was 'saved' by someone in high office - namely Winston Churchill.[115]

A symbol of hope

After the Liberation and with the national economy in ruins, France was in urgent need of a revival of her industries. To this end, Raoul Dautry, the Minister of Reconstruction and Urbanism, set up *L'Entraide Française,* a national charity, to begin war relief. *Haute couture* led the field. At the suggestion of his friend, Robert Ricci - joint founder with his mother Nina of the Ricci fashion house - it was decided to hold a fashion exhibition organised by the *Chambre Syndicale de la Couture Parisienne* in conjunction with the charities. The proposal met with enthusiasm and support from the designers, as well as the associated trades, but there were severe problems with shortages of materials and the industry in the doldrums.

Not to be deterred, Ricci's deputy, General Paul Caldaguès, suggested that dolls were the answer to the problem. Throughout the freezing winter and amid food shortages, the fashion industry worked with verve to produce one of the most spectacular exhibitions ever, its greatest attraction being that it was all crafted in finely detailed miniature. The greatest French designers, artists and craftsmen produced the finest *couture* garments, complete with silk underwear, Cartier and Van Cleef & Arpels jewels and tiny shoes, all displayed in a miniature theatre, designed by Christian Bérard, with lighting by Boris Kochno. The dolls were each seventy centimetres tall, exquisitely made of wire frames, with their heads sculpted in white plaster and hair styled by top hairdressers.[116]

All those working on the project gave their services free and large sums were raised to help those in need. Everything was perfection and represented every aspect of the best of French fashion. With thirteen miniature stage sets, and 237 beautifully crafted dolls, the exhibition opened on 27 March 1945 to the accompaniment of music by Henri Sauguet and with a guard of honour by the *Garde Républicain.* The excitement of the Paris audience was palpable, and more than one hundred thousand people were to visit the Pavilion Marsan in the Louvre over the following weeks. This was the boost that Parisians needed after the grey years of the Occupation. It was like a breath of fresh spring air in a city looking to rejuvenate itself. The dolls had even further success when the exhibition toured London, Barcelona, Copenhagen, Stockholm and Vienna. In September 1945 it was opened at the Prince's Gallery in London, by the Duchess of Kent and Madame Massigli, wife of the French ambassador. The British called it 'The Fantasy of Fashion' and in the course of the next six weeks 120,000 visitors queued up to view the breathtaking dolls in their spectacular settings.[117]

In spring 1946, the all-important American market was to see the exhibition. It was doubly important, as the Americans had developed their own industry in the four years that they had been cut off from Paris and doubted that *haute couture* could regain its superiority. The exhibition was updated to show 1946 fashions and housed in the opulent Whitelaw Reid mansion at 451 Madison Avenue. New Yorkers were stunned, Paris had not lost its touch and the supremacy of Parisian fashion was confirmed.[118]

Carlisle celebrates peace

Flags were flying and celebrations were held in Carlisle. 1945 would be remembered for a lifetime, as men and women returned home from the horrors of war to the joy and delight of their families. Carlisle railway station was the scene of many ecstatic reunions as kit bags were dumped on the cobblestones and men and women hugged each other, together again after years of separation. Proud grandparents stood by holding on to the hands of children who barely remembered their fathers, and had only known their 'paper Daddy' from photographs. It was a scene being played out all over Britain as families were re-united.

But the euphoria was not to last. All too soon the parties were over and men wearing their ill-fitting 'de-mob' suits were out looking for jobs and better homes for their families. The stresses of returning to civilian life, in a country which had won the war but was still paying heavily for it, made these hard times indeed. There were housing shortages, fuel shortages, food and clothing rationing continued: it was still a time of 'make do and mend'.

The hero of the war, Winston Churchill, found that men returning from war in Europe, Singapore, Burma, the Middle East and the Western desert, did not take kindly to the privations to be faced in their home country. Disillusionment set in and in the 1945 General Election, the unthinkable happened as Churchill lost his Premiership to Clement Attlee, the Labour leader. It was called 'The Age of Austerity' - it was a time of change.

It was also a time that presented new challenges for Linton Tweeds and by New Year 1945, after her several house moves during the war and with Geltsdale House having become a hostel for the Women's Land Army, and then an orphanage, Nessy bought a large property with land at Oakland House, Brisco, just outside Carlisle. This was to be her permanent home, and the home of the Geltsdale Kennels for the rest of her life.[119]

Nessy invests in the future

After the war there was a gradual expansion at Linton's, as the textile industry began to return to normal. The khaki military cloth was banished from the looms. Once again soft, colourful tweeds were produced as heather pink, damask rose, lilac, sky blue, moss green and every shade of coffee and cream yarns replaced the dun coloured military cloth. The yarn store glowed with a myriad of colours.

With the heart-lifting sight of bale upon bale of Linton tweed being produced, Nessy began making trips to the United States of America. She travelled first class on the great ocean-going liners, a journey taking six days. Her custom-made trunk was packed with hundreds of samples of exquisite tweed that spilled out an array of colour, and which were shown exclusively to ten or twelve chosen manufacturers. The great Cunard liners, the *Queen Mary* and the *Queen Elizabeth* were back to normal service, after being used as troopships in 1942, carrying military personnel from New Zealand and Australia to war, when they had been named 'the grey ghosts' due to their wartime camouflage.

Hardy Amies, the British designer, was given financial support from Nessy Linton to set up his own fashion house in London

Nessy was also acutely aware of the problems of the British textile and fashion industry after the war. When Hardy Amies was posted home from SOE shortly after VE-Day and awaiting demobilisation, he describes visiting his old friends, the Lintons, at the tweed mills in Cumberland. No doubt he discussed his plans for the future with them, and Nessy was supportive of those plans.[120] By 1946, he had decided not to return to Lachasse and, although he was offered a place on the Board of the newly created joint business of Worth-Paquin based in London and Paris, he decided to set up a couture house in London under his own name.

In later years Sir Hardy was to write, 'It is a truth universally acknowledged that a young designer in possession of a good *clientèle* must be in want of capital.' [121] Although some customers had shown an interest in investing capital if he should start his own house, he was fearful that it would mean undue interference in the running of the business.

There were, however, three customers who offered to become shareholders, which enabled him to open his house at 14 Savile Row London in 1946. The actress Virginia Cherrill, the star of Charlie Chaplin's film 'City Lights' and former wife of Cary Grant, now married to George Child-Villiers, 9th Earl of Jersey, was a fan of the chic suits that were made of Linton tweed. Together with her friend Mrs Dickie Gillson, she backed the new enterprise. The third backer was Agnes Linton, showing the foresight that marked so much of Linton's business sense. Sir Hardy recalled appreciatively in 1954:

> 'I was very disappointed in the lack of financial support I got from the cloth merchants and manufacturers... they preferred to assist by giving good credit: by supplying cloth without asking for quick payment, rather than tying up their own capital... An exception was Miss Agnes Linton, of the famous Linton Tweed

Mills in Cumberland. She immediately subscribed the amount suggested by my accountants. I am proud to be associated with this distinguished Mill. Old Mr Linton, Miss Linton's father, the founder of the firm, worked in close collaboration with the great Chanel, and a little later with Schiaparelli. Together they devised many wonderfully-coloured tweeds, which delighted and startled the world of fashion in the late 'twenties and early 'thirties. Mr Linton is now dead, but Miss Linton and her cousin George still continue the tradition of taking a trunk full of tweed patterns twice a year to New York to show the big manufacturers there. They have never bothered to advertise their name in England but it is a household word in dressmaking circles in America.' [122]

By giving him her help, Nessy proved not only her loyalty to her old friend but her appreciation of the need for investment in the British fashion industry, at a time when the whole nation was struggling to put a recovery programme into operation.

In spite of the problems that service men and women faced on returning to 'Civvy Street,' 750,000 of them were back in jobs by the end of 1945, with the government implementing many re-training schemes. Food rationing was still in place, with bread rationing being brought in for the first time from June 1946 for two years. Sweets remained rationed until 1953 when once again children could spend their pocket money on toffee apples and liquorice sticks. [123]

Optimism and belief in a better future were everyone's watchwords and, by September 1946, the Victoria and Albert Museum in London were staging an exhibition promoting the best of British design sponsored by the Council of Industrial Design. Called 'Britain Can Make It', the exhibition promoted the country's manufacturing prowess and attracted crowds to view the six thousand products produced by British firms. [124] But in cash-strapped Britain it also caused disappointment, as most of the goods were for the export market only. A long road to recovery lay ahead.

***

39
1947... The New Look

In France, the phoenix had indeed arisen from the ashes. In the aftermath of war, with France looking for revival and renewal, there was a search for new thinking and new ideas. In Paris, a new star was about to burst onto the scene.

Christian Dior has been described as looking like a country priest, with his kind, gentle face and his shy, self-effacing manner. A dreamer who was never happier than when working in his gardens, in tune with nature. But he was also a creative genius. He was born in 1905, in the town of Angers, in the lush Loire valley, not many miles from Saumur, Coco's birthplace. He later lived at Granville in Normandy, his family moving to Paris in 1911, where his father, Maurice, set up the headquarters of his booming phosphate and fertiliser business. Christian was to describe himself in his memoirs as a well brought-up and well behaved little boy. As a child, he loved nothing better than to draw sketches of fancy dress costumes for his brothers and sisters to wear at Carnival time in Granville, working with the family seamstress in making them up. [125]

After gaining his *baccalaureat,* Christian expressed his wish to go to art school, but his parent's were totally opposed to the idea. Giving in to family pressure, he agreed to study political science and enrolled at the *École des Sciences Politiques* in Paris: his mother hoping that one day he would become a diplomat and ambassador. [126]

The sensitive, affectionate, artistic youth drifted into the company of the bohemian and artistic set of Paris, much to his wealthy parents' chagrin. Among his friends were Jean

Cocteau, Christian Bérard and Max Jacob and he shared with them a bohemian lifestyle. Eventually, after a spell as Director of an art gallery, he started to work in fashion design and in 1935 was selling his sketches to many of the top fashion houses. By 1938 he had been offered a post as designer for Robert Piguet at his fashion house on the Champs Elysées, which had opened five years earlier. Piguet was Swiss-born and had worked for both Redfern and Paul Poiret, and now made beautifully cut suits and tailored dresses, as well as romantic gowns. But he wanted Dior to design Dior.

Christian was to admit that, until then, he had been influenced by Chanel and Molyneux and was to famously write of Coco: '... with a black pullover and ten rows of pearls she revolutionised fashion.' [127] He would also pay her the compliment of acknowledging her place in fashion history when he wrote: 'That was the era of the great couturiers. Outstanding among them was Mlle Chanel, who dominated all the rest... Her personality as well as her taste had style, elegance and authority. From quite different points of view she and Madeleine Vionnet can claim to be the creators of modern fashion.' [128]

12 February 1947 - Christian Dior's famous 'Bar' suit launches the New Look

Dior's designs were an instant success and he was soon introduced to Carmel Snow, the energetic and powerful American editor-in chief of *Harper's Bazaar*, who later played such a fortuitous role in his story. Of this meeting Christian wrote:

> 'Marie-Louise [Bousquet] introduced me to Mrs Snow, the editor of Harper's Bazaar. It was then that I began to have a place in the world of fashion which, even a short time before, had been entirely unknown to me.' [129]

At the outbreak of war, Dior had been assigned to military service, working on the land in the unoccupied zone, but when the French armistice was signed in 1940 he was demobbed and stayed on for a year at the farm in Mehun-sur-Yèvre. He loved the rural life and later moved to Callian in Provence where his parents were living. On his return to Paris in 1941, he joined Lucien Lelong, where the young Pierre Balmain was operational.

A fateful meeting with Marcel Boussac, a textile millionaire, head of the Cotton Industry Board, and famous for his newspapers and horseracing stables, set Dior on the path to opening his own house. On 16 December 1946, one week after his father's death and with his mother decreeing that the name Dior should never appear on a shop front, Dior stepped over the threshold of 30 avenue Montaigne, and began the journey to fame and fortune which would only end with his premature death eleven years later.

Millions of words have been written about Dior's first collection. It appeared upon the post-war fashion scene like a sunburst, a total surprise, an exquisite silhouette: it was

156

named the 'New Look'.

He had long planned the launch of the 'Corolle' collection and, with his life-long empathy for nature and the world of flowers, the line burgeoned like the sepals of some delicate flower enhancing the feminine shape of women. After the non-fashion of the war years with its short skirts, square padded shoulders, and platform shoes, women embraced it. The years of austerity and shortages were as nothing compared to this extravagance of curves, pleats and femininity. Not since Chanel had launched her 'Garçonne Look' in the twenties had a style so quickly made everything else look out-moded.

12 February 1947 - the day would go down in the annals of fashion history. Maison Dior showed its first collection, and nothing would ever be the same again. Perhaps no-one was more surprised by the acclaim than Christian, who wrote:

> 'I do admit that if I had been asked about my work and what I hoped to achieve on the eve of my first collection, the one that launched the New Look, I certainly would not have talked about a revolution. I could never have foreseen the reception it was about to receive. I had so little inkling of it, but merely tried to do my best.' [130]

It was the last show of the Spring Collections that year, and amid great excitement and expectation the fashion press assembled in the elegant grey and gold salon. With Carmel Snow ensconced on her grey velvet settee, the models began to sashay down the catwalk. Nothing like it had been seen before, the dresses and suits with their full skirts, their flat pleats stitched down twelve inches from the waist, and some billowing out to an amazing forty yards in circumference, were only twelve inches off the ground, the waists were nipped and the shoulder line rounded.

Perhaps the most stunning suit was called 'Bar' with its full black wool skirt and its pale pink shantung jacket. The rest of the collection was in neutral tones of grey, black and navy, but with brilliant accents of red, green and pink. The applause never ceased throughout the show, and by the end reached its crescendo with Christian in tears, and crying out, 'My God what have I done?' Carmel Snow had no doubt, 'It's quite a revolution, dear Christian. Your dresses have such a new look.' [131] These were the words that gave the style its name, and which will ever remain in the story of fashion.

The New Look was to put Parisian fashion back where it had been before the war started - the world leader. It dashed the hopes of American designers, who had assumed that the *couture* would never again re-establish its supremacy and that American-designed ready-to-wear was about to dominate international fashion. With the advent of Dior, this became a non-issue. Against all odds, this war-torn city again revived its textile and fashion ateliers and reigned supreme. Paris was back.

Coco in Switzerland

At the end of the war, Coco had gone to live in Lausanne in Switzerland where Spatz was also in residence. She and Spatz were always seen together and there is no doubting the affection she felt for this rather weak but elegant man. Still she watched like a hawk what was happening to the *couture*, and she loathed it. It was everything that she had sought to banish from women's clothes and lives; everything she had replaced with her spare elegant designs - and here was *a man* taking women backwards. Back to wearing waspies to gain the corseted cinched waist, back to restriction of movement with padded skirts, heavy linings and yards of material. It was an abomination. In her view, 'Dior does not dress women, he drapes them.'

Coco was bored. To a woman used to running her own fashion house and designing twice-yearly collections, the dilettante life of retirement was not really for her. These are almost the missing years of her life. She was in exile. In private, she grew waspish in her comments about the male designers who now dominated the Parisian couture scene.

She amused herself by instituting law suits against the perfume company, with whom her ongoing disputes became more acrid. She was convinced that the Wertheimers were trying to deprive her of the true wealth due to her. There were visits to La Pausa every summer, to her friends in America, skiing in Switzerland, life with Spatz - none of these things would fulfill a woman who had turned her back on marriage to the Duke of Westminster in favour of her independence and her fashion house. She missed so much, the dresses, the women, the work - and the power of being at the centre of this hive of activity. But most of all she loathed what the male designers who had come to the fore, were doing to fashion.

But she kept quiet, kept a low profile. The question is why?

Ghosts from the past

The answer to this may be found in the *Modellhut* affair, because it really wasn't over. There were many loose ends. In the closing stages of the war, Schellenberg had gone to Sweden on behalf of Heinrich Himmler, to see Count Folke Bernadotte, still with the hopes of negotiating peace with the Allies. Count Bernadotte had liaised between Heinreich Himmler in passing a peace offer to the British and Americans - but there was no chance of acceptance at this late stage of the war. Bernadotte was the nephew of King Gustavus V, and became President of the Swedish Red Cross in 1946. Towards the end of the war he arranged for the evacuation of Norwegian and Danish prisoners from the

German concentration camps. He proved a good friend to Schellenberg, advising him to write details of his peace efforts in a memorandum. In 1948 the Count was appointed United Nations mediator in Palestine only to be assassinated in Jerusalem later that year by Jewish extremists known as the Stern Gang.[132]

As the war ended on 7 May 1945, Schellenberg was extradited back to Germany in June for the Nuremberg Trials. He remained in prison until 1948, awaiting his trial. In April 1949 he was sentenced to six years imprisonment, running from June 1945. The lightness of his sentence in comparison to the other twenty-one of Hitler's henchmen, of whom all but seven received death sentences, was due to his attempts to make peace, his attempts to aid prisoners in the concentration camps at the end of the war and his role as spymaster, rather than involvement in criminal activities.

In 1949, he was extremely ill with liver disease and underwent surgery. He wrote to Mömm thanking him for passing on *Modellhut's* - or Coco's - good wishes. [133] When he was released in June 1951,

Chanel with Hans Günther von Dincklage, 'Spatz' or 'Sparrow,' in Switzerland

Schellenberg took refuge in Switzerland, changed his name, and was helped financially by Coco. He was contracted to Scherz Verlag, a Berne publishing firm to write his memoirs, [134] and perhaps she feared what he might reveal of her role in wartime affairs. He made no secret of his links with Coco but the Swiss police, perhaps aware of the furore his presence might cause, asked him to leave the country. He went to Italy, to Pallanza on the shores of Lake Maggiore, again financed by Coco.

To her concern, Coco found herself being blackmailed by an unscrupulous literary agent who had got hold of the story - and she paid him off. By the summer of 1951 Schellenberg was a very sick man and invited a young German journalist, Herr Harpprecht, to assist with editing the memoirs. The draft was a thousand pages long and Schellenberg anxious to finish it, delayed having an operation that he badly needed to relieve his condition. With his health deteriorating, Schellenberg went into a clinic in Turin, but it was too late and he died on 31 March 1952.[135] His wife then found herself in litigation with Swiss agents who thought they owned her husband's copyright. Through Theodor Mömm, she sought Coco's help, but Mömm, ever loyal to Coco, discouraged her from making contact.[136] His wife later went to a German publisher and the memoirs were eventually produced in 1957 under the title *The Labyrinth.* Coco's name is not mentioned in them.

Another version of the story came to light in the American National Archives where documents relating to Schellenberg's post-war interrogation by the Allies in 1945 became available in the 1980s. He declared that he intended to inform Churchill of the turmoil within the German Government, with Himmler planning Hitler's demise. He claimed that, in April 1944, a man named Schiebe told him that 'a certain Frau Chanel' should be used to contact Churchill in London, saying that she was: 'a person who knew Churchill sufficiently to undertake political negotiations with him, as an enemy of Russia and as desirous of helping France and Germany whose destinies she believed to be closely linked together.' Schellenberg invited her to visit him in Berlin, where she was accompanied by Spatz. Chanel proposed - and Schellenberg agreed - that she should write a letter to Churchill, which would be taken to the British embassy in Madrid by her friend, Vera Bate Lombardi. As Vera was interned in Italy at this time, she was released and travelled to Italy with the letter. On arrival in Madrid, she scuppered the whole scheme by denouncing Coco and others as German agents to the British authorities.[137]

All this becomes even more bizarre when one considers Chanel's love of all things English and of the English way of life. She had many friends among the English aristocracy and upper classes, since the days of her affairs with Boy Capel and the Duke of Westminster. At this time of espionage and counter-espionage it is interesting to note that she knew Sir Stewart Menzies, head of the British Secret Intelligence Service and Churchill's spymaster, who was known as 'C'. In his book on the life of Sir Stewart Menzies, Anthony Cave Brown relates that Coco was deeply interested in politics and especially fascism, as she detested Bolshevism.[138]

Menzies had married Pamela Garton, one of the four daughters of Hon. Major and Mrs Rupert Beckett who lived at 34 Grosvenor Street, London, part of the Duke of Westminster's estates. The Hon. Major Beckett was chairman of the Westminster Bank Ltd and of the *Yorkshire Post* newspaper and would become Chancellor of Leeds University.[139] Her mother, the former Muriel Paget, was a celebrated society beauty and both mother and daughter were friends of Coco.

Intriguing questions remain: who was Coco working for? Was the affair her own idea? Or was she undertaking a mission for someone else? The true sequence and detail of these events, which were not revealed until thirty years later, is difficult to ascertain. Was Coco the sole instigator, or is there a deeper web to be unravelled which might involve those who were at the very top of the British Establishment? We may never know.

It is unlikely that Churchill would have agreed to a negotiated peace at this stage in the war, the Allies were out to win – nothing less. Given that Coco was not tried for collaboration with the enemy after the war, and that she had freedom to travel wherever she wished, including America, it would seem odd. Is it just one more of Coco's secrets, or will the true reasons for Coco's quest for peace one day be revealed?

Spatz was deported from France on 9 July 1947 on ministerial decree.[140] After living in Switzerland with Coco, for some years after the war, he went to live on a Mediterranean island, supported by an allowance from Coco.[141] Vera died in Italy in the same year, and with Schellenberg dead, Coco must have felt some relief that the main players in the *Modellhut* affair could say nothing further. She could put it behind her and look to a new start.

A further blow fell in 1950, with the death of her old friend, Misia Sert - the woman whom she had relied on all those years ago and who had witnessed the highs and lows of her extraordinary life. Now she would hurry to Paris, there to dress her friend, once the toast of Paris, in beautiful clothes for the last time.[142]

The old order was giving way to the new.

***

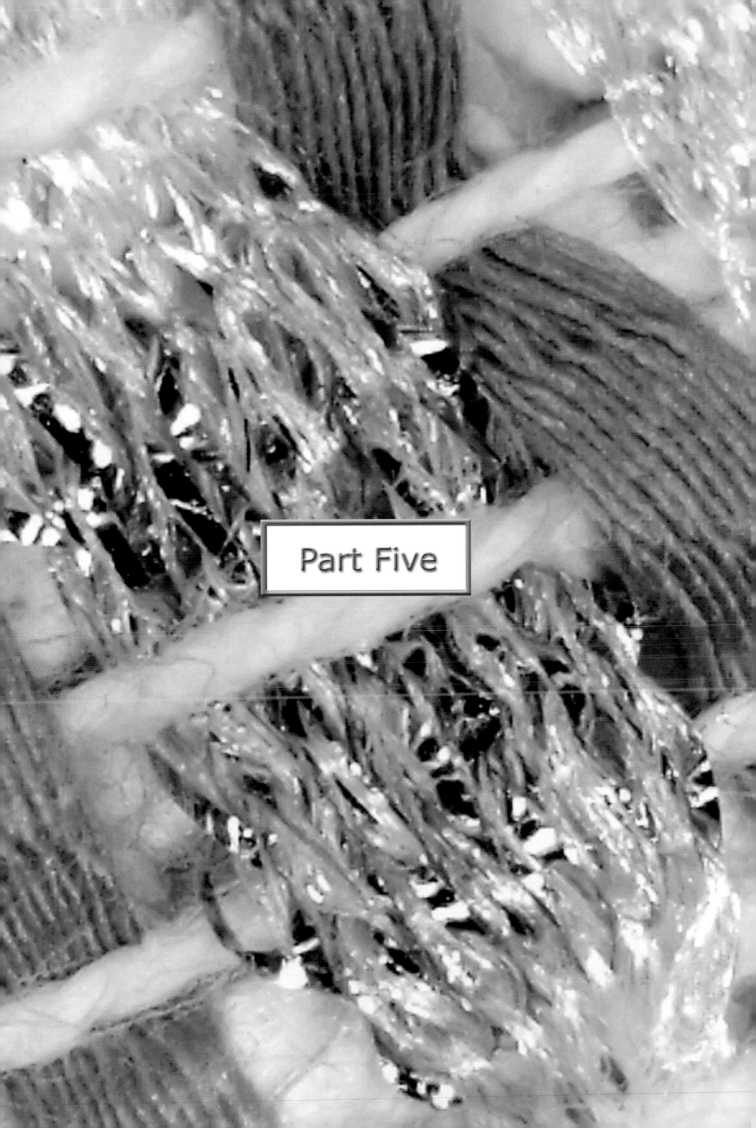

Part Five

40

The comeback

1953 and, from her home in Switzerland, Coco had looked increasingly askance at the turn that haute couture was taking in the hands of the new breed of male designers. She was not only scathing about their personal sexual persuasion, but also saw their designs as a backward step, which would put women back into restricting and unwearable fashions. She had to make a comeback.

In deciding to re-enter the fray, her aim was to once more spread the gospel of Chanel to the world. Elegant simplicity in chic, wearable clothes - clothes to live in, clothes to work in - nothing had changed.

It was not a question of money: with the perfume sales she was an extremely rich woman and no longer needed to think of her financial situation. But she had a passion and enthusiasm for her belief in her timeless creations and the zeal to come back and put them into production. Never mind that she was seventy years old, and that the Parisian pundits would say that she was finished: she had total self-belief, which would inspire her to say:

> 'There is an increasing tendency to consider dress designing as an art when not as a veritable philosophy! It seems to be forgotten that dress designing is a craft. There are some people who know this craft and others, more numerous, who think they know it. The present crisis is due to this. I have thought it all over and have come to believe that I still have perhaps two or three things to say.' [1]

Her credo was declared to her friends in her usual pithy manner: 'Fashion has become a joke; the designers have forgotten that there are women inside the dresses. Most women dress for men and want to be admired. But they must also be able to move, to get into a car without bursting their seams! Clothes must have a natural shape.' [2]

Carmel Snow, the editor in chief of *Harper's Bazaar* in New York, was contacted with the news by Marie-Louise Bousquet, the Paris editor of the magazine, acting on Coco's behalf.

She immediately cabled Coco:

> 'KNOW TOP WHOLESALE MANUFACTURER WHO WOULD BE INTERESTED IN COPYING THE MODELS YOU WILL CREATE. MARIE-LOUISE VAGUE AS TO DETAILS. WHEN WOULD YOUR COLLECTION BE READY. DO YOU ANTICIPATE COMING OVER WITH IT. WILL YOU SUPPLY FABRIC TO COPY. DELIGHTED TO BE OF ANY HELP. CARMEL SNOW.' [3]

On 30 September 1953 Carmel received a hand delivered letter from Coco. It was in reply to her cable of 24 September. Coco wrote:

> 'This will acknowledge your cable and confirm my reply. During the summer I thought it would be fun to work again because work is my entire life. I probably told you before that one day or another I might resume my activity of creating a new style adapted to a new mode of living and I was waiting for the proper time to come. I feel that this time has come.

> 'The paradoxical Parisian atmosphere of today, where more and more women go to collections of dresses they cannot afford to buy, has led me to do something entirely different.

> 'One of my prime objects is naturally to wholesale through one manufacturer in

162

the United States on a royalty basis. Nevertheless I feel that what I am doing will have a tremendous appeal throughout the world.

'My first collection will be ready on November 1, and I think it would be wise not to make any move before receiving the offer of the top wholesale manufacturer whom you have in mind. Possibly the best would be for him to fly over to Paris. Of course nothing would please me more than having you over here, too. For the time being I do not anticipate presenting the collection myself in America, but that might come later.

As ever,

Gabrielle Chanel' [4]

Carmel had a scoop: this was red hot news, perhaps the best any fashion editor would ever get. After fifteen years the 'Chanel look' was to return, with its easy, elegant, informal wearability. Carmel had long admired Chanel and, in the days when she worked for *Vogue*, had said, 'My first allegiance was to Chanel, because the freedom of her clothes was so congenial to me.' [5]

Coco makes her move

Coco had additional motives. As she pondered, she realised the vast expense of opening the couture house again, even though she had immense wealth. That sort of money was only available from the perfume company.

She had already approached Pierre Wertheimer, meeting him at the Hotel Beau Rivage at Ouchy in Switzerland, and suggested the launch of a new perfume. He had not agreed, saying that a new perfume would harm the sales of No.5, and be tremendously expensive to launch at this time. He must have been surprised when she accepted.

Not one to waste time, she was back living in her apartment at the Ritz in Paris within a few days. She would not be written off as an out-of-touch old lady yet. Her hands might have some arthritis, but she still had vigour, and ideas. But she needed a new source of funds and she recruited an unwitting press to achieve this. Her letter to Carmel Snow, indicating that she would sell to the garment manufacturers on New York's Seventh Avenue, was something of a ploy and bargaining counter. Her lawyer, René de Chambrun, revealed that 'Coco wanted to be able to say to herself and to others: "I can make a comeback on my own. I don't need the Wertheimers".' [6]

The Wertheimers, only too aware that, in America, she could also sell new perfumes not covered by their buy-out agreement or other merchandise in boutiques and department stores under her own name, were anxious to reach an agreement with her. They had to protect the exclusivity of Chanel No.5 at any cost.

The Board of the perfume company at Neuilly were concerned by her motives and her determination: the memory of thirty years of Coco issuing law suits must have haunted them. However, Pierre Wertheimer had faith in her, and

Chanel and Carmel Snow, editor-in-chief of Harper's Bazaar

when the company's financial advisor, Robert Chaillot spoke to him about re-opening the fashion house, and asked if it interested him, he replied, 'It is too fantastic. Obviously, it interests me.'[7]

The agreement finally signed was a tribute to Coco's business acumen and to Pierre Wertheimer's belief in his old adversary. It made the perfume company responsible for half of the fashion house expenses, as a publicity investment on behalf of the perfumes.

Pierre was going to need his staunch belief in Coco. She had estimated to Robert de Nexon that the collection would cost no more than fifteen million francs. This was wildly optimistic. By the end of a year, both she and the perfume company had each lost thirty-five million francs, and rue Cambon was out of cash.[8]

Coco's motives in reopening her couture house at the age of seventy have been the subject of long debate by fashion writers. Bettina Ballard of *Vogue* would state, 'Chanel didn't re-open in 1954 to worry about a successful couture business; she went back to designing to escape boredom and to keep young.'[9]

Ten green years

Back in Paris, rumour was rife. To whip up a little interest, Coco began giving exclusive interviews to the French press, as well as the *New York Herald Tribune* and British *Vogue*. In February 1954, she informed *American Vogue* that she would again make women look pretty and young. 'A dress isn't right if it is uncomfortable... buttons must have buttonholes, pockets be in the right place, usable... Elegance in clothes means the freedom to move freely.'[10]

The fashion magazines and newspapers were having a field day; besides quoting her edicts on fashion, they were running stories of Coco's life and loves, and the younger generation were hearing stories of her colourful life and glittering career. Once more she was a celebrity, and once more she was back at the Ritz and inviting her friends to her rue Cambon apartment. She told *Vogue,* 'I am no longer interested in dressing a few hundred women, private clients; I shall dress thousands.'[11]

As Michel Deon, her journalist friend, wrote:

> 'She sometimes walked through the deserted workrooms where pieces of fabric, dress dummies fallen over onto tables, rusting sewing machines were left trailing about. Life had stopped there in 1940, having barely survived the Popular Front strikes. Mademoiselle had no regrets and no bitterness, never imagining that one day she might bring back to life this graveyard from which so many fashion criteria had sprung.'[12]

As she looked at her deserted salon, perhaps she saw it come to life, saw the future. Perhaps she was looking for happiness. 'Someone to love, something to look forward to, and something to do,' was Coco's philosophy.

When the call came, her old staff were only too willing to answer it. Mademoiselle was back, there would be dresses again at rue Cambon. 'Come quickly,' she said, 'we have only ten green years before us.'[13]

Mme Lucie, her old *directrice*, even gave up her own shop in the rue Royale to return as head of the rue Cambon establishment. Coco asked her to bring along Mme Manon, she recalled:

> 'That is how we reopened the house, with two workrooms. We were all greatly excited. Mademoiselle had such guts! At that moment, we didn't think that we would become so important again.'[14]

The fashionable Fifties

The Forties had seen the end of the war and with it the growing expectations of millions of people. In Britain, this surge of newly charged hope found expression in developments in the arts. Never mind that food was still rationed and everything from dresses to doormats were in short supply, houses were almost unobtainable and political change was in the air: the post-war years were seen as a time of hope and progress, a time to get back to normal. In 1951 the Festival of Britain was a national celebration of the country's contributions to the world of arts and science. In London the Festival Hall was built and work on the National Theatre started, as the concrete mass of the South Bank arose from the rubble of the blitz. By 1953 Roger Bannister had run the four-minute mile and Sir Edmund Hillary had conquered Mount Everest.

The Fifties saw a gradual return to normal in the fashion world. In London, fashions from Jaeger, Susan Small, Dereta and Mary Black were best-sellers. The idea of the 'teenager' crossed the ocean from America and young women, no longer wishing to dress like their mothers, developed their own style. Suddenly men too were interested in fashion and soon the advent of 'Teddy Boys' would be seen, as music hit the streets and the sound of jazz, skiffle, rock n' roll and Elvis Presley burst onto the Fifties scene, like a sunburst to light up the post-war sky.

The influence of Paris, regaining its place on the international scene since Dior's bombshell 'New Look', was surging forward, and although Dior was the name on everyone's lips in these years, others were coming to the fore. In America, the ready-to-wear designers went from strength-to-strength and Hollywood promoted high glamour in film. In London, designers were working to regain their position. Norman Hartnell, for example, striving to enhance the reputation of British fashion had toured South America in 1946 with a collection of all-wool designer garments. By 1947 he had designed the wardrobe for Queen Elizabeth, the late Queen Mother, to wear during the Royal Tour of South Africa, and created the beautiful ivory duchesse satin wedding dress for Princess Elizabeth on her marriage to Prince Phillip, Duke of Edinburgh. He would also design the magnificent gown for Queen Elizabeth to wear at her Coronation in 1953.[15]

Harry Yoxall, the editor of British *Vogue*, opined that the British fashion industry, although not on a par with the French industry, was an acceptable alternative. However, once Paris was back, he watched with dismay as the British industry - from designers to government - failed to drive things forward with the commitment and imagination needed to match the French competition.[16] It was a time to look forward.

Carlisle expects

Back at Linton Tweeds, having weathered the Second World War, the news of Coco's return must have made sweet reading. In Carlisle, Agnes Linton had a building ready for new business. As she wrote at the time 'The factory is very well designed, on one level, beautifully light and airy and the machinery is of the most modern. We are very proud of our canteen, extremely up to date, and of our garden with its lawn and herbaceous borders, its evergreen trees and shrubs. In spring the crocuses are a delight.' [17] All that was missing was a resurgence of the old Chanel/Linton Tweeds partnership. 1954 was to be that year to remember. Coco was back and, with her, requests for Linton Tweed. Once again the beautiful cloth would be up there on the Chanel catwalk. Agnes and George were very proud.

Although Coco had used Linton Tweeds in every one of her collections since 1928, when the designer Captain Edward Molyneux had introduced her to William Linton, she now had ideas for a new concept in tweed suits: her own new contemporary look in tweed. This was the time when today's iconic Chanel suit was first conceived: Coco knew how she wanted it to look, and that she would use Linton Tweed. It became the most famous suit in the world, and the subject of Coco's wise words, telling *Vogue*, 'Certain women wear a suit, certain suits wear women. In the first case the woman is bad; in the second, the suit is not good.' [18] The Chanel suit was one of the good, of course.

They had both survived, Agnes and Coco, and now in 1953, with whatever difficulties they had endured in the previous fifteen years receding, they were both looking forward to the future with confidence and relish.

Coco meanwhile was preparing to return to Paris, once again to light up rue Cambon and start creating her dresses. At the age of seventy, she did not doubt that she still had a lot to contribute to the future of style, and to women's comfort in dress.

Different lifestyles, the same ideal

For the first time Agnes Linton would be leading negotiatons with Coco. Although nineteen years Coco's junior, and without her reputation and profile, Agnes Linton was still something of a rarity in the business world: a woman in a man's world.

Agnes and Coco were two women linked by their work, but perhaps scarcely acknowledging it. Both women would spend sixty years of their life dedicated to the same ideal – creating beauty, elegance and style for women. Coco with her easy-to-wear, simple but stylish fashions, and Agnes with her designs for the beautiful tweeds from which the renowned Chanel suits were made.

Their lifestyles were very different. Coco lived in the 'city of light', a leader of Parisian society, patron of the arts, and friend of artists, musicians and writers. Agnes, based in Carlisle amid the soft green landscape and gentle hills of the Eden Valley, ran the tweed mill and bred deerhounds. Agnes had proved that she could run both businesses, and was striving to do new things at Linton Tweeds, where a new designer, Desmond Mathews, had been appointed that year.

It is likely that these two extremely independent women would have understood each other very well, had they had the opportunity of friendship. Both shared a common work ethic: Agnes's inherited from her Scottish forebears, and Coco's from her will to succeed in life, and to escape the memory of her upbringing in a convent orphanage. They were both strong women who combined enthusiasm with good sense and business acumen, and both succeeded enormously in their chosen fields.

Some notes written by Agnes in the 1950s vividly describe the activity at Linton's:

> 'The work is seasonal and very hard. Twice each year a Director goes to North America with new designs, orders from which have to be executed with considerable speed if repeats are to follow. It is then "all hands to the plough".

> 'There are also frequent visits to London and Europe, not only to take orders but to remain conversant with the trend of fashion.

> 'We are proud to number a large percentage of the Haute Couture, past and present both in Paris and London, as users of our materials for their collections.

> 'In America we sell only to the best manufacturers and stores with most of whom we have done business for thirty years or more.

> 'The staff work with a will - the Queen Mary sails a day early this week - so the van must be loaded by British Railways on Friday evening - the Queen Elizabeth sails later the following week, so the final packing need not be complete until Saturday lunch time. And so it goes on and the last repeat orders are barely executed before the designs for the next season have to begin and the wheel has turned full circle.' [19]

***

41
The comeback collection

Launch day was 5 February 1954, chosen because of the auspicious number, 5. At two o'clock in the afternoon, the world's press gathered, perched on the little gilt chairs and sharpened their pencils, waiting to pass judgement on Mademoiselle's return. Tension was high as they viewed the refurbished salon, its new mirrors gleaming, reflecting the assembled *fashionistas*. There was an air of excitement and anticipation, with journalists and fashion editors craning their necks, standing on their chairs, afraid of missing the first Chanel creation in fifteen years.

Coco was nervous as she stood once again at the top of the mirrored staircase with a few close friends, surveying the throng below. Her old customers were back, looking round with an air of nostalgia and casting surreptitious glances up the staircase, but Mademoiselle was not in sight.

John Fairchild's influential *Women's Wear Daily* reported to its American readers on 8 February:

> 'A long wait downstairs, and seating mix-ups when press and buyers were finally allowed up into the salon, gave the Chanel 1954 opening the air of the New York rush hour... Before the first model appeared everyone was irritated and the general attitude was: This had better be good - or else.' [20]

Coco had created one hundred and thirty models, and everything depended on how they were received. The first suit appeared: it was a cardigan suit in black jersey. Shades of the old but with a new twist. The rest of the show had the same simple, elegant look. Black and navy suits in jersey or tweed, with cardigan style jackets and pencil skirts. A navy sailor suit worn with a white blouse and straw boater still remembered and copied years later. The trademark features were all there, with print shirts matching jacket linings or open cuffs showing pretty linings. Coats were lined to match the dresses worn underneath. Evening dresses were white, with touches of red and pink. They were classy, confidence-giving clothes for the modern woman.

A hostile press

The show had taken place in cold, mirrored silence, no music, no pizzazz, only cool mannequins parading with numbered cards. The reception was hostile. Bettina Ballard, fashion editor for American *Vogue,* covered the Paris collections that year and described the atmosphere of the Chanel opening: 'The French fashion press lay in wait for her first post-war collection like cats in a rat hole... She sat at the top of her stairs... watching the faces of the spectators in the mirrors, knowing that they had come with closed minds and venomous pens. The blast in the press the next day was blindly violent, as if the fashion writers could in some way deny the strength of this voice from the past by ranting and raving.' [21]

Michel Deon was sitting next to Chanel and saw it all. He was appalled at her treatment by the French press, with their comments about her age and being out of touch. The show then progressed in stony silence and the end was greeted with more loud jibes.[22]

She fared no better with the British press. The English *Daily Express* was equally scathing, the headline howling 'A Fiasco - Audience Gasped'.[23] In the *Daily Herald*, Marge Proops wrote 'How sad are these attempts to make a come-back. How very rarely they succeed... Once you're faded it takes more than a name and memories of past triumphs to put you back in the spotlight.' [24]

The tabloid press, as ever, looked for its pound of flesh.

Whatever Coco must have felt at this cruel reception she was not a woman to give in - rather she would fight back and show her detractors what the name Chanel really meant. Simone Baron wrote in *France Soir*:

> *'It is then that I saw her for the first time. She was wearing a white tweed suit, a straw sailor hat, lots of gold jewellery, and very little makeup. She was vehement and passionately excited. I heard her speak: "Pooh! People don't know what elegance is anymore. It is the contrary of vulgarity. Me, I think only of women and not of fashion houses. It is not possible to bamboozle them to such a degree. Once I helped us to achieve liberation; I am beginning again. For fifty years I have done everything – the accounts, the dresses, the administration, everything. They will see what I am still capable of doing".'* [25]

The next day she was back in the salon, telling her faithful staff, 'At least we will be comfortable, we will work in the main salon.' [26] Pierre Wertheimer found her there, on her knees, creating dresses. He had shown his faith in her when he agreed that the Wertheimers and Parfums Chanel would pay fifty percent of the collection costs, which he charged to the company's publicity budget. Now he could see her quiet determination to continue. [27]

His faith in her would be more than justified, within four years, the new Chanel suit was born, and Coco had regained her place at the top.

It was not all disaster, however. The Americans loved the collection and the American fashion press heaped praise on it. Perhaps they saw further than the Europeans, saw that the neat, stylish dresses and suits were the perfect outfits, whether for business or pleasure. The clothes were fresh, elegant, modern, and they had the look of youth. Perhaps also, the Americans lacked the European capacity to put down success. For them, this was the woman who had led fashion since the 1920s - and she had not lost her touch. By March, for example, *Life* magazine was claiming 'She has influenced all today's collections. At seventy-one, she brings us more than a style- she has caused a veritable tempest. She has decided to return and to conquer her old position- the first.' [28]

Her champion Bettina Ballard gave three full pages of the March issue of Vogue to the Chanel models, with a frontispiece featuring the unknown Marie-Hélène Arnaud in a navy jersey suit, with white lawn blouse and a navy straw sailor hat with ribbon streamers. As Ballard admitted, 'I wanted this costume for myself – I had missed comfortable, reliably young clothes like this, and I was sure that other women would want them, too, if they saw them.' [29]

The British fashion writer Iris Ashley commented: 'I thought that Mademoiselle Chanel had started another revolution of fashion. Just how she put it across was hard to define in writing. The clothes were so undramatic... It was chiefly the colours, the fabrics, the sheer feminine softness of outline, that made you realize how hard and forced the silhouette of fashion had become.' [30]

The young Karl Lagerfeld, then an apprentice at the Chambre Syndicale de la Couture Parisienne, would say that he 'loved this look that harked back to a pre-war world I hadn't known but found more intoxicating than any current fashion.' [31]

Later, Coco commented 'I brought off something when I recaptured my place at the top. Now the working people know me. When I go to the flea market everyone says *bonjour* to me. People come up and kiss me. I let them - it doesn't cost anything and it gives pleasure, as Picasso says.' [32]

A collection is born

Coco was famous for her refusal to draw sketches of her designs; instead she worked directly with a live model. She could be seen on her knees, perfectly dressed in one of her own creations, complete with hat, with scissors on a ribbon around her neck, with those strong hands working the material until she found the perfect fit. 'I do not sell bits of paper,' she would say.

Diana Vreeland, the incomparable fashion editor of *Harper's Bazaar* experienced this at first hand in Coco's private atelier six floors up on rue Cambon: 'Coco was a nut on armholes. She never, ever got an armhole quite, *quite* perfect, the way she wanted it. She was always snipping and taking out sleeves, driving the tailors absolutely crazy.' [33] She would mercilessly rip out sleeves time after time, until she got the perfect high fitting sleeve that enhanced the body shape, gave small, neat shoulders and long arms and became a trademark of her designs. But it paid off. Diana testified 'She was extraordinary. The *alertness* of the woman! The *charm*! You would have fallen in love with her. She was mesmerizing, strange, alarming, witty... you can't compare anyone with Chanel. They haven't got the *chien!* Or the chic. She was French, don't forget - totally French!' [34]

The production of a twice-yearly collection in any fashion house must, for practical reasons, follow a certain pattern, but it also relies on the skill of the designer, to pull forth inspirational ideas. The nightmare is to know that you have to do it to order, and on time. This is made even harder by the fact that the designer is always working six months ahead and, therefore, always out of season. Chanel's 'hands-on' approach, forsaking drawings and sketches to translate into *toiles* or muslin models, left her tailor and *première* taking note of her requirements directly.

Her models had a hard time in this pursuit of perfection, with Mademoiselle studying the subtleties of the textiles, watching their fall and movement from the body in the surrounding mirrors, as her models walked round the salon. One of them, refusing to be named, told Pierre Galante:

> 'Mademoiselle did not create, she enveloped us in material. For example, she made a shoulder on which she mounted a sleeve. Then she made us walk and for half an hour we had to raise and lower our arms. Mademoiselle wanted to see what the new material would give. This exercise would occur five, ten times during the afternoon. By evening I was all in, swearing not to return the next day. Then she would smile charmingly and say 'See you tomorrow.' And the next day we were all there. One day I cracked and left. I shall always regret it.'

The model went on to explain how she then worked for many other top fashion houses, for designers who were less tyrannical than Coco, with shorter hours and less tiring work.

> 'The models were first sketched, then constructed. When we wore them they were in there final form. Only a few fittings were required before the opening day of the collections... Nothing compared to Mademoiselle's interminable sessions. Nevertheless, with her, I had the impression that I was more than just a mannequin... we participated. The dress was created on us, was modelled after our reflexes and the movements of our body. We almost felt the fusion of our skin with that of the fabric... we had the feeling that it was made for us, even in a small way, by us. I have never again had this impression... Mademoiselle had shown me, what fashion was all about and what it really could be. Yes, Mademoiselle was someone.' [35]

The Chanel tweed suit

The comeback was to see the further development of the famous tweed suit and by 1957 Coco had it there in all its perfection. She had developed and enhanced it: now it was a masterpiece of design and craftsmanship.

Claire B. Shaeffer writing in her book, *Couture Sewing Techniques* describes it thus:

> 'The classic Chanel suit appears to be a loosely fitted cardigan and skirt with a well-coordinated blouse. Casual in appearance, the ensemble is actually assembled with meticulous attention to details. Nothing is left to chance, either in the way the suit is to be worn or in its construction and fit. Linings for jackets and skirts are often cut from the same fragile fabric as the blouse, which means it's almost impossible to wear the suit with a different blouse. In fact... many of the skirt and blouse ensembles designed by Chanel are actually dresses that look like separates.' [36]

In the book accompanying the Metropolitan Museum of Art's Chanel exhibition in 2005, her 'design secrets' are described thus:

> '... they were neither arbitrary nor impulsive, determined as they were by Chanel's unyielding functionalism as demonstrated by the largely invisible gilt chain and quilted lining of her post-1954 suits. While the gilt chain was intended to anchor the hem of a jacket, the quilted lining was designed to preserve its shape and structure.' [37]

The feature, of matching the lining to the blouse or dress underneath, was one of Coco's favourite looks for many years, and is still seen today. Coco had a favourite range of colours which always included beige, black, navy together with pink, red and pale green, and these were the fabrics she required from her tweedmaker. But for now, she had other things on her mind.

Financial security at last

Coco was undeterred by the snipes of the fashion press; she knew they were wrong and before long she would prove it. Her self-belief was vindicated when the board of the perfume company, Les Parfums Chanel, after some persuasion from Pierre Wertheimer decided to back her and renegotiate their contract with her.

In the original agreement made in 1924, when the Wertheimers took over the production and marketing of Chanel No.5 and its stablemates, they provided 90 percent of the working capital. To protect her fashion house Coco had signed away all but 10 percent of the perfume company.

The Wertheimers had fled France for America during the war and sold their shares to *Chanel Inc.,* a new company established by them in New York. Chanel No.5 was then manufactured in America. When Coco found out, there was endless litigation on the interpretation of clauses in the agreement. To add further intrigue, Coco had craftily had some samples of a new perfume, a twin of No.5, made up in Switzerland, which she named *Mademoiselle Chanel No.5,* and sent as gifts to Neiman Marcus in Dallas, Texas, and to Sam Goldwyn in Hollywood. She believed she could legally do this, and eventually sold it in her boutique. If she was trying to antagonise the Wertheimers she succeeded. By 1947 law suits were flying on both sides of the Atlantic, each party accusing the other of counterfeiting, and the new perfume was seized from the Paris boutique, by court order.

After long hours of negotiations, and to the relief of all concerned, Coco accepted a deal whereby she received two percent of the worldwide sales on all Chanel products, instead of ten percent of the French sales only. In addition, she would receive a vastly increased royalty from the American war-time sales, and agreed not to use 'No.5' in the name of her new Swiss perfume. She was an even wealthier woman now, than she had ever been.[38]

Now, in 1954, with House of Chanel reopened for business and Mademoiselle determined to succeed in bringing back her fashion, Les Parfums Chanel and Pierre Wertheimer were ready to talk business. Coco got an amazing deal: the perfume company would take over the entire cost of running the couture house at rue Cambon, and she retained sole control of the collection. They would pay all her personal expenses and taxes, her apartment at the Ritz, her personal staff, even her postage stamps: in return she gave them complete ownership of the Chanel name as applied to perfumes and cosmetic products. She also gave up the right to manufacture the Mademoiselle Chanel perfumes in Switzerland.[39]

Already a very wealthy woman, she was now mega-rich. Never again would Coco have to be concerned about the cost of creating couture: it must have felt a far cry from the day in 1910 when, with a financial loan from another man who believed in her, Boy Capel, she set up her millinery salon at 21 rue Cambon – just down the street.

***

42

The Canadian connection

Desmond Mathews had spent the war years serving in the Royal Air Force, and one of his greatest friends was fellow-airman Bill Waddell, the nephew of Cranston Waddell. Des and Bill were making plans for after the war, and the two friends agreed that Des would study the Textile Design course at the Scottish College of Textiles in the Border town of Galashiels, and then join Bill in running the Waddell mill at Warwick Bridge. Sadly, this was not to be as Bill, a pilot, lost his life on 24 February 1945 at the age of twenty-four. He is buried in Holme Eden churchyard, just outside Carlisle, alongside his uncle, Cranston. A plain white memorial marks his grave, and each year on Remembrance Sunday, a small wooden cross was placed on his gravestone by his friend: a tradition that was repeated until Desmond's own death in 2010.

Des continued with his plans to study textile design and, after graduating from the College, took a post with a company in the north of Scotland. In an interview, Des recalled that in 1953, 'the Principal there rang me up one day to say there was a position going in Carlisle, at Linton Tweeds, if I was interested. So I got in touch with them, and did, in fact, come down for an interview with them, and was appointed... and the Principal, Doctor Martindale had already been in touch with George Linton and said that he would get in touch with me and tell me about the job, so that's how it came about.'

A kindly man who cared for his students, Doctor Martindale had remembered that Des had said to him 'I quite like it up here in the north of Scotland, but I would much rather be down in the Borders.'

Des joined Agnes and George at Linton's, and when Jimmy Jamieson from Gretna, a Director who had worked at the mill for many years, retired, three or four years later, Des became a Director of the company. At this time, all three of the Directors were involved in designing, but Agnes curtailed her visits to America.

The company recruited local workers and George Linton would ask Bill Heaney, a teacher

Bill Waddell's gravestone in Holme Eden churchyard - the nephew of Cranston Waddell, he planned to run Warwick Mill with Des Mathews after the war, but his early death left this dream unfulfilled and Des joined Linton's

at St. Patrick's School, if there were any good lads who would like to work at the mill, recruiting George Taggart among others. Staff were loyal and stayed with the company for years, Tommy Ellis worked on the hand-looms for special fancy designs and Richard Bradbury produced patterns.[40]

As well as designing the cloth, George and Des would travel to the USA and Canada, seeing clothing manufacturers and taking orders for the tweed. The manufacturers at this time would not always be aware of the large variety of cloths available and large numbers of samples were taken, as Des remembered:

'It consisted of two or three hundred bunches... which we had produced in the previous six months or so, it used to take a long, long time, a tremendous number of patterns were produced... I suppose they suffered from insufficient knowledge of the actual manufacture... but you would pick up an idea yourself from what they bought from you, what they were interested in... you could develop then... and we had American customers, here in Carlisle, and staying at the Crown and Mitre hotel, and coming down to the mill during the day, to give us the benefit... of what they might be interested in.'

During this time, trends and predictions in seasonal colours were not as developed as they are today. As a result, 'we pretty well went our own way with the colours, when we produced the collection. Obviously we would bear certain things in mind: how they liked to buy quite a lot of yellow in the States, which we wouldn't perhaps go in for as much in this country.'

The manufacturers were mainly Jewish or Italian, but the latter gradually faded from the picture, leaving the Jewish companies as the main buyers. In Canada the largest customer was in Montreal, a Russian Jew named Auckie Sanft, while in New York it was the two Davidow brothers (also Russian Jews, making Chanel-style clothes), and who sold to major stores such as Saks Fifth Avenue and Bloomingdales.[41]

Auckie Sanft was a well-known Montreal-based clothing manufacturer, who made news in the early '60s when he hired the gifted young Canadian designer, John Warden, to become the first designer associated with a clothing manufacturer. Warden produced his first forty-item ready-to-wear spring signature collection for Sanft in 1964. It was an immediate success, and the fashion press loved the pure lines of his modern and timeless designs, mainly in cream, black and white. He opened his own boutique in 1966 when his clients included Margaret Trudeau and Ivana Trump. From 1968 to 1980 John Warden worked in association with many other Canadian clothing manufacturers, and his designs were distributed world-wide. In 1974, the Canadian Association of Fashion Designers was formed, demonstrating an important shift in the Canadian fashion world, with the emphasis on ready-to-wear. In 1978 Warden shared the prestigious 'Designer of the World' award with Yves Saint Laurent. In 1983 'The Canadian Designer of the Year Award' was one of many awards he received before his untimely death in 2007.[42]

Another talented designer, Jean-Claude Poitras designed his first line in the early 1970s for Beverini & Auckie Sanft and introduced a bridge label named BOF! later that decade. In the same period, he founded *Fashion Société Design* with Arthur Sanft, his business partner. He is known for his couture style clothing and for his promotion of Quebec's fashion industry word-wide.[43]

On a trip to London's theatreland with his wife, Des met a couple of Jewish Canadian ladies who each had a dress business in Montreal. In conversation he mentioned that he knew Montreal. They said 'How do you know Montreal, dear?' and Des replied that he had a customer there, named Auckie Sanft. They said, 'Ah, poor Auckie.' 'What's the matter with Auckie? asked Des. 'Well, he's dead dear.' 'And this went on, and another chap at Auckie's, Sol, was Auckie's right hand man really, a chap called Solomon Domer. As I said this, they said, "Ah, poor Solly." And I said "What's the matter with Solly", and they said "Well he's dead, dear." Most of these people have died, very sad.'

George Stirling Linton

Today, the clothes made of Linton Tweed by Auckie Sanft occasionally appear for sale on Vintage Fashion web-sites, and they have stood the test of time. A 1960s chartreuse lime tweed coat with a lemon yellow lining, in a chic classic style and with fringing on the pockets, looked as fresh and modern as when it was first made. It also looks typically Chanel.[44]

Bettina Ballard described developments in New York fashion in the 1950s, and the Paris influence on Seventh Avenue:

> *'New and young designers began cutting into extravagant fabrics to create luxurious fashions independent of Paris. The most important name, James Galanos, in this group belongs to an out-of-space character who describes himself as "an asparagus with eyes". He is a true designer, a fanatic perfectionist, and strangely enough, a shrewd businessman.'* [45]

Greek in origin, he had some training in Paris with Robert Piguet and Davidow, but these designs were all his own.

Harry Yoxall was the engaging and perceptive Chairman of British *Vogue* in these years and described how the British dress manufacturers were surging ahead in this period after the Second World War:

> *'Our people also learned manufacturing techniques from New York's Seventh Avenue, without sacrificing our higher finish and workmanship. They used better materials than the Americans, and the comparative smallness of their market gave them greater speed in production.* [46]

At last the quality of British design and workmanship was being recognised: if Britain had only entered the Common Market, Yoxall felt it would have been unstoppable. With the American invention of the teenager, and the upcoming young British designers such as Mary Quant, John Bates and Jean Muir, British exports soared and 'suddenly American department stores, chains, pattern publishers, were all fighting to commission young British designers to provide them with young designs.' [47]

Of Christian Dior, agents and the White Rabbit

With the return of Coco Chanel, Linton's decided to appoint an agent in Paris. M. Robert Burg had his premises just around the corner from rue Cambon; a convenient way of doing business, both for the supplier and for the couture house. His efforts, combined with those of Agnes, George and Des, regained export markets on the Continent.[48]

In fact, Burg was the first agent anywhere for Linton's, because neither George nor Agnes really favoured the idea. Des Mathews was the initiator. Visiting Christian Dior in Paris with some samples, he remembered vividly the great man's reaction to seeing them: 'Yes, they're very nice, but I really can't work like this, I have to be able to ring up somebody here in Paris, and say, "I want this and this, and I want it when I want it".'

From the customer's perspective this clearly made good retail sense, and Mathews asked Dior how he could find one. Dior then made a suggestion which was to shape Linton's business practice with the couture industry in future years when he said, 'Well, it's up to you, of course, but on your way out, call in on Monsieur Richard, who is our Treasurer, and he might be able to give a suggestion of two or three names, perhaps.'

Des Mathews went to see M. Richard who recommended Robert Burg. But before interviewing him, Des decided to take advice from the British Chamber of Commerce's office in Paris. He wanted to ensure that contracts and arrangements would be absolutely correct, and to obtain the services of an interpreter.

As luck would have it, the contact turned out to be a war hero with significant connections in haute couture.

> 'It was a Mr Yeo-Thomas that I saw, who was a very famous, sad figure, who had been a leader of the opposition in Paris against the Germans during the war. He was there all the time, and had been interrogated by the Gestapo and had his finger nails pulled out, and when I saw his hands on the desk, I could see how dreadful they were.' [49]

As part of the Special Operations Executive (SOE), Wing Commander Forest Yeo-Thomas had operated behind enemy lines under the code name of 'The White Rabbit'. He was captured and tortured by the Gestapo before being sent to Buchenwald Concentration Camp, from where he led a successful escape in 1944. Before the war he had worked in Paris, as Director for Captain Edward Molyneux at his fashion house in rue Royale, and resumed his position there when peace came.[50] His help proved invaluable to Des Mathews. (In 2010, he became the first secret agent to be commemorated with an English Heritage blue plaque, unveiled at the house in Camden, North London where he once lived.[51])

Linton Tweed at rue Cambon

Once appointed, Burg came over from Paris to Carlisle on a regular basis, selecting bunches of tweed samples that he thought suitable to sell and taking them back to Paris. He would show the tweed collection to the different Fashion Houses, with Chanel being the main buyer, and send orders back to Carlisle for six-yard lengths of different fabrics. Supplying these short lengths in many different colours was a time-consuming and costly business. At this time Chanel, for example, would make up to a hundred models for each of her collections, many of them in Linton Tweed. But, for the tweedmaker, this was a crucial way of keeping the Linton *marque* in the headlines. And it worked, much to the chagrin of their competitors.

Des Mathews recalled one occasion at the showing of a Chanel collection, when Mr Bratman, the Managing Director of Jersey Crafts (who supplied top quality jersey to Chanel) was sitting behind him watching the parade of models wearing Linton Tweed.

Leaning over to Des, he said, 'Is this supposed to be a Linton collection or a Chanel collection, I'm fed up with Linton's cloth coming out one after another.'

But it was a friendly rivalry as Mathews recalled one trip to New York when all the power went down in the city: 'George Linton and I were staying on the 31st floor, so it was a long way down, and we started to walk... on the way we met Bratman carrying a chandelier, with half a dozen candles in it, and he lighted us down and we went into his apartment for a drink.'

Chanel – fashion immortal

Such was Chanel's impact on the American fashion scene that in September 1957, on the fiftieth anniversary of the opening of Neiman Marcus stores, Stanley Marcus invited her to attend the celebrations. But he had to resort to a clever piece of flattery to get her there.[52]

The name of Neiman Marcus is renowned not only in America, but throughout the world. It opened in Dallas, Texas, in 1906 and is recognised as the most luxurious store in America. Its founders were Herbert Marcus, his younger sister, Carrie Marcus Neiman, together with her husband, Al Neiman. To honour those who

Des Mathews, Director of Linton Tweeds in the 1950s, responsible for design and sales with George Linton

worked in fashion, the company established the Fashion Oscar's in 1938, celebrating with a gala evening fashion show, and in 1947 Christian Dior received the 'Neiman Marcus Award for Distinguished Service in the Field of Fashion'.[53]

Writing in his book *Christian Dior and I* in 1957, Dior would say of Dallas:

> 'I had no idea what to expect of a city answering to such a romantic name. In fact, Dallas is a massive block of skyscrapers, grouped around a central square, and so the church, the town hall, the school and the hotel are situated exactly as they would be in a French village, except that the height of everything is multiplied twenty or thirty times.' [54]

Ten years later, having now totally regained her place at the top of the couture tree, Coco accepted Stanley Marcus' invitation to attend the store's celebrations.

That he persuaded the seventy-four year old lady to attend was no mean feat.

Her friend, Marcel Haedrich, recounts how he did it. Marcus was lunching with Coco and her lawyer, René de Chambrun, at Château de Lagrange, which René had turned into a museum dedicated to French-American friendship and commemorating Lafayette, Washington and all the heroes of the American Revolution. One of the silk banners in the museum announced a production of Hamlet starring Macready, the famous English Shakespearean actor. In huge letters the banner announced that General Lafayette would attend.

Showing Coco the banner, Marcus told her that this is how he would announce the store's fiftieth anniversary 'Mademoiselle Chanel will attend.' Coco agreed immediately but only as it was being made a special award, unique to her![55]

In his memoirs *Minding the Store* Stanley Marcus related: 'She came accompanied by the president of her American perfume company, the tall, gregarious, loquacious, encyclopaedic, and charming Gregory Thomas.'

On hearing that Coco wanted to visit a ranch, Marcus laid on the entertainment at his brother's place: ranch-style food, roping, bronco riding and a bovine fashion show, with the cattle dressed in fashion hats.

Marcus met Chanel through a mutual friend, Marie-Louise Bousquet of *Harper's Bazaar*. He found her a bit overwhelming at first, commenting on the rapidity of her speech, 'It would be an exaggeration for anyone to claim that they had ever had a conversation with Chanel, for she conducted a one-woman filibuster. Supreme egoist she was, but with justification.' [56]

On his trips to Paris, Leslie Walker would also have this problem in talking to Mademoiselle.

Speaking of her fashions, Stanley Marcus wrote:

> *'Coco Chanel revolutionised clothes... She made little suits of Linton tweeds from England, to be worn with white silk shirts, and borrowed the convenience of pants pockets from men's trousers for her skirts. Having stripped the clothes down to a basic simplicity, she then proceeded to adorn them with copies of her lavish personal jewelry, given to her by her lover, the Duke of Westminster. She had two vogues, one when she started in 1915, and the other when she came out of retirement in 1954. In the '50s and '60s her little tweed suits became a worldwide mass fashion.'* [57]

In 1963, Coco was honoured by the London *Sunday Times* by being named a Fashion Immortal. As ever, she would refuse any award that any other designer had previously received, as she did with the Légion d'Honneur, before the war. Refusing to go to London to receive the Fashion Immortal award, she did accept its delivery to her in Paris, but referred to it dismissively as 'a pretty piece of crystal.' [58]

The magic of rue Cambon

The 1950s and early 1960s were a successful time for Linton's, when more than 85% of production was exported mainly to America and Paris. Besides Chanel, other top couture houses were demanding Linton products, including Dior, St Laurent, Nina Ricci, Givenchy and Courrèges.

The salon at 31 rue Cambon, however, retained a special place in the affections of the tweedmakers. Des Mathews recalled:

> *'It's quite a big room. The wall is lined all the way round with mirrors... long mirrors, and Chanel used to sit halfway up the stairs, watching, and she could see everything with these mirrors, from where she sat, more or less see the whole affair, and when whoever was announcing said, "La collection est terminee." Then the fournisseurs as they were called, all the suppliers of braid, cloth, buttons, everything, used to make their way to the stairs and go up to give their best wishes, say how the collection was beautiful. You realised you were dismissed, as she was talking over your shoulder to the next man behind you... she always said the same sort of thing, a few words about Mr Churchill, or Mr "Currkeel" as she called him, and the Duke of Westminster... and she was sitting in a suit of our material, I can tell you the number, H1804, that's the number of the pattern, and she sat there in this suit always, but the buttons had gone and it was held together with a safety pin, quite a big safety pin, but she was a rebel of course.'* [59]

At this time all the tweed collections were piece-dyed and, therefore, single colours, or made in black and white, or grey, black and white, and dyed after the pieces of cloth were woven. There were no multi-coloured fabrics. Chanel had a favourite personal fabric, designed by Mr Jamieson, and it was simply numbered H1804: it was ecru white, wool and mohair, and the mohair made a check through the wool, so that when it was dyed the mohair dyed a slightly different colour from the wool, and the darker mohair made an overcheck.

Years later Leslie Walker, now Chairman of Linton's recalled:

> 'She said, "I want that fabric" and it went on for years and years and she would just re-colour it, and I've got a photograph in my office that she gave us, of herself wearing the fabric - a fabric she wore all the time and just used to wear it in ecru white, not mixed. That was her favourite fabric. It's too bulky and loose a fabric for today, she lined it and quilted it... and it looked lovely. She always wore a hat too.' [60]

***

43
Changing times at Linton's

The 1960s brought modernisation to Linton Tweeds as new appointments came with fresh ideas. Robert Thomlinson joined the company in 1960 after receiving his accountancy training with two large national companies. He found a very different working environment from the one he had known in the wider business world beyond the factory gates. His first impressions were of antiquated office procedures and autocratic management. George and Agnes Linton held undisputed sway and their rule was absolute. Robert recalled that, 'To be "ticked off" by either George or Agnes was not a pleasant experience. But for me it was an incentive to improve my performance and avoid another "ticking off". You had the choice of either leaving or improving. For me it was a valuable learning experience for I learned that your boss had the right to expect your very best work.'

Agnes and George could, however, be generous and thoughtful to those employees who served them to the best of their ability, and there were 'perks' to the job. There were no Trade Unions to represent the workers interests, but they received better rates of pay than elsewhere and were never paid off when the work slackened off.

Robert was given a free hand to modernise the office systems, and the shipment of tweed orders to clients was also updated. All large export orders went by boat either from Southampton or Liverpool, with samples and orders for Paris going by air from Manchester airport. Robert said, 'Eventually, by grouping all our orders for America into one consolidated shipment, we got a cheaper rate from the airlines, which enabled us to send all our exports by air to Prestwick airport at a cheaper rate than by sea freight. Way back in the 1960s that was something innovative, giving our customers a much better service and at the same time reducing our costs to the point of shipment.'

Old customs still endured, however, and Robert recalled the mill girls with affection:

> 'The most important part of the day for them was the evening and particularly the weekend when they went out to enjoy themselves. It was not unusual to see the girls turn up for work in hair curlers and wrapped up in a head scarf, all part of their advance beauty treatment in preparation for the night out. One of the customs always carried out when any of the girls were getting married was, on

the final work day before the wedding, the future bride was all decked up with ribbons, balloons and paint, and frog-marched from the Mill and up through the city centre, escorted and linked, with a dozen girls there to ensure that she was on full display with all her adornments. All with broad smiles, giggling and laughing, except for the unfortunate prospective bride.' [61]

Back in 1963 - the same year that Coco was named a Fashion Immortal - Leslie Walker had been a bright young Scottish designer engaged in work-study at Heather Mills in Selkirk before being head-hunted for a permanent post by Linton's.[62] It was to prove a fortuitous day for Linton's when he began working alongside George Linton and Desmond Mathews for, in later years, he would play a crucial role in the business. But for now, he was learning about the glamorous world of haute couture and it wasn't long before he, too, fell under the spell of rue Cambon.

By this time, George Linton was at the helm of Linton Tweeds and Desmond Matthews was a Director. Agnes Linton, although still owner and Chairwoman of the company, gradually became less involved in the day-to-day running of the business, and concentrated on developing the renowned Geltsdale Kennels and breeding deerhounds.

In June 1965, on a visit to New York with Desmond Matthews, George Linton told a journalist from *Women's Wear Daily* that Linton's had no plans to expand, but rather to modernise equipment. A dozen top firms in the American market were taking about 110,000 yards annually, and this represented 60% of the mill's output. For Spring 1966, Linton's were showing 2,000 patterns, with a further 2,000 for the autumn.

Since 1956, Coco Chanel had employed two design assistants who knew her every wish, they were Jean Cazaubon and Yvonne Dudel and Chanel trusted their judgement completely. Leslie Walker recalled his first visit to rue Cambon with George Linton in the 1960s, to show them fabrics for selection. While they were all looking at the tweeds, Chanel would often wander in from her room next door, and make suggestions on the colour and type of tweed. Orders would be placed, but as this fabric was for couture only, the business was loss-making to Linton's.

Leslie succinctly explained why this was the case:

'Jean and Yvonne would choose fabrics, and at the end of the day we would be given twenty colours in a fabric. So we had to make the fabrics and then dye twenty different colours, but they would choose round about fifty fabrics, sometimes in one colour, but most times, in three or four or five or even up to twenty colours, and all these were sent over free - free, and they only paid for what they used, and we took back afterwards.' [63]

Amusingly recalling his first visits to the showroom, to see the couture collection and his meeting with Chanel, Leslie remembered:

'I was taken very quickly in the sixties by George Linton... we would get invited to the first show at rue Cambon, and although we were never in the front seat, we were always in a good seat in the row behind - we were always a special customer and Chanel very rarely came into the salon, she sat on the stairs, and I can remember one time, there was a photographer and she came down the stairs, and she must have been eighty, and she came right down the stairs, grabbed him by the collar and she pushed him down the stairs and out - one storey up, and she did it herself. Along with Mr Robert Burg, who was our agent... we would be invited to her inner sanctum which is now kept as a museum, just up the stairs at rue Cambon, and we would have a glass of wine and she would say how lovely the Linton Tweed fabrics were... twice a year we were invited to the first show and it was exciting and I would see Givenchy and Saint Laurent and all the shows, sitting on those little, hard, gilt chairs.' [64]

The agent played an important role and his assistance was beneficial to both Linton's and Chanel. The couture house would order anything up to one hundred and fifty lengths of cloth, and if they required repeat fabric on any length, it had to be sent again from Carlisle. With Linton's ability to send bulk fabric to their agency in Paris, it meant that when Chanel required another three metres for a suit, she just had to go round the corner to Maison Burg.[65]

Tricks of the trade

Chanel was well aware of the tricks her competitors would resort to and took practical steps to thwart them, as Mathews discovered. 'She had a right-hand man who was front of house in the salon, a Monsieur Tranchant... because there were people, who would copy, of course, if they could.'[66] Pierre Tranchant had been appointed by the perfume company as Director of the fashion house, and was responsible for the administrative and commercial affairs of the company. He and Coco did not always see eye to eye, of course, as she regarded the perfume company her sworn enemy. He was Director from 1956 to 1967, when Coco fired him. He did, however, acknowledge her talent, describing her as 'above all a colourist'.[67]

Linton's success in Paris was also impacting on their domestic business. Jeffrey Wallis, the founder of Wallis Shops, was one of the growing band of British mass retailers who looked to Paris for their designs in the 1950s and 1960s. Des Mathews remembered that:

> 'Jeffrey Wallis used to be in Paris when I was there and he would track me down, wherever I was, because he would want to buy some of the particular cloths that he'd taken a fancy to. But, of course, Tranchant used to go mad if he thought that anybody was selling Wallis something. Wallis hadn't bought the model; you could only get the name of the manufacturer of the cloth, if you bought the model, and the same with the buttons, and the braid and everything else. But Wallis' mission in life was to circumvent Monsieur Tranchant, who was bright red-faced and stoutish, very furious, about Monsieur Wallis - he used to play war about him, but, of course, we had to tread very carefully, we didn't want to miss a sale. We sold a lot of cloth to Wallis, but on the other hand we didn't want to upset Chanel or Monsieur Tranchant either.'[68]

This state of affairs was soon regularised, as Wallis Shops became noted for re-introducing the classic Chanel suit to the British market, and by the end of the 1950s were buying so many models, in the form of *toiles* - a calico copy of the design - that they were offered concessionary prices by Chanel. At this time, copies of a Chanel original costing £350 would sell for £40 in Wallis Shops.[69]

Brian Godbold, head of the coat and suit design room at Wallis in the late 1960s (and later Design Director at Marks and Spencer), described Wallis as one of the great high street entrepreneurs when he introduced the Pick of Paris range in the late 1960s. Godbold chose models from the Paris collections, which were then adapted in London to fit the price and style of the Wallis range - the manufacture had to be achieved within four weeks to get the garments in store by the release date and to get newspaper coverage.[70] Marks and Spencer employed the British couturier Michael as a consultant designer for mass-production styles and bought Paris models in the 1960s to inspire their designers.[71]

Synthetic fibres change the ground rules

The development of modern technology had advanced in leaps and bounds since the end of the war and traditional textiles, using natural fibres and natural dyes, soon faced stiff competition from synthetic fibres. Manufacturers now had a huge choice of man-made fibres and no longer relied on traditional cotton, silk and wool. It also meant that fabrics now boasted advantages previously unheard of, and gave us permanent pleats, faux fur, nylon stockings, Lurex to add sparkle and even thermal underwear! The other advantages were the easy care they offered, with drip-dry, water-proof, crease-resistant, moth-proof, shrink-proof and washable properties becoming the norm.

The effects on the textile and clothing industries were far-reaching and women revelled in the freedom offered by the new materials. It was now possible to wear light-coloured easy-care clothes in the office or for sport, with materials such as Courtelle, Orlon and Dralon.[72] The large chemical companies, such as Du Pont, ICI, Monsanto, Eastman Kodak and Phillips Petroleum led the field in textile development, and have had a massive impact the fashion scene ever since.[73]

The Swinging Sixties

By now, London's own fashion revolution was in full swing. It was the time of Carnaby Street and the King's Road, of the rise of boutiques, of Mary Quant, Twiggy and miniskirts and an explosion of fashion for the young. In the music world, the Beatles were storming America, and the decade earned the name the 'permissive society' as young women found sexual freedom with the introduction of the contraceptive pill. It was also a time of social consciousness. It became the age of youth as young people joined in protest marches against nuclear weapons and, in America, the Civil Rights movement demonstrated for equal rights for black Americans. It was a decade of enormous political and social change: in Paris there were student riots, the Berlin wall was built, China saw the Cultural Revolution, man first landed on the moon, photo-journalists captured the horrors of the Vietnam War and the world held its breath over the Cuban missile crisis.

In the world of fashion, the Sixties were a time of great development for the House of Chanel and for Linton Tweeds. Coco was now firmly back at the top. Even though by now she was well into her seventies, there seemed to be no end to her indefatigable energy. Marketing was the new buzz word, as not only the fashions, but the perfumes made news. Andy Warhol considered the distinctive square bottle of No.5 perfume to be a twentieth century icon and, in 1964, immortalised it in a series of colourful screenprints. The following year Jacques Helleu was appointed Artistic Director at Chanel and eventually became Artistic Director for the perfumes and beauty products. The House of Chanel was a great success.

Locally, Linton's brought a bit of Paris chic to their hometown. In October 1963, the *Carlisle Journal* was reporting:

> *'You too can have the Paris haute couture look; you can buy tweeds from the famous Parisian fashion houses here in Carlisle. Linton Tweeds Ltd have opened a small shop… where lengths of tweed of all colours and textures can be bought, the same tweeds that are supplied to leading fashion houses in America, Canada, Japan, Australia, Paris and the Netherlands. The odd lengths not required by the designers are returned to Carlisle for sale. And remember, tweed is in fashion this winter.'*[74]

It was definitely a fashionable winter for the ladies of Carlisle.

Life at Oakland House

Christmas 1964 and fifteen-year-old Linda Nelson had started her first job as kennel maid to Agnes Linton. It was a job she really loved. The work was hard, with early morning starts at 7.30am, and the day not finishing until she had given the daily progress report to Miss Linton on her return from the Mill at 4.00pm.

The deerhounds were beautiful and she loved every one of them: there were seventeen in all, together with the puppies or 'tiddlers', as they were called.

Linda walked them every day in groups of five, and they were truly gentle giants. The conservatory was ablaze with colour, with dozens of pink, red, lilac and white pot plants delivered by the florist, which were to be Nessy's Christmas gifts to her friends.

The dogs were Nessy's life, and now, in her early sixties, she still spent the middle hours of the day in her management role at the Mill but then came back to Oaklands, which was her retreat and haven of peace from the cares of business. It was now almost twenty years since she had moved here, and the hardships of the war years, with their restrictions on textiles and government edicts, were a fading memory, as were the problems of making a home for homesick evacuee children.

Nessy liked an ordered life and everything at the house ran like clockwork, with enough staff to ensure that it was self-sufficient. There was a chauffeur to drive the two cars, and the cook, Evelyn Jackson, lived in for six days a week, going home to her parents in the village of Slaggyford every two weeks. She would serve Nessy's meals in the library, but when there was a dinner party, the dining room table would be glowing with the family silver and fresh flowers. Ralph Watson, the gardener, lived in the flat above the kennels, tending the lovely gardens and growing fresh vegetables to supply the house, as well as nectarines and other fruits in the three greenhouses.

Every Thursday afternoon, the chauffeur picked up Christine, an eighty-year-old lady, who was a former mill employee and came to the house each week to clean the silver, with another cleaner coming in for three days each week. Nessy was a firm but fair employer, a very proper country lady, and treated her staff with generosity. She was rewarded with great loyalty, many of the staff remaining with her for a lifetime. Every week, on her instructions, the cook would make afternoon tea for the staff, with the nectarine fool being described by Linda as 'to die for'.

A fit and vigorous woman, Nessy had a great sense of humour. She loved to read, a fact attested to by the ceiling to floor bookshelves in her library - there were hundreds of books. Sometimes the dogs were allowed into the library to sit on a huge sofa, covered with a throw of exquisite tweed. She loved beautiful, elegant things around her, but did not flinch when a deerhound accidentally brushed against a four foot Chinese vase - one of a pair - and crashed it to smithereens. To the dismayed Linda, she would say 'It's alright, my dear, it's only a vase, it's not breathing!'

A kind, often shy woman, she may have been, but when it came to the welfare of the dogs, she was formidable. One day driving along behind a gypsy caravan, she noticed a sick-looking deerhound tied to the back and trailing along behind. She stopped the caravan and insisted that the owner sell the dog to her, now, on the spot. Confronted by a lady who was not to be trifled with, he did so, and the deerhound was taken back to Oaklands to be cared for.

The house and its grounds were extensive, almost a small estate, with Nessy owning woodlands, adjoining fields and Red Cat House opposite, where her friends, Mr and Mrs Atkinson, lived with their deerhound, Flora. Red Cat House had formerly been a public house, and was next door to a poultry farm, where Linda's future husband, Dave Nelson, worked. On Linda's marriage, she received a congratulatory card from her deerhound charges - with all their names on it!

The deerhounds were Nessy's life and Linda describes her as being totally dedicated to preserving the purity of the deerhound breed. She would study pedigrees going back six or seven generations, and any dog not quite matching up would be kept as a pet,

Oakland House, Brisco

Linda Nelson with the 'tiddlers'
at Geltsdale Kennels, 1964

Oakland House with its extensive
kennels

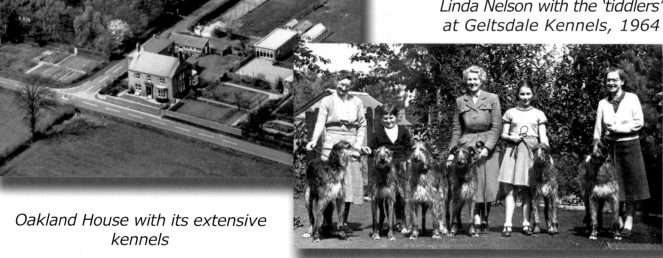

Mrs Trotter, Morna Trotter, Nessy,
Linda Trotter and Miss Maymie
Linton with the Geltsdales, 1954

Red Cat House, Brisco

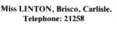

Advertising the Geltsdales in 'Our Dogs
Christmas Annual,' 1976/77 - a
thriving business

but not for breeding. Nessy's Geltsdale Kennels were one of three major breeders in the United Kingdom, the others being her friend, Norah Hartley's Rotherwood Kennels in Peterborough and Ardkinglas in Scotland. In those days the breed was rarer than it is today.

The dogs had the best of everything. There was a separate dog kitchen to prepare their food, complete with a Bendix automatic washing machine - this at a time when many homes did not possess one. The kennels were centrally heated, with a separate hospital kennel, a nursery for the pups, and an annexe for the dogs. When photographs were needed for advertising or show purposes, the leading photographer of dogs, Thomas Fall, was called in.

Like-minded ladies

Perhaps it was because she was surrounded by beautiful tweeds, and news of fashion houses and couturiers all day long, that Nessy herself did not care too much about clothes. Or perhaps her true vocation was really in being a country lady. She had always had a lady companion: initially Miss Kidd, who had travelled with her to America on her selling trips to the New York buyers. Miss Kidd had also served as a part-time Kennel Manager, helping with the deerhounds until she died in the 1960s.

Her friend, Norah Hartley, writing at the time of Nessy's death, recalled:

> *'A year before the outbreak of the Second World War Mr Linton died and Nessy found herself the Managing Director of Linton's Cumberland Homespuns, a name which was afterwards changed to Linton Tweeds. It was a challenging position because the firm, though small, numbered among its customers many of the great couturiers and fashion houses of London, Paris and New York. That it kept its high position was due to her outstanding ability - a fact which she tried, often too successfully, to conceal. But it meant heavy responsibility and very hard work and though she loved and cherished her dogs there was little time to devote to them as a kennel. Without the wonderful help and companionship of her great friend Miss Kidd she could scarcely have carried on, but Kiddiekins loved both Nessy and the dogs and devoted herself unstintingly to both.'* [75]

Miss Kidd's successor was Miss Sivewright, who came as a live-in companion and owned an old house at Skinburness near Silloth, a small Victorian town on the west coast of Cumbria. Of her, Norah Hartley wrote that 'a fresh impetus was given to the kennel's success by the advent of Miss Sivewright. She loved all dogs and quickly identified herself with the Geltsdales. Her part-time work allowed her to give Nessy much actual help, her training in physiotherapy provided much knowledge and her comradeship in good times and bad was an inspiration and source of strength.' [76]

At this time the post of full-time Kennel Maid was created and Linda Nelson joined Geltsdale Kennels. Miss Sivewright had an enhancing effect on Nessy's fashion sense, as she now started wearing beautiful tweed suits, with short Chanel-style jackets and box-pleated skirts: she had lots of them. It was all a far cry from the days when she wore her three good suits in succession. But she still wore her sensible country shoes.

As a designer, Nessy had always appreciated colour and well-cut, beautifully sewn clothes. On going to her first dog show in Darlington, Linda asked Nessy what she should wear for the occasion, and recalls Miss Linton said 'Oh my dear, whatever you put on will be fine.' As Linda's mother was a talented seamstress, she had just finished making her a heather wool skirt and had almost finished knitting a toning jumper. Linda wore this outfit on the day, and it was greatly admired by Nessy. Asking where she had got it from, and hearing that Linda's mother had made it from material bought in Carlisle Market, she later brought home a large pile of tweed lengths, and left them with a note for Linda to look at them, 'and hope you find them of some use.' Linda left a message that she had chosen the green roll, whereupon Miss Linton said 'My dear, you are meant

183

to have all of them.' Linda was very happy wearing couture tweed - and was the best dressed Kennel Maid in town.[77]

***

44

Mannequins in Moscow, suits in the States

Meanwhile, Chanel was branching out. 1967 saw seven of Coco's mannequins in Moscow, along with the Director of the House, Pierre Tranchant. This was the first official trip of a Western couturier to Moscow, but Coco herself, now eighty–four, did not attend in person.

The invitation to show a collection of her clothes behind the Iron Curtain came out of the blue, but Coco relished the chance: 'This amuses me. I think this experiment is worth making. I've only had one aim in life: to send my models out into the street. And now here they are on Red Square.'

The show was a great success with thirty-five thousand people, paying two roubles each and crowding to see the epitome of French style, during the two-day event.

On his return to Paris, Monsieur Tranchant reported:

> 'No-one in the U.S.S.R. can afford to dress in high fashion, not even in ready-to-wear as we think of it. But an evolution is taking place. I even think that in the future we might be asked to act as fashion advisers for the Ministry of Light Industry, which is in charge of couture... In any case, the Russians plan to come to Paris for the winter collections... The only trade agreements we came to concerned the perfumes. Chanel perfumes, which for a year now have come under an import agreement, will from now on be sent in greater quantities to the U.S.S.R. But here again, the market is a limited one due to insufficient buying power.' [78]

His words were prophetic: Russian fashion had to wait until the 1980s before it took off, with an influx of imports from the Far East. Valentin Yudashkin, one of Russia's leading fashion houses, started in 1987 and now has showrooms in Moscow, Paris and Milan, as well as a network of boutiques in Russia and the rest of Europe. He was chosen to design the Russian team uniforms for the Atlanta Olympic Games and his work, based on the beauty of Russian culture, is represented in the Louvre Costume Museum in Paris.

Chanel tweed suits America's first lady

The Chanel tweed suit, with its boxy jacket and elegant cut became a fashion favourite in America. Jacqueline Kennedy was one of the women who loved it. A winner of American *Vogue's* Prix de Paris in 1951, when she cited Charles Baudelaire, Oscar Wilde and Serge Diaghilev in her essay *'People I Wish I Had Known'*, fashion and style were her forte.[79]

She was a fan of the Chanel look which suited her simple, elegant, well groomed persona. Her husband John F. Kennedy bought her jewellery from Chanel and one of the most poignant items was a brooch pin - a dragonfly with an articulated tail - which she lost on the edge of the ocean at New Mexico, on her honeymoon. She was heartbroken when the search that she and JFK made to retrieve it proved fruitless.[80]

A less happy memory of the Coco-Kennedy connection came on 22 November 1963, President Kennedy tragically lost his life in Dallas and the photograph of Mrs Kennedy, her skirt covered in his blood flashed around the world. The pink suit she was wearing was made by Chanel. By then Coco was eighty years old, and her only comment was 'Yes, Jackie Kennedy was wearing a Chanel suit in Dallas.' [81]

In 1966, three years after the President's death, Coco had the chance to repay Jackie's love of her work when she was told how the dragonfly brooch had been lost. Chanel made a replica for her, and Jackie is reported to have wept when she saw it. Today, the brooch is in possession of her daughter, Caroline.

Fashion is news when it happens

John Fairchild, the publisher of New York's prestigious fashion trade newspaper, *Women's Wear Daily*, said in 1965 'Fashion is news when it happens, that day, not a month after.' [82] In his book, *The Fashionable Savages*, he wrote of meeting Coco, whom he calls the 'Eighth Wonder of the World', when she had Monsieur Tranchant telephone to invite him to lunch at her apartment at rue Cambon. To him and her other guest, Hervé Mille, she held forth:

> *'Couture is architecture. It's proportion, the shape and length of the neck, the shape of the head, its proportion to the body... Fashion is not illusion. It is the colour of the cloth, the choice of mannequins, the setting. I try to present the least vulgarity possible, under lights like those of a cathedral.'* [83]

Jackie Kennedy, wearing a Chanel suit, arrives at Dallas airport, 22 November 1963, just hours before the fatal shooting of the President

In 1965, he saw Coco at her Spring/Summer collection: for him she was still the best.

> *'Right after the showing I went upstairs to see Mademoiselle Chanel. She looked wonderful, even though she had been confined to her bed for two weeks in the middle of making the collection. The small, outer salon was filled with people. Coco smiled at me and we embraced. She wore a rusty orange coloured plaid suit, a thick sable round her neck, fastened with an ordinary safety pin, a diamond sunburst with a huge cabochon ruby pinned casually to her bottom jacket pocket, and she held a glass of champagne in her hand. "I want to have dinner with you alone tonight," she said.'* [84]

Such was the appeal of this eighty-one year old woman. At dinner she told him 'that fashion really was a daily thing, today, not yesterday, or tomorrow.'

The copyists

If imitation is the sincerest form of flattery, then Coco was the most flattered woman in the world. The beautifully cut suits of Linton tweed, with their contrasting braid-bound edges, jewelled buttons and silk shirts matching their jacket linings, were her greatest success and copied at all levels. Sometimes they had matching coats, which enhanced the look even more. When she introduced them in 1957, three years after her comeback, she could not have known that that they would become the most copied clothes in the Western world.[85]

Copying was anathema to all the couture designers; it meant that their ideas and designs could be pirated when the models were scarcely off the catwalk. Some manufacturers would go to extraordinary lengths to be the first to get a copy on to the high street, and to protect the designers the *Chambre Syndicale de la Couture Parisienne* sought to prevent such practices.

Coco herself recognised that it was almost impossible to prevent cheap copies. She understood that all women wanted to look stylish and was delighted one day when her secretary, Lilou Grumbach, brought back a fifty franc 'Chanel' that was being sold, next to the vegetables, at a street market. Made in white coarse linen, with a plaited braid border, it gave Coco the idea of using raffia: two could play that game - if they stole her ideas, she would borrow from them.

But she reserved her real contempt for the trade association: for her it was simply a device for protecting the interests of dressmakers.[86] In 1957, she broke with the *Chambre Syndicale,* after a dispute over allowing photographs of the collection to be made before the agreed dates. She wrote to the President saying: 'I have the honour to submit to you, as President... a resignation that you desire but that, out of a courtesy for which I thank you, you hesitate to request of me. This will resolve the conflict that has existed between your association and myself.' [87]

Gavin Waddell, discussing this problem in his book *How Fashion Works,* has this to say: 'Copying may be so much part of the fashion process that, no matter how much regulation is supposed to govern copyright it may be impossible ever to counteract plagiarism in fashion. The promotion of the success of shorter lead times from catwalk to high street has meant that the original designers' input and their protection seems to have been quite forgotten.' [88]

The stuff of which legends are made

Cecil Beaton was tearing out his hair. He had been invited to design the sets and costumes for the stage musical of Coco's life. Life was difficult with two prima donnas to contend with not only Coco, but Katherine Hepburn who was playing her onstage.

In 1965, Alan Jay Lerner had been looking to follow his successful musical *My Fair Lady* (for which Beaton had designed the sets and costumes) with another stage musical. He had the idea of portraying the life of Coco Chanel. Lerner and Loewe had also had big hits with *Gigi* and *Camelot* and Lerner felt the time was right for a modern story - Coco's life.

Frederick Brisson, the film and stage producer, who was married to the actress Rosalind Russell, had been trying to persuade Coco to agree to the idea since her comeback in 1954 but without success. It was another ten years before she finally agreed, with her lawyer, René de Chambrun, negotiating the rights for her.

A lunch was held in the home of her great friends, Hervé and Gerard Mille in rue de Varenne. The brothers were well-known society figures, and Hervé had connections with the French newspaper magnate, Jean Prouvost, who owned *Paris-Match* and *Marie-Claire* among many other publications.

Frederick Brisson met with Coco and put forward his ideas - an autobiography, a musical comedy and then a film. She rejected the book and film out of hand, perhaps not wishing writers probing her secrets, but she did agree to the musical comedy. Yes, she thought, perhaps the story of her youth from 1913 when she started to make a name for herself, perhaps played by Audrey Hepburn? It would be amusing *and* let her detractors see what she had achieved.

Alan Jay Lerner had something altogether different in mind. He had written a libretto suitable for the middle-aged Rosalind Russell, and it portrayed Coco's life from 1954, when she made her comeback at the age of seventy. He explained how he saw her 'Coco is a woman who has sacrificed everything for her independence and who, having gained it, pays the exorbitant price of loneliness for it.' This was a true assessment, but one likely to traumatise Coco.[89]

In 1966, the musical trio of Brisson, Lerner and composer André Previn came to Paris with the finished work. Coco was invited to the Hotel Meurice, where Lerner ran through the libretto, singing all the songs to Previn's accompaniment on the piano. She was in tears at the portrayed prediction of her grandmother, singing the words that she would know fame and fortune but would always be alone.

The work went forward, with Beaton having a series of meetings both with Coco and with Katherine Hepburn. In July 1969, he had his first costume fittings with Katherine Hepburn in London. It was not an easy experience, with Hepburn and her advisors, making constant suggestions for changes to the designs. Beaton describes the fittings as a war of nerves, and saw part of the problem in the fact that Katherine Hepburn had never 'worn' women's clothes, but had her own style of polo-necked sweater and wide-legged slacks, topped with a Dutchman's cap. On being presented with Chanel-type styles, she would say 'No, I've never worn anything like this.' [90]

In all, Beaton made two hundred and fifty-three costumes for the fifty-three actors, and criticism by the fashion world did not go down well. It was thought that they were too different from Chanel's style. But Beaton would explain that they were what Coco would have designed for the stage, and they had to be not only an interpretation, but an exaggeration of her style.[91]

Of the designs, Beaton would say 'I don't think they are very exciting but then Chanel's work is not theatrical. It is in perfect taste and always has been.

> 'I have not enjoyed the job as much as I should, as the background to the whole project is hysterical and changing. As soon as one has made one gesture of good faith one is rewarded by a slap in the eye of disappointment. At the moment Hepburn is being difficult and wants to look like Hepburn and not Chanel.' [92]

Eventually, on 13 November 1969, after months of costume alterations, arguments about the stage sets and frayed nerves, the ticket office opened at the Mark Hellinger Theatre on Broadway. The queues stretching around the block, and the box office advance receipts, setting a record at $2 million.

The great day dawned - it was Thursday 18 December 1969 - the First Night of *Coco*. Cecil Beaton attended with Princess Lee Radziwill, Jackie Kennedy's beautiful sister. In his diaries he describes his feelings:

> 'Our seats were in the second row... I enjoyed the evening, for the show has improved enormously and goes with a zing. There are lots of things that could and should be changed, but Alan is above everything stubborn.

Beaton was pleased to see how positively the choreography, the sets and little black dresses and other costumes were received, but was concerned to hear people saying that 'there was no show but for me.' The problem seemed to lie in the casting of Katherine Hepburn: for Beaton, she was lacking the magic he associated with Chanel, even though the finale was greeted with rapturous applause. [93]

The show was spectacular with the action taking place after the so-called failure of Chanel's 1954 come-back collection, and then celebrating her success in the American market. Hepburn had worked on her almost non-existent singing voice for eight hours a day, and played the part with aplomb. Throughout the action there were film flashbacks on-screen, showing the men who had been important in Coco's life. To the aroma of No.5 drifting from the stage, the finale was spectacular, a parade of the dresses she had created from 1916 until 1969 - a time-span of fifty-three years, an amazing record.

The next day the newspaper critics panned the show, but praised Hepburn's performance, which worried Brisson because of the effect it would have when the time came for her to leave the show.

In spite of Beaton's misgivings, Katherine Hepburn remained in the show until 1 August 1970, when her part was taken over by Danielle Darrieux, a French actress, who was a great success. However, the show failed to bring in the audiences and it closed on 3 October 1970 after 329 performances. Beaton's prediction that it would not open in London came true.[94] But Katherine Hepburn returned to the show, to take it on a tour of major American cities, where she again triumphed.[95]

Cecil Beaton won a coveted Tony Award for his costumes,[96] but back at Linton Tweeds, George Linton was disappointed that the company had not been more involved.

Coco had mixed feelings about attending the Broadway first night opening, even though she would have been given a tumultuous welcome by the American audience. She would say 'To be loved... When you're badly treated, America comes to your defence. America is the Salvation Army.' She had a white sequin dress made, but still had doubts. She had some irreconcilable differences with the production: Lerner had written that, after the first comeback collection, an American dress designer had injected youth into her designs and brought in American customers to the house. This, only partly true, was perhaps good theatrical licence for an American audience, but anathema to Coco. The second reason was Cecil Beaton's costume designs for the show - with which she was not impressed. Of the libretto, she was to say: 'I don't do very much - I just sit there and everyone marches past me. They come and sing me the songs that I liked.'

It was fate that decided the issue, a week before the opening she suffered a mild stroke, which affected one of her hands. As her songs were sung on Broadway, Coco lay fuming in the American Hospital at Neuilly. It was to take three months for her to recover, and as she returned to rue Cambon, wearing a black and gold elastic wrist support, her staff, paid her the compliment of acting as if they hadn't noticed anything. Mademoiselle was a survivor.[97]

✱✱✱

45

A fresh impetus for Linton's

By 1968 further changes were afoot at Linton's, as George Linton retired due to ill-health and Desmond Matthews left the company to move to Cornwall. This left Leslie Walker as the only working Director and designer. In 1969 he was appointed Managing Director, a move that marked the birth of Linton's modern era.

Leslie Hope Walker, like William Linton, was born in the Scottish border town of Selkirk and had a longstanding family background in tweed production. His grandfather, David Walker, had moved south from Innerleithen in the Tweed Valley to Selkirk in the 1890s. An interesting document that has survived from 1885 shows he was a leading light in the Innerleithen Debating Society. Although Innerleithen had five mills at this time, Selkirk was a larger town with greater opportunity. He started Heather Mills in the town around 1894. David had gained a considerable reputation in the textile world when he brought in the successful innovation of selling tweed direct to tailors, cutting out the middle-man, the wholesaler. Like most of the Selkirk mills, Heather Mills was a 'vertical' mill, meaning that it had its own wool spinning mill to produce its own yarn and feed the weaving sheds. Large warehouses were obtained in Selkirk, to store the woollen cloth and tweed, and fulfil orders. Twelve sales representatives were employed to take 'bunches' of the swatch samples and sell the cloth to tailors throughout the United Kingdom.

Tragically, in 1905, David died of peritonitis while still a young man, leaving his wife, Nellie Hope, with a young family to care for. Nellie was forced to take money out of the Mill to bring up the young family of five children under the age of nine, which included her seven-year old son, Jack, who would become Leslie's father.

Jack served in World War 1 before making his career in Heather Mills. His wife, Alice, was a schoolteacher. By the time Leslie had gained his Scottish Highers examinations and left school, he had decided not to go into the family business, but to pursue his keen interest in sport and train as a Physical Education Instructor at Jordan Hill College in Glasgow. However, Leslie had spent his school holidays working at the mill and, with his two brothers pursuing other careers, he gave further thought to joining the family business. He decided to study textile design at the Scottish College of Textiles in Galashiels, splitting his weeks between working two days in the mill and studying three days at the college. As a result, he rapidly acquired an all-round knowledge and expertise of the textile manufacturing process.[98]

And he started at the very bottom to learn the business: sweeping the floor in the room where the wool was sorted before being washed, carded and spun at the nearby Whinfield Mill, after which it was returned to Heather Mills. Leslie soon progressed through all the processes of the mill and its tweed production, a background that left him thoroughly equipped for his later career at Linton Tweeds.[99]

In those days the mill owners also 'owned' the town, being involved in many aspects of civic life. My interviews with him showed that Leslie had vivid memories of his early life in Selkirk and he recalled as a child hearing the mill hooters sounding at seven-thirty in the morning, from the eight mills down by the riverside. 'Most people stayed on the hillside so there were buses that would go down in the morning... my father worked on a Saturday morning, and they didn't get Christmas Day either you know, it wasn't a holiday in Scotland... we got New Year... but my father, because he was a Director of the company would be home for a long lunch with us, but he still worked.'

Leslie's maternal grandfather worked on the estate of the 8th Duke of Buccleuch, whose son, the Earl of Dalkeith, was a close friend of Princess Margaret and married the beautiful Jane McNeill, a fashion model for the house of Norman Hartnell.

'All the townspeople were connected with the mill – it was just a way of life, you know, somebody would say their granny was a weaver and their mother was a darner – they all worked in the factory.' Selkirk slang

David Walker (seated, 2nd left front row), grandfather of Leslie Walker and the founder of Heather Mills, pictured in 1905

finally got the better of Leslie's mother, Alice, who was not from the border country. One day when she was teaching, she said to the children 'What are you going to do when you leave school?' The reply had her baffled, 'In gear, Miss'. It turned out to be Selkirk slang for 'In-giver' - a process that described the first job that boys and girls started with at the mill.

Leslie explained:

> 'They were really saying an In-giver, who separated each thread in its correct order and gave it to the person sitting at the other side who pushed a hook through and pulled it back through, and that was the first job they all got... Strand by strand and they had to pick it, they had to give it to a more skilled person who was at the other side with a hook... so the In-giver had to give the right thread – so that's what everybody did – everybody in Selkirk. There was no other... other than shops, the normal thing, the butcher, the baker, the candlestick maker, everybody went into... six large mills that would all employ 150 to 200 people each one, the only one that's left, really of any size, is Heather Mills... it now belongs to Edinburgh Woollen Mills, it makes fabric.' [100]

(Heather Mills were bought by Edinburgh Woollen Mill in the 1980s.[101])

Just across the yard...

Boom times for Linton Tweeds also meant stability for their suppliers, such as Robert Todd & Sons, just across the yard from the tweedmaker. This was an enduring business relationship, dating back to the Linton's beginnings. In 1968, four girls from Agnes Linton's old high school visited Todd's woollen mill and Lintons, and described the production processes they saw in the High School Magazine. It makes amusing and interesting reading today. At Todds, the girls described how they tracked down as many old men as they could find, and Mr Burrows, the Production Manager, to learn the history of the mill. Mr Coulthard, the lift man, was the tenth generation of his family to work at the mill, and recalled bygone days, when workers in clogs and shawls, worked from six in the morning until six at night, with only one week's unpaid holiday and a bonus of 2s 6d at Christmas.

Conditions had improved since then, and the factory had been modernised with new machinery, lighting and ventilation.

On the ground floor, the sacks of scoured wool entering the factory process, was of different origins and quality, with the best coming from Merino sheep. A coarser quality, 'Shetland', came from all over England. A wide colour range was available to customers and, after the four-hour dyeing process in large dye-baths, the wool was rinsed and dried before been put into the teasing machine for blending. It was now ready for packing into tight bales.

The second floor of the factory was home to the carding department, where the dyed wool was fed through the machine in seven–ounce hanks, rolled onto wooden balls and then onto spools. It was now ready for spinning.

The noise of the machinery in the third-floor Spinning Department was deafening, with the winding frames, spinning frames and spinning mules. Here the wool was spun into yarn of various thickness or ply's, and wound onto cones (although some customers preferred it wound into hanks). Finally, it was graded as heavy or light, and was now ready for dispatch to firms throughout the United Kingdom. 90% of it was then exported, mainly to America.

And some of it just crossed the yard to Linton Tweed, where it went through the weaving process, and the finished product became beautiful tweed.[102]

The challenge of the future

It was a difficult time for Leslie Walker to take over the running of Linton's. The boom times of the previous decade were gone. Events over which the company had no control were having an effect on the business and a dangerous downward spiral began. At this time Linton Tweeds employed over a hundred workers, many of whom had been with the company for years. Closure would have meant the devastating loss of jobs to a skilled staff group who had always been extremely loyal and hard working.

The reasons for the downturn were many and complex.

Traditional practices endured in the fashion industry, at a cost to Linton's. Robert Burg, the old friend and agent in Paris, was still running the business to the couture houses, but most of these, and Chanel in particular, would only order six-yard lengths, then use just a small number. It was not a lucrative business, even though the prestige was great.

In addition, Linton's, a member of the Scottish Woollen Trades Employer's Association had, until this time, always used 100% pure virgin wool and mohair or natural fibre, and there was much competition from larger firms in Yorkshire, many of whom produced 'shoddy' (regenerated blended wool and a cheaper cloth), as well as from Scotland who could apply economies of scale and produce cheaper cloth.

Even more problematic were the new man-made products that were coming onto the market, offering different design opportunities and greater production challenges.

The situation was further aggravated by events in the United States, where quota systems introduced in the 1950s to protect American manufacturers, and Trade Union agreements in the 1960s, affected Seventh Avenue and helped to close most of the manufacturers who were Linton's customers. As this was Linton's main market, with 85% of production exported to America, the outlook was grave. Agnes and George Linton had traditionally sold to ten prestigious customers exclusively, in America, providing them with a first-class service, but the downturn in trade threatened the closure of Linton's for lack of new customers.

Bill Blass, the American designer was one of those who at first would not see Leslie when he went to show his samples, having previously been denied the tweed. Blass threw the samples across the room in a fit of temperament. However peace soon reigned and, eventually, Leslie Walker was even invited to the Blass penthouse suite where orders were placed. It was not always so congenial and Leslie recalls, with some feeling, the day he visited a designer and found the staircase guarded by the Mafia, complete with machine guns.[103]

Staff at Linton's pause for a photo opportunity, 1930s

Leslie had grown up with the tweed trade in his blood and had belief in the quality of Linton products, but could see that this was a new age in the textile trade and in the fashion world. He had to fight to turn the business around - and so he made his plans.

At this point, Linton's could have gone the way of many long-established family businesses, where specialist skills and practices could not compete in a world making great technological and commercial advances. Many small businesses who were closed down or were taken over by the large conglomerates. Leslie Walker was driven by the determination not to let this happen to Linton Tweeds.

Changing the product – a momentous decision

His belief in the company was to prove both inspired and justified, but he could not know this in 1969. He set to work with a determined ambition to make the product different from its competitors. It needed to be unique and it needed to be attractive to the designers of the new era - the 'Swinging Sixties' were drawing to a close, but the changes they had brought about in the fashion world would reverberate into the future.

As a member of the Scottish Woollen Trade Employers Association, Linton's could only use 100% pure virgin wool or natural fibres. This meant they were prevented from designing innovatory fabrics with man-made fibres. But the company was based in England, not Scotland, so Walker made the bold decision that Linton's should withdraw their membership from the Trade Association.

Agnes and George were at first sceptical, wanting to preserve the traditional methods of production, but they were finally persuaded to agree with Leslie. It was decided that Linton's would leave the Association so as to have the freedom and ability to design new and exotic fabrics with mixed yarns. It was a momentous decision and major change in the dynamics of the company.

Perhaps Agnes and George were concerned about the effect of change on their relationship with Chanel. Leslie knew their worries had no foundation:

> *'The original Mr Linton was connected with Chanel in Paris... and she used only wool and mohair fabrics, but there were no synthetics. So the original Chanel suit was all in wool and mohair, with texture. I wanted to change things and Chanel was very happy to change, so that we then started using multi-coloured fabrics...*
> *I showed to Coco Chanel herself, and she was happy that we were doing something different... and in my opinion, if we hadn't changed then, we would have gone out of business'* [104]

Those Scottish firms who stayed with producing cloth in virgin wool alone soon found there was too much competition within this shrinking market. It then became a matter of price and, as small firms could not compete with larger ones, their only recourse was to do something different or go out of business. Eventually more companies followed Linton's lead.

Leslie described the situation then:

> *'You see, in the good old days in this country, there were worsteds, Huddersfield were the men's worsteds, the whole of Yorkshire was shoddy, which meant they were using cheaper wools, and Scotland used 100% virgin wool... and we were the first to step outside that because I felt we're not Scotland, we're not Yorkshire, so we could do what we liked, we were the first to step out of line.'* [105]

The wedding of Leslie and Carole Walker at Selkirk, 1960

192

At Linton's, new yarn-dyeing machinery was installed, enabling an extended colour range to be produced. Originally the Dyeing Department only dyed plain, single coloured cloth, but the new machinery meant that they could dye multi-coloured yarn. Leslie recalling this time says 'It was a major investment and a major turn too, you know, in thinking.'

But Linton's were still buying a lot of wool. Eighty percent of wool was bought from Robert Todd's mill, and no transport was needed. By 1968, Todd's were producing different blends of wool, such as lambswool and mohair, lambswool, angora and nylon, and lambswool, alpaca and nylon.

Leslie recalled:

> 'At Linton Tweeds we had some very subtle things that we used to buy from Robert Todd, which was owned by Mick Potts... we got them to make six different shades, going from very light grey to dark grey - see them all now - we had bordeaux shades, we had very light bordeaux to dark bordeaux and very light blue to dark blue. They were fast to cross-dye, so we could do a check in a cloth, make a check with green and blue and white, and whatever we wanted, and then after it was made into cloth we would dye in a range of colours. So you see, instead of just black we could have black and grey and bordeaux and then dye on top of it, and it gave some very nice cloths.' [106]

Tweed by design – warping and wefting

Now, all of Leslie Walker's experience as a young man at Heather Mills came into its own. So how is all that beautiful tweed created? Are there trade secrets or some potent ingredient which adds sparkle and sheen to the fabric? Not so: the talent it requires has many qualities - imagination, an eye for colour, patience and hard work play no small part.

Leslie visualised the colour mix and pattern he wanted to create in the tweed, and then selected all the appropriate yarns from the yarn store. The yarns might be natural, such as wool, mohair, silk, cotton or linen. Or they might be a selection of man-made fibres, or a mix of both, giving a wide variety of texture or finish to the cloth. Selecting his colour palette came next, whether it was vibrant pinks, soft blues, groovy greens, buttery yellows or the soft muted natural tones which were always popular.

With a sheet of black cloth in front of him, and his choice of yarns on the table close by, he started to lay out and build up the pattern he saw in his mind's eye. 'I designed the same way as I had known at Heather Mills, I'd have a sheet of black cloth and I would have all my colours and yarn and lay them out.'

If it was a check pattern, the balance of colour, and light and shade, had to be considered. As the pattern emerged, the sequence of the colours and yarns were recorded for the weaver. Other factors had to be kept in mind, the texture and weight of the finished fabric were important to the finished garment, as was the type of finishing to be used. 'Then you went to the handloom weavers, you would have them in the room... and you could spend a lot of time getting them to change things.'

The handloom weaver would now work from the recorded instructions with the designer alongside. At this point, with the warp and weft of the yarns meshing, the pattern and colour of the cloth unfolded as it came off the loom. Modifications to colours or textures could be made at this stage, by changing a yarn, to create the desired effect.

A lot of time could be spent in modifying a design before the final sample was woven, ready to show to the clients. 'Then after that we would take it to Chanel and Jaeger and they would say "I like that, but could I have my mauve in here, and could I

This page: Late 1970 - Coco aged 87 in Switzerland. One of the last photos taken of her.

Opposite page, clockwise from top left:

a) Jersey suits and hats designed by Chanel. Published in magazine 'Les Élégances Parisiennes,' March 1917;
b) 1954 - Chanel at work in her office at 31 rue Cambon, wearing her signature jewelled pins;
c) 1960s Chanel silver tweed coat with ruby lining and matching dress;
d) Chanel on the mirrored staircase of her fashion house, ca 1954;
e) 1960 - mustard and gold tweed suit with toning blouse and lining;
f) Coco Chanel puts the finishing touches to a new creation, 1959;
g) Chanel jersey suits 1934, illustrated by Karsavina (M.K.S.);
h) 1954 The Comeback Collection - Chanel's iconic navy wool jersey suit with boater hat.

have my special green in there?", and so you came back and did some more alterations... I could use multi-colours, colours that come and go, random colours.' [107]

Inspiration for the season's shades and designs would come from the fashion designers themselves, as Leslie described:

> 'By visiting, by being the salesman yourself, going out to see today's collections, going to see Chanel... and you get criticism... what they want changed, next season more smooth fabrics, or smooth in part and rough in others, lighter weights or heavier. I'm not arrogant enough to think I knew what was coming the next season – you found out by speaking and listening... you spoke to clothes designers in Paris and New York and London and they'd tell you... Someone like Karl Lagerfeld was a leader, Chanel was a leader, Chanel didn't care what others did, she didn't care, she did her own thing, and I would say Karl Lagerfeld has taken on from there.' [108]

The traditional piece-dyed fabrics were also redesigned and reduced in weight. Lightweight cloths were in great demand in the fashion trade, giving a flexibility to design and cut. The company's products changed irreversibly:

> 'We changed and we used cotton yarn for the basis for this cloth, and fancy yarns with acrylic to give sheen or a matte finish. And it meant that we had to change the Finishing machinery for the fabrics... Finishing was different from a wool fabric.'

Leslie would consider almost any yarn to provide the lighter, multi-coloured, textured cloth which the fashion trade demanded. 'People selling us yarn used to say "Oh, I've got a yarn here, but it's for the upholstery trade."... and I would say, "No, no, let me see it and if it's something different I might be interested".' [109]

Brinksmanship and survival!

In these early days of reshaping the business, Linton's had a near-empty order book and Leslie had to draw on all his skills to ensure the company survived.

An example is the way he won orders from the prestigious Aquascutum fashion retailer. On a trip to London, Leslie showed Linton's fabrics to Sir Charles Abraham and his design team at Aquascutum, a long-established company, started by John Emary as a high-quality menswear shop in Regent Street, London in 1851. By 1853 Emary had produced the first waterproof wool fabric, which he patented. The coats were favoured by royalty, in particular the fashion leader, King Edward VII, who wore his coats in Prince of Wales check. The company extended their range into women's wear and developed other ranges, such as the lightweight Eiderscutum and the multi-coloured wool-yarn weave Aquaspectrum in 1962.

When Leslie arrived at the Regent Street store, the fine tweeds were laid out and the team studied the colours and weave; handled the soft fabric; and admired the beautiful quality. They knew what they wanted. The sticking point was price. They said they never paid more than £1 per metre, and Linton Tweed costs very much more. 'So I looked at them all, and I said, "Well, Sir Charles you're wasting my time, and I'm wasting your time". So I quietly picked the whole lot up - and I was desperate for orders, absolutely desperate - and packed my case and said goodbye'. There could be no compromise.

Three weeks later, back at the mill, Leslie was in the weaving shed when a telephone call came through. 'I've got Sir Charles Abraham of Aquascutum and he wants to speak to you.' When Leslie got up to the office to take the call, Sir Charles himself was hanging on, and said 'Mr. Walker, I want to see a Linton collection, are you coming down to London soon?' Without missing a beat Leslie replied 'Well, I was coming down on Monday, Sir Charles... before I come down, the prices haven't changed, I've told you what the prices are… I told them that I thought a company with the reputation of Aquascutum, should be buying this quality, and we sold to them quite a lot after that. So I wasn't to be browbeaten.' Quality had won the day.[110]

Press Leslie Walker to tell you what qualities were needed to turn the company around in 1970 and create an upsurge in trade, and he will modestly say that the main reason was: 'Changing the product… yes, and changing it from all wool fabrics that were dyed after they were woven into fabric, to multi-coloured yarns and making multi-coloured tweed.' [111] This may be true, but it takes more than a product: it takes business acumen, having the best skilled staff, marketing and good public relations with clothes designers and manufacturers, hard work and just a little luck to ensure a small, specialist company's survival in the modern world.

It was a fortuitous insight and, thanks to him, Linton Tweeds have continued to grace, not only the world's catwalks, but to give pleasure to thousands of women who could never afford the real thing, but for whom a good copy would do just as well. They have been able to wear a Chanel-style jacket, in beautiful tweed and feel a million dollars.

Japan beckons

Once the transition to innovatory fabrics had been achieved, Leslie quickly looked for new markets to fill Linton's flagging order book. He found them in Japan.

Japanese women were increasingly looking for Western fashions and manufacturers sought to fulfil their insatiable desire for quality fashion goods. One of their favourite looks was the classic Chanel suit. In 1969 Leslie packed his bags and flew to Japan, with samples of beautiful, colourful tweeds. This was the start of a partnership with Japanese garment manufacturers which is still strong today.

Leslie Walker recalled 'I was lucky because they were interested in what we sold to Chanel, but I couldn't sell to them what we sold to Chanel because it was exclusive.' [112]

George Linton had appointed two Englishmen to be agents for Linton's in Japan, they also represented Reid and Taylor, a high class menswear tailoring company, based over the border in Langholm. A Japanese agent, Mr Takahara Uchinuma, worked with them, and eventually Reid and Taylor in partnership with Linton's, set him up on his own, to work on their behalf. When Leslie went to Tokyo, Mr Uchinuma sat in on his meetings with manufacturers, acting as interpreter. Leslie recalled them sitting cross-legged on the floor, examining the tweed and making their choices. It proved a long and successful relationship.

***

46

A woman without love

In her later years, Coco appeared to live in a state of tension. It manifested itself as intolerance. She was famous for expressing her opinions, her sharp *mots,* her clipped witticisms, but these did not constitute her deepest private thoughts and feelings. There was another Coco - she was called Gabrielle, and what Coco talked about was not important to Gabrielle. That was something very different.

Gabrielle was lonely, alone and perhaps afraid. The television interview that she gave to Jacques Chazot in 1969 when she was eighty-five years old, shows a strong confident woman with strong views on all aspects of fashion, the fashionable world, and of women's place in it. The most telling passage comes when she speaks of love. 'A woman without love is nothing, she may as well be dead.' Her eyes seek the interviewer's, looking for understanding. And that was Gabrielle speaking from her heart. Her face has the expression of a woman definite in her views; sure of the truth she is speaking, but unsure of the response from her listener.

Uproar is what would greet these sentiments today, but a grain of truth may be hidden there, and in the loneliness of the night, might it not be true?

Mademoiselle's last perfume

In old age Coco found, as those of every generation who live until old age find, that many of her friends and acquaintances were no more. Living in a world depleted by time of the friendly and familiar, the loved and the loving, there was only one recourse: hard work. How else to fight boredom and fill the hours which otherwise hang so heavy? Not for Coco a future of card games or measuring out her life with coffee spoons.

At eighty-three Mademoiselle still had fresh ideas and plans for the future. This remarkable woman was planning to launch a new perfume to coincide with the musical: it would be called simply *Coco*.[113] She had created it many years before.

But it was not to be. The perfume company did not think *Coco* a suitable name for a perfume, and there were also fears that it would harm the sales of No.5.

Mademoiselle did not give up. In 1970, at her request, Henri Robert created Chanel No.19, inspired by her birth date, 19 August 1883. It is described as a daring and sophisticated fragrance. 'A burst of neroli for gaiety and a powdery composition of Tuscan iris, Centifolia rose and narcissus for a bold heart recall the young Coco in her days at Royallieu, where she would fuel her insatiable appetite for life in the highly charged atmosphere of the race tracks.' [114]

By Christmas Eve, there were queues in rue Cambon waiting to buy the new perfume. Coco was even stopped in the street by a young man, who asked what perfume she was wearing, whereupon she proudly took him round the corner to the boutique in rue Cambon and sold him some!

As she said, 'To be stopped in the street, by a man at my age, that's not bad, is it?'

'But how old are you, Mademoiselle?'

'A hundred and forever.' [115]

She may have been eighty-seven years old, but Mademoiselle was still capable of feeling that *frisson* of delight when complimented by an unknown man.

(Her perfume *Coco* would not be put into production until 1984, when model Inés de la Fressange played Coco in a series of commercials advertising the new perfume and directed by Jacques Helleu. It was a great success.[116])

Never on a Sunday

Coco hated Sundays. Sunday was the only day of the week when she would rest, the only day she would spend away from her beloved 'House' - when the tweeds, silks, tulle, and jersey were not being kneaded and forced into submission, by those strong, elegant hands. She did not know it, but Sunday, 10 January 1971 was her last.

That morning she spent time with her friend, Claude Baillén, who had called on her, chatting to her as she finished dressing. Coco was dressed in her tweed suit, her hat on her dark curls, her jewels round her neck. They took the lift down to the Ritz restaurant, where she ordered her lunch, her usual choice of an unsalted ham starter followed by a minute steak and boiled potatoes, then melon, with a well-chilled Riesling.

By coffee, she was discussing romanticism and the people off to Longchamps to watch the races.

Remarking that it was ten years old, she put on her tweed coat, and got into the Cadillac. They took her usual route, driving up the Champs-Elysées and round the race-course, through the cold mist and wintry sunshine, and back past the Trocadero to the Ritz. Leaving her friend at the door of the Ritz, Coco said, 'I'll be working tomorrow.' [117]

Later, the news would filter through the grand hotel, which had been her home for so many years. *Mademoiselle est mort.* Mademoiselle is dead.

Coco had returned from the drive exhausted, telling her maid, Celine, that she was very tired. With tears in her eyes, Celine, whom she always called Jeanne, her mother's name, described the sad events to Pierre Galante.

> *'She lay down on her bed, in her clothes. I couldn't get her to take them off. Only her shoes. She watched the television for a few minutes and then asked me to turn it off. She lay there in the twilight, drowsing. I never left the room.*
>
> *'Later, she sat up. "I'm going to eat here," she said. She read over the restaurant's menu. It was 8:30 in the evening.*
>
> *'"I'm suffocating... Jeanne ... the window." I rushed over. "It hurts."' She held her hands over her chest, her face taut. I grabbed the syringe. She tried to break the phial without success while I bared her hip. I stuck the needle in. She pushed the syringe herself. As I was taking out the needle she murmured:*
>
> *'"So that's the way one dies." I knew immediately that it was all over. I rushed to the phone.'* [118]

Celine dressed Gabrielle in her favourite Linton Tweed suit, with its green, pink and beige tones, soft colours in the pink lamplight from her night table, with Stravinsky's icon, given so many years ago, beside her.

Last goodbyes

On Thursday, 14 January, the church of La Madeleine, in the centre of Paris, was crowded to capacity. Requiem Mass, according to the rites of the Roman Catholic Church, was celebrated for Gabrielle. She had never forgotten her roots.

She had told Lilou Grumbach, her secretary, and François Mironet, her *major domo*: 'No nonsense after I'm dead, because I'll still be there beside you, in another dimension.' [119]

The imposing marble and gilt-decorated church, with its colonnade of Corinthian columns and its beautiful sculpture by Charles Marochetti of 'Mary Magdalene Ascending to Heaven', rising up behind the high altar, provided a magnificent backdrop, for the last rites of a woman who, throughout her life, valued simplicity above all else.

Her coffin was a mass of flowers, all white, orchids, a cushion of camellias, gardenias, a shield of laurel leaves, with her scissors depicted in lilac, from her models. There was a cross of white azaleas, the name simply inscribed, François. Masses of white sweet-smelling blooms. Luchino Visconti, her friend and lover from long ago sent red, red roses. The *Chambre Syndicale* did the same. Whatever disputes they had had with Mademoiselle over the years, they knew that she alone, over the long years of her reign, had done more than anyone else, for Paris fashion, for the *couture*.

They were all there to acknowledge that fact: all the top couturiers, Pierre Balmain, her old friend Cristobal Balenciaga making what would be his last public appearance, Yves Saint Laurent in glasses and beard, Paco Rabanne, Courrèges, whose mini-skirts she had decried, Michel Goma, and Marc Bohan who had taken over at Dior.

They may have all suffered Coco's scorn and harsh tongue at one time or another but, nevertheless, at heart they all acknowledged what Paris owed to this brave, courageous, brilliantly gifted woman.[120]

Her models were all wearing Chanel and stood to the right of her coffin, in the front row for the whole ceremony. In the rows behind them were the sad faces of all her staff, the forewomen, seamstresses, everyone who had made the House of Chanel, the most important force in fashion.

Parisian society thronged the crowded church to the doors, her old friends, Serge Lifar, Hervé Mille, Lady Abdy, Salvador Dali, the Rothschilds, Jeanne Moreau, and Robert Bresson were among the many who came to pay homage and to give thanks for the life of this vibrant woman.[121]

Her family gave the responses to the immortal words of the requiem.

Requiem aeternam et lux perpetua - eternal rest and perpetual light - for Gabrielle.

Gabrielle had left instructions with her great-niece, Mme Gabrielle Labrunie, the daughter of her favourite nephew, André Palasse, that she was to be buried in Switzerland, in Lausanne.

Today, Coco rests in the cemetery at Lausanne, her grave marked by a pink marble stele, with five small lions' heads carved on it, depicting Leo, her sign of the zodiac, in the shape of medallions. The lions' heads are in the same style as those engraved on the buttons she used on her suits.[122]

The news had flashed around the world and the obituaries appeared in the world's press. Mademoiselle was no more.

Part Six

47
After Mademoiselle

The show that Coco had been working on immediately before her death went ahead and, on 26 January 1971, the first collection that she had designed but not watched from her mirrored staircase was shown. It was for Spring/Summer 1971. The salon was packed to the doors, the world's press waiting to report this last collection perhaps even more hungrily than the comeback in 1954. The past fifteen years had seen Coco triumph, but now at this historic moment, truly Mademoiselle's last collection, the fashion world waited with bated breath.

The first model, wearing a pink suit stepped onto the catwalk, followed by the easy suits, dresses and pleated skirts of Chanel's usual show. It ended with the traditional three white evening dresses that Coco used instead of a wedding dress to end her shows. It was all over and it was the end of an era.

The *New York Times* reported, 'The audience remained seated in the stifling closeness, glancing covertly toward her famous staircase, as if, by their clapping, they could summon that ageless figure to take a bow.' [1]

And perhaps Gabrielle was there, watching, in another dimension.

She had appointed no successor; had trained no up-and-coming designer in her ethos. Perhaps she believed that no one could follow her, or perhaps she didn't want them to.

The only designer she empathised with was the young Yves Saint Laurent. In 1967 his autumn *couture* collection had been an affectionate *hommage* to her, showing inspirational little black dresses and suits, with a retro look influenced by the hit film of the year, *Bonnie and Clyde.* Coco was impressed enough to announce in a television interview in 1968, that she was naming him as her successor, commenting 'one day, someone will have to take over from me.' [2] But Saint Laurent had received public acclaim on a grand scale since leaving Dior and opening his own couture house in 1962. He was not about to give this up, even for the great Mademoiselle. So the question of her successor remained unresolved in her lifetime.

Now Gaston Berthelot, another designer from Dior stepped into the breach at the House of Chanel.

As a young man of twenty, Christian Dior, always with an eye to encouraging young talent, had employed him as a milliner for his boutique collection. He had joined the House of Dior when it opened on Avenue Montaigne in 1946, and became one of Dior's closest colleagues. [3] In 1969 he moved from the Paris house to take over Christian Dior-New York in succession to Guy Douvier, who had moved to Guy Laroche. (Douvier himself had worked for Chanel in 1955 before moving to Dior and transferring to Christian Dior-New York, based on Seventh Avenue, in 1961.). [4]

During his time in New York, Berthelot built a traditional home near Hammamet in Tunisia, where he relaxed on holidays. He was still in charge of Christian Dior-New York when, following Coco's death, he was head hunted for the House of Chanel.

In the years immediately after her death, no one would take the risk of re-interpreting Coco's style in a fresh way and each season's designs stayed close to her tradition. It was deemed safer to produce the Chanel suit beloved by so many women without deviation. Gaston Berthelot produced several such collections at rue Cambon, before he left in 1973. [5]

In 1974, with Alain Wertheimer in charge of the company, Jean Cazaubon and Yvonne Dudel, Coco's two steadfast design assistants who had worked alongside her since 1956, took over management of the *couture* side of the business. [6] The move was met with great enthusiasm at Linton Tweeds, as Jean and Yvonne had both worked closely with Leslie Walker over the years, choosing the perfect fabrics on Coco's behalf.

Leslie always kept faith with Chanel, even in the lean years after Coco's death, when the small quantities of individual tweeds ordered were loss-making for Linton's. When Chanel launched their ready-to-wear collection in 1978, one of the last couture houses to do so, Leslie's faith was vindicated. Once again, the names of Linton Tweed and Chanel were synonymous.

The revolution of ready-to-wear

Fashion styles in the 1970s reflected wide-ranging trends, from the wholesome fresh floral look depicted by Laura Ashley designs to the advent of the dark and dangerous designs of Punk fashion, with its safety pins and Mohican hairstyles promoted by Vivienne Westwood. It was not just the age of ready-to-wear but also of wear-what–you-please, as the mini-skirt gave way to the long and flowing midi and maxi lengths, and trouser suits for women became acceptable. Many of the couture houses had slipped into the doldrums at the changes brought about in the 1960s, and the emergence of youth culture. Their failure to take on the changes emanating from the 'London scene' made them appear dated. Young women no longer dressed like younger versions of their mothers; they now had their own fashion identity and they revelled in it.

Gavin Waddell, in his book *How Fashion Works,* describes the three-level waterfall process that galvanizes the fashion industry:

> '*Without the impetus of new ideas, industries like fashion soon shrivel and die. Inventive and original design needs the hotbed environment of the highest level, couture, to nurture its experiments. The second level, ready-to-wear, although also inventive and original, relies on couture to "soften-up" the market and translate avant-garde notions into a truly marketable product.*' [7]

In turn, several seasons later, the mass market benefits from the designs as the third level, mass production, copies and translates the designs for all to wear.

One of the most influential groups in the seventies was the new breed of *créateurs*: young designers with something new to say who were leading the ready-to–wear revolution. In London these included Zandra Rhodes, Barbara Hulanicki with the decadent Biba look, Ossie Clark, Vivienne Westwood and Jean Muir.

In Paris the couture houses fought back with their own young designers, typified by André Courrèges with his 'space-age' designs, and Pierre Cardin with his unlimited ideas. In America, Ralph Lauren and Calvin Klein were designing stylish tailored clothes for women, taking the lead on the ever-changing fashion scene.

The textile world was changing rapidly too, as man-made fibres brought greater versatility to fabrics, and enabled designers to achieve many different textures and finishes to their products. The stretchy Lycra yarns developed by Du Pont now meant that leggings, ra-ra skirts, sweat-shirting and jumpsuits became must-have fashion items, and the American designer Norma Kamali was instrumental in introducing them.

The 1970s also saw expansion in luxury goods, as designer labels became collectable items and the couture houses sought new ways to promote their exclusive name. The increasingly affluent youth market meant that there was demand for new affordable luxuries. As Chanel herself had said, 'Luxury is a necessity that begins where necessity ends.' [8]

At the House of Chanel a new eau de toilette, *Cristalle,* was launched in 1974. It was a bright, citrus sharp perfume, said to recall Gabrielle's carefree life at Deauville and Biarritz.[9] The following year a beauty care and cosmetic line, *Noir et Or,* was introduced. Back in 1968, the company had begun a new era in advertising its perfumes when it launched Catherine Deneuve, the beautiful French film star and friend of Coco, as the 'face of Chanel' to promote the sales of No.5 perfume in America. Photographed by Richard Avedon and Helmut Newton, over fifty commercials were filmed.[10] The new lines, however, were a statement for the future.

But the couture business was carrying on in its traditional way, without the spark and panache of Coco's ideas. It was still selling its designs to its faithful clientele among the wealthy society women who had always patronised rue Cambon, but the company knew it was missing out on sales to the youth market and needed a new approach to attract that market, projecting a more exciting image.

Prêt-à-porter gets carried away

By 1977, the Wertheimers were actively looking for ways to revitalize the business and decided to take forward an idea that Coco had suggested to Carmel Snow in 1953. It was to prove one of the most important decisions that the House of Chanel would ever make. Inspired and commercially sound, the idea meant that Chanel would make *prêt-à-porter*, or ready-to-wear collections, and sell them in Chanel boutiques, rather than in department stores. They appointed Philippe Guibourgé as Director to undertake the task. He had trained with Jacques Fath, one of the first designers to introduce a ready-to-wear line, launched in America in 1948. Following this he had worked at Dior in Paris as Marc Bohan's assistant for fifteen years from 1962. (Bohan had taken over from Yves Saint Laurent who, after a mental breakdown following military service, left Dior and set up his own couture house.)

Guibourgé launched this immensely successful new venture in America in 1978. His brief was to continue the Chanel look, an all-time favourite with American women, keeping the youthful, elegant style, but to ensure that it was in touch with modern times. He succeeded beyond the wildest dreams of the Paris House. He took Coco's favourite jersey fabric and turned out the sleekest navy cardigan suits, trouser suits with wide legs and collarless braided jackets, and a little black dress sporting a white peter pan collar and flared chiffon skirt.

Ernestine Carter, a former Associate Editor of the London *Sunday Times,* wrote:

> 'Within a year there were nineteen boutiques in major stores in major cities stretching across the USA from coast to coast and from north to south, as well as one in Canada. Europe followed suit as boutiques were opened in Belgium, Germany, Switzerland and France. Then came the Far East with Hong Kong and Japan.' [11]

In 1979 a boutique was opened on the ground floor of the House of Chanel in Paris, as part of a Chanel festival. The London boutique was opened with a shop all to itself. Jean Cazaubon and Yvonne Dudel continued to design the *haute couture* and in 1980, another designer, the Basque-born Ramon Esparza, joined Chanel. He was a friend of the Spanish designer, Cristobal Balenciaga, Coco's old friend and rival, for whom he had designed millinery since 1948. [12]

***

48
Shaddon Mills and all that jazz

Back in Carlisle, Linton Tweeds and their suppliers faced their own particular challenges throughout the 1970s. The woollen spinning industry had fallen victim to a general slump in the 1970s textile trade and Todd and Sons, one of Linton's key suppliers, were among the most seriously affected. This is not just the story of one small mill: its problems were symptomatic of the challenges facing many mills throughout the United Kingdom in the years when the textile trade hit rock bottom.

At the time Todd's were managed by a man who was to become revered as a jazz legend as well as the champion of his workforce: Mick Potts.

Mick was born on 1 July 1935 in Carlisle. From an early age music was his passion: he was a pianist and self-taught trumpet player, also teaching his older brother Al to play clarinet.

In 1953, while still at Carlisle Grammar School, Mick, Al and a friend, trombonist Norman Heeley-Creed, formed the Gateway Jazz Band. They played at the Garrett Club, above the Modern Milk Bar in Devonshire Street, Carlisle, and it became a favourite venue with young people. Al became a professional musician and left to work with a jazz band in Leeds, while Mick and the Gateway Jazz Band went from strength to strength locally, giving Carlisle its halcyon days of jazz. A highlight for Mick and his jazzmen was when they were invited to play several times for Prince Philip at Greystoke Castle, when the Prince took part in the horse-carriage driving events with George Bowman at the Lowther Show. An impressed Duke of Edinburgh later invited them to Windsor Castle to play for foreign visitors.

Shaddon Mill and Dixon's Chimney, home of Robert Todd & Sons until the demise of the business in 1975

Combining business acumen with musical talent, Mick opened two Carlisle nightclubs, Mick's One, from which Radio Cumbria made broadcasts, and Mick's Two in Fisher Street. Border Television made a series of twenty-four half-hour shows called 'Take the Mick', which were networked nationally and to Holland. Mick would appear on the shows, with his elegant, relaxed manner, a glass of whisky in one hand, a cigarette in the other, and with his perfect diction get the shows rolling.

Tim Belford, a former Gateway jazzman, described him as, 'a natural musician, a pianist, could sing, play trumpet, and his great forte was in speaking to audiences.' [13] Not only a jazz trumpeter but a gifted pianist, he enjoyed playing classical music, as well as jazz on the piano.

Stewart Jessett, another Gateway jazzman, who played double bass with the band for fifteen years, recalled Mick's sense of fun and many wonderful stories of these years. His clubs booked major artists such as Chris Barber, Humphrey Lyttleton, and Oscar Peterson to appear at Carlisle. George Chisholm and William 'Wild Bill' Davison became personal friends, often staying at Mick's home and playing with the Gateway. 'Wild Bill' would recall the golden days of Chicago Jazz in the 1920s when he played the cornet in and around the windy city at the same time as Bix Beiderbecke and Jelly Roll Morton.[14] For many years, they were a fixture at the Coach House, at Heads Nook, just outside Carlisle, playing to a packed house. Mick's signature tune *Up a Lazy River* became well known throughout the area.

By the early 1970s, Mick had formed another band, Britain's Greatest Jazz Band, which played on tour and at the Montreux Jazz Festival, where the superb Freddie Randall often took Mick's place on the trumpet seat, and on one occasion he managed to bring Teddy Wilson from the States to play piano with them. Although a traditionalist at heart, Mick could, and did, play mainstream and modern jazz.

One of the most famous photographs of Mick Potts was taken in 1970, when builders were repairing the top of Dixon's Chimney; he climbed up there, taking along a silver teapot, which held not a strong brew of tea, but his favourite tipple, whisky.

*Mick Potts and the Gateway Jazz band at Windsor Castle,
playing for the Duke of Edinburgh, 1983*

He was far more than a charismatic jazzman and entertainer, however: Mick Potts played an important role in the business life of Carlisle at a time when the local textile industry was at its lowest ebb. His own business struggled to survive throughout the early 1970s but eventually found the odds too great.

Robert Todd bows out

In 1975, Robert Todd and Sons closed its doors for the last time. Shaddon Mills was empty. There was no hum of machinery, no rush to deliver orders, no chatter at lunchtimes – the mill was silent.

It did not go down without a fight.

It says much for Mick Potts and his workers that they fought so long and hard for many months to save the mill. But in May 1975, the Receiver had to be called in and, week after week, in that long hot summer, *The Cumberland News* carried reports of the battle that was raging. In previous years, the company had followed Government directives for companies to invest in new machinery and plant: Todd's had spent £500,000 on modern machines, enabling them to meet national and international orders, and to develop new and fancy yarns.

On 23 May, the one hundred and eight workers, offered to take a £10 per week pay cut, to help save the ailing mill. Mick Potts, then Managing Director, said, 'I have been tremendously moved by the expressions of support from all the work force. Their offer to take a cut in wages is a wonderful gesture... I advised them against signing wage reductions because problems could arise if the company is eventually taken over by another concern.' [15] The workers' gesture was typical of the family feeling at the yarn-spinning mill, even though it had been badly hit by the cash crisis and the world recession in textiles.

The workers were determined and signed a 'Save Our Company' petition, which was rushed to London by express post to beat the Parliamentary recess. Its aim was to secure

206

a £150,000 short-term government loan from Tony Benn, Trade and Industry Secretary. Ron Lewis, Carlisle's Labour MP, added his support to the fight, talking until after midnight to Gregor McKenzie, the Under Secretary at the Department of Trade and Industry. As a result, the Department agreed to reconsider its earlier refusal of the loan.

Of the workers, Ron Lewis said, 'These people are militants in the right sense – they have said they are prepared to sacrifice pay in order to help the company out of its difficulties. This is most unusual in these days – the good side of industrial relations.' Of the government he said, 'I would hope that Mr Benn will look upon this case favourably, because it is as important for Carlisle, as Rolls Royce or Leyland are for the country.' [16]

At a press conference the following week, Ron Lewis announced plans to turn the textile firm into a workers' co-operative. He had telephoned Gregor McKenzie and 'he will now have received a red despatch box, containing my suggestion.' The aim was to avoid the possibility of another firm buying the company and asset stripping the new machinery. Mick Potts believed that the co-operative would be the first experiment in genuine industrial democracy in Carlisle and emphasised his commitment: 'I am a sixty percent shareholder in Robert Todd and Sons, but I am prepared to sacrifice my personal position to keep the firm going.' [17]

The drama continued when, on 5 June, Ron Lewis and Mick Potts were pictured posting more than a hundred letters to companies and firms in the city, as well as to individual trade unions. The letters, signed by Lewis, Potts and Don Gribbon, the General and Municipal Workers' Union senior shop steward at Todd's, sought active support for the co-operative by asking the recipients to send a reply slip to Gregor McKenzie, who was working in his Glasgow constituency during the Parliamentary recess.

At a shop-floor meeting of workers and management representatives, Ron Lewis said that the North Regional Conference of the Labour Party had voted unanimously to support the workers' co-operative scheme, and their resolution was being sent to Mr McKenzie and Transport House, Labour Party headquarters. A two thousand-signature petition of support was handed to Mr Lewis, to add to the six-thousand-signature petition already sent to Whitehall.

Todd's Financial Director, Jim Johnson, told employees that the more they could produce between now and the end of June, the more chance they had of convincing the Receiver that operations at the mill should carry on.

With the Mayor of Carlisle, Mr Tom Bisland, the city Labour Party and the General and Municipal Workers Union adding their support, there was an air of hopeful optimism at the meeting.[18]

Hard times

On 10 July, the blow fell. To the chagrin of Lewis, Potts, the trades union, the workers and all the thousands of people in Carlisle and beyond who had supported the idea of the workers' co-operative, the answer was a resounding 'No'. The letter was received from Gregor McKenzie and it incensed Mick Potts in its unfairness.

Mr McKenzie wrote: 'Without Todd's securing a substantially increased share of a diminishing market there is no possibility in the department's view of the firm achieving viability.' He doubted that the workers co-operative would

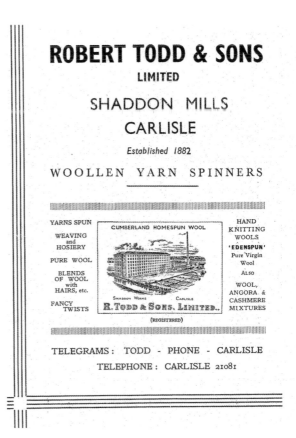

ROBERT TODD & SONS
LIMITED

SHADDON MILLS
CARLISLE

Established 1882

WOOLLEN YARN SPINNERS

YARNS SPUN
WEAVING and HOSIERY
PURE WOOL
BLENDS OF WOOL with HAIRS, etc.
FANCY TWISTS

CUMBERLAND HOMESPUN WOOL

R. TODD & SONS, LIMITED.
(REGISTERED)

HAND KNITTING WOOLS
'EDENSPUN' Pure Virgin Wool
ALSO
WOOL, ANGORA & CASHMERE MIXTURES

TELEGRAMS : TODD - PHONE - CARLISLE
TELEPHONE : CARLISLE 21081

Advert for Robert Todd & Sons, 1954

solve the problem of a 'lack of sufficient marketing drive'. Potts rejected this, pointing out that 'this is very offensive and completely untrue. I totally refute the charge. A high official in the trade once told me that among woollen spinners Todd's had the best public relations and the best sales promotion team in the whole of Europe.' [19]

Ron Lewis broke the news that their dreams had foundered to the one hundred and eight workers that afternoon. The government had remained unimpressed, in spite of the tremendous efforts of all concerned.

He gave one ray of hope: 'We are currently in touch with a company who may be interested in taking over Todd's and preserving employment in Carlisle.' [20]

A Portuguese businessman, one of Todd's big foreign customers, visited the mill at the end of July, and was baffled by the threat to production. He had spent £37,000 on yarn in the first six months of the year and was now desperate for more. The prospect of finding a new supplier at short notice presented a major problem.

At Linton Tweeds, Leslie Walker found himself in the same position.

As Jim Johnson said, 'We could be working round the clock now if only we'd had the money at the right time.' Recounting the failure, he said that they installed expensive machinery the previous year on three to four years hire purchase, as they were aware of the need for more modern production. 'It was then that the market dried up on us. We lost a fortune and our lines of finance were taken away from us. But when the installation was coming to an end the work returned. But it was too late.' [21]

It summed up the tragic plight of the doomed mill: plenty of demand, but no money.

Todd's workers were on a two-week annual holiday at the end of July, but when they returned on 4 August there was still no prospect but the dole queue.

Mick Potts pouring whisky from a silver teapot on the top of Dixon's Chimney, 1970.
Others in the picture are (left to right) Gerard Brady, Steve Gill and Alan Fitzgerald

Not one to take defeat easily, however, Ron Lewis continued his efforts on behalf of the company. He approached the new Chairman of Courtaulds, Sir Arthur Knight, enquiring if he would be interested in making a bid for Todd's. In his reply, Sir Arthur said that he had taken a close look at the position of Todd's and consulted with colleagues. He had concluded that 'Although we are customers of theirs to a minor degree, we do not feel that we would wish to get more deeply involved in their type of business and should their supplies not be available to us we would be able to make other arrangements. All in all therefore, I fear that we are not going to be able to help in this matter.' [22] Disappointed, Ron Lewis said that he would continue to approach industrialists to see if he could get them interested in Todd's. He did not succeed and Todd's closed.

(Mick Potts was to go on to open a textile consultancy business, Suttle Textiles, which he and his family ran, with offices in Carlisle and Leicester. It was named after Suttle House, the ancient mansion house that was his home. He died on 22 April 1993 at the age of fifty-seven.[23])

The life of Shaddon Mills and Dixon's Chimney had turned full circle, from the day that Richard Wright and his steeplejacks and builders left in 1836. The seven hundred cotton weavers employed by Dixon's had come and gone, followed by the workers spinning woollen yarn for Robert Todd and Sons. It had seen Mick Potts leave and, in the years that followed, numerous small industries inhabited the mill. One thing did not change: across the yard, the weaving sheds still stood and with them, Linton Tweeds.

***

49
Japan's fashion goes global

The ups and downs of the textile industry in Carlisle were no more than a microcosm of what was happening internationally. With the decline of many of the traditional major textile producers, new developments world-wide threatened the traditional manufacturing industries of the Western world.

Japan was one of the countries that, in the aftermath of World War 2, had seen a gradual development of its fashion industry. An economic and industrial boom began in the 1960s and continued throughout the 1970s. During this time the Japanese love affair with fashion and consumer goods began.

Nicholas Coleridge, in his book *The Fashion Conspiracy*[24] describes the development as major manufacturers, Renown, Kashiyama, Bigi and Sanyo Shokai, made licensing deals with foreign manufacturers of luxury goods, bringing vast quantities of high fashion and designer labels into the country. Japan's own high fashion industry also took off in this period when Hanae Mori, a Tokyo–born designer, opened her designer shop in the prestigious Ginza shopping area in Tokyo in 1955. By the early 1970s she had established a salon in New York and, by 1975 Mori had become famous for her adaptations of the kimono, designing soft, ethereal evening gowns, belted with the traditional obi. She gave her first couture showing in Paris in 1977.

It was the beginning of a period when designers such as Kenzo, with his use of vivid colour and draping, and Issey Miyake, a master of the layered and wrapped look, were showing their designs on the international catwalks and making a vast impact. In the early 1970s, Kansai Yamamoto became famous for his dramatic clothes, influenced by the powerful and exotic elements of traditional Japanese dress, which he dramatically combined with Western day wear, producing a high fashion look. The House of Kenzo opened in Paris in 1970, with Hanae Mori following in 1977.

Yohji Yamamoto, who showed his first collection in Japan in 1976, was a non-traditional designer, who produced the unstructured, loose, voluminous garments similar to those of Rei Kawakubo of Comme des Garçons. Both were bringing new and inspirational design to the catwalks, with their loose wrapped styles, sombre colours, and non-cut cutting, the opposite of form-fitting Western dress, and which caused a storm on the catwalks. The Japanese designers were adept at combining a traditional look with the use of modern fibre technology and synthetic materials to effect layering techniques and sculptural forms.[25] By 1985, the Council of Fashion Designers in Tokyo had been established with thirty-two designers[26] and the stage was set for future developments.

Back in Carlisle, at Linton Tweeds, Leslie Walker's far-sighted forays into the Japanese fashion market in 1969 had paid off and by 1981 a substantial trade had been established, as the *Cumberland News* reported:

> '*Japanese women have a yen for tweed and that means a lot of trade for a Carlisle textile firm. Linton Tweeds of Shaddon Mills sell over £100,000 worth of material each year to one firm alone. And today, buyers from the Sanki Shoji Company paid their first visit to the city factory. Mr Takemoto and Mr Hayashi are here together with Mr Uchinuma to discuss new designs for next year. "We decided to take them on a tour of our mill and shop", explained Linton Tweeds Managing Director, Leslie Walker. "Sanki Shoji – based in Tokyo and Osaka are our best Japanese customers, although we do also deal with other firms." '* [27]

Nessy dies - a break with the past

Throughout the 1970s, Nessy had been coming to the mill less and less. By 1978, aged 76, she was in poor health and weakened by illness. She had been diagnosed as having cancer of the colon and this must have seemed a cruel twist of fate, as she had won her battle with breast cancer in 1950. She still had the kennels with her beloved Geltsdales, but worried about their future should anything happen to her. Her old friend Norah Hartley visited her, and they talked it over. Early in 1979, she called in her solicitor John Assheton of Aldwych, London, and her Chartered Accountant, Fergus Culley of 17 Fisher Street, Carlisle, and on the 31 January made her Will.

Nessy died on 25 May 1979 at Oakland House, on the anniversary of her father's birth in 1872. A small notice appeared in *The Cumberland News* announcing that she had been cremated at Carlisle on 30 May.[28] In her Will, Nessy had left the care of the deerhounds to her dearest friend Norah Hartley, together with a bequest and the request that she find good homes for those dogs that she could not keep herself. Other legacies were

Nessy in 1976

left to the four children of her cousins, and to a number of friends, employees and charities. Red Cat House at Brisco was to remain rent-free accommodation for her friend Mrs Atkinson until its sale, after which she was to be re-housed rent-free elsewhere. The final residual value of the estate was to be shared between her four cousins.

Afterwards Norah wrote, 'It is pleasant to think that this great kennel, closed now by its owner's death, went out in a blaze of glory. Its name will live whenever and wherever deerhound pedigrees are read.' [29]

There is much that we do not know about Nessy's life. Her circle of friends was wide, from top international fashion designers to dog-lovers of the deerhound world and the people who gave such stalwart service at the mill, yet there is no extant record of her thoughts on life and love, no writings to give a chink of light into her private world, no small whisper to say who Nessy really was. Like Chanel her work was her *raison d'être,* whether at the tweed mill or with the deerhounds. Unlike Coco, her personal world remains private. She left no diaries or letters for future biographers: only Norah knew her secrets, and she was not telling.

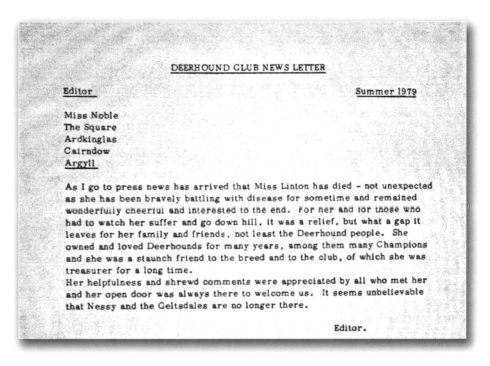

Obituary of Nessy in Deerhound Club Newsletter, 1979

Norah had learned such caution following her experience with the biographers of her brother, Leslie P. Hartley. His biographer, Adrian Wright would report on his conversations with Norah, and then on the fact that she left instructions for the family papers, and the archive of Leslie's personal papers to be burnt after her death.[30] Did she do the same for Nessy? It seems likely. But she did preserve the photos of the shimmering salad days of the 1920s, of family and friends and deerhounds, enjoying a world of innocence and simplicity in a time of hope and joy.

Nessy left all her shares in Linton Tweeds, in equal parts, to her cousin, George Linton, and to Leslie Walker, his fellow Director of the company. Perhaps this action illustrates the fact that, although Nessy and George worked well together for the company, there was an underlying tension in their relationship.

It also illustrates that Nessy realised and appreciated how much the company owed to Leslie Walker's vision and hard work in keeping it ahead of the game through good times and bad. He had worked steadfastly to turn the company's fortunes around and establish a firm footing for a thriving company in the future. Before she died Nessy was to tell Leslie, 'Leslie, you've kept the mill going for the last ten years...' In my interviews with him, Leslie acknowledged that 'It was nice that it was appreciated that I did.'[31] Leslie had been good to her, but as he recalled, she had also been good to him.

Leslie's hard work to keep the company going had been necessary, not only due to Nessy's ill health, but also that of her cousin George. George Linton, Chairman of the company, had suffered serious ill health during the 70s, and had not held an executive position at the mill since 1970. A widower with two children, William and Margaret, he died on 10 April 1986, aged seventy-two. The *Cumberland News* reported his death the next day under the headline 'Tweed Chief dies.'[32]

It was a sad report and the reign of the Linton family, who had started the renowned tweedmaking company in 1912 and had influenced so many of the top designers and couturières over the years, was now finally over. Neither of George's children went into textile design, but his grand-daughter did choose a career in the world of fashion.

One family dynasty may have ended but another remained and it was not the end of Linton Tweeds. Leslie Walker consolidated the firm's position and looked to the future. Leslie remembered those years, when he and his wife, Carole, borrowed money from his mother, to buy the mill, together with a £75,000 bank loan. His mother asked:

'Leslie, do you know what you are doing?' His hesitating reply was: 'I think so.' [33] In later years, looking at bales of glittering, glowing, cobweb-soft tweed waiting to be shipped off to Chanel, Carole Walker could say, 'Thankfully, Leslie got it right.'

Leslie Walker eventually became Chairman of the company he joined in 1963. A charmingly modest and perceptive man, he demonstrated the business acumen he used to develop the company with an easy humour. At Nessy's death his belief and passion for the company and product he had saved so many years before was as strong as ever. But this was a time to look forward, a time of more change. Soon his son Keith would join him in the business and, at Chanel, a man would be appointed who would take Mademoiselle's couture house to new heights on the stage of international fashion. His name was Karl Lagerfeld.

* * *

Part Seven

50
Karl Lagerfeld arrives

1982 was an important landmark in the history of the House of Chanel when Karl Lagerfeld was appointed Artistic Director and tasked with bringing the house back to the greatness of its founder.

Today Karl Lagerfeld is as much an iconic figure as Coco Chanel was. Recognized everywhere as a man of superlative style, white powdered ponytail flowing, black suited and booted, high white collar upright, fingers aglow with silver rings, he is a colossus of the fashion world. But back then, the eyes of all *fashionistas* were on him as the new man at Chanel. Could he do it? Could he fill the great Mademoiselle's shoes? Could he once again make the House of Chanel great? And as the world watched Karl Lagerfeld proceeded to answer all the questions with a resounding 'yes'.

Born in Hamburg, Germany, on 10 September 1938, the son of Christian and Elisabeth Lagerfeld, as a fourteen-year-old he was sent to Paris to further his studies. His father was a successful businessman and his mother, a beautiful, cultured woman who played the violin, spurred on the young Karl with sharp criticism. Influenced by his mother, and with a natural gift for art and fashion, he applied himself to his studies at the Chambre Syndicale School with zest.

By 1954, at the age of sixteen and in the year that Coco made her comeback, he won first prize in a competition sponsored by the International Wool Secretariat. Out of six thousand entries, his design for a long yellow wool coat caught the eye with its elegant, sleek design. His fellow prize winner, designing a black cocktail dress and winning first prize in the dress category, was Yves Saint Laurent. They were pictured standing together, receiving their prizes, two gifted young men on the cusp of their careers. Lagerfeld has been quoted as saying, 'I won on coats, but actually I like designing coats least of all. What I really love are little black dresses.' [1]

Karl Lagerfeld was on his way and would never look back. His delight must have been great when one of the competition judges, the distinguished Pierre Balmain, offered him an apprenticeship in his couture house. He stayed with Balmain for the next three years, learning the couture business from the ground up and becoming Balmain's assistant.

By 1958, at the age of twenty he moved to the House of Patou as Artistic Director. Before his death in 1936, Jean Patou had established a House famous for its easy, wearable styles, pleated skirts, long sleeveless cardigans and lace dresses, not unlike those designed by Coco Chanel. Sporting clothes were his *métier,* and he had designed clothes in jersey for the modern woman. After his death, Patou's family kept the House open and a number of well-known designers worked there, including Marc Bohan and Christian Lacroix.

Lagerfeld kept true to the traditions of the House, designing collections in the style of Patou.

Karl Lagerfeld discusses with top model Inès de la Fressange the last details of the preparation of 1987-88 Autumn-Winter Ready-To-Wear collection shows, March 13, 1987

Reports on his Spring 1960 collection noted that his clothes had an understated chic and elegance reminiscent of Molyneux and Mainbocher.[2]

But he found life as a couture designer too restrictive, believing that there was more scope for innovative and fresh ideas in the world of ready-to-wear, and in 1961 he left Patou to pursue his creative muse. Couture, he said, 'became very dowdy and very bourgeois and it was just not trendy.'[3]

Ready-to-wear had been developing through the century, particularly in America where designers such as Hattie Carnegie, Norman Norell and Claire McCardell led the field. In Europe the development was slower, due to the dominance of the couture houses, but by the 1960s a new breed of designer influenced by the Swinging Sixties, the fashion revolution that began in London, were looking to bring the youthful trendy images seen on the streets onto the catwalk. The couture houses catering for the older, wealthier woman seemed *démodé,* and by the 1970s the new designers were influencing style – they were the *créateurs,* whose inventive grasp of street style established the place of ready-to-wear on the world stage. Lagerfeld became one of the leaders of this trend.

Carole Walker in the showroom, wearing Linton Tweed

More than just clothes

He had always been interested in more than just the clothes; he was fascinated by how trends develop, how they come up from the street, how they reflect an individual's perception of themselves, and how social and economic development influence the shifting styles of each new generation. He was also an avid reader of fashion magazines and newspapers, clipping the articles and building up a vast resource of both historical and modern fashion history, which he could dip into for inspiration. He was soon recognized as a world authority on the history of fashion. With his capacity for multi-tasking, his endless creativity and ability to illustrate his designs in quick vital sketches, annotated with detailed descriptions of cut, fabric and embellishments, Lagerfeld worked as a freelance designer for many of the top establishments.

He became head designer at the House of Chloé producing elegant, simple, fluid clothes for them from 1965 to 1982 and was famous for his quality collections, expressed in positive, unhesitating terms. Chloé was founded in 1952 by Gaby Aghion and aimed to fill a gap in the market by creating 'luxury prêt-à-porter', top quality designs made from fine fabrics, but without the demands of haute couture and its many garment fittings. The garments became favourites with celebrities such as Jackie Kennedy, Brigitte Bardot, Maria Callas and Grace Kelly. Known as a meticulous, confident stylist, Lagerfeld would accessorize his clothes with flair and sophistication. (He would design again for Chloé from 1992 until 1997, when Stella McCartney joined the company.)

Always a prolific designer, he worked for Krizia, Cadette and Valentino in Italy as well as the shoe manufacturer Charles Jourdan in France, bringing to each his different interpretations and re-interpretations of their style, but always with an eye on the latest trend and a nod to humour. Passionate and enthusiastic about everything he undertook, he shocked and shook the establishment with his never-ending flow of innovative ideas.

By 1967 Karl Lagerfeld was working for Fendi in Rome, the old-established company who produced soft leather handbags and furs. The house, founded in 1918 by their

Leslie Walker with the photo that Coco Chanel presented to Linton Tweeds

mother Adele Casagrande, was run by the five Fendi sisters, and by the 1960s the classic fur coat was seen as out-moded and with little appeal to the young. Lagerfeld designed the now famous double 'F' logo, using it on many of the leather products. He was like a breath of fresh air and revolutionized the treatment of fur and revitalized the Fendi image with his original designs, producing innovatory, unusual and modern styles. By blending fur with leather, creating kimono-styled furs, reversible fur coats and giving denim coats a whole new life lined in fur and sporting the double 'F' logo, he introduced a new generation to Fendi fur. This modern and sought-after look brought Fendi international acclaim.

His strength lay in his ability to take the classical and make it topical, using his creativity to break down the boundaries of tradition and designing with unfashionable furs, such as rabbit, squirrel and mole dyed in vibrant colours. By 1977 the company launched women's wear designed by Lagerfeld, which was very successful. This plethora of originality, while keeping to the original concepts of the company, was an indication of Lagerfeld's genius for updating the image of a traditional company and moving it forward into the future. Since the mid 1970s he has been regarded as a major force in fashion.[4] He was later to use this gift to great effect at Chanel.

In 1980, the twenty-three year old Hervé Léger, who had been a milliner and knitwear designer, moved to Rome to assist him at Fendi. When Lagerfeld went to Chanel in Paris in 1982, Léger moved there also, but left Chanel in 1985 to start his own company. By 1989 Léger was being acclaimed for introducing the curvaceous silhouette of his 'bandage' dresses, made from elasticized wool, silk or lycra, which clung to the body and were regarded as modern high glamour.[5] He too was a visitor to Linton Tweeds, where Leslie Walker helped him select suitable textile designs for his creations.

In the spirit of Chanel

Lagerfeld's arrival at the House of Chanel was regarded as its third incarnation since Coco first opened it and then re-opened it in 1954. It was to prove to be a monumentally right, if dramatic, decision by the company. Still privately owned by the Wertheimer family, who looked to increase sales and develop into the youth market, while still retaining the approval of its staunch traditional clientele, the appointment was crucial. The House of Chanel may have been in the doldrums, but within a year it was once again leading fashion and, under Lagerfeld, the house has achieved the 'glittering prize' of sustained success in the global market.

The fashion press were as excited about Lagerfeld's first collection at Chanel in January 1983 as they were in 1954 at Coco's comeback. This time the verdict was very different: phones were ringing in London and New York, news was spinning around the fashion world, as journalists and fashion editors spread the word - Chanel was back and then some! Karl had succeeded beyond their wildest dreams.

Lagerfeld described how he prepared for taking over Mademoiselle's shining mantle, before signing his contract. Going through his large collection of archived fashion magazines and newspapers, he cut out the references and photographs of Chanel's designs over the years. These were pasted into volumes of large scrapbooks or concept books, suitably annotated, and provided a valuable source for studying and absorbing the spirit of Chanel. The task ahead then fell into place.

He was keen to point out, however, that while he had studied Mademoiselle's designs and key looks, respect was not an issue:

> 'Absolute respect would have been fatal to creativity, I took the Chanel codes, or language and I mixed them up. Mademoiselle's basic idea was timeless modernity. But my job was primarily to reinvent Chanel. So I played with the codes, manipulated them, sometimes even eliminated them before bringing them back. Fashion is not respect; it is first and foremost fashion. I don't like nostalgia. At times, my 'reinventions' shocked the purists who thought I was destroying Mademoiselle's elegant simplicity. But I was not afraid.' [6]

So shocked were many of Coco's clients and others in the fashion world by this apparent disregard for Mademoiselle's credo, that newspaper reports began dubbing him 'Kaiser Karl' and the name stuck.

But he was right not to be afraid and, over his years at the helm, he has repeatedly proved his total grasp of the Chanel look. As Coco herself always looked for the new, adapting it to fit with the Chanel look, so Karl Lagerfeld has successfully brought the designs to total modernity, while still keeping that remarkable style that only ever says 'Chanel'. It takes no small genius to do this.[7] The late Nina Hyde, Fashion Editor of *The Washington Post* saw this from the beginning and wrote, ' A lot of people have been concerned that Lagerfeld means the end of Chanel, but the House is too smart to throw out the suit. It works and Karl is likely to continue with it.' [8]

That first collection referred back to Coco's shows of the 1920s and 1930s showing some of her favourite looks: white satin evening pyjamas with short jackets, her little black dress, the cardigan jacket, suits with long slender jackets and short panelled skirts for ease of movement and tweeds were once again multi-coloured checks with texture. There were brocades richly embroidered by Lesage and accessories reflecting the long-established Chanel look with long ropes of pearls, faux jewels and gilt chains blending with the iconic interlocking double C's on belts, bags and shoes.[9]

Keeping the Linton Tweeds connection

All through the 1980s and early 1990s the little tweed skirt suit reigned supreme, given a plethora of looks in colour, texture and design, but always retaining its essential appeal. Karl Lagerfeld was keen to continue Coco's connection with Linton Tweeds, still featuring the lovely tweed as a major part of his creations.

With exclusivity being of prime importance in the luxury fashion world, any fabrics chosen by Chanel may not be sold to anyone else, and the type of fabric and its colour are confined to his designs. Even fabric eventually not used by the House has to be stored by Linton's for two years before it may be sold in Linton's own shop. This protects the exclusivity of the cloth, as it is the fabric that makes each couture collection unique. Designers take the best fabrics from the international textile specialists, and for tweed it is Linton's. Their efforts were formally recognised in 1991 when Linton's were awarded with the prestigious Queens Award for Export Achievement.

Leslie Walker described how Karl Lagerfeld would send his inspirational ideas, often in the form of abstract paintings, a colour picture, a photograph of a vineyard or other artefacts, asking for a fabric to be designed to capture the essence of the picture, with colours and textures being all important to a faithful interpretation of his muse. Such is the skill of Linton's designers, dyers, weavers and finishers that they always succeeded. To produce these unusual and different effects, Linton's use many complicated yarns, some made exclusively for them by other companies in Italy or elsewhere, but many are made by themselves. As Leslie said, 'anywhere that makes something different.' [10]

It would not have been possible to produce such wide variety had they continued using wool alone. With special machines, they now have the ability to use many fancy mixes, mixing tweed with silk, linen, cotton, Lurex with stretch and even raffia and rubber. 'Imagination' and 'innovation' are the designer's watchwords, experimentation is the key word.

Consistency in quality and colour are always paramount to clients, and fabric ordered must be of the highest quality. It is not always easy to maintain this, as the variation in wool's natural colouring can affect the dyeing process. Leslie explained, 'the starting off point is not always the same and it's very difficult...a thousand metres will all be bleached at the same time... and it is a commercial match: computer print-outs will tell you it's a commercial match.' But if the client does not agree, they may request it to be re-done, 'if it goes back in the pot to get bleached it would all [turn into] felt, if it happens to be an old-fashioned wool cloth... the texture will go.'

This process starts with the yarn itself. To produce the weight required 'the fibres must be fine enough to spin to a yarn, small enough to produce a cloth of the necessary weight or thickness; not so fine that the eye cannot distinguish the individual fibres; not so coarse as to be harsh to the touch; of a good natural colour so as to be able to display the dyes well and of a lustre sufficient to reflect the light satisfactorily.' [11] Quite a tall order and different yarns will have some or all of these properties. Yet all through the 1980s and early 1990s the little tweed skirt suit reigned supreme, given a wide variety of looks in colour, texture and design, but always retaining its essential appeal.

The age of the supermodel

By the 1980s, the age of the supermodel had dawned, with Linda Evangelista, Claudia Schiffer and Naomi Campbell strutting the catwalks. It seemed that nothing was too flashy or sexy for this new age of couture.

Linton Tweeds were featured at Chanel as they had never been seen before; there was an influence of the biker culture with quilted leather trimmings and the jangling chains of the rapper's world, suits with bare midriffs, bejewelled bra-tops, shorts or mini-skirts worn under the chain and logo-laden jackets. The tweeds were lighter, brilliantly coloured and incorporated many different textures, presenting a dramatic picture on the catwalk.

The glossy magazines featured a parade of celebrities wearing Linton Tweed: the late Princess of Wales in a cool blue suit, Joanna Lumley looking absolutely fabulous, Stella Tennant in red and white houndstooth check, and many more. They grabbed the headlines; the ladies who lunched appreciated the fun and drama safe in the knowledge that they could order the more conventional, longer skirt to match their jacket. Headlines matter in the world of luxury goods, and the bags, boots, watches, jewels and perfume, all sporting Coco's famous logo walked out the door.

The clothes and accessories appealed to the young as never before; beautiful tweed jackets with matching tweed or leather quilted bags were worn with leggings, ripped jeans, city shorts, trainers, spike heels or boho boots. And it worked, it was fabulous, it was street-style. In 1998 a beautiful skirt cut 'from feathery tweeds, the top layer comprising pleats that fluttered over the layer beneath', had both movement and a clean silhouette.[12] The modern sporty look was in and a new squashy amoebic-style Chanel bag was invented. It proved a huge success, but did not replace the covetable classic 2.55 with its quilting and gilt chain, so beloved of Mademoiselle.

Arson strikes Linton's

But it was not all plain sailing at Linton's during these years. On 5 November 1992 an arsonist burnt down the staff canteen, which at the time was full of expensive and exclusive yarn. The insurers stipulated that a claim could only be made if the canteen was rebuilt, and this was the start of the development of the visitors' centre, with its large coffee house, conservatory and a retail fabric showroom selling a brilliant array of tweeds, and a Designer Knitwear Boutique.[13] By turning calamity into success, Carole Walker epitomised the commitment of the Walkers that has been so crucial to ensuring the business won through in hard as well as good times.

219

Reminiscing about these times, Carole recalled how the new development grew from modest beginnings: 'I tried for years to get them to open a coffee shop but there was a wool storage down here, and on 5th November [1992] it was set fire to and everything was ruined and all the yarn inside it was ruined, but we were insured. They would only pay out the insurance if we put up another building... that was how it started. I started having little parties like WI parties, church visits, everything like that and it was so popular that Margaret Duffy and I were doing it for four nights a week, for years... we never advertised once... and in all that time they got a talk, they got a tour round the mills and a nice supper and it was a nice evening. And in the meantime, the coffee shop just took off... and we did do it ourselves... it was an instant success.' [14] Perhaps this has always been the secret of Linton's success as, under the Walker family, the local community has felt involved and welcomed; no small achievement for an international company.

**

51
Very Jean Muir, very Linton's

On a happy day in April 1993, the phoenix had truly risen from the ashes. The elegant British fashion designer Jean Muir led the celebrations and opened the new visitors' centre. Standing alongside Leslie Walker and dressed in one of her own designs - a chic inky navy three-quarter length coat with an undulating edge, worn over a matching dress, made from Linton's fine wool crêpe - Muir plunged the scissors into a swathe of Linton Tweed and declared the new centre open.

Jean Muir had always been a friend of the company, having known Linton Tweeds since the early days of her career when she was a young designer at Jaeger and often extolled the virtues of the British cloth suppliers. Her diktat was 'to buy the best and buy British wherever possible.' [15]

Jean loved the northern landscape from Yorkshire to Cumbria to the Scottish borders and would say of it, 'Oh, there's definitely something about the place, it's grand and it's straightforward and that is what the people are like... I think it's magnificent... it never lets you down. It's simply wonderful at any time of the year.' [16]

Her belief in British textiles led her to seek out the skills and expertise of the local knitwear and textile companies. Linton's with its world-class cloth fitted her brief exactly. She may be regarded as the British Coco Chanel, for she shared many of the same personal

Jean Muir with Leslie Walker, opening the new visitors' centre at Linton Tweeds, 1993

220

attributes and views on style as the great French couturière, some of her favourite fabrics being matte jersey and tweed. Her use of tactile fabric combined with simple but superb cut had connotations of Coco. Largely self-taught she was proud of her Scottish heritage, and ascribed her characteristic determination and self-assured tenacity to her Celtic roots.

Historian Sir Roy Strong says of her 'All fashion is either classic or romantic and Jean Muir is the former, rarer bird. Within the context of the history of dress in our own age she belongs to a line of descent from Fortuny and Chanel, those designers whose concern has been the creation of the timeless.' [17]

After working for Jaeger, she worked under the label Jane and Jane, before setting up her own company based in Bruton Street, London in 1966. Her husband Harry Leuckert was co-director and looked after the business side of the venture, while Jean concentrated on designing. This was the decade when London was regarded as the fashion capital of the world, and soon Jean Muir would receive international acclaim, becoming arguably the greatest British designer of her generation.

Always a passionate supporter of the British fashion industry, she had highlighted the old problem of lack of government support for the industry and the training of designers in the 1980s, with the subsequent loss of British talent overseas. Speaking at the Royal Society of Arts in 1981 and quoted in the London *Times* by fashion writer Suzy Menkes, she said:

> 'Of course I want to see instinctive, marvellous, creative designers. But at best you are going to find one of those a year. The rest aren't even taught properly the way the system works, let alone how to do good pattern making and cutting. I don't expect them to be able to cut like Balenciaga – or even to be as good as me. But I think that far too much emphasis is put on the sketch.' [18]

On the day of her visit to Linton's, she paid tribute to the company describing them as wonderful suppliers to work with, and went on to say:

> 'As a designer I am looking for the weight and the hang of a cloth to produce high quality garments. Designers sculpt clothes, fabric is our medium and Linton Tweeds produce the best cloths with which to work. They are wonderful to work with – we work very well together producing fabrics specifically for my collections.' [19]

Jean Muir had almost as many *bon mots* and aphorisms as Coco Chanel and among her wise words are:

'Life is for living and you might as well live it as attractively as possible.' [20]

And 'Getting the clothes right for the body they're on. The handwriting is mine, but the reading is the wearer's...' [21]

She would also say, 'Wool has always been part of our lives. It dyes to the most luminous colours...' [22]

When I spoke to him, Leslie Walker had many fond memories of Jean Muir, not least her insistence on exactness. He described her as:

> 'An eccentric, and a very talented eccentric – she didn't use what you would think of as Linton Tweeds now, she used more of a plain cloth – but we had our own dye house and could dye things, and she wanted all her own colours... it had to be right, yes, there was no good sending it down and one of her staff saying it was OK. I wouldn't accept that – had Jean Muir seen it herself? Her husband was financially involved in the business, and I think he was one of her great fans too.' [23]

Tour parties were always welcome at the visitors' centre, where hand loom weavers could be seen using machines over a hundred years old, as well as the most up-to date in modern technology.[24] Many of the machines were supplied by the German firm,

Doing business at Première Vision, Monsieur Robert Burg, Linton's long-standing agent (back to camera), and Leslie Walker with a client

Dornier, famous for their aircraft manufacture during World War 2 but who, after the war, developed modern weaving machines. Sadly, today, due to health and safety regulations the weaving sheds are no longer open to visitors.

During the 1990s, when recession hit much of the British textile industry, Linton's were on a roll as Leslie Walker recalled, 'Our turnover went roughly one million, two million, three million from 1990 to 1992. It hit £3.8million last year [1993]. We were sending out 50% of orders to be machined elsewhere. I wouldn't like production to go any higher than that.'

It was the specialism, the difference and the 'un-tweediness' of the fabric that made Linton Tweeds so popular with the couture designers. Holding a swatch of pink tweed, Carole Walker demonstrated this in an interview with Charles Darwent of *Management Today* in 1994. 'The texture, she says, ruthlessly shredding it "comes from this. Touch it. It feels like rubber. It is," says Mrs. Walker. "Then there's this" – she extracts a filament of what looks like etiolated tinsel – "that's Christmas tree yarn, and this... is tissue paper yarn. We're constantly having to push back the boundaries of what people think tweed is. Karl Lagerfeld won a prize for this cloth," notes Mrs Walker, "but it was The Boss who designed it." '

Leslie Walker himself observed, 'When I went into the textile industry after my National Service, the fashionable work-study buzz-word was 'rationalisation'. Everyone else in Scotland... was busy saying: "Get rid of yarn-dyeing," for example. "Farm it out to a specialist." Well, all they've ended up with is sheds full of weaving machines and anyone can do that.' [25]

1994 - Change at the top and another loss

By August 1994, after a quarter of a century as Managing Director, Leslie Walker had decided to move into semi-retirement and hand over the reins of running the company to his son, Keith. Like his father, Keith was a keen rugby player and had a background in banking before joining the family business in 1988. An energetic and articulate man, trained in banking, he worked hard to continue and extend his father's innovatory ideas. Looking back on those days he said, 'I was always involved because my Dad was doing the travelling and discussing everything that was happening at Linton. I felt like I already knew the business before I came in and I'd always been interested to come in.' [26] His father urged caution, feeling that textiles were a precarious industry, particularly as Keith had a successful banking career. But as Keith explained, 'In the end the discussion centred on my saying it was my decision and if I wanted to take the risk.' [27]

Keith became Managing Director at the age of thirty-two, with Leslie staying as Chairman of the company he had revitalised with his forward-thinking and modernity, and retaining a keen interest in its development.[28]

Linton's is still truly a family affair, in the same way that it was in the days of William and Agnes. As well as Leslie's wife, Carole, and their son Keith being involved, their other son Bruce also works for the company as Mill Manager. Given the many problems that can occur in the tweed business, Leslie recalled saying to his sons, ' "don't come into textiles" - and there they are, both in it now.'

1994 also saw the end of another link with the Linton family, when Norah Hartley died on 27 September at the age of ninety-one.

In the final year of her life she had given permission for Adrian Wright to write the biography of her celebrated brother, Leslie Poles Hartley, who had died in December 1972. Six months before his death he had been honoured by the Royal Society of Literature when he was made a 'Companion of Literature', 'in honour of his great gifts as a writer and in gratitude for his excellent contribution to English letters.'[29]

It was not an easy decision for Norah. Since Leslie had died she had turned away many would-be biographers, seeking to protect the privacy of her brother's life, and prevent sensationalist stories about his sexuality. It was not publicly acknowledged in his lifetime that he was homosexual, but now it seemed that Norah was prepared to allow a writer who had said, 'I want to write a truthful book about Leslie.' permission to do just that.[30]

Norah had lived on the beautiful Fletton Tower estate all her life, but the last years must have been lonely after her sister Enid died in 1968, even though she had the support of a long-serving and friendly staff. The Rotherwood Kennels and the deerhounds had been her life and she

Keith Walker, Managing Director of Linton Tweeds

had won many honours and awards, having bred twenty-four champions by 1971, outranking all other kennels in the breed. By 1979 she had been elected to the Committee of the Kennel Club, one of the first women to serve in the Club's one hundred and fifty-four years lifespan and as a judge at Cruft's, she presented the 1989 Supreme Championship Cup to the winner.[31]

In her long life she had been a steadfast friend to Nessy Linton, from their early days as bright young women at Cheltenham Ladies' College, and through the difficult war years. Later, when Nessy was struggling with the stress of serious illness and running the tweed mill, Norah had been there, her strength and stay. Now she too was gone, and her loss was felt keenly in the deerhound world. Two of the greatest kennels were now lost, but they had left a legacy which still goes on today in the breeding of deerhounds. In her Will, Norah left assets of more than £3million pounds. These included provision for the deerhounds, requesting that Mrs Pauline Maxwell, one of her staff, dispose of her dogs, with two thousand pounds for their upkeep while this was done. All her papers, photographs and trophies were left to the Deerhound Club. Her links with Linton Tweeds were finally severed as she directed that her shares in the company be sold, but with the proviso that her Trustees had 'the widest possible powers to dispose of these shares to such persons and at such times and at such price... and to postpone the sale for such period... [as they] think fit.'[32] In other words, Norah was ensuring that her shares in Nessy's former business went into the right hands and that nothing would harm the business.

Eastern promise pays off

In October 1994 the local paper reported a trading boom and a future filled with Eastern promise, as Linton's took on extra staff to meet the growing demands of their well-established Japanese markets. It quoted Keith Walker as saying: 'In money terms, Japan is by far our biggest market,' with the firm selling up to £1.5 million worth of its textiles to the Japanese market every year. 'The Japanese will buy anything if it is the

**Pink and black check
Linton Tweed suit
made for Japanese
Export 1990s**

right quality. Our products are at the top of the quality range and that is why they are doing so well. We don't sell as well in Britain because of the price. Over there the price doesn't matter. All the Japanese have large savings which they tended to hang on to and have only recently begun to spend.'[33]

Later in the 1990s, the Japanese economy was to have a serious downturn and the value of the yen dropped against the strength of sterling. This affected orders from the buyers and Keith Walker found himself in search of new markets once again. He was to find them in America and Europe and supplied mail order fashion companies in America.[34]

The fourth generation of the Walker family in the business, he had a clear view of his priorities from the outset:

> 'My task has been primarily to look after the reputation that has already been established for Linton Tweeds. You know, when you are already one of the best suppliers of certain things, my stewardship has got to ensure that we enhance that and try and develop it if we can. The way to develop was to ensure that where there were new markets, we were part of the new markets. In the past Linton Tweeds was in Japan when it became a new market, but there have been others since then, Korea, and now Hong Kong and China, new customers, so we've developed into new markets as they have come, but still the most development has been in our existing markets.
>
> 'We have continued to develop in Japan, America, France and Germany and they have developed even further over the last ten or fifteen years, because our product is not a cheap product, it's a high quality, but also high priced item and tends to gravitate towards the richest economies in the world. There is a small market in every country for our type of product but the most customers will always be in the traditional markets.'[35]

As a result of his efforts, Linton Tweed became popular with German women and, by 2004, the German firm Escada's orders meant a boom in business once again for them. They found themselves unable to recruit enough skilled workers in the Carlisle area, and had to recruit workers from Poland, under the European Union agreements, in order to have three shifts working at the mill, day, evening and night. Keith Walker commenting at the time said: 'The Germans like the fact that we produce such a high quality product... We've taken on fifty extra staff this year alone, some of them from Poland because they were the only weavers we could find who had the necessary expertise and knowledge to work with our machinery. We were really struggling to find local weavers for the extra shifts.'[36]

Two other German companies, Basler and Rena Lange, also use Linton Tweed in their distinctive ranges, and the Italian market is growing.[37]

Travel became a way of life for Keith Walker and his designers, always keeping in touch with clients and responding to their requirements, as well as developing new contacts. Keith did the Far East trips, with the head designer doing the USA, and the rest of the overseas work being shared between him and all three designers.[38] Nessy would have recognised the lifestyle and would have been well-pleased, although for today's modern businessman flying off to global destinations is a far cry from voyages to America by luxury liner.

America is still one of Linton's largest markets, with designers such as DKNY and Daks Fifth Avenue buying the tweeds and having garments made up for them. A major growth area over the last ten years has been in sales by party plan, whereby women invite their friends to a social evening and sell the tweed directly to them. There is a huge network throughout America which gives customers easy access to luxury tweed.

The ups and downs of the global market mean that Linton Tweeds have to keep a close eye on world economies, and balance their reliance on any one market with developments in others. Keith Walker, well aware of the danger of relying on a single market, has acknowledged this tension:

> *'It gets dangerous and in the history of Linton Tweeds that has been shown, because we did nearly all of our business in the United States and then there was a problem there and we nearly collapsed because of it, and... since I've taken over as Managing Director, Japan represented about forty-four percent of our turnover, and that's far too high, it's risky in one market... now that's not the case, our bigger markets are fairly equal, so we don't have one market dominating our business.'*

The company still looks for new markets and South America is an area of potential growth, but it is the established markets that give the company its stability. As Keith Walker commented, 'You know, if we are sitting here in ten years time and I look at the make-up of our business I would imagine that because we are so well established, because our name is so well known, it's easier to develop more business in our existing market, than trying to establish new markets. It's only when people have heard about us and what we do, it translates well.' [39]

***

52
Trouble in paradise

By 1999, on the eve of the new millennium, there were cream tweeds offset with cloche hats, harking back to the 1920s, and soft fluid shapes which moved away from the decorative gilt chains and bejeweled look. Jackets sported fringed edges as deconstruction became the fashion theme that carried over into the new century. On the surface, it was business as usual in the world of haute couture. But there was trouble looming in paradise.

There are around three thousand women in the world who can afford to buy haute couture, and with only three hundred of these buying regularly, the couture houses sell about 1500 items per year. Of these women, there are around 150 who will invest in a couture Chanel suit; women with old money - the Rothschilds, the Guinnesses - but also the wives of wealthy business men, men who are Presidents of large corporations and whose wives will always dress in couture.

In addition, as well as the Hollywood stars, there are other celebrities from the worlds of pop music, television, sport and fashion, who can afford the high prices (a couture suit may cost in excess of £20,000) and look for the cachet of wearing couture.

The ladies of the old money, however, will not be seen in the same designs as the celebrities, or often even attend the same showings. The red carpet is a definite no-no.

High fashion demands high prices: the prices are more understandable if you look at what is involved in the original creation of the haute couture suit, the hours of work which go into the perfect hand-sewing, and the fine detail which every garment requires.

The House of Chanel, for example, has a number of features and techniques which, in the 1960s, the editors of *Vogue* described as 'Chanelisms'. These features, such as exclusive, luxurious material which may cost £100 per metre, quilted linings, chains in the jacket hemline which weight the garment, buttonholes which are handsewn on the outside but bound on the inside, and signature buttons are only a few of the techniques that give the suit its perfect balance and hang, and its high price-tag. It may take three fittings on the client and 100-150 hours of manual work to achieve the required look of perfection. An embellished evening dress may take 1,000 hours of work, with thousands of hand-sewn beads and can cost over £50,000. [40]

Each separate element requires the unique contribution of a select group of artists and craft workers. Linton's are one of this band of specialist suppliers that have helped

Chanel sustain its unique style and quality over the years, together with traditional French crafts companies such as François Lesage, Madame Pouzieux and André Lemarié.

Unlike Linton's, however, who had diversified their markets and reshaped their organisation over the years, by the new century many of these smaller providers depended on an ageing workforce and the unique skills of a few talented individuals. With each passing year, the continued supply of their goods was under threat: for fashion houses such as Chanel, self-interest dictated a change in their historic relationship.

Reworking tradition

Although these are often seen as traditional skills dating back centuries, new developments are constantly been sought, with many contemporary variations. In 2000, for example, Chanel funded an exciting new creation in the cloth used for its suits which required the Lesage workshops to develop 'reworked' tweed with stunningly beautiful results. 'In the early days,' explained M. François, 'threads were twisted together recalling a luxurious mop. Today the work done on tweeds in the couture embroidery workshops is amazing: sequins, feathers, braids and trimmings and even crystal splinters provide an endless array of garnishes, further enhancing the beautiful tweed that leaves Linton's weaving sheds to give it an air of total luxury. The result is a stunning fabric that Karl Lagerfeld uses for both his Prêt-á-Porter and Haute Couture collections.' [41]

Lesage, who died on 1 December 2011, ran a prestigious embroidery school, to train the embroiderers of the future. Karl Lagerfeld has said, 'I cannot conceive of any fashion without embroidery... Nor of any embroidery without Lesage.' [42] The handwork is exquisite, a jacket might take six hundred hours of work. The embroidery for a 1980s Chanel bleu de Chine dress, for example, took eighteen hundred hours of work and two hundred thousand miniature pearls to complete. François Lesage said, 'When a couturier phones me he sometimes merely says 'crocodiles' or 'Braque'. Then it's up to me to interpret.' [43]

At the other end of the scale, Madame Pouzieux combined her work as a *passementière* or an expert at making intricate braiding with farming. Her artistry enhances the edges of the tweed jackets on the famous haute couture suits. She uses a loom invented many years ago by herself and her brother, and is the only one who can master its intricacies. She has made Chanel braid for many years, since first making it for Coco and takes pride in her craft, using lengths of the tweed being used to make the suits for the collection. Spreading it on her work-table, she teases out the yarn, taking long lengths of it in proportion to the colour mix in the fabric, and from it sets about the laborious task of making her braid. Lengths of yarn are twisted round a complicated series of hooks; Madame sits down at her loom and begins to create.

The braid is often finished with other touches sent down from Chanel, a gold thread may be woven in, and Madame Pouzieux will set about the delicate task of hand-sewing it in. The result is a beautiful, and a uniquely crafted, finishing touch to set off the jackets made from Linton Tweed. That finishing touch says Paris. [44] In French legislation, her art only exists as a mechanized process for home furnishings! She has never been able to declare her craft and so her official trade is breeding horses. [45]

Flowers also feature prominently in many Chanel designs: this dates back to Coco herself. Her favourite flower was the camellia, the perfect creamy-white, scentless flower, often known as the Asian rose. She was to be seen wearing it in the earliest photographs of her designs, and her models would wear it pinned to a chic tweed suit, or to dramatise a little black dress. It became a constant to her look, and when Karl Lagerfeld took over, he too used it, dyed in many colours, and made from every material from silk and feathers, to leather and tweed. There was even a fabulous diamond brooch made in this style.

In the workshops of André Lemarié, the last *plumassier* or feathermaker in Paris, these luxurious hand-made artificial flowers are crafted. He makes 20,000 a year for Chanel. [46]

When he retired in 2000, Eric-Charles Donatien from the menswear atelier at Hermès was appointed Creative Director. While retaining the old techniques, he modernized the output and launched a line of jewellery influenced by tribal art, using feathers, rhinestones and precious metals.[47]

The Paris fashion designers have always relied on the hundreds of craftspeople such as Lesage, Pouzieux and Lemarié, who have traditionally made the 'extras', the embellishments which give the total look of luxury and perfection to the beautifully sewn garments. From embroidery to jewels, from buttons to shoes, there cannot be a collection without the work of these dedicated crafters.

And the demand extends to the accessories that the catwalk models wear with their haute couture suits. Maison Massaro of 2, rue de la Paix, Paris makes boots and shoes for some of the world's greatest couturiers. Raymond Massaro has been designing and supplying shoes that appear in the shows of Chanel, Dior, Christian Lacroix, John Galliano and Thierry Mugler, to name but a few, for over fifty years. The firm was founded by his grandfather and there are no heirs to follow him in the business. Private clients such as the Duchess of Windsor, Elizabeth Taylor and Marlene Dietrich have also been enthusiastic customers in the past, and today's socialites and celebrities still flock there. Karl Lagerfeld works closely with M. Massaro on the new designs for the couture collection, honing them to perfection, and says, 'Do you want to be one step ahead of the rest? Step out elegantly and walk tall with tailor-made shoes!'[48] It takes forty hours to craft a pair of hand-made shoes, and the retail customer will have to pay at least £1,500 for them.

Hats, too, are an important part of the couture look, whether it be a chic black beribboned straw boater or a froth of pink feathers, shaped like a camellia, it is likely to have come from the atelier of Michel, a milliner founded in 1936 and whose eleven workers produce four thousand hats each year. The wooden blocks are handmade, and the felt and straw shaped around them, before being dried in a large oven and then assembled and trimmed with ribbon or tulle.[49]

In the hands of the Desrues workshop, a button becomes an object of fashion and symbolism. The company was founded in 1929 by Georges Desrues, making buttons and costume jewellery, and has expanded from employing twenty people in 1984 to 170 today, relocating to a modern factory outside Paris. A million buttons are crafted each year for Chanel, made from gilt or pearl they include those embossed with Mademoiselle's signature lion's head, commemorating her Leo birth sign; three thousand are used in the couture collection.

The women who undertake the meticulous handwork required by the fashion houses, the *petites mains* or 'tiny hands', work long hours on fine, painstaking work to meet the needs of couture.

Saving an endangered species

At the beginning of the 21st century, the specialist craft workshops or *fournisseurs* that Chanel and other couture houses relied on were under threat. Many had been in existence for over a hundred years, and were almost becoming an endangered species. The reasons for this were several: the decline in the number of women buying haute couture; young women not inclined to undertake the long hours and close work of the craft ateliers; and the effect of cheap foreign competition. Where there had been ten thousand French embroiderers in the 1920s there are now about two hundred.[50]

François Lesage, owner of the famous Parisian embroidery workshop, founded in 1868, has fulfilled the dreams of every couturier with his exquisite embroidery. He described the problem to Susie Rushton of *The Independent* in 2003:

> *"Since the Gulf War in 1990 we have lost 50 per cent of couture clients," says Lesage. The core clientele of haute couture – the Middle Eastern princesses who spent hundreds of thousands of their petro dollars on Lesage's beaded wonders –*

were no longer enjoying their biannual spree in Paris. Lesage announced his concerns at a dinner hosted by the chairman of Chanel, Madame Montenay, and attended by his fellow master-artisans: Desrues, a costume jeweller; the milliner, Michel; Massaro a shoemaker; and Lemarié, a supplier of feathers and silk flowers. "I said, 'Madame, you have in front of you all the reasons why there is haute couture in Paris. If we were not here, the couture will fly away.'" She said, "I have something in mind. Let me think about it".' [51]

Madame Montenay's thoughts meant that, in July 2002, the House of Chanel decided to purchase all five of the suppliers, seeing them as essential for the continuation of the requirements of couture, as well as ensuring that the skills and crafts were not lost to future generations. The workshops would continue as before, and still sell to other couturiers, but under the mantle of Chanel. Monsieur Lesage says, 'I was approached by several other houses, but I accepted an offer of marriage from Miss Coco Chanel... She is not so young but she's quite rich!' [52]

The President of Fashion at Chanel, Bruno Pavlovsky said, 'It is a real investment in creativity which, aside from preserving a unique heritage and know-how, should help the still-independent companies to not only grow and break new ground but also shape new skills to ensure the future existence of our business lines.' [53]

Together with the two additional businesses acquired - the goldsmith and silversmith, Goossens, who opened his workshop in 1950, purchased in 2005, and the silk flower-maker Guillet, founded in 1896 and acquired in 2006 - the seven satellite ateliers d'art are known as 'Paraffection' and employ three hundred staff with a turnover of €35m. Chanel honours the craftspeople by showcasing their work annually in a special Métiers d'Art show staged each year in a different fashion capital and shows have been held in Paris, Tokyo, New York, Monte Carlo and London.

Elizabeth Hayt writing in *The New York Times* explains, 'The demand for high fashion ready-to-wear in the last 15 years - made ever more deluxe by couture embellishments – has caused a business shift in many of the ateliers. At Lesage and Lemarié, for instance, 80 percent of the workmanship is done for ready-to-wear and 20 percent for haute couture.' [54]

***

53
Hard times, but business as usual

2005 started badly for Linton Tweeds – and for many of their neighbours. The Carlisle Floods had a devastating effect on them when, along with many other Carlisle businesses in the Caldewgate and Shaddongate areas of the city, they were closed for a month.

The disaster occurred when three rivers - the Eden, the Caldew and the Petteril - burst their banks and, in combination with high tides on the Solway coast, caused the worst floods in the city since 1822.

Carole Walker could not believe how much damage the flood waters did at Linton Tweeds and gazed in horror at the mud all over the car park and the devastation and damp smell in the coffee shop and Visitors Centre. Rolls of brilliant tweeds, expensive knitwear, £300 Reid and Taylor men's suits, tables, chairs and crockery all lay destroyed and dripping wet.

Recalling the horror of that day she said:

'The floods happened over Friday night, on Saturday morning the cook turned up for work and couldn't get in, it was very bad, the mobiles didn't work... and Radio Cumbria was absolutely wonderful, because you could only get information from

them. We could only get in when the waters had receded, the tables and chairs from the conservatory had all warped before the next day so that when we tossed them out everything had to go in the bucket... the staff were absolutely wonderful. I got in on the Sunday morning with hosepipes, and that was the good thing about not having flood insurance because I didn't have to wait for assessors. With six feet of water swirling up the walls... it was as though a hundred vandals had come in because the water had swept in and swept out and it took the heavy tills, it left about a foot of solid mud on top of everything.

'It was absolutely astonishing, we had customers who came to help, coats off, everything was thrown out, we had no electricity to start with... I got twelve dozen pairs of rubber gloves and everything was sterilized, everything was scrubbed, anything that could be kept was scrubbed, because you can't take any risk in a public place... we hired humidifiers and they drew out the damp and we saved these tables which we scrubbed with toothbrushes but the staff were absolutely superb and they came and got us up and working again within the month.' [55]

As the huge clean-up began, a mood of optimism soon overtook the horror, the absolute disaster of it all. Carole said: 'Yesterday was bad, today has been a bit better, and tomorrow will be better than today. You have to take one day at a time and get on with the cleaning. The staff have been absolutely brilliant and we've had a lot of regular customers phoning up and popping by to see if they can help in any way. That makes the situation bearable.' [56] While the shop and coffee shop had extensive damage, it was fortunate for the couture business that the factory, the weaving sheds with their costly machinery, escaped serious damage.

'That would have been the end,' said Carole. 'That would have been totally the end. The water lapped up onto the steps... then it started to recede, had it got into the machines that would have been it, finished, it was lucky that it didn't go in any further, and we were blessed with the staff - we survived, you have to be quite optimistic... we recovered you know and its very popular.' [57]

But something irreplaceable was lost: the Linton Archives - scrapbook upon scrapbook of photographs, tweed swatches and memorabilia going back beyond the 1950s which were Carole Walker's pride and joy. Here was the company history, with signed photos of Coco Chanel, handwritten letters, drawings and designs; it was a treasure trove of priceless artefacts of the company's heritage which could never be replaced. But the flood waters of 2005 saw its demise and Carole Walker still speaks wistfully today of her lost treasure.

In the medium term, however, the floods proved an opportunity for more development and

Flood damage at Linton Tweeds caused by the Carlisle floods of 2005

as Linton's recovered and cleaned up, Carole Walker looked to the future: the attractive conservatory was extended and a patio garden was added to the restaurant. As a lasting reminder of one of the worst days at the mill, the floods are graphically depicted in a vivid collage of photographs that Carole has hung on the wall. Now, once again, the Bobbin Coffee Shop, with its pretty tweed tablecloths, home-baked food and collection of vintage sewing machines, is one of Carlisle's most popular meeting places, where one can meet friends for a gossip and admire the beautiful fabrics.

Keith Walker, Managing Director of Linton Tweeds, and Design and Sales Director, Rob Irvine

Meanwhile, back in Paris... Karl has arrived!

The House of Chanel at 31 rue Cambon is in a state of suspended animation. Telephones ring, white coated seamstresses answer and hear the news – 'Monsieur Karl est là.' Now the hive of activity will roll into action. The studio manager remarks, 'It'll be crazy, once it starts.'

A 2005 film sets the scene. In he walks, dress immaculate, white ponytail coiffed, wearing signature shades, high white starched collar, boots and fingers full of silver rings. As stylish as Mademoiselle herself and now it is all systems go at Chanel.

Holding court in Mademoiselle's former office, surrounded by assistants hanging on every word, he begins his sketches. Working rapidly, never pausing, the designs seem to run over the paper like quicksilver, light quick sketches, but full of detail and written notes, as he is explaining all the while to the head seamstress who is watching like a hawk. She has to understand every line on the sketch. In a few moments the design is complete, and it is perfectly lovely. Often he will have drawn the designs at home, rapidly recording his thoughts and inspirations, even occasionally recalling dreams where he has seen the whole theme of the collection. He works hard and with concentration, his ideas flowing from his fingertips.[58]

In the large white airy workrooms on the top floors of rue Cambon, Madam Jacqueline, the Head of Tailoring, shows the sketches to the seamstresses, they crowd around looking at the lovely designs, and know they will be working flat out to get them ready for the fashion show in just a few weeks time. There are two couture collections shown each year, traditionally in January and July, but in between there are as many as seven shows for prêt-a-porter, cruise collections and the satellite collection.

Over the years Lagerfeld has shown some amazing collections, and every one of them has referenced Coco.

In March 2005, for example, *Vogue* reported that the 2005/6 Autumn/Winter Ready-To-Wear collection included 'a taste of the English countryside with tweed plus fours inspired by the ones Coco herself used to wear in the days of her liaison with the Duke of Westminster.' [59]

For this show, Lagerfeld did not disappoint, using a spectacular setting to show the new collection, a stark white spherical podium, with rows of steps disappearing in ever-diminishing circles to the top. As *Vogue's* Camilla Morton reported: 'a procession of girls, head to toe in black, started to circle the set, circling and climbing the layers of steps... Capes, gowns, coats and macs – all in black- all trailed and mounted the layers of the set as if it were a massive life size wedding cake... following the opening high priestess. Audrey Marney in a classic Coco Chanel-style quilted coat, black tweeds, and 60s PVC style macs.'

When all were in place, the models shrugged off their top coats and capes and, like exotic butterflies emerging from their chrysalis, showed suits in brilliant hues. As the spiral unfurled to cocktail and evening dresses, only the last girl was left at the top. 'The lining of the top layer coordinated exactly with the butterfly that has come out of her cocoon: proof from Mr Lagerfeld that you must never judge a book by its cover. Shift dresses and frayed tweeds, salmon pinks and piped pastel sculpted blue jackets brought in a new palette and the softer mood was lapped up by onlookers.'[60] At the top of the 'wedding cake' the model slipped off her cape and emerged in one of the most enchanting wedding dresses ever, a gown covered in twists and ruffles of white chiffon ribbons, where she was joined by the elegant black-suited and silver-gloved Karl Lagerfeld who took her hand, before blowing a kiss to the crowd and running off to receive his congratulations.

By October 2007, American influences were evident in a collection that included star-spangled navy blue dresses cinched at the waist with red and white stripes, denim jeans worn with the iconic bouclé wool jacket in red and white, and heather-mix tweed jackets shrugged over blue denim bustiers and glittering star brooches.[61]

That year, it was the Paris-Londres show that caught the headlines: the first major Chanel show in London with its 'English chic' theme inspired by the Englishmen who were not only Coco's lovers, but would influence her interpretation of the Chanel style in the 1920s and 1930s - Arthur 'Boy' Capel and the Duke of Westminster. From both men she would keep her lifelong love affair with all things English, including her love of English tweed.[62]

La collection – c'est si bon!

Interviewed before the Paris-Londres Exhibition, Karl Lagerfeld told Geordie Greig of *Tatler* magazine:

> '"The danger is when designers think they are artists". He stresses that Chanel and Balenciaga didn't have exhibitions during their lifetimes: "They made dresses for people, which was the purpose of their job." For him there are three moments of excitement that need to work separately and together in fashion: the sketch, the fitting and it all coming together in a collection. "Like cooking, you have to put the ingredients together and sometimes it does not work, and if you do not feel the excitement you should begin the whole process again."'[63]

Chanel's links with Russia were honoured in the seventh Métiers d'Art show in December 2008, held at the Théâtre Ranelagh in Paris and it was a spectacle Coco would have appreciated. In her lifetime she had embraced the Russian elements in her life and used her talent in embodying the influences in many aspects of her business. Prince Dmitri, her lover from the 1920s, had introduced her to the splendour, jewels and perfumes of the Russian court, which would directly lead to the creation of Chanel No.5, and through his sister, Marie, to the richly embroidered designs of the Chanel collections. Her friendship and collaboration with Russian artists such as Diaghilev and Stravinsky enhanced her feel of the Russian ethos and involved her in the theatricality of live performance.

Karl Lagerfeld cleverly transposed these influences into a show where all the traditional Chanel looks appear, but with Lagerfeld's own special twist. Tweeds appeared in a white fringed snow-queen ensemble complete with white boots and gold Tsarina-style head-dress, and in a striking scarlet-red skirt suit trimmed with black braid and worn white fringed snow-queen ensemble complete with white boots and gold Tsarina-style head-dress, and in a striking scarlet-red skirt suit trimmed with black braid and worn with an elaborate head-dress. All the skills and talents of the satellite ateliers were showcased in a brilliant show enacted in a recreation of a 1920s Parisian nightclub, complete with marble pillars and red table lamps. [64]

Karl Lagerfeld - Chanel's driving force in the 21st century

Two years later, in January 2009, it was white, white all the way: there may have been snow on the ground in London, bankers being held responsible for the recession, but at Chanel it was business as usual. Karl Lagerfeld may have felt restrained by the times in producing an all-white, trimmed with black collection, but luxury had not lost its place. It was one of Mademoiselle's favourite colours and it was used to scintillating sparkling effect in a stunning show held at rue Cambon. As Karl Lagerfeld commented recently, 'Bling is over. Red carpetry covered in rhinestones is out. I call it "the new modesty".' [65]

Linton Tweed was featured in a cropped magnolia jacket with a wide funnel neck, teamed with an A-line skirt sporting a single front pleat, and in a series of white short-sleeved, silk-braided jackets. Carola Long of *The Independent* reported on the neat simple styles that enabled the embroiderers and feather-makers to display their craft and embellish to perfection, with bouquets of tiny white paper roses, butterflies, bows and embossed petals on headdresses, flowers made from sequins and lace covered with paint-sprayed feathers. The white embellishments on white dresses enhancing the look of purity and femininity, as fresh as a spring morning. [66]

In spite of the fact that the normal week-long catwalk shows have been cut to three days, Chanel's President of Fashion, Bruno Pavlovsky was bullish. 'Haute couture is for everyone... The message of couture is creativity. Couture exists to keep our customers dreaming. Not only the customers who buy the clothes but the other Chanel customers who see the show.'

He also pointed out that couture provides employment for highly skilled specialist craftspeople, because the intricate garments are made entirely by hand in the Paris workshops. [67]

Jess Carter-Morley reporting from Paris for *The Guardian* wrote: 'Just one – of the outfits on yesterday's catwalk – a dress in white percaline cotton, embroidered with pearls and sequins and trimmed with leaves and flowers each cut separately by hand in the famed Lemarié embroidery atelier – took 800 hours of workmanship to complete.' [68]

Chanel may have announced the cutting of two hundred jobs in December 2008, but they had also reported twenty percent growth in sales. Bruno Pavlovsky reported that the company had seen large growth in the last five years, and even if it were less strong this year, comments:

> *'I don't worry about couture. Couture is very special and Karl is so strong. I am not sure there is a direct link between what you saw on the catwalk today and the economic situation.'* [69]

***

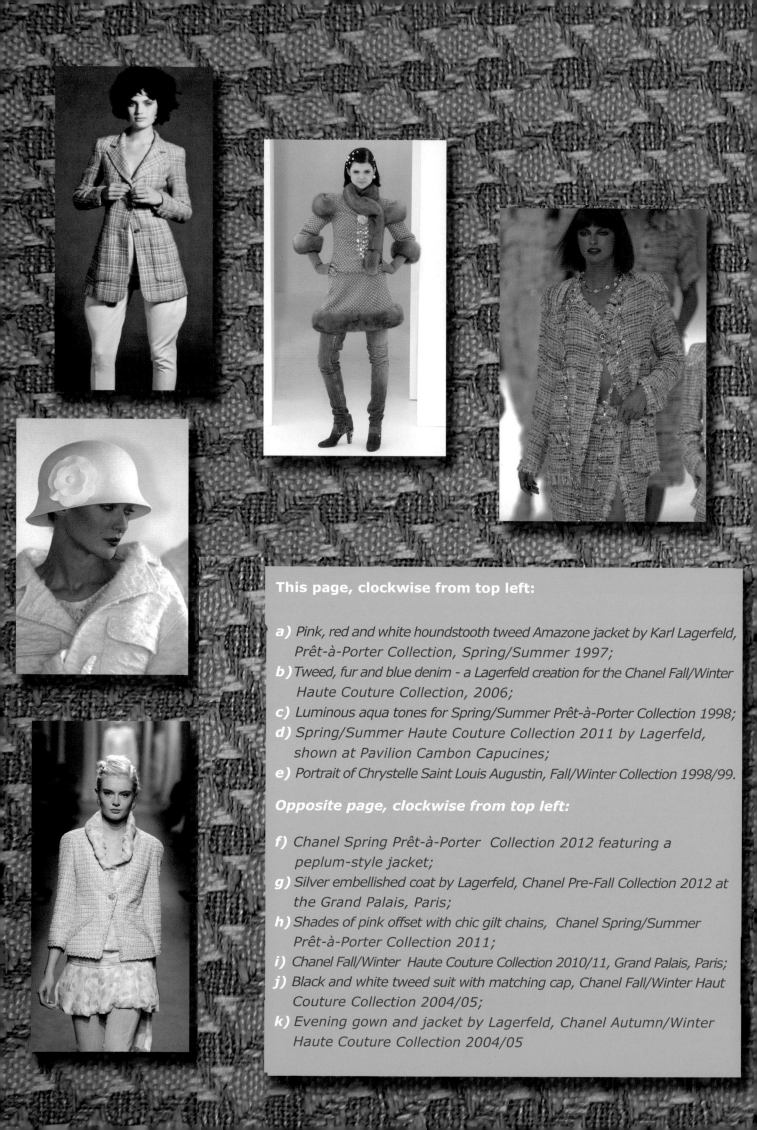

This page, clockwise from top left:

a) *Pink, red and white houndstooth tweed Amazone jacket by Karl Lagerfeld, Prêt-à-Porter Collection, Spring/Summer 1997;*

b) *Tweed, fur and blue denim - a Lagerfeld creation for the Chanel Fall/Winter Haute Couture Collection, 2006;*

c) *Luminous aqua tones for Spring/Summer Prêt-à-Porter Collection 1998;*

d) *Spring/Summer Haute Couture Collection 2011 by Lagerfeld, shown at Pavilion Cambon Capucines;*

e) *Portrait of Chrystelle Saint Louis Augustin, Fall/Winter Collection 1998/99.*

Opposite page, clockwise from top left:

f) *Chanel Spring Prêt-à-Porter Collection 2012 featuring a peplum-style jacket;*

g) *Silver embellished coat by Lagerfeld, Chanel Pre-Fall Collection 2012 at the Grand Palais, Paris;*

h) *Shades of pink offset with chic gilt chains, Chanel Spring/Summer Prêt-à-Porter Collection 2011;*

i) *Chanel Fall/Winter Haute Couture Collection 2010/11, Grand Palais, Paris;*

j) *Black and white tweed suit with matching cap, Chanel Fall/Winter Haut Couture Collection 2004/05;*

k) *Evening gown and jacket by Lagerfeld, Chanel Autumn/Winter Haute Couture Collection 2004/05*

54
To Russia with love – and beyond

The High Street shops may be in serious financial trouble as their customers suffer the effects of the economic down-turn and tighten their belts, but in the heady atmosphere of the couture showrooms, where the models strut their stuff, all is well. The super rich ladies from Russia, China and the Middle East, the celebrities and the ranks of the old money, can still buy their six-figure dresses.

The popularity of the Chanel look and Linton Tweeds is on the ascendant in growing markets such as Russia and China, as Keith Walker has described, and Bruno Pavlovsky agrees: 'Yes, Russia is a booming market, and this is a nice way to support it. Russian consumers know a lot about fashion. They like something special and unique.' [70]

When asked if the economic climate was right for such extravagance, Lagerfeld said, 'I'm not sure, but the collection isn't in the shops until June, and thanks to Mr Obama things may be OK. I'm not a marketing person, I don't ask myself questions, I do things by instinct.' [71]

The Russian connection - supplying the top couturier Slava Zaitsev with Linton Tweed - is a strange coincidence after Coco's own exhibits in Moscow in 1967. She would never have imagined that forty years later, in the autumn of 2007, the State Pushkin Museum of Fine Arts in Moscow would host an exhibition, 'Chanel. L'Art Comme Univers', dedicated to her life and the history of the House of Chanel.

The Director of the Pushkin Museum, Dr Irina Antonova, speaking at the opening of the exhibition, said, 'We have supported this project with great enthusiasm as 20th century fashion plays such an integral role in contemporary culture... we owe so much to Gabrielle Chanel, as her design creations and approach were very much akin to the artistic pursuits of her century. What's more, the Russian public will be more than delighted to discover the links that Mademoiselle Chanel had with Russians and how they profoundly influenced her life and her life's work.' [72]

Fashion design has boomed in Russia over the last ten years, with the number of designers rocketing from a handful to one hundred and twenty. They show at two main events, Russian Fashion Week and Fashion Week in Moscow. While some designers also show on the international catwalks of Milan and New York, many prefer the vast potential of the home market. Robb Young, writing in the *International Herald Tribune* said, 'Aside from household names like Slava Zaitsev and more recently Valentin Yudashkin, virtually all the designers toiling away in Moscow and St Petersburg's ateliers are products of the post-Soviet economic explosion. They are the same generation and, whether they know it or not, they are jockeying for position as future heritage brands. Essentially, the history of Russian fashion design begins now.' [73]

Since 2002 the shows have been a resounding success and looking to the future Lagerfeld states 'They would love me to do something on China next. Perhaps China Express – the trip Chanel never made.' [74]

China: the East–West connection

Throughout the ages, China has been a key player in trade with Europe. Since the second century BC the Silk Road from Xi'an was the famous trade route connecting the Imperial court of China and the far eastern markets, to the Mediterranean, the Roman Empire and the European markets in the west. This was the information super highway of its age, serving not only as a conduit for goods, but as a pathway for the interchange of culture, ideas and knowledge between east and west, and was instrumental in the development of the great civilisations.

Today after thirty years of market reform that has taken place since the Cultural Revolution, this ancient country with its 5,000 years of history is taking its place on the of Chinese citizens look forward to a new prosperity. After decades of social and political upheaval in China, trade with the West is booming and the luxury goods business taking off at the speed of light.

As the second fastest growing economy in the world, after the USA, the Chinese economy is set to continue to grow. The global economy is not always ready to assimilate this. In 2005, the famous 'bra wars' erupted between China and the European Union when the thirty-year-old Multi-Fibre agreement, a textile tariff and quota system, which set annual clothing export limits for each country, ended. With seventy five million Chinese garments set to flood the European market, the clothing was piled up in European ports. After marathon negotiations it was agreed to release half of the blocked clothing and count the rest against 2006 quotas. With agreement finally made, UK Prime Minister Tony Blair, told the BBC that the strategic partnership between the EU and China was 'vital'. 'The difficulty is that we are trying to balance a number of interests here because obviously people want less expensive goods... But then you have the textile producers across Europe who are worried about their jobs and unfair competition.' [75]

By 2008 the EU no longer imposed quotas on Chinese textiles, but opted for a year of surveillance on the levels of imports. The French textile industry, which has undergone massive restructuring in the last twenty years and has seen a forty percent decrease in the number of people employed from 1995 to 2005, reducing to 82,000, is said not to be worried by the Chinese garment influx. They cite diversification and new supply sources, such as northwest Africa and eastern Europe as their buffer.[76]

The USA was also embroiled in a war of words with China for similar reasons, and led to calls for American quotas to be introduced. An agreement was reached allowing limited increases in Chinese imports until 2008, with the National Council of Textile Organisations claiming victory. The Chairman, Jim Chesnutt said, 'The US industry will know with certainty that China will not be able to flood the US market.' [77]

Luxury brands – what's in a name?

China may be exporting cheap garments to America and Europe but, on the other side of the coin, they are importing luxury items on a grand scale. Consumer wealth is growing at an unprecedented rate and, by 2006, China had three hundred thousand millionaires, with a vast consumer potential. Dana Thomas in her book *Deluxe* quotes Tom Ford telling her, 'This is the century of emerging markets, we are finished here in the West – our moment has come and gone. This is all about China and India and Russia. It is the beginning of the reawakening of cultures that have historically worshipped luxury and haven't had it for so long.' [78]

From Beijing to Shanghai, the 1990s saw Chinese men embracing luxury brands, and responsible for 90% of luxury goods sales. Favourite brands were Boss, Vuitton, Rolex and Givenchy or Armani suits, as they sought the look of the Western businessman. By 2000, women were catching up, and by 2004 accounted for forty percent of all luxury goods sales, and it is not only the wealthy who are buying Chanel or Prada handbags. There is the cult of wanting the best, and secretaries will spend a month's salary on their favourite designer brand.

Vogue China editor, Angelica Cheung says, 'Most Chinese buy luxury as a status symbol rather than taste. They

Chanel jacket, made of Linton Tweed, featuring signature double-C buttons, now part of the Tullie House collection

like logos. They want people to know they are carrying something expensive... they can't pronounce the names and they don't know where it comes from. They just want it because it's expensive.' [79]

Consequently, in today's fashion markets, logos are not only about brand image, a stylish touch to catch the eye or signify one's fashion status. They have a more mundane but strategic use. No one understands this better than Karl Lagerfeld.

Speaking to Susanna Frankel of *The Independent Magazine* he said:

> 'I don't remember the first time I saw the Chanel logo. But I noticed it when I took over Chanel, when real logo power started all over the world. For a company it is very important today, because, much more than in the past, we all sell in parts of the world where they cannot read our writing or understand our languages. In one part - a very big part – of the world it is all about signs when they write. They can memorise perhaps the famous "CC" but they have difficulties reading the name first. They find out later. In the past we sold mostly to people who knew our culture and could read English or French. Now it is only a part of our clientele. Logos are the Esperanto of marketing, luxury and business today.' [80]

In its original form, the double C was the fastening on the 2.55 bag which Coco first introduced in February 1955 and named after its birth date. It was to become one of the most sought-after bags of the century, as the easy-to-wear, over-the-shoulder style epitomised elegance, class and practicality by freeing the hands. Today the bag, with its quilting and gilt chain, is as popular as ever, and is made in many colours and style variations, still retaining its chic and cachet.

Fashion is now big business, with Chinese women studying the latest copies of *Elle*, *Cosmopolitan* and *Vogue China* just as keenly as the fashionistas in London, Paris or New York. People crave luxury, something which Coco Chanel herself understood very well, and she had many *bon mots* on the subject. As she was fond of saying, 'Luxury is a necessity that begins where necessity ends.'

There is evidence that motivation is changing and people now want more than just the 'bling' factor. Fashion magazines and media are increasingly playing an educative role in informing women of the choices available and of the creative differences between the various designers and brands. Two of the leading magazines in this field are *i-Look* and *Vision* and Hung Huang, CEO of China Interactive Media Group has said, 'Our flagship brand is *i-Look* and it focuses on affluent female customers. We have a magazine and a TV show that target the same market... Our message about luxury consumption is that fashion is not skin deep. To be intelligent as a luxury consumer the Chinese have to get over buying status. They have to buy for their personal enjoyment... We want them to feel that their purchases have really given them pleasure, rather than simply encouraging other people to perceive them as rich people.' [81]

Hung Huang also noted that, 'The entire aesthetic of fashion, of luxury, of lifestyle is dominated by western culture. There is no single luxury manufacturer in China. In practical terms there is no choice but to follow international trends.'

Describing one of the first fashion shoots done in China with local staff she said:

> 'When Chanel launched its first ready-to-wear collection in China we took two no-name models up into the mountains. We lined up a bunch of herdsmen, Chinese cowboys leading horses and had a girl dressed in Chanel on each horse. This was Chanel entering China. Chanel loved it, but most Chinese hated it. They said, "These people are poor, they have nothing to do with fashion." It doesn't matter! The whole thing symbolizes Chanel landing in China and that glamour, that bling, versus all the normal perceptions you have of China – rice paddy fields and so on. It's a great sign of changes to come in the future. The Chinese hated it... Nationalism becomes an issue and people say: "you're trying to humiliate us".' [82]

The desire for luxury goods has seen the market become the fastest growing in the world, galloping ahead at twenty per cent a year, with sales of luxury goods predicted to reach $12billion by 2010.[83]

Ten years on from opening the first Chanel boutique in Beijing, 25 November 2009 saw Chanel opening its fifth boutique on the Chinese mainland when a new flagship store was opened in the city known as the 'Paris of the East', Shanghai.

New York architect Peter Marino had taken his inspiration from Coco's luxury apartment in rue Cambon to create a new boutique concept, displaying artwork and antiques in salon-style rooms, in the luxurious Art Deco style Peninsula Hotel located on the Bund, the waterfront promenade in Shanghai. Karl Lagerfeld had designed an exclusive collection, with limited edition signature quilted bags, tweed jackets trimmed in gold and sling-back shoes, all zinging in bright pink, dragon red and jade green recalling the colours of Imperial China.

The grand opening was followed a few days later, on 3 December, by the eighth Métiers D'Arts show, the annual display of work honouring the Chanel satellite craft workshops in Paris. The setting was magnificent, the concept grand, and the clothes everything Coco would ever have dreamed of. On a custom-built barge moored on the banks of the Huangpu River, officials of the People's Republic of China brushed shoulders with the world's fashion press, Shanghai billionaires and Chinese fashionistas, all seated in a huge glass box and looking across the neon-lit sky to the financial district of Pudong, with its sky-line of futuristic high-rise buildings lit with neon. Karl Lagerfeld described the scene as, 'magical, with colours that look somehow different to Europe, and a kind of transparency about them.' [84]

The exotic theme of the collection was set by an atmospheric film directed by Karl Lagerfeld, entitled *Paris-Shanghai A Fantasy*, *The Trip Coco Only Made in Her Dreams*. Here we see Coco falling asleep in her rue Cambon apartment and dreaming of visiting Shanghai in the 1930s and 1940s and, later, in the Cultural Revolution of the 1960s. Along the way, she is seen in the company of the Duchess of Windsor and Marlene Dietrich in exotic gambling dens and night clubs, and touchingly exchanging her famous ecru Linton Tweed jacket for a young girl's denim blue Chairman Mao jacket, which, she muses, may inspire a collection.

The collection of 71 garments which followed was inspired and showed little red dresses and little red bags, flower-printed blouses, the iconic Linton tweed jackets and suits in lacquer red and jade green worn with thigh-high black shiny boots, embroidered mousseline tweed jackets, Mao jackets and filmy courtesan dresses, all embellished with braid, beads, flowers and feathers in an interpretation of Chinese crafts. The lust for luxury is alive and well in the People's Republic, but as Karl Lagerfeld commented at his pre-show press conference, 'If you are against luxury, then you are for unemployment. The luxury industry employs millions of people.' [85] It is a point of view.

Keith Walker has seen this booming economy and desire for luxury goods for himself and comments, 'In China, there are so many people there, that even if only one or two percent are quite wealthy, that still represents a lot of people and they're looking for the luxury items... We don't do so much direct selling , but the customers that we sell to in our traditional markets sell on into China and India, the place of the up and coming economies.' [86]

Those with a social conscience may look at the boom in luxury in world-wide markets, at the growth of the affluent society, at the sheer extravagance of those who can afford to pay thousands of pounds for luxury brands, and find it difficult to reconcile this with the millions of poor people, scraping a living in these countries. The many Chinese, Russians and Indians who live on the edge of poverty while millions of pounds are spent on exclusive shopping malls and designer labels, may not be aware of this disparity, or if they are, can do little about it.

It is an issue for our time and one of the most compelling images of our time is a photograph taken by Jeremy Sutton-Hibbert in the Shinjuku district of Tokyo. It depicts a homeless man standing outside a Chanel luxury clothing store selling *The Big Issue*. There are no easy answers.[87]

＊＊＊

55
Of media, marketing and high fashion

Over the years, marketing and the media have become increasingly important in the world of haute couture, particularly since the advent of prêt-à-porter. From very simple origins, it is now a highly sophisticated industry.

Rose Bertin, the first international couturière and 'minister of fashion' to Queen Marie-Antoinette of France in the eighteenth century, used dolls to show her designs to women and it was from these small beginnings that the modelling industry began. Designers had to have a means of showing their fashions to the women who held the purse strings. The society ladies who first showed the creations of Lucile, Poiret and Chanel, were soon overtaken as model agencies sprung up, and young women aspired to this new and glamorous profession. Charm schools turned out hopeful aspirants to the new cause.

It was to continue to develop through the decades until by the 1980s the new breed of supermodels were celebrities in their own right and commanded huge sums, showing the latest styles at the highly produced and glitzy catwalk shows which continue today.

It was a three-pronged development, as the women's fashion magazines developed, and those such as *Harper's Bazaar* and Condé Nast's *Vogue* took the lead. They were read avidly by women wanting to find out the latest look in Paris fashion's. At first the magazines used illustrators sketching the garments but then started to use photographers who were to become celebrated names, from Norman Parkinson, Man Ray, Horst, Hoyningen-Huene, Cecil Beaton, to David Bailey, Terry Donovan, Patrick Lichfield and right up today, with Patrick Demachelier. The women editors of the top magazines became powerful: Edna Woolman Chase, Carmel Snow, and Diana Vreeland through to Anna Wintour could make or break a designer's collection with a few choice words.

The glossy fashion magazines were not the only media to make an impact on the women of the world: soon every daily newspaper would have its fashion editor, devoting pages to the latest reports on the new season's styles and with hints on beauty and how to achieve the model look. As a schoolgirl, I recall devouring the fashion page of *The Daily Telegraph* where fashion editor Winefride Jackson would describe the latest Ascot hats by Simone Mirman or Aage Thaarup, or the clothes that royalty would be wearing on their latest overseas tour, while in *The Sunday Times,* Ernestine Carter would cover the Paris collections, all elegantly illustrated by the great Robb. It opened the door to a magical world. The growth of teenage magazines in the sixties spawned a whole new generation of fashion addicts queuing up to buy the latest in mini-skirts or try the newest make-up and hairstyles.

Today the glossy fashion magazines are full of adverts, not only for the clothes, but for a whole lifestyle: they have become purveyors of dreams. The trendy photographs of luscious models are often less about the clothes, than about the luxurious tropical locations and the artistic interpretation of the photographer.

It is a far cry from the days in 1936 when the editor of American *Vogue*, Edna Woolman Chase fought a losing battle with photographers to have the detail of the clothes shown. She would say, 'I'm sick and tired of having women say to me, "How is this dress made? What is it like?"... Concentrate completely on the dress, light it for this purpose, and if that can't be done without art then art be damned.' [88]

Photography is all important in showing the collections to a world-wide audience: those women who still buy couture but do not travel to Paris to see the shows will receive videos of the collection. At Chanel, Karl Lagerfeld himself takes the photographs, and Jacques Helleu, who joined Chanel at the age of eighteen in 1965, is still producing advertising campaigns for Chanel perfumes that rank with the best.

Now the cult of the celebrity has taken over from the role of the high society woman as the arbiter of the latest style, and celebrity-led magazines, such *Hello* and *OK* are as influential as *Vogue*, *Elle* or *Marie-Claire* in educating the eye of today's woman.

This means that today's woman is probably more knowledgeable about the world of fashion than at any other time in fashion history. The exclusive, chic designs of haute couture may be a million miles away from the pockets of most women, but the dream is attainable from the local High Street, with a bottle of designer perfume.

The publicity and huge media attention that the catwalk show attracts for the couture house means that they will always promote the glamorous, often loss-making, million-pound collections each season. With the collections accounting for less than ten per cent of gross profits, it is the perfumes, cosmetics, accessories and boutiques which bring in the vast profits that fulfill the dream for most women, and enable the world of haute couture to look to the future.

Première Vision, Paris – where it all begins

If you have ever wondered how the high street shops all manage to show similar colours and styles each season, or how fashion writers predict 'this year it's violet' or 'it's black, black all the way', the answer lies in Paris. As international trade shows go, Première Vision in Paris, known to *aficionados* as P.V., is one of the largest fabric trade shows in the world, and it is here that the wheels of the fashion industry start turning. It is where textile manufacturers find new customers, where garment manufacturers view the latest fabrics and where new trends for forthcoming seasons are displayed. Held at the Parc d'Expositions de Paris–Nord Villepinte, this is textile creativity at its best, fulfilling an important role in the international textile industry.

Keith Walker is no stranger to its portals , having been Chairman of the Selection Committee and exhibiting Linton Tweeds textiles twice each year. It is an influential position, and as Keith says, 'You can't have influence if you're not there... they invite some of the people who head the suppliers that use the show, and get them to help guide Première Vision, to ensure that they are doing the right thing... it helps because I can put forward Linton Tweeds opinion on issues that affect the way they do the show, the way they conduct it and how they attract their customers... P.V. is one of the best for finding new customers.' [89]

P.V. has been a fascinating development since it started in 1973, when a group of fifteen weavers in Lyons decided to present a joint fabric collection at the International Trade Centre in Paris. This totally new concept took off, and soon they were meeting ahead of production to plan the trends and colours for each new season. By 1980 European manufacturers were invited to exhibit and, since 2002, non-European weavers also take part. Their influence is immense and the look and colours found in all the high street shops each season starts here.

The forecasting of fabric and colour trends is now a very sophisticated business, and starts two years before the clothes actually appear. In 1997 an international observatory was established globally to identify emerging fashion trends. Meetings of these networks eventually decide on colours and trends, and forecasts are analysed leading to the seasons look. The results of the research are used to produce textile performance codes covering everything from water-proofing to anti-UV protection. P.V. sees its aim as being 'to choose a colour for its strength, an idea for its meaning, and a fabric for its fibre.' [90]

The event goes from strength to strength, with satellite shows held in New York, Moscow, Tokyo and Shanghai. In Paris, the shows are held twice each year and seven hundred weavers from twenty-eight countries take part, with fifty-thousand professional visitors from one-hundred-and-six countries visiting the amazing displays. Here developments in technology vie for position with the world of ideas as the constant search for the new in fashion goes on, season after season. Here among the vast array of stunning silks, crushed velvets, brilliant jerseys and glitzy Lurex, the exquisite fabrics of Linton Tweeds take their place and Keith Walker competes to fill his order book.[91]

Keith travels the world meeting buyers from the fashion houses, and his client list reads like a copy of *Vogue* magazine, or a Who's Who of fashion designers. They are all there: Dior, Armani, Yves Saint Laurent, Lacroix, Bruce Oldfield, Donna Karan, Calvin Klein, Jaeger, Aquascutum, and this list is not exhaustive. But new names are always being added – as new fashion houses and high-profile customers discover Linton's quality and style.

Nothing stands still and, in the UK, Linton Tweeds are often in the news. In November 2008 it was reported that Victoria Beckham was considering a feisty black and rubber mix tweed for her next collection. In February 2009 her second collection for autumn/winter 2009/10 was launched at the Waldorf Towers in New York, showing twenty-three garments. As well as her perfectly tailored pencil-slim dresses she featured a series of foxy capes in rubberized tweeds, 'NOT waterproof' as she emphasised. The capes knotted at the neck and featured long bold gold zips running down the front and up each of the semi-sleeves, 'to add interest, so that you can wear it in different ways' she said. The clothes are made in London and feature hand-sewing as part of their aspirations to couture style class. Retailing at between £850 and £4,900 the clothes are popular in Russia and Dubai as well as being a success story in America at top stores, Bergdorf Goodman and Neiman Marcus.[92]

America's First Lady favours Linton's

If the American presidential elections hit the news in November 2008, as Barack Obama and John McCain fought it out at the at the polls, excitement was high at Linton Tweeds when with the Obama victory, an order was placed by Thai-born American designer Thakoon Panichgul for Linton tweed destined to be used for the new First Lady. Thakoon has become noted for his feminine, elegant clothes spiced with wit so, when Michelle and Barack Obama left Washington D.C. on 31 March 2009, bound for London at the start of their first presidential European tour, the world's media watched and Keith Walker at Linton Tweeds knew they had a hit. The First Lady, being dubbed the new 'Mrs O' in America following the celebrity of Jacqueline Kennedy Onassis, was wearing an elegant ivory tulle Linton Tweed coat with grosgrain piping over a black Michael Kors dress enlivened with one of her signature oversized brooches.

Keith Walker said:

> *'Thakoon selected two of our fabrics last year and we were thrilled when we were told they were using them for custom made items for Michelle Obama. Since then we have been waiting to hear that she has worn the garments and couldn't have hoped for more prominent occasions than the Inauguration and European Tour. We are delighted that such a prominent figure loves the garment designs of our customer "Thakoon" and ultimately loves Linton fabrics.'* [93]

Gemma Smith, Linton's Commercial Manager admitted, 'We were chuffed to bits when we finally saw Michelle looking stunning in our fabric.' [94] The fashion press described the outfit as elegant and '50s ladylike, with *Elle* magazine saying that it 'radiated hope, optimism and a bright future'.

Not just the First Lady wore Linton Tweed, as her mother, the chic Marian Robinson, sported a pink tweed suit at the Inauguration ceremony, and is now being dubbed the 'First Granny' as she settles into the White House to help take care of her grand-daughters.

And a new breed of designer has come to acknowledge Linton's qualities. In January

2009, Carlisle-born designer Stuart Stockdale, as well-known for making Pringle knitwear sexy as for being an assistant to Jean Paul Gaultier in Paris, was saying of his new job as Creative Director for Jaeger, 'Linton Tweeds in Carlisle has a great pedigree, supplying Jean Muir and Chanel. I intend to support northern and Scottish mills.' [95]

Linton's have always been associated with the young designers who will take fashion to new heights in the future. William Linton may have given Charles Creed his grounding in design in the early years of the company,

Michelle Obama wearing Linton Tweed, departing the White House en route to Europe, March 2009

but the Walker family too still supports young talent. They helped the Carlisle-born designer Stuart Vevers by sponsoring him in the early days of his career, when he was securing his job with Calvin Klein.[96] Vevers went on to design for top names such as Givenchy, before becoming the successful Creative Director at Mulberry in 2005, where he won the British Fashion Council's Accessory Designer of the Year award in 2006. In 2008 he became Creative Director at Loewe, the Spanish leather and luxury-goods company which is part of the LVMH group and is based in Madrid.[97]

But above all, it is their most prestigious customer whom they have to please. Karl Lagerfeld continued Coco's long association with Linton Tweed when he took over at Chanel in 1983 and has sustained it ever since. As Keith Walker says:

> 'We have a fantastic relationship with all our customers, but the Chanel connection, which goes back to the very start of our business at the beginning of the last century, is better than it has ever been... There has never been a Chanel collection that did not contain Linton Tweeds fabric, and Karl Lagerfeld, their chief designer, is the man we have to impress.' [98]

***

56

Weavers of dreams

When Karl Lagerfeld requests a tweed that looks like 'an old wall covered with lichens and mosses,' it is translated by Linton's top designer Rob Irvine into a cloth of burnt umber and clotted cream.[99] The design brief on these occasions has more to do with ideas, auras, feelings and creativity than specifics, but nonetheless the designer must be able to combine his inventive skills with his practical skills and knowledge of what his machines will produce, and with his perception of what will sell to buyers. His skills, then, range from the creative to the commercial. The skill is in experimenting with the cloth, colours, dyes and yarn, and in the finishing and surface treatments, to ensure that the end result is exquisite.[100]

Today's couturiers and designers are just as likely to request a cloth containing rubber, raffia or Lycra as they are to request natural fibres. These requests can be met, thanks to the great strides made in the technology of textile production. There are virtually no constraints on what can be achieved, and with international developments in textiles, the possibilities with new fabrics and techniques are limitless. The traditional role of the textile designer has thus come a long way in the last forty years.

One of the earliest attempts of the man-made fibre industry was to manufacture artificial silk to meet demand for this lovely cloth. This was due to the high cost of producing natural silk, which put it beyond the pocket of ordinary shoppers. It was soon realised that the development of artificial textile fibres could be more successful than trying to copy natural fibres, and by the 1920s, the first man-made fibre, rayon, was being produced. The industry developed apace and today there are almost no boundaries to what can be achieved. It makes for exciting and innovative textiles.

Innovative textiles are what the top designers crave, the constant need for new and different looks, and it is this that Rob Irvine has to capture in his work at Linton's for Chanel. Keith Walker sets the scene for Linton Tweeds most prestigious work:

> 'We get invited, myself and Rob Irvine to go to the shows, which of course, is a fantastic honour, because so few people are invited, and it is a good idea for Rob, the Design and Sales Director to see the show.' On meeting Karl Lagerfeld, Keith recalls the buzz and excitement of the day: 'I went behind the stage and met Karl Lagerfeld... it was like trying to speak to the President who had about four hundred other people trying to speak to him at the same time, just after the show when he is all excited.'

> 'Although it is very important for Linton Tweeds to have Chanel as our customer, I think it is important to them that there are people like Linton Tweeds supplying them, so it's a two-way street, not just one-way.' By its very essence, the Chanel look needs a constant supply of the components that keep it at the top. 'It's important to them because that's how they keep this mystery and this label, to keep it very high and they are the best at it. It's good to see that these things develop , because if they stay the same, if they stand still, if Chanel stands still they can't maintain their exceptional standing and Karl Lagerfeld has been absolutely brilliant, as well as in design terms, in bringing them forward and still retaining the integrity of Chanel.' [101]

Fabulous fabrics - the Linton Collections

Today, Karl Lagerfeld communicates his ideas to Linton's through his personal assistant Kim, who is the main link between the fashion house and the designers.

The design team is headed by the Design and Sales Director, Robert Irvine from Troon. Rob has been at Linton since 1979, after working in the mills at Galashiels. His designs remain as fresh as ever – no easy task in the demanding world of textiles. He comments: 'If you get a good result with people like Chanel, it keeps you enthused. If the suppliers come up with something new and exciting I get a buzz. We've even had our fabrics on the front of *Vogue* – that's pretty good.' [102]

Kim may bring a picture, examples of colour or a description to help her translate Karl Lagerfeld's ideas and thoughts to the Linton team. As a result of Kim's visit, the designer will produce anything up to a dozen new fabrics; each will be unique and be exclusive to Chanel. Out of these tweeds, Lagerfeld may choose two or three to be put into production, when Linton's will weave twenty-five to thirty-five metres of each and from these samples prototype garments will be made for the ready-to-wear show in Paris.

There is no computer-aided design here, everything is worked out on a paper ticket, before being tried and tested on the hand looms. As Rob remarks, 'we did think of getting computer-aided design... but people want something in their hands, they want something they can touch.' With the company's fabric archives dating back to the 1950s, clients may peruse them for that essential unique element, and Linton designers will work with them to develop a fresh modern fabric.[103]

The managers of the world-wide Chanel shops operate almost like an independent business or franchise and have complete autonomy over what they sell. They attend the Paris show to see the collection and decide on their choice of garments. This in turn affects the orders that Linton's receive. As Keith Walker says, 'If every Chanel shop in the world decides they like the one with Linton Tweeds then that's quite a big order for us, but if two or three do, we might get a couple of hundred metres. That's fine, that's how it works, composite orders.

'At the end of the day, our product has to be good, because first of all Mr Lagerfeld has to choose it, then he has to make the garment, and then the people who run the shops have to choose to buy it, before it's picked up and becomes an order, so yes, it has to be something that everybody likes.' [104]

This may seem a precarious system, but it is how Linton Tweeds have always received orders from Chanel. As Keith Walker says, 'I suppose it's a big plus that we are able to keep coming up with... the interpretation of their ideas of the things they want.' [105] And as Rob Irvine says, 'We are constantly searching for new yarns. We'll try to weave anything.' If the yarn makers have not moved ahead as quickly as Linton, they will spin their own yarn.[106]

With more than six hundred new fabrics being produced annually there is a frenetic production schedule, and this ability to interpret the clients' wishes and produce innovative weaves has given the company its world-renowned status. From Burberry to Max Mara to John Rocha, the interpretation of individual designers' needs is paramount. The *nouveau technique* fibres and weaves introduced by Leslie Walker in the 1960s are still being created and re-created today using confetti yarn, variegated chenille yarn and metallic threads to make up the lightweight bouclé tweed which is woven in a plaid design in the softest colours. The yarns used are key to the overall look of the tweed, and Linton's designers use a wide variety to create many different looks.[107]

The ability of the design team keeps Linton's ahead of the game. Twice a year Rob Irvine oversees the production of 150 designs for the two prestige fabric collections, the Linton and the Ullswater. These are beautiful collections of the finest quality, which provide unique fabrics in weights ranging from 250-450 gm/m². 'The Linton Collection' is aimed at the top of the range market and is made with an accumulation of wool, mohair and polyester blends with contrasting *nouveau technique* fibres. The boutique market requires a simpler style, and for this 'The Ullswater Collection' has been produced. This was developed as a diffusion range in 1995 and, while providing the same service and quality, it uses less fancy yarns. These are the collections that are shown twice each year at Première Vision, Paris, as well as at exhibitions in Japan, Milan, New York.

It is a far cry from the days when Des Matthews appointed M. Robert Burg, the first agent in

Lady Mayoress Elizabeth Wootton wearing Linton Tweed at the Lord Mayor's Show, London, November 2011

245

the late '50s as today, the collections are marketed internationally by a team of agents in Korea, Germany, Italy, the USA, the UK, Burg in France and Uchinuma in Japan. The collections are held by the agents and may be ordered from them in those countries.

The collections are also regularly shown by Mrs Margaret Duffy, the Fabric Showroom Manageress, at the craft and needlework exhibitions held each year in major cities such as Putney Sewing Rooms in London, Glasgow, Harrogate and Birmingham.

Carole Walker speaks highly of the contribution of their staff:

> *'The girls are wonderful, they pack that van, they drive it themselves, go all over the country, to London, Newcastle, Birmingham is always very good, they go to Putney at least twice a year and it's two sewing rooms there, absolutely laden with fabric and customers are so pleased to be able to buy it.'*

These services to customers are widely appreciated by crafters, fashion students and dressmakers alike and have largely replaced the times when, as Carole recalls:

> *'We've had busloads coming here... I took sewing parties round and they came from all over, and people who worked in fashion, students and people doing tailoring or similar at evening or day classes, would buy what they wanted and it was a very good scheme and a good PR job. Then people began to know that you would be at Birmingham every year and they would go to get their fabric when it was too far to come up here.'* [108]

Never resting on their laurels, Linton's have other new ventures: at Linton Direct it is possible to order accessories such as hats, scarves and bags, and there is a made-to-measure service, where customers can order a professionally-made tweed jacket, choosing their own fabric and have the pleasure of wearing Linton Tweed at a small fraction of the cost of its couture cousin. It is a venture that has long been Carole Walker's dream. As well as fashion, at Linton Lifestyle, there is a whole range of soft furnishings, cushions and throws which can be made in the customer's choice of fabric, and give the Linton look to the home.

Dreams don't just happen

Behind the scenes in any company like this, there has to be tight organisation and attention to the details of meeting customer's orders – it has to run like clock-work. As Mill Manager, Leslie's second son, Bruce, is responsible for this. In addition to his other duties as a Director of the company, Bruce has wider interests unconnected with the tweed mill, having studied for his degree in Botany at London University, and gaining a degree in Landscape Gardening from Edinburgh University.

His day job requires him to source all the many complex yarns that go to make the tweed, and ensuring that they come in on time. When a customer orders cloth, it may require five different yarns for each design: the yarn is ordered in white, as it is then dyed into perhaps ten colours, before it is ready to be warped on the loom and then woven into fabulous tweed. It will then go to the packing department ready to be dispatched in time to meet delivery dates of the customer. This is an ongoing process and requires well-honed organisational skills to meet the demands of Chanel and other top fashion houses.

Bruce combines his job of Mill Manager with running the company's market garden and garden centre, Westwood Nurseries, just outside Carlisle, and his attractive plants and shrubs are on sale in the patio garden shop of the mill. Westwood Nurseries are largely wholesale suppliers, who supply all the annual planting of 100,000 bedding plants to Carlisle City Council for the five hundred hanging baskets and for the numerous troughs and flower beds which make the city so attractive and of which Carlisle is so proud.

Part of the community

Linton Tweeds may be one of Carlisle's most prestigious companies, but are just as well-known in Cumbria for their involvement in sponsorship of local events and charities. From the 'Cumbria Women of the Year Awards' to 'Woolfest' (an event organised by 'The Wool Clip' cooperative to celebrate natural fibres), Linton's are involved. Of the Women of the Year Awards Carole says, 'We help, because it praises and honours people who work all their lives and most of the people like that don't even think about it, they just do it.' [109]

The input is both valuable and valued. One of 2008 Woolfest exhibitors, Naomi Harrison from Ireby, who won an award for her collection of modern clothing designs in vibrant reds and greens says: 'Some of the fabric has been woven locally by Linton Tweeds in Carlisle. I thoroughly enjoyed Woolfest as it gave me a great opportunity to showcase my work.' [110] And fashion students at Cumbria Institute of the Arts (now part of the University of Cumbria) are no strangers to Linton Tweed and often use the fabric in their designs shown at the Summer Exhibition.

Carole Walker has not only played her part in the development of the business, raising its profile in Cumbria, but for many years had her own separate career as a teacher. For thirty years she was involved in the care and welfare of physically handicapped children, working at the H.K. Campbell School in Carlisle, as well as spending time as a home tutor for children with severe social problems. Involved and passionate about this aspect of her life, she says, 'I absolutely loved it and when I stopped teaching, when they integrated children into ordinary schools, I took a lot of children here and gave them a talk, as weaving is one of the things they do at school, and often it is the children who show you how to cope with things. Physically handicapped children tend to have enormous courage. No matter what dreadful thing happens to them, they seem to come up smiling. They made me realise that my own problems weren't worth mentioning.' [111]

Asked if she has a favourite tweed, Carole says:

> 'No I don't because I adore so many of them; I can't say that I have a particular favourite. And I did go to Paris, and I went to the Chanel show, and I sat in the front row and I was wearing Linton Tweed at the time, I didn't meet either Chanel or Karl Lagerfeld, but it was very, very interesting. I think there were something like fifteen of ours in that one show. There's never been a show without Linton Tweeds, do you know that? I was there as a customer, the show was in Chanel's own place, all mirrors and they all came down the stairs, It is absolute magic... I had three young children at the time and it wasn't easy to get away...I've been to Paris, but I am not involved in that side of the business at all.' [112]

In fact, over the years, Carole has played no small part in the development of the company, always there to support Leslie and entertain clients, as well doing PR work and using her talents in the decoration of the visitors' centre and coffee shop.

She recalls many high spots over the years, seeing the Queen Mother, the Queen, Princess Diana, Margaret Thatcher and many other celebrities, including Victoria Beckham and Michelle Obama, all wearing Linton fabric. 'It was always lovely to see them and some of the fabrics being modelled in the fashion magazines by Escada and others.' [113]

Respect for Lagerfeld

Looking back over the decades, with the changes in tweedmaking and fashion, Leslie Walker is pleased to acknowledge that:

> 'We were always able to say that Chanel was in our fabric, and Chanel always stayed in fashion in our fabric... A Chanel suit was never really out of fashion.'

Coco herself was constantly bringing in the new, even though simple elegance remained the keynote.

> '*I'm not saying that she couldn't have developed in the same way as Lagerfeld, but what they produce now is vastly different from what she would ever have... but, she might have done, because she was the first to bring out pants, so she might just have done that... but he's kept the House of Chanel to the forefront... he realized that Chanel had left a legacy worth building on.*'

Of the more *avant-garde* fashions that appear on the Chanel catwalk today, Leslie understands that:

> '*They've got to have a talking point, even if they're not wearable, people still talk about it, then he's got something that is wearable. If he had kept to her [designs] strictly he would have gone out of business, I think. He had to do his own thing... and I think he's been very clever... he's designing in there but he's kept the spirit of Chanel. I think so. You see if Linton Tweeds had stayed the way it was, it wouldn't be here now, you've got to move on, ah yes.*' [114]

Weaving dreams for today and tomorrow

The dizzy world of fashion is perhaps the only one where the story of a small town tweedmaker could impact, not only on an international company, but on the global fashion scene. In 1912, William Linton could never have imagined the explosion of the fashion world into a multi-billion dollar industry, which would reach from the western world to the farthest flung reaches of the globe. It has been brought about by industrialization, by cultural development and, in no small measure, by marketing and advertising.

Survival is the name of the game in the fashion industry and at Chanel it is likely that secret discussions are afoot to plan for a successor to Karl Lagerfeld should he decide to retire. All fashion houses eventually have to consider their options on who leads them but it is not a subject they are willing to talk about - yet. In a statement to Reuters, the House of Chanel said, 'Karl Lagerfeld is the creative director of Chanel and enjoys a long-term contract which is absolutely not put into question. His succession is not on the agenda.' [115]

The survival of a brand can be down to having the right person at the helm, and Chanel has never looked back since Lagerfeld took on Mademoiselle's mantle in 1983 and spiced the collections with mystery and modernity. Now in his 70s and with a workload that would floor a much younger designer, he is as creative as ever. As the rumour mill turns, he insists, 'The world can count on me for a long time. Retirement is not one of the topics with which I deal. Why should I? I still have so many projects that I sometimes don't know where to begin. Chanel will still need some clothes when I am 89.' [116]

Kylie Minogue in Chanel Tweed at the Macy's Thanksgiving Parade, November 2010

When being interviewed on the BBC *Today* programme in 2009, Lagerfeld, on being asked if his products were expensive dreams to aspire to, responded:

> 'What is the real world? If you have no dreams, or if you don't try to improve real life of everybody, people would ask why they get up in the morning.

> 'You have to have drive. My drive is the work I do. People have different kinds of dreams... people need a handbag... if you can buy a beautiful one and if that's your dream to buy, why not?' [117]

When Coco Chanel died in 1971, it may have seemed inconceivable to her stylish followers that anyone could continue to keep her spirit alive into the 21st century, but Karl Lagerfeld has done just that.

At Linton Tweeds too, the company continues to meet the challenges of the modern global fashion world with its plans for the future.

A new dream of the future

Surprisingly, Keith Walker has a radical view of the future. Passionately describing his product, he says:

> 'Tweed is a rubbish description, people think hunting, shooting, fishing. But we're not that at all... We are the archetypal Chanel-style jacket... Tweed is an old-fashioned word. We are trying to shake tweed, we are pushing Linton, rather than Linton Tweed.'

His dream for the future includes Linton becoming a brand in its own right. As he told Sarah Newstead of *The Cumberland News,* his goal is to see *Fabric by Linton* labels nestling in the folds of couture garments. [118]

The UK fashion industry can never rest on its laurels, and the British Fashion Council is constantly looking to promote the industry. London Fashion Week showcases the pivotal role of cutting edge British design and attracts millions of visitors from around the world each year.

The Council's first major report on the industry, 'Value of the UK Fashion Industry' published in September 2010, highlights its importance to the UK economy. The direct value is worth £21 billion to the economy, with indirect and 'spillover' effects, such as tourism, bringing the value to £37 billion. Not a small figure.

The main factors behind this growth are the creation of desire and demand by the top end designer sector, with its influence on the high street retailers and supermarkets. Also the expansion of fashion brands into other product lines beyond clothing, such as perfume, accessories and homeware has seen an enormous leap forward.

By employing 816,000 people across a wide range of jobs, it is the largest employer of all the creative industries. But nothing stands still, and with some of the best designers, retailers and fashion colleges in the world, the report highlights the challenges ahead.

Harold Tillman CBE, Chairman of the British Fashion Council and Chairman of Aquascutum and Jaeger comments:

> 'Fashion is a great British success story and this landmark piece of research underlines its true scope and economic impact. This is just the first step, to creating a detailed national action plan for the industry which will help to support its future growth and success.

> 'I am committed to driving this forward and to ensuring that we come together as an industry to work with Government to discuss forthcoming challenges and agree the support required to overcome them.' [119]

It is this same spirit of looking to the future and facing new challenges which has driven Linton Tweeds since the Walker family took over almost fifty years ago. Today Keith Walker looks to diversify the family business and comments: 'I've overseen us diversify from textiles into one or two business areas. We don't want to find that one day we are out of fashion and we are gone.'

Those diversifications are impressive and include, a partnership in an £8million garden centre project, an internet enterprise for individual seamstresses and crafters wishing buy fabric for their own creations, a former pub offering lunches in addition to their own coffee shop and retail outlet, and a directorship with an international freight-forwarding business.[120]

The latest venture is one of the most exciting - the launch of the Linton Japan Collection at the British Embassy, Tokyo on 9 February 2012. The collection features Linton fabrics combined with knit and premium leathers and the garments are likely to find favour with the Japanese ladies.

No small feat: but perhaps today, a hundred years on from its small beginnings, in the minds of women who follow fashion, Linton will always mean tweed and Chanel.

Ask Leslie Walker what he sees as his greatest achievement at Linton Tweeds, over the years and he will say:

> *'Oh, I think going down to Buckingham Palace and getting the Queen's Award for Exports... there were three of us went down, me, and a foreman and someone from the shop floor. A recognition? – Oh, it was the company mainly.*
>
> *'And I think one of our successes is still being alive **today**... Yes there are so few left and it's because we've followed fashion and changed, changed what we make now for Chanel and everybody else, it's quite different from what we made in the Sixties. So we've changed our machinery and changed our attitude and life has changed and it's very difficult now, because of the economic situation and people can make stuff at a fraction of the price, and China or India – but, we're still here.'*
> [121]

So there it is: it's about survival, it's about the people working for the companies, it's about the product and it's about achievement. It's about ordinary people doing an extraordinary job, crafting a thing of beauty, creating the stuff of other people's dreams, and somewhere along the way, perhaps finding the fulfilment of their own dreams.

It is today, it is the future. It is Linton Tweeds, and it is Chanel. It's about weaving dreams.

***

A new logo for a new era - in 2012 Linton Tweeds celebrates its centenary

References
Acknowledgements
Photo Credits
Index

References

Part 1

1   R.L. Stevenson, *Edinburgh: Picturesque Notes,* Edinburgh, Robert Grant & Son Ltd, 1948, p.13.

2   C. Gulvin, *The Tweedmakers: A History of the Scottish Fancy Woollen Industry 1600-1914*, Newton Abbot, David & Charles, 1973, pp.70-71.

3   E. Charles-Roux (N. Amphoux, trans.), *Chanel*, London: The Harvill Press, 1995, pp.8-9.

4   P. Galante, *Mademoiselle Chanel,* Chicago: Henry Regnery Co., 1973, p.8.

5   E. Charles-Roux (N. Amphoux, trans.), *op.cit.*, p.8.

6   A. Madsen, Chanel*: A Woman of Her Own*, New York: Henry Holt & Co., 1990, p.7.

7   E. Charles-Roux (N. Amphoux, trans.), *op.cit*, p.34.

8   A. Madsen, *op.cit*, p8.

9   E. Charles-Roux (N. Amphoux, trans.), *op.cit*, p.37.

10 A.F. Young, *Old Selkirk*, Catrine, Ayrshire: Stenlake Publishing Ltd, 2005, pp.8-9.

11 J.B. Brown, *J.B. Selkirk: 1832-1904, Centenary Reflections,* Selkirk: Compiled by Wilma Derry, 2005, pp. 8-9.

12 *The Great Exhibition, A Facsimile of the Illustrated Catalogue of London's 1851 Crystal Palace Exposition,* New York: Gramercy Books, 1995, p.ii.

13 C. Gulvin, *op.cit*, p. 122.

14 J.B. Brown, *op.cit*, p. 11.

15 S. Roberts, 'The Textile Industry' in J.M. Gilbert (ed.), *Flower of the Forest*, Selkirk: The Commongood Fund, 1985, pp.112-119.

16 C. Gulvin, *op.cit*, p.102.

17 J.B. Brown, *op.cit*, p.110.

18 *Ibid*, p.112.

19 *Ibid*, p.117.

20 *Ibid*, p.116.

21 Leslie Walker, interview with author, 09.05.2007.

22 www.undiscoverdscotland.co.uk/hawick.

23 C. Gulvin, *op.cit*, p.72.

24 G Macdonald, *100 Years of Hawick Industry –The Hawick Tweed Trade*, paper for exhibition, Hawick, 2005.

25 *Ibid.*

26 'Marriage presentation to Mr William Linton, Designer,' *Hawick News*, 01.07.1898, p.3.

27 1901 Census, Hawick.

28 G. Macdonald, *op.cit.*

29 *Ibid.*

30 *Ibid.*

31 M. Haedrich, *Coco Chanel, Her Life, Her Secrets*, London: Robert Hale & Co., 1972, pp. 26-27.

32 *Ibid, p.28.*

33 E. Charles-Roux (N. Amphoux, trans.), *op.cit*, p.39.

34 G. Addecott, *Sacred Heart of Mary Girls' School, 75th Anniversary 1927-2002: An Account of its Progress and Achievements*, Upminster: 2002.

35 B. Barrière, *L'Abbaye Cistercienne d'Obazine en bas-Limousin, Les Origines – Le Patrimoine*, Tulle : Conseil Général de la Corrèze, n.d, p.22.

36 M. Haedrich, *op.cit*, p.25.

37 *Ibid*, p.30.

38 *Ibid*, pp.33-34.

39 E. Charles-Roux (N. Amphoux, trans.), *op.cit*, pp.45-46.

40 *Ibid*, p.48.

41 *Ibid*, p.47.

42 *Ibid*, p.56.

43 *Ibid*, p.50.

44 *Ibid*, p.63.

45 *Ibid*, p.65.

46 Wikipedia, Pauline Polaire.

47 E. Charles-Roux (N. Amphoux, trans.), *op.cit*, p.68.

48 J. Thurman, *Secrets of the Flesh, A Life of Colette,* London: Bloomsbury Publishing PLC., 2000, p.xii.

49 A. Madsen, *op. cit.*, p 26.

50 E. Charles-Roux (N. Amphoux, trans.), *op.cit*, p.71.

51 M. Haedrich, *op.cit*, p.57.

52 *Ibid*, p.58.

53 E. Charles-Roux (N. Amphoux, trans.), *op.cit*, p.76.

54   *Ibid*, p.77.

55   *Ibid*, p.79.

56   *Ibid*, p.84.

57   M. Haedrich, *op.cit*, p.61.

58   E. Charles-Roux (N. Amphoux, trans.), *op.cit*, p.91.

59   C. Baillén, *Chanel Solitaire*, London : Wm Collins & Sons, 1973, p.16.

60   M. Haedrich, *op.cit*, p.57.

61   www.genea-baf.org/BasesDonnees/geneologies/balsn.htm

62   A. Madsen, *op.cit*, p.28.

63   C. Vanderbilt, *The Glitter and the Gold*, New York: Harper & Bros., 1952, p.243.

64   E. Charles-Roux (N. Amphoux, trans.), *op.cit*, p.68.

65   L. Haney, *Naked at the Feast, A Biography of Josephine Baker,* London: Robson Books, 1995, p.95.

66   fr.wikipedia.org/wiki/Emilienne d'Alencon.

67   E. Charles-Roux (N. Amphoux, trans.), *op.cit*, p.101.

68   *Ibid*.

69   C. Baillén*, op.cit*, p.19.

70   D. de Marly, *Worth, Father of Haute Couture*, New York: Holmes & Meier, 1990, pp.31-32.

71   K. Murrey & M. Richards, *Decades of Beauty*, London: Hamlyn, 1998, pp.10-11.

72   *Ibid*, p.16.

73   M. Haedrich, *op.cit*, p.70.

74   E. Charles-Roux (N. Amphoux, trans.), *op.cit*, p.93.

75   *Ibid*, p.97.

76   *Ibid*, p.98.

77   General Register Office, Birth Certificate, Arthur Edward Capel, 7 Sept 1881.

78   Jardine Mathieson Archive, Cambridge University manuscripts /MS/JM/ .JM/PC34-39, 1860-1881 Prices current and market reports re: tea.

79   E. Charles-Roux (N. Amphoux, trans.), *op.cit*, p.108.

80   M. Haedrich, *op.cit*, p.73.

81   British Coastguards. 1841-1901, GENUKI.org.uk/big/Coastguards/index/html.

Provided to GENUKI by Stan Waight *et al.*

82   'Monsignor Capel's Effects. A Priest's Property to be sold at Sothern's Old Home,' *New York Times*, 24.02.1880.

83   C. Baillén, *op.cit*, p.139.

84   T. Carder, Encyclopaedia of Brighton, 1990. Royal Albion Hotel: Lion Mansion. www.mybrightonanndhove.org.uk/page_id_8716.aspx.

85   M. Haedrich, *op.cit*, p.73.

86   E. Charles-Roux (N. Amphoux, trans.), *op.cit*, p.111.

87   *Ibid*, p.115.

88   A. Mackrell, *Coco Chanel*, London: Batsford Ltd, 1992, p.19.

89   M. Haedrich, *op.cit*, p.75.

90   *Ibid*, p.78.

91   *Ibid*, p.74.

Part 2

1   W.S. Crockett, (Ed. W. Shaw-Sparrow), *In* 1906, p.61.

2   Sir F. Chance, *Centenary: Ferguson Brothers*, Carlisle: Charles Thurman & Sons, 1924, p.19.

3   D.J.W. Mawson, *Langthwaite Cotton Mill*. Offprint Transactions Cumberland & Westmorland Antiquarian Archaeological Society vol.xxxvi, 1976, pp.159-183.

4   D. R. Perriam, *Messrs Peter Dixon & Sons and their factory buildings*, (unpublished report for Carlisle City Council; copy in Cumbria Library: 1920 Dixon), (n.d.).

5   D.J.W. Mawson, *op.cit*.

6   D.R. Perriam, *op.cit*.

7   Sir F. Chance, *op.cit*, p.20.

8   W. Farish, *The Autobiography of William Farish, The Struggles of a Hand-Loom Weaver*, London: Caliban Books, 1996, p.11.

9   S. Towill, *Georgian and Victorian Carlisle, Life, Society and Industry*, Preston: Carnegie Publishing Ltd, 1996, pp.165-166.

10   Carlisle Journal of 12.07.1872, http://www.carlisleshistory.co.uk/page26.htm

11   N. Nicholson, 'Lore and More, A Touch of Festive Cheer for the Jobless Weavers,' *The Cumberland News*, 30.12.1993.

12   J. Morton, *Three Generations in a Family Textile Firm*, London: Routledge & Kegan

Paul, 1971, pp.182-185.

13 '170 Years of Printing: 1835-2005,' *Cumbrian Executive*, Spring 2006.

14 'New Local Company: Waddell's Ltd,' *Carlisle Journal*, 22.11.1912, p.4.

15 'Waddell's Ltd,' *Carlisle Journal*, 20.12.1912, p.4.

16 'The History Behind Otterburn Mill,' Euan J. Pringle, www.otterburnmill.co.uk/History.aspx.

17 D.J.W. Mawson, *op.cit.*

18 *Kelly's Directory of Cumberland*, 1910.

19 Linton Tweed Ltd, Company History.

20 Waddell's Ltd, Board of Directors' Meeting, 22.05.1914.

21 'Tweeds Are Not Stylish,' *The New York Times*, 9 November 1913.

22 http://en.wikipedia.org/wiki/Tariffs_in_United_States_history#Civil_War_protective_policy.2C_1861-1913 .

23 A.J.P. Taylor, *English History 1914-1945,* Oxford: Pelican Books, 1973, p.4.

24 *Ibid*, p.122.

25 A. Wilson, *An American President's Love Affair with the English Lake District*, Cumbria: Lakeland Press Agency, 1999, p.3.

26 Waddells Ltd, Board of Directors' Meeting, 04.06.1915.

27 'Obituary Notice: Mr Cranston Waddell, Warwick Bridge,' *Carlisle Journal*, 16.11.1917, p.5.

28 'The Late Mr C. Waddell, Funeral at Warwick Bridge,' *Carlisle Journal*, 20.11.1917, p.2.

29 E. Charles-Roux (N. Amphoux, trans.), *op.cit*, p.117.

30 S. Bowman, *A Fashion for Extravagance*, London: Bell & Hyman, 1985, p98.

31 E. Charles-Roux (N. Amphoux, trans.), *op.cit*, p.117.

32 *Ibid,* p119.

33 *Ibid*, p124.

34 *Ibid*, p125.

35 C.W. Beaumont, 'Enrico Cecchetti, a Memoir,' in A.L. Haskell, *Balletomania,* London: Gollancz, 1934, p.75.

36 G. O'Hara Callan, *Dictionary of Fashion and Fashion Designers*, London: Thames & Hudson, 1998, p.23.

37 *The New York Times*, 03.09.1911.

38 E. Charles-Roux (N. Amphoux, trans.), *op.cit*, p.128.

39 C. Baillén, *op.cit*, p.24.

40 M. Haedrich, *op.cit,* p.90.

41 *Ibid,* p92.

42 C. Beaton (1), *The Glass of Fashion*, London: Weidenfeld & Nicolson, 1954, p.162.

43 E. Charles-Roux (N. Amphoux, trans.), *op.cit*, p.133.

44 *Ibid,* p.139.

45 *Ibid.*

46 A.J.P. Taylor, *op.cit*, p.35.

47 *Ibid,* pp. 93-95.

48 G. Brook-Shepherd, *Uncle of Europe: The Social and Diplomatic Life of Edward VII,* London: Collins, 1975, p.269.

49 E. Charles-Roux (N. Amphoux, trans.), *op.cit*, p.151.

50 *Ibid,* p.152.

51 P. Galante, *op.cit*, pp.36-39.

52 E. Charles-Roux (N. Amphoux, trans.), *op.cit*, p.154.

53 *Ibid,* p.155.

54 F. Brachet, 'French Fashion During the First World War,' Champseur, Business History Conference, 2004.

55 E. Charles-Roux (N. Amphoux, trans.), *op.cit*, p.156.

56 M. Richards, *Chanel: Key Collections*, London: Hamlyn, 2000, p.14.

57 E. Charles-Roux (N. Amphoux, trans.), *op.cit*, p.154.

58 G. O'Hara Callan, *op.cit*, pp.178-179.

59 E. Charles-Roux (N. Amphoux, trans.), *op.cit*, p.159.

60 F. Delamere & B. Guineau, *Colour, Making and Using Dyes and Pigments*, London: Thames & Hudson, 2000, p.115.

61 National Archives WD339/55790 : Ref.12765/3(S.D.2.), letter from Arthur Capel to Brigadier-General, General Staff, Cavalry Corps, 03.03.1916.

62 A.J.P. Taylor, *op.cit*, p.115.

63 'Reflections on Victory,' *Times Literary Supplement*, 10.05.1917, p.227.

64 E. Charles-Roux (N. Amphoux, trans.), *op.cit*, p.166.

65 E. Holt, *The Tiger: The Life of Georges Clemenceau 1841-1929*, London: Hamish Hamilton Ltd, 1976, p.222.

66 E. Charles-Roux (N. Amphoux, trans.), *op.cit*, p.128.

67 J. W. Smith & T.S. Holden, *Where Ships are Born, Sunderland 1346-1946, A History of*

Shipbuilding on the River Wear, Sunderland: Thomas Reed & Co. Ltd, 1947, pp.55-56.

68   Robert Thompson & Sons, Yard Lists, Tyne & Wear Archives.

69   Website: crwflags.com, Prentout-Leblond, Leroux et Cie (Shipping Company, France); website: uboat.net, ships hit during WW1.

70   D. Simpson, *Barry Merchant Seamen – History and Tribute,* 2007, website:

www.barrymerchantseamen.org.uk.

71   C. Beaton (2), *The Unexpurgated Beaton, The Cecil Beaton Diaries,* London: Phoenix, 2003, p.196.

72   M Egremont, *Under Two Flags, The Life of Major-General Sir Edward Spears,* London: Phoenix Giant, 1998, p.75.

73   A.J.P. Taylor, *op.cit*, p.34.

74   M Egremont, *op.cit*, p.55.

75   Liddell Hart Centre for Military Archives, Kings College, London. File Ref. Spears to Lord Derby, Hankey and Kirke. Written as Head of British Military Mission – re: Spears, date 1917 Sept. 20 – Dec. 30. LSI60 Capel's view on shipping control, 01.11.1917.

76   M Egremont, *op.cit*, p.81.

77   *Ibid,* p.16.

78   Liddell Hart Centre for Military Archives, *op.cit*, Kings College, London. File Ref. M283. Letter from Arthur Capel to Hankey enclosed, 21.12.1917.

79   *Ibid,* Letter from Spears to Hankey concerning Clemenceau's decision to call up 270,000 men, 24.12.1917.

80   *Ibid,* Letter from Spears to Kirke on Clemenceau's attitude to Inter-Allied Council, 30.12.1917.

81   A.J.P. Taylor, *op.cit*, p.28.

82   J. Demornex, *Lucien Lelong*, London: Thames & Hudson, 2008, p.10.

83   E. Charles-Roux (N. Amphoux, trans.), *op.cit*, p.132.

84   M. Sert, *Two or three muses: the memoirs of Misia Sert*, London, Museum Press, 1953, p60.

85   *Ibid*, p.107.

86   *Ibid,* p.108.

87   A. Gold & R. Fizdale, *Misia, The Life of Misia Sert*, New York: Alfred A. Knopf, 1980, p.197.

88   *Ibid*, pp.197-198.

89   L. Field, *Bendor, The Golden Duke of Westminster*, London: Weidenfeld & Nicolson, 1983, pp.37-39.

90   *Ibid*, p. 132.

91   J Fane, *Memories of My Mother*, London: Hamish Hamilton & St. George's Press, 1987, p.40.

D. Taylor, 'Diana (nee Lister) Countess of Westmoreland 1893 - 1983 - another interesting member of the Ribblesdale Family,' http://www.gisburn.org.uk/gisburnvillage/ribblesdales2.htm

92   National Archives WO339/55790 REG. NO. 127665/3(S.D.2.) Letter from Army Council to British Military Representative, British Section, Supreme War Council, Versailles 12 May 1918.

93   E. Charles-Roux (N. Amphoux, trans.), *op.cit*, p.169.

94   *Ibid*, p.170.

95   D. Dutton (ed.), *Paris 1918: The War Diary of the 17th Earl of Derby*, Liverpool, Liverpool University Press, 2001, p. xiv (quoting J. McEwan (ed.), *The Riddell Diaries 1908-1923*, London, 1986, p.312.)

96   *Ibid*, p.xxvi.

97   *Ibid*, p.119.

98   M. Haedrich, *op. cit*, p.76.

99   D. Taylor, 'Laura Lister (Lady Lovat)1892-1965,'

http://www.gisburn.org.uk/gisburnvillage/ribblesdales2.htm

100   General Register Office, Edinburgh: Register of Marriages, 03.08.1918, Arthur Capel and Diana Wyndham.

101   D. Dutton (ed.), *op.cit*, p.134.

102   *Ibid,* p.143.

103   *Ibid*, p.161.

104   J Fane, *op.cit*, p.47.

105   D. Taylor, 'Laura Lister (Lady Lovat) 1892-1965,' *op.cit*.

106   E. Charles-Roux (N. Amphoux, trans.), *op.cit*, p.171.

107   M. Gilbert, *A History of the Twentieth Century, Volume One: 1900-1933*, London: Harper Collins, 1997, p.527.

108   *Ibid*, p.529.

109   *Ibid*, p.483.

110   A. Wilson, *op.cit*, p.57.

111   D. Bennett, *Margot, A Life of the Countess of Oxford and Asquith*, London: Arean Books, 1986, p.251.

112 'Sale of Property: Warwick Bridge Woollen Mill,' *Carlisle Journal*, 14.10.1919, p5.

113 'Linton Tweed File notes', Tullie House Museum and Art Gallery, 25.06.1985.

114 'Rise and Fall of Messrs. Dixon', *Cumberland News*, Denis Perriam, 19.07.1996.

115 'Dixon's Chimney to be a Monument', *Carlisle Journal*, 18.10.1963.

116 G. & P. Hitchon, *Sam Bough RSA: The Rivers in Bohemia*, Lewes: Book Guild, 1998, p.8.

117 'Dixon's Chimney to be a Monument', *op.cit*.

     Carleola: The Carlisle & County High School for Girls Magazine, No. 76, July, 1968.

118 E. Charles-Roux (N. Amphoux, trans.), *op.cit*, p.176.

119 L. Field, *op.cit*, p.181.

120 J. Fane, *op.cit*, p.48.

121 E. Charles-Roux (N. Amphoux, trans.), *op.cit*, p.178.

122 J. Fane, *op.cit*, p.54.

123 E. Charles-Roux (N. Amphoux, trans.), *op.cit*, pp.178-179.

124 J.J. Norwich (ed.) *The Duff Cooper Diaries, 1915-1951*, London: Phoenix, 2006, pp.113-114.

125 *Ibid*.

126 E. Charles-Roux (N. Amphoux, trans.), *op.cit*, p.180.

127 Death certificate of Arthur Edward Capel, General Register Office, Registered 04.06.1928.

128 *The New York Times*, 25.12.1919, p.6.

129 *The Times*, London, 29.12.1919.

130 'The Probate Registry: Last Will and Testament of Arthur Capel, January 13, 1919,' *The Times*, —.02.1920.

131 J.J. Norwich (ed.), *op.cit*, p.118.

132 J. Fane, *op.cit*, p.53.

133 Website www.thepeerage.com P7110.htm#i71095,

134 E. Charpentier, *Coco Chanel: Le drame de sa vie au bord d'une route varoise*, 03.06.2009, varmatin.com/puget-sur-argens.

135 P. Whiteside & J. Gee, 'Found Coco Chanel's Secret Memorial to the British Love of Her Life,' *Mail on Sunday*, 14.08.2005.

136 Ref. WO 339/55790, The National Archives, The War Office, London, Register No. 127665/7.

137 *Ibid*, Letter War Office to Edith Capel, ref. 127665/8(C.2.) 18.09.1925.

138 *Ibid*, Letter Edith Capel to War Office, ref. 127665. 20.02.1935.

139 *Ibid,* Letter War Office to Edith Capel, Ref. 127665/9(R. Records), 14.03.1935.

140 *Ibid*, The War Office file, Ref. LN/127665/10 29.11.1938.

141 F. Zefirelli, *Zefirelli: The Autobiography of Franco Zefirelli*, London: Weidenfeld & Nicolson, 1986, p.101.

142 E. Charles-Roux (N. Amphoux, trans.), *op.cit*, p.185.

143 P. Galante, *op.cit*, p.54.

144 V. Mendes & A. de la Haye, *20th Century Fashion*, London: Thames & Hudson, 1999, p.60.

145 F. Baudot, *A Century of Fashion*, London: Thames & Hudson, 1999, p.38.

146 E. Wilson & L. Taylor, *Through the Looking Glass: A History of Dress from 1860 to the Present Day*, London: BBC Books, 1989, p.67. P. White, *Poiret*, London: Studio Vista, 1973, p.64.

147 P. White, *op.cit,* pp.117-118.

148 F. Baudot, *op.cit*, p.50.

149 E. Carter, *Magic Names of Fashion*, London: Weidenfeld & Nicolson, 1980, p.37.

150 M. Etherington-Smith, *Patou*, London: Hutchinson, 1983, p.52.

151 K. Mulvey & M. Richards, *Decades of Beauty, The Changing Image of Women 1890s – 1990s*, London: Hamlyn, 1998, p.65.

152 L. Haney, *op.cit*, pp.51-52.

153 E. Carter, *op.cit*, p.71.

154 E. Maxwell, *I Married the World*, London: William Heinemann Ltd, 1955, p.145.

155 E. Carter, *op.cit*, p.71.

156 D. Blum, *A Pictorial History of the Talkies*, Feltham: Hamlyn, 1968, p.5.

157 G.L. Routledge, *Miracles and Munitions*, Cumbria: Arthuret Publishers, 2003, p.47.

158 K. Mulvey & M. Richards, *op.cit*, p.65.

159 *Ibid*.

160 K. Eve, '100-year-old Annabella's Loyalty to the city,' *Cumberland News,* 03.11.2006.

161 *Carlisle Journal*, 04.01.1921.

162 *Carlisle Journal*, 11.01.1921.

163 Linton's Cumberland Homespuns, Minutes of Directors' Meeting, Tullie House Art Gallery & Museum, 23.07.1921.

164 *Carlisle Journal*, 11.01.1921.

165 M.M. Chin, *Sewing Women Immigrants and the New York City Garment Industry*, New York: Columbia University Press, 2005, pp.7-10.

166 Lower East Side Tenement Museum Encyclopedia, Chapter 6: Garment Industry, New York, 2006. www.tenement.org/ency clopedia/garment.htm

167 E. Wilson & L. Taylor, *op.cit*, p.69.

168 Carlisle & County High School for Girls, Admissions Register, Vol. 2.

169 St Hilda's College, Oxford, Report and Chronicle, 2000-2001.

170 A. Wright, *A Foreign Country: The Life of L.P. Hartley*, London: Tauris Parke Paperbacks, 2001, p.26.

171 *Ibid*, p.19.

172 M. Liquorice, *The Hartleys of Fletton Tower*, March, Cambridge: Cambridgeshire Libraries Publications, 1996, p.19.

173 A.N. Hartley (1), *The Deerhound*, Peterborough, 1972, p71.

174 A.N. Hartley (2), *Random Rotherwood Recollections*, Peterborough, 2006, p.2.

175 A.N. Hartley (3), 'The Geltsdales - Obituary of Miss Agnes Linton,' *The Deerhound Club Newsletter*, Summer 1979, p.5.

176 G. O'Hara Callan, *op.cit*, p.81.

177 A. de la Haye (ed.), *The Cutting Edge, 50 Years of British Fashion 1947-1997*, London: V&A Publications, 1996, pp.13-14.

178 G. O'Hara Callan, *op.cit*, p.239.

179 N. Hartnell, *Silver and Gold,* London: Evans Bros Ltd, 1955, p.40.

180 H. Amies (1), *Still Here*, London: Weidenfeld & Nicolson, 1984, p.21.

181 ANSWERS.COM.Digby Morton.

182 A. Mackrell *op.cit*, p28.

Part 3

1 M.E, Jordan Haight, Paris *Portraits, Renoir to Chanel: Walks on the Right Bank*, Utah: Gibbs Smith Publisher, 1991, p.127.

2 E. Charles-Roux (N. Amphoux, trans.), *op.cit*, p.195.

3 *Ibid*, p.196.

4 M. Fonteyn, *The Magic of Dance*, London: BBC, 1980, p.127.

5 P. Morand (E Cameron, trans.), *The Allure of Chanel*, London: Pushkin Press, 2008, p.88.

6 S. Walsh, *Igor Stravinsky, A Creative Spring: Russia and France 1882-1934*, London: Pimlico, 2002, p.150.

7 *Ibid*, p.285.

8 T. & D. Strawinsky (S. Walsh, trans.), *Catherine and Igor Stravinsky, A family Chronicle, 1906-1940*, London: Schirmer Trade Books, 2004, p.25.

9 *Ibid*, p.66.

10 *Ibid.*

11 *Ibid*, p.149.

12 I. Stravinsky (A Knodel and I. Dahl, trans.) *the Poetics of Music in the Form of Six Lessons*, Cambridge, MS, Harvard University Press, 1947, p.77.

13 Marie, Grand Duchess of Russia, *A Princess in Exile*, London: Cassell & Co. Ltd, 1932, p.158.

14 J. Van Der Kiste, *The Romanovs 1818-1959, Alexander II of Russia and his family*, Stroud: Sutton Publishing Ltd, 1998.

15 Marie, Grand Duchess of Russia, *op.cit*, pp.69-70.

16 *Ibid*, p.71.

17 E. Charles-Roux (N. Amphoux, trans.), *op.cit*, p.204.

18 Marie, Grand Duchess of Russia, *op.cit*, p.187.

19 S. Bowman, *A Fashion for Extravagance, Art Deco fabrics and fashions*, London: Bell & Hyman, 1985, p.56.

20 Brunel, J. *F. Lesage: A Golden Embroiderer*, Ministry of Foreign Affairs/Label France/magazine, March 1996. www.france, diplomatique.fr/label_france/ENGLISH/ DOSSIER/MODE/les.html.

21 *Ibid*, p.57 and p.102.

22 Marie, Grand Duchess of Russia, *op.cit*, p.159.

23 *Ibid*, p.160.

24 *Ibid*, p.163.

25 Marie, Grand Duchess of Russia, *op.cit*, p.174.

26 *Ibid*, pp.172-173.

27 *Ibid*, p.110.

28 S.A. Irvine, *Perfume, the Creation and Allure of Classic Fragrances*, New York:

Crescent Books, 1995, p.1.

29 *Ibid*, p.108.

30 F. Kennet, *Coco, the Life and Loves of Gabrielle Chanel,* London: Victor Gollancz Ltd, 1989, p.47.

31 P. Galante, *op.cit*, p.76.

32 *Ibid*.

33 *Ibid*, p.77.

34 International Perfume Museum, Grasse.

35 J. Josephs, 'The Nose: Interview with Jacques Polge,' *Saga Magazine,* April, 1998.

36 A. Kerr, 'Channelling Chanel,' *The Scotsman*, 01.04.2006.

37 *Ibid*.

38 D. Teather, 'Channel 5 for Chanel No. 5,' *The Sunday Express*, 15.12.1996.

39 T.J. Mazzeo, *The Secret of Chanel No. 5: The Intimate History of the World's Most Famous Perfume,* New York: HarperCollins, 2010, p.95.

40 www.bymnews.com/classics/html/nadine.html.

41 www.forbes.com.

42 M. Haedrich, *op.cit,* p.134.

43 E. Charles-Roux (N. Amphoux, trans.), *op.cit*, p.215.

44 P. Galante, *op.cit*, p.135.

45 *Ibid*.

46 F. Kennett, *op.cit.*, p. 57.

47 *Ibid*, p.58.

48 M. Haedrich, *op.cit,* p.134.

49 P. Galante, *op.cit*, p.138.

50 R. Ingleby, *Christopher Wood. An English Painter*, London: Allison & Busby, 1995, p.86.

51 F. Steegmuller, *Cocteau. A Biography*, London: Constable & Co., 1986, p.82.

52 Jean Cocteau, en.wikipedia.org/wiki, Jean-Cocteau.

53 F. Steegmuller, *op.cit*, p.87.

54 E. Charles-Roux (N. Amphoux, trans.), *op.cit*, p.164, quoting Paul Morand.

55 R. Ingleby, *op.cit*, p.101.

56 P. Galante, *op.cit*, p.89.

57 F. Steegmuller, *op.cit*, p.297.

58 E. Charles-Roux (N. Amphoux, trans.), *op.cit*, p227.

59 *Ibid*, p.233.

60 *Ibid*, p.236, quoting Chanel's maxims in French edition of *Vogue*, 1947.

61 E. Maxwell, *op.cit*, p.147.

62 A. Mackrell, *op.cit*, p.33.

63 B. Ballard, *In My Fashion*, London: Secker & Warburg, 1960, p.60.

64 *Ibid*, p.61.

65 *Ibid*, p.62.

66 F. Kennett, *op.cit*, p.102.

67 P. Mauriès (B. Mellor, trans.), *Jewelry by Chanel*, London: Thames & Hudson, 2000, p.36

68 W. McBrien, *Cole Porter. The Definitive Biography*, New York: HarperCollins, 1999, p.158.

69 M. Haedrich, *op.cit,* p.184.

70 C. Baillen, *op.cit*, p.37.

71 H. Nicolson, *King George the Fifth: His Life and Reign*, London: Constable, 1950, p.310.

72 L. Field, *op.cit*, p.177.

73 wikipedia.org/wiki/Eaton_Hall,_Cheshire.

74 Loelia, Duchess of Westminster, *Grace and Favour*, London: Weidenfeld & Nicolson, 1961, p.145.

75 L. Field, *op.cit*, p.156.

76 *Ibid*, p.157.

77 *Ibid*, pp.183-184.

78 *Ibid*, p.185.

79 C. Baillen, *op.cit*, p.40.

80 L. Field, *op.cit*, p.184.

81 Loelia, Duchess of Westminster, *op.cit*, p.155.

82 *Ibid*, p.212.

83 L. Field, *op.cit*, p.197.

84 *Ibid*, p.205.

85 *Ibid*.

86 P. Galante, *op.cit*, p.117.

87 *Ibid*.

88 R. Cameron, *The Golden Riviera*, Honolulu: Editions Ltd, 1984, p.48.

89 *Ibid*.

90 Loelia, Duchess of Westminster, *op.cit*, p.157.

91 *Ibid*, p.159.

92 M. Etherington-Smith & J. Pilcher, *The 'It' Girls: Lucy, Lady Duff Gordon, the couturière 'Lucile' and Elinor Glyn, Romantic*

Novelist, New York: Harcourt Brace Jonavitch Publishers, 1986, p.73.

93   *Ibid*, p.153.

94   *Ibid*, p.163.

95   E. Carter, *op.cit*, p.71.

96   M. Etherington-Smith & J. Pilcher, *op.cit*, p.198.

97   *Ibid*, p.202.

98   F. Carter, *op.cit*, p.71.

99   Linton Tweeds, Queen's Award for Exports, framed certificate.

100   C. McDowell, *Forties Fashion and the New Look*, London: Bloomsbury, 1997, pp.10-11

101   *Ibid*, p.11.

102   P. Balmain (E. Lanchberry with G. Young, trans.), *Pierre Balmain, my years and seasons*, London: Cassell & Co. Ltd., 1964, p.34.

103   G. O'Hara Callan, *op.cit*, p.74.

104   C. Creed, *Maid to Measure, Jarrolds*, London: Quality Book Club edition, 1961, p.17.

105   G. O'Hara Callan, *op.cit*, p.74.

106   L. Watson, *Vogue: Twentieth Century Fashion. 100 Years of style by decade and designer*, London: Carlton Books Ltd, 1999, p.121.

107   C. Creed, *op.cit*, pp.62-63.

108   *Ibid*, pp.63-64.

109   *Ibid*, p.63.

110   *Ibid*, p.65.

111   'The Principles of Colour, Paper 4, November 1932,' The National Association of Scottish Woollen Manufacturers, 1956.

112   C. Creed, *op.cit*, pp.65-66.

113   *Ibid*, p.75.

114   P. White, *Elsa Schiaparelli, Empress of Paris Fashion*, London: Aurum Press, 1995, p.130.

115   *Ibid*, p.154.

116   A. Gold & R. Fizdale, *op.cit*, p.275.

117   A. Scott Berg, *Goldwyn, a Biography*, New York: Riverhead Books, 1998, p.160.

118   P. Galante, *op.cit*., pp.155-156. Quoting Goldwyn interview with Laura Mount, *Colliers*, April 1932.

119   A. Scott Berg, *op.cit*, p.214.

120   G. Swanson, *Swanson on Swanson*, London: Hamlyn Paperbacks, 1982, pp.414-415.

121   *Ibid*, p.417.

122   P. Galante, *op.cit*., p.164.

123   A. Mackrell, *op.cit*, p.95.

124   G. Howell, *In Vogue: Six Decades of Fashion*, London: Allen Lane, 1975, p.104.

125   Sir F. Chance, *op.cit*., p.18.

126   'Bought by the Duchess,' Ferguson Scrapbook 1929, Carlisle newspaper cutting, no date.

127   G. Howell, *op.cit*, p.128.

128   *Ibid*, p.104.

129   P. Galante, *op.cit*, p.164.

130   A. Mackrell, *op.cit*, p.47.

131   Ferguson Brothers Archive, Carlisle, letter 12.10.1932.

132   *Carlisle Journal*, 24.01.1933.

133   G. Howell, *op.cit*, p.136.

134   'Queen and a Local Firm,' *Carlisle Journal, Illustrated Supplement*, 22.02.1935.

135   M. Egremont, *op.cit*, p.126.

136   *Hansard*, Vol.279, cols 1836-1853, 30.06.1933.

137   *The Cumberland News*, 05.08.1933.

138   M. Egremont, *op.cit*, p.126.

139   *Ibid*, p.133.

140   E. Charles-Roux (N. Amphoux, trans.), *op.cit*, pp.275-276.

141   *Ibid*, p.291.

142   P. Galante, *op.cit*, p.140.

143   G. O'Hara Callan, *op.cit*, p.128.

144   E. Charles-Roux (N. Amphoux, trans.), *op.cit*, p.279.

145   P. Poiret (S. Haden Guest, trans.) *King of Fashion, the Autobiography of Paul Poiret*, London: V&A Publishing, 2009, p.48.

146   P. Galante, *op.cit*, p.34.

147   D. Chierichetti, *Edith Head, the Life and times of Hollywood's Celebrated Costume Designer*, New York: First Perennial edition, 2004, p.14.

148   E. Charles-Roux (D. Wheeler, trans.), *The World of Coco Chanel : Friends, Fashion, Fame*, London: Thames & Hudson, 2005, p269.

149   E. Charles-Roux (N. Amphoux, trans.), *op.cit*, p.284.

150   *Ibid*.

151   *Ibid*, p.285.

152   P. Galante, *op.cit*, p.140.

153 P. Mauriès (B. Mellor, trans.), *op.cit*, p.24.

154 S. King, *Princess Marina, Her Life and Times*, London: Cassell & Co. Ltd, 1969, p.139.

155 *Ibid*, p.120.

156 *Ibid*, p.94.

157 *Ibid*, p.140.

158 'Obituary of William Linton,' *Hawick News*, 14.01.1938.

159 A. Packard, *HRH The Duchess of Kent*, London: Pitkins, no year, p.14.

160 *Ibid*., p.22.

161 J. Wentworth Day, *HRH Princess Marina, Duchess of Kent: the First Authentic Life Story*, London: Robert Hale Ltd, 1962, p.107.

162 S. King, *op.cit*, p.151.

163 *Ibid*, p.153.

164 C. Beaton (3), *Cecil Beaton Diaries, 1963-74, The Parting Years*, London: Weidenfeld & Nicolson, 1978, pp.80-81.

165 J. Wentworth Day, *op.cit*, p.124.

166 C. Beaton (3), op.cit, p.81.

167 J. Flanner, *Paris was Yesterday, 1925-1939*, London: Virago Press, 2003, pp.134-135.

168 E. Charles-Roux (N. Amphoux, trans.), *op.cit*, p.292.

169 *Ibid*, p.293.

170 P. Galante, *op.cit*, p.140.

171 E. Charles-Roux (N. Amphoux, trans.), *op.cit*, p.296.

172 *Ibid*, p.300.

173 A. Madsen, *Chanel, A Woman of Her Own*, New York: Henry Holt & Co., 1991, p.216.

174 C. Mann, *Paris, Artistic Life in the Twenties and Thirties*, London: Laurence King publishing, 1996, p.196.

175 E. Charles-Roux (N. Amphoux, trans.), *op.cit*, p.300.

176 E. Schiaparelli, *Shocking life; The Autobiography of Elsa Schiaparelli*, London: V&A Publications, 2007, p.78.

177 H. Amies (2), *Just So Far*, London: Collins, 1954, p.63.

178 *Ibid*.

179 E. Longford, *The Queen Mother: A Biography*, London: Weidenfeld & Nicolson, 1981, p.67.

180 'Textile Exhibition,' *Carlisle Journal*, 07.05.1937.

181 C. Mann, *op.cit*, p.161.

182 E. Charles-Roux (N. Amphoux, trans.), *op.cit*., plate 78, p.302.

183 'County Enterprise: Local Firms' Exhibits at Paris Exhibition,' *Carlisle Journal*, 02.07.1937.

184 'Local Works Outing,' *Carlisle Journal*, 23.07.1937.

185 'Obituary: William Linton, Great Corby,' *Carlisle Journal*, 11.01.1938.

186 'The Late Mr William Linton, Former Hawick Designer,' *Hawick News*, 14.01.1938, p.6.

187 *Our Dogs Magazine*, 14.01.1938.

188 Deerhound Club Library Scrapbook, p.72.

189 Deerhound Club Library Scrapbook, p.73.

190 P. Mauriès (B. Mellor, trans.), *op.cit*, p.79.

191 D. Vreeland, *D.V.*, New York: Da Capo Press Inc., 1997, p.129.

192 M. Richards, *op.cit*, p.64.

Part 4

1 J. Flanner, *op.cit*, p.266.

2 A.J.P. Taylor, *op.cit*, p.526-528.

3 E. Charles-Roux (N. Amphoux, trans.), *op.cit*, p.305.

4 *Ibid*, p.306.

5 P. Galante, *op.cit*, p. 170.

6 A. Mackrell, *op.cit*, p.52. Quoting S. Menkes, 'Chanel, Lagerfeld's New Look,' *International Herald Tribune*, 26.07.1989.

7 E. Charles-Roux (N. Amphoux, trans.), *op.cit*, p.307.

8 *Ibid*, p.308.

9 E. Woolman Chase and I. Chase, *Always In Vogue*, London: Victor Gollancz Ltd, 1954, p.280.

10 *Ibid*, p.282.

11 E. Charles-Roux (N. Amphoux, trans.), *op.cit*, p.307.

12 P. Galante, *op.cit*, p. 178.

13 I. Ousby, *Occupation: The Ordeal of France 1940-1944*, London: Pimlico, 1999, p.43.

14 *Ibid*, p.67.

15 M. Curtis, *Verdict on Vichy: Power and Prejudice in the Vichy France Regime*. London: Phoenix Press, 2004, p.66.

16 *Ibid*.

17 I. Ousby, *op.cit*, p.69.

18 *Ibid*.

19 E. Charles-Roux (N. Amphoux, trans.), *op.cit*, p.312.

20   P. Galante, *op.cit*, p. 179.

21   The *Abwehr* was a German Intelligence Organisation between 1921 and 1944, when it was abolished and its activities taken over by the Reich Security Head Office under Major General of Police Walter Schellenberg. The *Abwehr* under Admiral Wilhelm Canaris was to a large extent anti-Nazi, and often in conflict with SS intelligence activities under Heydrich and Schellenberg. en.wikipedia.org/wiki/Abwehr.

22   D. Veillon, *Fashion Under the Occupation*, Oxford: Berg, 2002, p.101.

23   *Ibid.*

24   E. Schiaparelli, *op.cit,* p.104.

25   *Ibid,* p.106.

26   E. Woolman Chase and I. Chase, *op.cit,* p.286.

27   V. Mendes & A. de la Haye, *op.cit,* p.106.

28   E. Woolman Chase and I. Chase, *op.cit,* p.287.

29   F. Baudot, *op.cit,* p.108.

30   J. Demornex, *op.cit,* p.84.

31   www.encyclopedia.com Lucien Lelong information. Copyright 2002 Gale Group, a Thomson Corporation Company.

32   A. Beevor & A. Cooper, *Paris After The Liberation*, London: Penguin, 2004, p.250.

33   G. O'Hara Callan, *op.cit,* p.152.

34   V. Mendes & A. de la Haye, *op.cit,* p.106.

35   C. McDowell, op.cit, p.138.

36   *Ibid.*

37   www.encyclopedia.com Lucien Lelong, *op.cit.*

38   F. Baudot, *op.cit*, p.108.

39   I. Ousby, *op.cit*, p.134.

40   F. Baudot, *op.cit*, pp.109-110.

41   E. Woolman Chase and I. Chase, *op.cit*, p.273.

42   G. Spanier, *It Isn't All Mink*, London: Collins, 1959, p.84.

43   S. Lifar, *Ma Vie,* London: Hutchinson & Co. Ltd, 1970, p.192.

44   *Ibid,* pp.203-204.

45   E. Charles-Roux (N. Amphoux, trans.), *op.cit*, pp.324-325.

46   *Ibid,* p.325.

47   *Ibid,* p.326.

48   *Ibid.*

49   *Ibid,* p.327.

50   J. Bryan III & C.J.V. Murphy, *The Windsor Story*, London: Book Club Associates, 1980, pp.431-433.

51   P. Brendon & P. Whitehead, *The Windsors: A Dynasty Revealed*, London: Hodder & Stoughton, 1994, p.117.

52   *Ibid*, p.110.

53   E. Charles-Roux (N. Amphoux, trans.), *op.cit*, p.323.

54   J. Bryan III & C.J.V. Murphy, *op.cit*, p.394.

55   E. Charles-Roux (N. Amphoux, trans.), *op.cit.,* pp.334-335.

56   *Ibid*, p.337.

57   *Ibid*, p.339.

58   *Ibid*, p.343.

59   A. Madsen, *Chanel. A Woman of Her Own,* New York: Henry Holt and Company, 1990, p263. C. Higham, *Mrs. Simpson, Secret Lives of the Duchess of Windsor,* London: Pan Books, 2004. p416.

60   E. Charles-Roux (N. Amphoux, trans.), *op.cit*, p.345.

61   S. Lifar, *op.cit*, p.203.

62   P. Galante, *op.cit*, p.181.

63   'The Late Mr. Robert Linton   Over Forty Years in Edinburgh Town-Clerk's Office,' *The Scotsman*, 15.11.1939.

64   L. Walker interview with author, 09.05.2007.

65   D. Mathews interview with author, 08-08-2006.

66   Heriot-Watt University Archive, Edinburgh.

67   Acting Corporal G.S. Linton's Diploma and Presentation Programme, 03.07.1942.

68   42nd Air Base Wing: History: World War 11 Era. www.au.mil/42abw/42abw/ history_ world_ war_ two _era.asp.

69   *Carlisle Journal,* 30.06.1939.

70   I. Jackson, *Gardiner's Tweed Adventures: The Story of a Tweed Mill 1945-1988*, Melrose, 1998, p.19.

71   F. Beddows, telephone conversation with author, 14.02.2007.

72   'The Out Of Doors Page: Great Corby,' *Carlisle Journal*, 05.07.1963.

73   T. Nunn, *World War II Evacuees*, www.tnunn.ndo.co.uk/evacuees.htm.

74   S. Goodman, *Children Of War*, London: John Murray, 2005, p.88.

75   *Cumberland News*, 16.02.1996.

76   'In Search of Sanctuary,' Carlisle Journal, 05.09.1939.

77   A.N. Hartley (1), *op.cit*, p.46.

78   *The Scotsman*, 15.11.1939, *op.cit*.

79   *Our Dogs Magazine*, 06.09.1940.

80   *Ibid*.

81   'Doing Fine, Newcastle's Lord Mayor Among Child Evacuees,' *Carlisle Journal,* 29.09.1939.

82   *Ibid*.

83   'Lest We Forget War Evacuees,' The *Sunday Sun*, 11.06.2006.

84   *Our Dogs Magazine*, 30.08.1940.

85   Our Dogs Magazine, 21.11.1941.

86   'How Cumberland did its bit for the war effort,' *Cumberland News,* 16.02.1996.

87   *Ibid*.

88   N. Nicholson, 'Lore and More: County's Dad's Army rallied to the call,' *Cumberland News*, 09.12.1994.

89   *Cumberland* News, 16.02.1996, *op.cit*.

90   D. Perriam, 'Past and Present in Cumbria: How Carlisle bought a Spitfire for £5000 to help beat Hitler,' *Cumberland News*, 01.08.1997.

91   E. Wilson & L. Taylor, *op.cit*, p.90.

92   G. O'Hara Callan, *op.cit*, p.172.

93   C. McDowell, *op.cit*, p.147.

94   A. de la Haye (ed.), *op.cit.*, p.15.

95   M. Constantino, *Fashion Marketing and* PR, London: Batsford, 1998, p.12 for full information on La Chambre Syndicale de la Couture Parisienne'

96   H.W. Yoxall, *A Fashion Of Life*, London: Heinemann, 1966, p.71.

97   *Ibid,* p.70.

98   C. McDowell. op.cit, p.8.

It was not until 2000 that it became known that Sir Hardy had organised assassinations of senior Nazis, when coordinating 'Operation Ratweek', in January 1944, SOE's campaign in Western Europe on the eve of D-Day, *vide* 'Obituary,' J. Mulvagh, *The Independent*, 06.03.2003.

99   I. Jackson, *op.cit*, p.20.

100   *Ibid*, p.21.

101   *Utility Furniture And Fashion 1941-1951*, Exhibition Catalogue CC41, London: The Geffrye Museum Trust, 1995. p.2.

102   *Ibid*, p.33.

103   *Make Do And Mend*, London: Board of Trade, 1943. Reprinted London: Imperial War Museum, 1997, p.31.

104   *Ibid*.

105   *Utility Furniture And Fashion 1941-1951, op.cit*, p.33.

106   D. Kearns Goodwin, *No Ordinary Time, Franklin And Eleanor Roosevelt: The Home Front In World War II*. New York: Simon & Schuster Paperbacks, 1994. p.358.

107   P. Cook, *I Know Where I'm Going*, London: BFI Film Classics, 2002.

108   *Ibid*, p.8.

109   *Dog World*, 21.12.1943 and 07.12.1945.

110   M. Churchill, *Deerhound Club Newsletter*. Summer 2005.

111   S. Lifar, *op.cit*, p.278.

112   A. Beevor & A. Cooper, *op.cit*, p.49.

113   S. Lifar, *op.cit,* p.279.

114   M. Haedrich, *op. cit,* p.148.

115   *Ibid*.

116   F. Baudot, *op.cit*.

117   S. Garfinkel. *Thèâtre de la Mode, Fashion Dolls: The Survival of Haute Couture,* 2nd Edition, Oregon: Palmer/Pletch Inc., 2002, p.47.

118   *Ibid*, p.48.

By the 1950s, with the French fashion industry once again riding high, the Thèâtre de la Mode was abandoned and presumed destroyed. The dolls and sets had in fact been stored in the City of Paris department store (now Neiman Marcus) in San Francisco by Paul Verdier, President of the store, who, with the agreement of the Chambre Syndicale sent them to Maryhill Museum at his own expense in 1952. They were rediscovered in 1983 and sent to Paris where they were restored or recreated and exhibited in the Musée des Arts Decoratif in 1990. They now have a permanent home in the Maryhill Museum of Art, in Goldendale, Washington, USA.

119   *The Dog World Annual,* 1945.

120   H. Amies (1), *op.cit*, p.48.

121   *Ibid*, p.49.

122   *Ibid,* p.50.

123   *Working Life in Britain 1900 to 1950*, London: Futura, 2007, p.170.

124   E. Wilson & L. Taylor, *op.cit*, p.155.

125   M-F. Pochna (1), *Christian Dior; The Man Who Made the World Look New,* New York: Arcade Publishing Inc., 1996, p.13.

126   M-F. Pochna (2), *Fashion Memoir Dior,* London: Thames and Hudson Ltd, 1996, p.6.

127   P. Rowlands, *A Dash of Daring: Carmel Snow and Her Life in Fashion, Art, and Letters*, New York: Atria Books, 2005, p.44.

128   C. Dior (A. Fraser, trans.), *Christian Dior and I*, New York: E.P. Dutton & Co. Inc., 1957, p.31.

129   P. Rowlands, *op.cit*, p.362.

130   M-F. Pochna (1), *op.cit*, p.128.

131   P. Rowlands, *op.cit*, p.365.

132   En.wikipedia.org/wiki/Folke_Bernadotte.

133   E. Charles-Roux (N. Amphoux, trans.), *op.cit*, p.357.

134   L. Hagan (ed.), *Walter Schellenberg, The Memoirs of Hitler's Spymaster*, London: André Deutsch, 2006, p.15.

135   *Ibid*, p.17.

136   E. Charles-Roux (N. Amphoux, trans.), *op.cit*, p.360.

137   A. Cave Brown, *"C", The Secret Life of Sir Stewart Graham Menzies, Spymaster to Winston Churchill*. New York: Macmillan Publishing Co., 1987, p.566, from National Archives, Modern Military Records Branch, captured enemy documents section. Washington. DC: interrogation of Walter Friedrich Schellenberg, in record group 165 (records of War Department general and special staffs) undated but c.1945, p.65.

138   *Ibid*.

139   *British History Online,* www.british-history.ac.uk/

140   P. Galante, *op.cit*, p. 179.

141   *Ibid*, p. 189.

142   A. Gold & R. Fizdale, *op.cit,* p.302.

Part 5

1   P. Galante, *op.cit*, pp.200-201.

2   *Ibid*, p.200.

3   *Ibid*, p.206.

4   M. Haedrich, *op.cit*, p.179. The words 'top wholesale manufacturer' and 'As ever' were in English in the original letter.

5   P. Rowlands, *op.cit*, p.86.

6   P. Galante, *op.cit*, pp.206-207.

7   *Ibid*, p.207.

8   *Ibid*.

9   B. Ballard, *op.cit*, p.64.

10   *American Vogue*, 15.02.1954, quoted in A. de la Haye & S. Tobin, *Chanel the Couturiere at Work,* London: V&A Publications, 1994, p.90.

11   G. Howell, *op.cit*, p.205.

12   P. Galante, *op.cit*, p.200.

13   *Ibid*, p.202.

14   *Ibid*.

15   *Norman Hartnell – 1901-1979,* Exhibition Catalogue, Brighton: Royal Pavilion Art Gallery and Museum, 1985, p.36.

16   H.W. Yoxall, *op.cit,* p.73.

17   A. Linton, *Notes on Linton Tweeds – 1950s,* Carlisle: Tullie House Art Gallery and Museum.

18   G. Howell, *op.cit*, p.205.

19   A. Linton, *op.cit*.

20   M. Richards, *op.cit*, p.79.

21   B. Ballard, *op.cit*, p.64

22   E. Charles-Roux (N. Amphoux, trans.), *op.cit*, p.365.

23   *Ibid*, p.366.

24   A. de la Haye & S. Tobin, *op.cit*, p.90.

25   P. Galante, *op.cit*, p.210.

26   E. Charles-Roux (N. Amphoux, trans.), *op.cit*, p.366.

27   A. de la Haye & S. Tobin, *op.cit*, p.90.

28   P. Galante, *op.cit*, pp.210-211.

29   B. Ballard, *op.cit*, p.65.

30   A. Mackrell, *op.cit*, p.72. Quoting I. Ashley, 'Coco,' *Paris Fashion, the Great Designers and their Collections*, R. Lynam, ed., London: Michael Joseph, 1972, p.127.

31   *Ibid,* quoting R. Tredre, 'Discrimination and the Elusive Taste of Coco,' *The Independent,* 09.10.1990, p.19.

32   M. Haedrich, *op.cit*, p.178.

33   D. Vreeland, *op.cit,* p.127.

34   *Ibid,* p.128.

35   P. Galante, *op.cit*, p.213.

36   C. B. Shaeffer, *Couture Sewing Techniques*, Newtown, Connecticut: The Taunton Press, 2000, p.182.

37   J. P. O'Neill, Editor-in Chief, *Coco*, New York: The Metropolitan Museum of Art, 2005, p.135.

38   The financial dealings regarding *Les Parfums Chanel* company are described in M. Haedrich, *op.cit*, pp.156 -161 and in P. Galante, *op.cit*, pp.146-153 and 190 -193, 205, 216, 217 and at length in T.J. Mazzeo, *The Secret of Chanel No.5,* New York: Harper Collins, 2010.

39   T.J. Mazzeo, *op.cit*, p.183.

40   D. Mathews, interview with author, 06.02.2007.

41   D. Mathews, interview with author, 08.08.2006.

42   A. Hustak, *The Gazette*, 30.06.2007, © CAN-WEST INTERACTIVE, www.canada.com . Also www.johnwardendesigner.com

43   www.thecanadianencyclopedia.com

44   www.prototypevintage.com

45   B. Ballard, *op.cit,* p.278.

46   H.W. Yoxall, *op.cit,* p.74.

47   *Ibid.*

48   Linton Tweeds reference file, Tullie House Art Gallery and Museum (Carlisle).

49   D. Mathews, interview with author, 08.08.2006.

50   B. Marshall, *The White Rabbit*, London: Cassell, 2000, p.9.

51   'Why the White Rabbit Deserves a Blue Plaque,' *Daily Mail*, 01.04.2010.

52   M. Haedrich, *op.cit*, p.192.

53   C. Dior (A. Fraser, trans.), *op.cit*, p.65.

54   *Ibid,* p.64.

55   M. Haedrich, *op.cit*, p.193.

56   S. Marcus, *Minding the Store,* New York: Signet Books, 1975, p.211.

57   *Ibid,* p.210.

58   E. Carter, *op.cit,* p.65.

59   D. Mathews, interview with author, 08.08.2006.

60   L. Walker, interview with author, 20.10.1998.

61   Memories of working at Linton Tweeds, Nov. 1960 – Jan 1973. Letter to author by Robert Thomlinson.

62   J. McGlone, 'The Fabric of Time,' *The Scotsman Magazine*, 23.10.2004.

63   L. Walker, interview with author, 20.10.1998.

64   *Ibid.*

65   *Ibid*.

66   D. Mathews, interview with author, 08.08.2006.

67   P. Galante, *op.cit,* p.248.

68   D. Mathews, interview with author, 08.08.2006.

69   E. Wilson & L. Taylor, *op.cit*, p.180.

70   N. White & I. Griffiths, *The Fashion Business, Theory, Practice, Image*, Oxford: Berg, 2000, p.107.

71   E. Wilson & L. Taylor, *op.cit*, p.180.

72   M. Constantino, *op.cit*, pp.35-36.

Three main categories of synthetic fibres have enabled far-reaching developments in the textile and clothing industries to take place.

1. Cellulose, derived from wood-pulp and some protein materials obtained from maize, peanuts and soya beans, are formed into filaments by chemical process. These are known as regenerated fibres and the end result is viscose, acetate and tri-acetate used for permanently pleated fabrics.

2. The synthetic's are made from coal and petroleum, and include polyester, nylon, acrylics for knitwear, elastenes for Lycra-stretch fabrics, polypropylene for sports knitwear and thermal clothing and modacrylics used for faux-fur fabric.

3. There are other miscellaneous types, which include substances like metal and glass. Gold and silver thread had long been used in fine embroidery, but modern metallic filaments, such as Lurex, which is based on coloured aluminium foil, is budget priced sparkle.

73   *Ibid,* p.40.

74   'Paris Fashion House Tweeds for Carlisle,' *Carlisle Journal*, 11.10.1963.

75   A.N. Hartley (3), *op.cit*, p.5.

76   *Ibid*, p.6.

77   L. Nelson, interview with author, 08.10.2006.

78   P. Galante, *op.cit*, p.234.

79   B. Holme, K. Tweed, J. Daves, & A. Liberman, eds., *The World in Vogue* , London: Secker & Warburg, 1963, p.301.

80   P. Katz – as told on QVC TV Show 10.03.2006.

81   E. Charles-Roux (N. Amphoux, trans.), *op.cit*, p.372.

82   I. Barmash, E. Gold, M. Klapper, S. Parker,

S. Rutberg, M. Sheinman, & S. Siegelman, 'Fashion Retailing in a Bygone Era,' *Women's Wear Daily*, Washington DC: Beard Books, 2005, pp,13-14.

83   J. Fairchild, *The Fashionable Savages*, New York: Doubleday & Co., 1965, p.36.

84   *Ibid,* p.176.

85   E. Carter, *op.cit*, p.62.

86   M. Haedrich, *op.cit*, p.187.

87   *Ibid*, p.189.

88   G. Waddell, *How Fashion Works*, Oxford: Blackwell Science Ltd., 2004, p.174.

89   M. Haedrich, *op.cit*, p.208.

90   C. Beaton (4), *Beaton in the Sixties - More Unexpurgated Diaries,* London: Phoenix, 2004, p.391.

91   P. Galante, *op.cit*, p.271.

92   Cecil Beaton (4), *op.cit*, p.389.

93   *Ibid,* p.470.

94   *Ibid,* p.417.

95   P. Galante, *op.cit*, p.273.

96   L. Watson, *op.cit*, p.112.

97   C.Baillén, *op.cit*, pp.155-157, and also, M Haedrich, op.cit, p209.

98   L. Walker, interview with author, 09.05.2007.

99   L. Walker, interview with author, 13.11.2007.

100   *Ibid.*

101   I. Jackson, *op.cit,* p.147.

102   *Carleola, op.cit.* Robert Todd & Sons were to own the mill until they ceased trading in 1975.

103   L. Walker, interview with author, 09.05.2007.

104   L. Walker, interview with author, 19.06.2007.

105   *Ibid.*

106   L. Walker, interview with author, 20.10.1998.

107   L. Walker, interview with author, 19.07.2007.

108   *Ibid.*

109   L. Walker, interview with author, 19.06.2007.

Since the end of the war there had been developments in textile manufacturing machinery, but the new machinery was only available from European and American manufactures, as many of the great British manufacturers had not survived the war. The world-wide renowned German company Dornier, had been one of the great aircraft manufacturers before the war, but as aircraft manufacture was forbidden by the Allied forces after the war, the company looked for new activities and began to make textile machinery. The Lindauer DORNIER GmbH company was founded in 1950 and began making shuttle weaving machines, and by 1967 had achieved an international reputation with the introduction of the rapier weaving machine and textile finishing machines. They now have subsidiary companies in the USA, China and India. www.dornier.com.

110   *Ibid.*

The company has always dressed the rich and famous, from royalty and film stars to politicians such as Sir Winston Churchill and Baroness Thatcher. In recent years the company has won numerous awards, including GQ style awards, and continues to promote its sought-after brand image as well as its international luxury appeal.

History of Aquascutum, www.wikipedia.org/wiki/aquascutum.

111   L. Walker, interview with author, 19.07.2007.

112   L. Walker, interview with author, 19.06.2007.

113   M. Haedrich, *op.cit,* p.209.

114   F. Aveline (S. Petch, trans.), *Chanel Perfume*, New York: Assouline, 2003, p.13.

115   P. Galante, *op.cit,* pp.275-276.

116   F. Aveline (S. Petch, trans.), *op.cit,* p.75.

117   C. Baillén, *op.cit,* p.190.

118   P Galante, *op.cit,* p.279.

119   M. Haedrich, *op.cit,* p.268.

120   Pierre Galante, *op.cit,* p.280.

121   *Ibid.*

122   *Ibid.* p.281.

Part 6

1   *New York The Times*, 08.02.1971, quoted in A. Madsen, *op.cit*, p.332.

2   G. Emerson, 'Saint Laurent Does Chanel - But Better,' *New York Times,* 01.08.1967, p.26, quoted in A. Rawsthorn, *Yves Saint Laurent*, London: HarperCollins, 1997, p.94, Jacques Chazot TV programme, *Dim, Dam, Dom,* Interview with Coco Chanel, 11.02.68.

3   M-F. Pochna (1), *op.cit*, p.237.

4   *New York Times,* 04.10.93.

5   A. de la Haye & S. Tobin, *op.cit*, p.113.

6   E. Carter, *op.cit,* pp.65-66.

7   G. Waddell, *op.cit*, p.xii.

8   U. Okonkwo, *Luxury Fashion Branding, Trends, Tactics, Techniques,* Basingstoke: Palgrave MacMillan, 2007. For the history of luxury fashion branding, see Chapter 2, 'What's in a name?'

9   F. Aveline (S. Petch, trans.), *op.cit,* p.13.

10   *Ibid*, p.75.

11   E. Carter, *op.cit,* p.66.

12   L. E. Miller, *Balenciaga*, London: V&A Publications, 2007, p.68.

13   T. Belford & S. Jessett, interview with author, 14.03.2007.

14   D. Guide (1), 'So Long Mick, Swinging Tribute to City's Jazz King,' *Cumberland News*, 30.04.1993.

15   R. Groom, 'Workers beg for paycut in bid to save plant,' *Cumberland News*, 23.05.1975.

16   *Ibid.*

17   'City Crisis Mill,' *Cumberland News*, 30.05.1975, p.32.

18   'City Mill Workers set up Campaign,' *Cumberland News*, 06.06.1975.

19   D. Guide (2), 'Government "no" to Todd Co-op blames Bosses, "Untrue" says Chairman,' *Cumberland News,* 11.07.1975.

20   *Ibid.*

21   'City Yarn Mill stays Silent,' *Cumberland News*, 01.08.1975, p.11.

22   'Textile Giant turns down City Mill plea,' *Cumberland News*, 15.08.1975.

23   V. Addison, 'Mick Potts Tribute Night,' —.02.2007.
     D. Guide (1), *op.cit.*

     T. Belford & S. Jessett, *op.cit.*

Mick Potts had suffered three heart attacks in the previous years, and had still kept up his hectic lifestyle. His funeral was held at St Bede's Roman Catholic Church, on Wigton Road, Carlisle, as hundreds of mourners arrived to pay their respects to Carlisle's own jazz legend. Among them were business associates from Italy. Famous faces were seen among the mourners, George Melly and Stan Stennet were there, while George Chisholm was too ill to attend. Outside the church there were unprecedented scenes, as jazzmen from both sides of the Border jammed New Orleans style and played Mick's favourite tunes, among them, Tishomingo Blues, Black and Blue, the Old Rugged Cross and Just a Closer Walk with Thee. Mick's own Gateway Jazz Band played, as did Les Bull's Festival Jazz Band from Kendal, and John Cowen who used to lead the Riverside Band in Dumfries, but now had his own professional outfit. Mick's brother Al was there playing clarinet.

At the requiem mass, Mick's sons read from Dylan Thomas, and Father John Watson, speaking of Mick's charismatic life said: 'It was a life lived to the full and one which people remember with gratitude and affection. No small achievement for a human being. There is a jazz band to see him off, and who knows, there might be a jazz band to welcome him into another shore. It would be entirely appropriate if there was.'

The next day *The Cumberland News* reported the scenes on its front page. Mick Potts may have left the people of Carlisle, but he is still remembered today wherever jazzmen meet, to talk over the good old days and to swap stories about gigs. Carlisle Jazz Club still hold Tribute Concerts and Dixon's Chimney still stands as a permanent memorial to this truly gifted man.

Today, former members of the Gateway Jazz Band, including Stewart Jessett, double bass player, and Tim Belford, pianist, together with some of Mick's old friends, Leslie Walker included, play outdoor bowls. The two teams, The Suttle Strikers and the Corby Hill Killers compete for the Mick Potts Memorial trophy.

24   N. Coleridge, *The Fashion Conspiracy*, London: Heinemann, London, 1989, p.82.

25   www.metmuseum.org/toah/hd/jafa/hd_jafa.htm

26   www.jetro.org/trends/fashion_history_japan.php

27   'A Yen for Tweed,' *Cumberland News*, 01.05.1981.

28   Death notice for Nessy Linton, *Cumberland News*, 01.06.1979.

29   A.N. Hartley (3), *op.cit.*

30   A. Wright, *op.cit*, p.274.

31   L. Walker, interview with author, 19.06.2007.

32   'Tweed Chief Dies,' *Cumberland News*, 19.06.2007.

33   J. McGlone, *op.cit.*

Part 7

1   en.wikipedia.org/wiki/Karl_Lagerfeld.

2   *Ibid.*

3   J. Colapinto, 'Where Karl Lagerfeld lives,' *The New Yorker*, 19.03.2007.

4   G. O'Hara Callan, *op.cit*, p.98 and p.145.

5   *Ibid*, p.150.

6   D. Bott, *op.cit*, p.44.

7   *Chanel*. A film by Eila Hershon and Roberta Guerra, Phaidon, VHS, ©RMS Arts 1986.

8   M. Richards, *op.cit*, p.122.

9   *Ibid*.

10   L. Walker, interview with author, 19.06.2007.

11   'The Principles of Colour, Paper 4, November 1932,' *op.cit.*

12   L. Armstrong, 'Karl's back to give Chanel a sporting new chance,' *The Times*, 17.10.1998, p.7.

13   M. Campbell, 'Weaving Success,' *Cumbria Life,* No. 57, March/April 1998.

14   C. Walker, interview with author, 06.07.2009.

15   S. Stemp, *Jean Muir: Beyond Fashion*, Suffolk: Antique Collectors Club Ltd, 2007, p.74.

16   *Ibid.*

17   *Ibid,* p.142.

18   E. Wilson & L. Taylor, *op.cit*, p.212, quoting S. Menkes, 'Yes but is it an art or a craft.' *The Times*, 05.07.1984, p.8.

19   T. Walker, 'Dressed to Thrill,' *News & Star,* —.04.1993.

20   S. Stemp, *op.cit*, p.110.

21   *Ibid*, p.120.

22   *Ibid,* p.102.

23   L. Walker, interview with author 13-11-2007.

In her lifetime Jean Muir received the highest accolades and played an important role in the development of British design. In 1995 she was the first British designer to be the subject of a television documentary, when Channel 4 produced the three-part series, 'Very Jean Muir'. Sadly, Jean Muir died on 28 May 1995 at the age of sixty-six. Her husband kept on the company Jean Muir Ltd., for a number of years before closing it in 2007.

She had been fundraising for the Museum of Scotland Project in Edinburgh shortly before her death and the Jean Muir Archive has been donated to the Museum by her husband. The Museum plans to hold exhibitions of her work in the future.

24   M. Campbell, 'Weaving Success,' East Cumbrian Gazette, p.16, 04.06.1998.

25   C. Darwent, 'UK: Money-Spinning in Carlisle – Linton Tweeds,' *Management Today*, 01.02.1994.

26   K Walker, interview with author, 13.5.2008.

27   *Ibid.*

28   'From Father to Son in the Tweed Trade,' *Cumberland News,* 19.08.1994.

29   M. Licquorice, *op.cit*, p.54.

30   A. Wright, *op.cit.*

31   M. Licquorice, *op.cit*, p.57.

32   Last Will and Testament of Annie Norah Hartley, HMCS Probate Office.

33   'Boom as Japanese take to Tweed,' *Cumberland News*, 07.10.1994.

34   J. McGlone, *op.cit.*

35   K. Walker, interview with author, 13.05.2008.

36   J. McGlone, *op.cit.*

37   J. Boys-Stones, 'Nicole's "Cold Mountain" Number,' *Cumbria Life,* June 2004.

38   *Ibid.*

39   K. Walker, interview with author, 13.05.2008.

40   www.fashion-era.com/haute_couture.

41   D. Bott, *op.cit*, p.49.

42   J. Brunel, *op.cit.*

43   *Ibid.*

44   L. Prigent, *Signé Chanel,* DVD, Lalala Productions, Arte France, 2005.

45   S. Lamy, Daily Luxury.blogspot, Daily Luxury.blogspot.com, 10.12.2007.

46   S. Menkes, 'A King of Haute Couture Feathers Reigns Supreme, André Lemarié is the Last of the Plumassier Breed,' *International Herald Tribune*, 15.12.1998.

47   Maison Lemarié, *www.lemarie-paris.fr.*

48   www.massaro.fr.

49   E. Hayt, 'The Hands That Sew Sequins,' *New York Times*, 19.01.2006.

50   *Ibid.*

51 S. Rushton, 'François Lesage: Dream Weaver,' *The Independent*, 08.07.2003.

52 *Ibid.*

53 S. Chhabra *et al*, press conference, *New Straits Times*, Malaysia, 20.07.2003.

54 E. Hayt, *op.cit*.

55 C. Walker, interview with author, 06.07.2009.

56 'Coffee Shop Returning to Normality,' *Cumberland News*, 14.01.2005.

57 C. Walker, interview with author, 06.07.2009.

58 L. Prigent, *op.cit*.

59 'Chanel Autumn/Winter 2005/6 Ready to Wear Show Report,' www.vogue.com , 04.03.2005.

60 C. Morton, 'Chanel. Autumn/Winter 2005-6 Couture,' www.vogue.com , 07.07.2005.

61 S. Frankel, 'Chanel casts aside French chic for a taste of Americana,' *The Independent*, 06.10.2007.

62 S. Lamy, Daily Luxury Web, Paris.

63 G. Greig, 'Inside The World Of Karl Lagerfeld,' *Tatler*, December 2007, excerpt in *The Independent*, 08.11.2007.

64 C. Long (1), 'Tsar Karl,' *The Independent,* 08.12.2008.

65 C. Long (2), 'Lagerfeld glows with his rhapsody in white,' *The Independent*, 28.01.2009.

66 *Ibid.*

67 J. Cartner-Morley, 'All white now, Chanel dismisses downturn talk,' *The Guardian*, 28.01.2009.

68 *Ibid.*

69 *Ibid.*

70 C. Long (1), *op.cit*.

71 *Ibid.*

72 www.chanel.-exposition.ru/en/exhibition copyright

73 R. Young, 'Russia, A Bread And Butter Market,' New York Times, 28.11.2007.

74 C. Long (1), *op.cit*.

75 BBC News, September 2005.

76 WWWRADIO 86, 10.01.2008.

77 BBC News, 05.09.2005.

78 D. Thomas, DELUXE, How Luxury Lost its Lustre, London: Allen Lane, 2007, p.300.

79 *Ibid.*

80 S. Frankel, 'Still Crazy About Coco,' *The Independent Magazine*, 22.03.2008.

81 L. Montgomery, 'Beijing bling: creative details and consumer choices in contemporary China. An interview with Hung Huang,' *International Journal of Cultural Studies,* Sage Publications,. 2006.

82 *Ibid.*

83 J. Picardie, 'Chanel in Shanghai: China goes from Mao to wow,' www.telegraph.co.uk, 06.12.2009

84 *Ibid.*

85 L. Movius, 'Karl Lagerfeld Talks Shanghai and Fashion,' www.com/fashion news. Fairchild Fashion Group, 04.12.2009.

86 K. Walker, interview with author, 13.05.2008.

87 Alamy Images.

88 H.W. Yoxall, *op.cit*, p.102.

89 K. Walker, interview with author, 13.05.2008.

90 www.premierevision.com/

91 J. Boys-Stones, *op.cit*.

92 H. Alexander, 'New York Fashion Week: Victoria Beckham's latest collection,' www.telegraph.co.uk/fashion/new-york. fashion-week , 17.02.2009.

93 E. Broughton, 'Michelle Obama's a fan of Linton Tweeds,' *News & Star*, 11.05. 2009.

94 J. Loughran, 'First Lady steps out in Linton Tweeds coat,' *Carlisle Living, Style in the City, Pride in the City*. May 2009.

95 J. Loughran, 'Carlisle's Coolest Export,' Carlisle Living, Style in the City, Pride in the City, January, 2009.

96 K. Eve, 'Cousin's prove all fashion design is relative,' *News & Star*, 03.11. 2006.

97 *Ibid.*

Stuart Vevers' cousin is Jonathan Kelsey a freelance shoe designer who has worked for Jimmy Choo, and designed items for Madonna and the late Amy Winehouse. Dubbed the 'British Louboutin' by the fashion press, Kelsey and his cousin have worked together on a collection for Mulberry and Luella. Their grandmother, the late Edna Murray, was a dressmaker and costume maker for the Carlisle Musical Society.

98 J. Boys-Stones, *op.cit*.

99 J. McGlone, *op.cit*.

100 C. Gale and J. Kaur, *The Textile Book*, Oxford, Berg, 2006, p38.

101   K. Walker, interview with author, 13.05.2008.

102   S. Newstead, 'The height of fashion,' *Cumberland News*, 15.04.2011.

103   *Ibid.*

104   K Walker, interview with author, 13.05.08.

105   *Ibid.*

106   M. Campbell, *op.cit.*

107   M. Murphy, 'Fine Fabrics - Linton Tweeds,' *Threads Magazine*, 01.02.2008.

108   C. Walker, interview with author, 06.07.2009.

109   *Ibid.*

110   'You wooldn't believe it – sheep event raises £1500,' *Cumberland News*, 04.07.2008.

111   C. Walker, interview with author, 06.07.2009.

112   *Ibid.*

113   *Ibid.*

114   L. Walker, interview with author, 19.06.2007.

115   A. Wentland & M-L. Gumuchian, 'Tough to let go for 70-something fashion designers,' Reuters, 15.12.2009.

116   L. Barnett, 'Karl Lagerfeld confirms that re tiring from Chanel isn't something he's planning to do anytime soon,' www.handbag.com/fashion, 12.11.2009.

117   'Cutting words from the master,' BBC Today programme, 2 January 2009.

118   S. Newstead, *op.cit.*

119   'Value of the UK Fashion Industry,' Report commissioned by the British Fashion Council, September 2010, London.

120   S. Newstead, *op.cit.*

121   L. Walker, interview with author, 13.11.2007.

✳ ✳ ✳

Acknowledgements

Of the many people who have helped with this book, I would particularly like to thank the following:

Leslie Walker – Chairman of Linton Tweeds – who brought alive the excitement of the company's history with unfailing patience and dry humour.

Carole Walker - Director of Linton Tweeds - who gave me an insight into everyday life at the mill and the spirit of dedication that prevails.

Keith Walker – Managing Director of Linton Tweeds - who gave me an understanding of the global market within which the company operates, and for his enthusiasm for having 'the best job in the world'.

The kindness and help of the Walker family throughout this venture has been outstanding.

Gemma Smith – Commercial Manager of Linton Tweeds, and Margaret Duffy, Showroom Manager.

Desmond Mathews – former Director of Linton Tweeds, for wonderful memories of Christian Dior and Coco Chanel. Also his wife, Teresa, for her support. Sadly Desmond died in 2010.

Margaret Robinson – who shared memories and photographs of her father, George S. Linton.

Linda Nelson – Agnes Linton's former kennel-maid, who told the story of Oakland House and the Geltsdale Deerhounds with such affection.

Frank Beddow, son of the late Mrs Jean Beddow, Secretary to Agnes Linton.

Robert Thomlinson, former Office Manager, Linton Tweeds.

Denis Perriam, Ashley Kendall, and the late Jim Templeton – all local historians, who generously shared their knowledge and photographs with me.

Stephen White and staff of Carlisle Library.

David Bowcock and staff at Carlisle Records Office.

Carlisle Register Office.

Melanie Gardner and Edwin Rutherford of Tullie House Museum and Art Gallery, Carlisle. Also Matthew Constantine, formerly of Tullie House.

Cumberland Newspapers. Carlisle.

Stewart Jessett, Tim Belford and Vernon Addison of Carlisle Jazz Club for their memories of Mick Potts and the Gateway Jazz Band.

Euan J. Pringle of Otterburn Mills for helpful information on the Waddell family.

The Deerhound Club for information on Agnes Linton, and in particular Mary Churchill and her husband Tony, of Lealla Deerhounds, who welcomed me to their home in Wrabness and gave me access to the club library, where Agnes Linton and Nora Hartley's records and photographs are kept. Their support and enthusiasm was inspirational and it was here that I met my first deerhound!

Other members of the Deerhound Club also showed me great kindness and support, particularly Mary Girling and Joan Wragg.

Pamela Brown, Sheillac Deerhounds, Newark.

Glenis Peach, Kilbourne Deerhounds.

David South, Harrogate.

The Hon. Julian Fane kindly gave me information about his mother, Lady Diana Westmorland and her second husband Arthur 'Boy' Capel, as well as introducing me to Boy Capel's grandson, Christopher Osborn, and giving me permission to use photographs of Lady Westmorland and Boy Capel's two daughters Ann and June Capel. Christopher Osborn for giving me permission to use the photograph of his grandfather, Boy Capel.

The Victoria and Albert Museum, London, in particular Mark Eastment, Head of Publishing and Dr. Lesley Miller, Senior Curator, Department of Furniture, Textiles and Fashion who reviewed my manuscript and gave me positive support and advice, also Sonnet Stanfill, Curator, Furniture, Textiles and Fashion.

The Kennel Club, London.

Austin Mutti-Meuwes of Hardy Amies, 46 Savile Row, London, for information on Sir Hardy Amies, and permission to use photographs.

Nathaniel Dafydd Beard, Royal College of Art, London.

The National Archives, Kew, London.

The British Library, London.

Probate Registry, York.

General Record Office, Southport.

General Register Office, Southport.

Rachel Roberts, The Cheltenham Ladies' College.

Elizabeth Boardman, Archivist, St. Hilda's College, Oxford.

Lisa Heighway, The Royal Photographic Collection, Windsor Castle.

Julie Snelling, The Royal Archives, Windsor Castle.

M. Jacques Audibert, Ambassade de France, Londres.

Sister Máire O'Donnell, Archivist, Religious of the Sacred Heart of Mary, Upminster, who tried to help me unravel the secrets of Aubazine, contacting the Mother House in France for me.

Mrs. B Williams, Sacred Heart of Mary Girls School, Upminster.

Richard White, Hawick Museum, Scotland.

Gordon Macdonald, Hawick, who kindly shared his vast knowledge of the Scottish mills and textile industry with me.

Ian Landles, Hawick.

Neil M. Horne, Rector, Hawick High School.

Susan Donaldson, Heritage Hub, Hawick.

Helen Taylor, Archivist, Heriot Watt University, Edinburgh.

Hawick News.

Rob Johnston, Arbroath.

John Beedle, Area Librarian, Hawick Library, for unfailing help with my many questions.

Helen Darling and Margaret Sellar, Scottish Borders Archive and Local History Centre, Selkirk.

Hollie Graham, General Register Office for Scotland, Edinburgh.

National Library of Scotland, Edinburgh.

Dawn McQuillan, Edinburgh Central Library.

R.G Watkins, Books and Prints, Ilminster

Tyne and Wear Archive Service, Newcastle-upon-Tyne.

Gwent Record Office.

James Arnold, Museum of Lakeland Life and Industry.

Lianne Smith, Kings College London Archives.

The Trustees of the Liddell Hart Centre for Military Archives.

New York State Archives, USA.

Chanel, Paris.

Office de Tourisme du Pays d'Aubazine Beynat, Limousin, France, for information on Chanel at Aubazine.

To my extended family:

Claude Jousselin for help with translation.

Jo Garrod for modelling my Linton Tweed suit so beautifully.

Noeline Wilson and the late Mrs. Lottie Wilson of New Zealand, for always giving me snippets of useful information.

Many of my friends and relatives have given me support and my sincerest thanks go to them, and in particular to:

My godmother, Alicia Grice who sadly passed away in July 2009, but who never lost her enthusiasm and belief in my work. Bill and Betty Hitchon, Bill hoped a film would be made of the book, he sadly left us in October 2008. My late cousin Bill Weston, Nick Weston, Edith Halvorsen who introduced me to Linton connections, Fr John Dobson for his interest and support, Dr Yvonne McKenzie who introduced me to the late Jim Templeton.

Three people provided unfailing support to me throughout the research and writing of this book:

Peter Perrin helped me with his far-sighted suggestions and penetrating insight. To my great sadness, Peter did not live to see its publication, as he died on 31 March 2010.

My sister-in-law, Elizabeth Hitchon, for her brilliant enthusiasm and constant support.

My brother, Gil Hitchon, who was my editor, advised, encouraged and unstintingly gave me the benefit of his wide journalistic experience, and helped me bring my book to fruition.

Finally, my thanks go to David Ramshaw of P3 Publications, for his exceptional support in publishing my manuscript.

Carlisle. January 2012

***

270

Photo credits

Apic/Getty Images, 19, 195 (a)

Archive Photos/Getty Images, 195 (f)

Art Rickerby/Getty Images, 185

Ashley Kendall, 35

Bettmann/Corbis, 103, 107

Bridgeman Art Library, 158

Bundesarchiv, Bild 101III-Alber-178-04A/Alber, Kurt/CC-BY-SA, 135

Chanel - photographer Karl Lagerfeld, 234(a)

Christopher Osborn, 28

Condé Nast Archive/Corbis, 195 (b), (d), and (h)

Cumberland News, Carlisle, 208, 215, 220, 231

Congregation of the Religious of the Sacred Heart of Mary, 16

David Martyn/Dreamstime.com, 6

Deerhound Club, 74, 76, 119, 121, 151, 182, 210, 211

Fiona Campbell, 245

Gordon Macdonald, Hawick, 11

G-P. Woimant-Malloizel, 24

Hon. Julian Fane, 57, 64

Hulton Archive/Getty Images, 93

Human Record, 81, 82

Joseph Hardman/Courtesy of Museum of Lakeland Life and Industry, Kendal, Cumbria, 138 (sheep shearing)

Keystone-France/Getty Images, 131, 156

Leslie H. Walker, 189, 191, 192

Linton Tweeds, 2, 3, 138, 139, 216, 217, 222, 230, 250

Louis Tauzin, Public Domain, 23

Lourens Smak /Alamy, 67

Marcus Brandt/epa/Corbis, 233

Mark Wilson/Getty Images, 243

Mary Evans Picture Library, 99

Mrs Linda Nelson, 182

Mrs Margaret Robinson, 140, 141, 173

Mrs Teresa Mathews, 175

National Archives, 47

Père Igor, CC-BY-SA, 17

Philippe Wojazer/Reuters/Corbis, 234 (b), 235 (k)

Pierre Guillaud/Getty Images, 214

Private Collection, 30, 42, 195 (g)

Public Domain, 26, 54, 112,114, 136

Rex Features, 194

Ronald Mitchell, 61

Sharok Hatami/Rex Features, 195 (c) and (e)

Sir Hardy Amies Archives, 117, 154

Startraks Photo/Rex Features, 248

Stephane Cardinale/People Avenue/Corbis, 235 (i) and (j)

Stewart Jessett,Carlisle Jazz Club, 206

Thierry Orban/Sygma/Corbis, 234 (c) and (e), 235 (h)

Time Life Pictures/Getty Images, 105

Tullie House Museum & Art Gallery, Carlisle, 237

Vanessak/Dreamstime.com, 44

Walter Sanders/Getty Images, 163

WWD/Condé Nast/Corbis, 234 (d), 235 (f) and (g)

Index